Inside Copilot

Inside Copilot is designed to teach users to master Copilot, Microsoft's generative AI assistant. Learn prompt engineering and use cases for Copilot in many Microsoft products at beginner, intermediate, and expert levels. Perfect for any professionals who find their schedules packed with repetitive computer tasks, Copilot can automatically generate PowerPoint presentations, draft emails on Outlook, write code on GitHub, and more. Both companies and individuals can learn to utilize Copilot to significantly speed up processes and gain an advantage.

More information about this series at `https://www.apress.com/series/17432`.

Introducing Microsoft Copilot for Managers

Enhance Your Team's Productivity and Creativity with Generative AI-Powered Assistant

Adeel Khan

Apress®

Introducing Microsoft Copilot for Managers: Enhance Your Team's Productivity and Creativity with Generative AI-Powered Assistant

Adeel Khan
Singapore, Singapore

ISBN-13 (pbk): 979-8-8688-0418-2   ISBN-13 (electronic): 979-8-8688-0419-9
https://doi.org/10.1007/979-8-8688-0419-9

Managing Director, Apress Media LLC: Welmoed Spahr
Acquisitions Editor: Smriti Srivastava
Development Editor: Laura Berendson
Editorial Assistant: Kripa Joseph

Cover designed by eStudioCalamar

Cover image designed by Freepik

Distributed to the book trade worldwide by Springer Science+Business Media New York, 1 New York Plaza, Suite 4600, New York, NY 10004-1562, USA. Phone 1-800-SPRINGER, fax (201) 348-4505, e-mail orders-ny@springer-sbm.com, or visit www.springeronline.com. Apress Media, LLC is a California LLC and the sole member (owner) is Springer Science + Business Media Finance Inc (SSBM Finance Inc). SSBM Finance Inc is a **Delaware** corporation.

For information on translations, please e-mail booktranslations@springernature.com; for reprint, paperback, or audio rights, please e-mail bookpermissions@springernature.com.

Apress titles may be purchased in bulk for academic, corporate, or promotional use. eBook versions and licenses are also available for most titles. For more information, reference our Print and eBook Bulk Sales web page at http://www.apress.com/bulk-sales.

Any source code or other supplementary material referenced by the author in this book is available to readers on GitHub. For more detailed information, please visit https://www.apress.com/gp/services/source-code.

If disposing of this product, please recycle the paper

*Dedicated to my loving parents, I can never thank you enough,
and my ever supporting siblings, wife, and daughters.
—Adeel Khan*

Table of Contents

About the Author

Adeel Khan is a distinguished Senior Technical Specialist at Microsoft, renowned for his expertise in driving enterprise-grade digital transformations. His nearly two decades of experience encompass a deep understanding of cloud solutions, AI and ML, and data management solution architectures that have consistently delivered customer success and profitability. Adeel's global professional journey has taken him across Pakistan, UAE, Malaysia, and Singapore, enriching his perspective and enhancing his ability to navigate complex technological landscapes. Adeel's academic achievements are notable, with an MBA from Coventry University and an AI certification from MIT. His multilingual fluency in English, Urdu, and Arabic complements his global leadership role. As an author and speaker, Adeel has shared his thought leadership at various regional and global events, inspiring audiences with his insights into the future of technology. In his role at Microsoft Operations in Singapore, Adeel has been recognized as an AI-Copilot Champion and has achieved the remarkable feat, helping Fortune 500 organizations adopt and transform the future of work. You can follow Adeel Khan and connect with him at LinkedIn: `www.linkedin.com/in/madeelkhan/`.

About the Technical Reviewer

Kasam Shaikh is a prominent figure in India's artificial intelligence landscape, holding the distinction of being one of the country's first four Microsoft Most Valuable Professionals (MVPs) in AI. Currently serving as a Senior Architect, Kasam boasts an impressive track record as an author, having authored five best-selling books dedicated to Azure and AI technologies. Beyond his writing endeavors, Kasam is recognized as a Microsoft Certified Trainer (MCT) and influential tech YouTuber (@mekasamshaikh). He also leads the largest online Azure AI community, known as DearAzure | Azure INDIA, and is a globally renowned AI speaker. His commitment to knowledge sharing extends to contributions to Microsoft Learn, where he plays a pivotal role.

Within the realm of AI, Kasam is a respected subject matter expert (SME) in generative AI for the cloud, complementing his role as a Senior Cloud Architect. He actively promotes the adoption of no-code and Azure OpenAI solutions and possesses a strong foundation in hybrid and cross-cloud practices. Kasam Shaikh's versatility and expertise make him an invaluable asset in the rapidly evolving landscape of technology, contributing significantly to the advancement of Azure and AI.

In summary, Kasam Shaikh is a multifaceted professional who excels in both technical expertise and knowledge dissemination. His contributions span writing, training, community leadership, public speaking, and architecture, establishing him as a true luminary in the world of Azure and AI. Kasam was recently recognized as the top voice in AI by LinkedIn, making him the sole exclusive Indian professional acknowledged by both Microsoft and LinkedIn for his contributions to the world of artificial intelligence!

Acknowledgments

It was a thrilling adventure to write this book, especially about technology that is changing faster than the speed of light. Every day, there is a new breakthrough that amazes everyone involved. I couldn't have done this without the continuous support from my dear wife Youshba and my lovely daughters (Zara, Zenubia, and Zoya) and their constant appreciation of my work.

I was lucky to spend time with my parents while I wrote this book. Their pure love, support, and enthusiasm motivated me during the hard times and kept me moving forward. They deserve all my gratitude, for the way they raised me and for instilling in me good principles and the passion for seeking and spreading knowledge.

I am grateful to my brother Junaid Khan for giving me great advice during the writing process, helping me shape the ideas from a business leader's perspective. I am also grateful to my leaders at Microsoft, Amit Pradhan, Vivek Chatrath, and Hui Li Lee, for encouraging me to challenge myself and embark on a "learn-it-all" journey.

A big shout-out to the Apress team for their professionalism, consistent support, and dedication to what they do and for creating a collaborative platform of learning and sharing.

Introduction

Today, Copilot is the talk of the town. Every software provider is infusing AI-powered experience in their software solutions, and every organization is evaluating how to embrace the future of work with AI-powered Copilot support.

Since the announcement in March 2023, Microsoft is leading the change and has successfully incorporated Copilot experience at various solutions. Today, the users of M365, Power Platform, or Business Applications like Dynamics 365 and Salesforce can leverage Copilot experience in their day-to-day interaction with these services and prepare for a hyperautomated new way of work.

The book is written for business managers who do not wish to be left behind during the current industry revolution. The book will help them understand the power of Copilot in business user–relevant applications and help them organize their team to embark on a transformative way of performing business operations. The content of this book will help them to make their journey smooth, with in-depth coverage and exercises for hands-on learning.

The content in this book is carefully curated in a way to introduce Copilot features and impact for personal productivity, team productivity, and business productivity, concluding with a discussion on how to create your own custom Copilot.

The book is divided into five parts, each one dedicated to Microsoft solutions relevant for business users. The first part introduces the concept of Copilot and how it works in a business-friendly language. The second part is dedicated to Copilot capabilities introduced in M365 services such as Word, PowerPoint, Excel, Outlook, and Teams. The third part is dedicated to Copilot advances in Microsoft Power Platform services such as Power Apps, Power Automate, Power BI, and Power Pages. The fourth part discusses in detail Copilot for Sales and Service, expanding beyond Dynamics 365 to cover Salesforce integrations as well. The book concludes with Part V where Copilot Studio is introduced and how organizations can build their own custom experience is discussed.

By the end of this book, readers will be empowered with the knowledge and skill set of working effectively with Copilots. Readers will feel confident using Microsoft productivity tools and will find their productivity level increased with the intelligent use of Copilot in daily business engagements.

PART I

Getting Started with Copilot

The first part of this book will introduce you to the concept of Copilot, setting the stage for a transformative experience of using Copilots in Microsoft suites of products and services. The objective of this part is to clarify the concept, provide insights on how Copilot works, and prepare you for what you are going to learn in this book.

Chapter 1: This chapter documents the journey of Copilot, its purpose, and the impact it has had since its inception. The chapter discusses the key fundamentals of Copilot and explains how our natural language ask is understood and transformed into information or action. The chapter provides a detailed examination of the underlying large language models (LLMs) that power Copilot, providing insights into its operational framework. The chapter concludes with a brief overview of how Microsoft has transformed the user experience of almost all of its products with embedded generative AI-powered assistant.

CHAPTER 1

Introduction

Welcome to the world of Microsoft Copilot. You are about to discover Microsoft Copilot, one of the most amazing technological breakthroughs that will transform how we create, collaborate, or communicate.

With this chapter, you are beginning your learning journey to master the art of working with the AI-powered intelligent assistant, Copilot, in various business user applications Microsoft provides. This chapter will establish the foundation for the readers and help them demystify the workings of Copilot.

In this chapter, we will talk about what Copilot is, how Copilot functions, how different solutions and services in the Microsoft ecosystem have integrated Copilot, and how the readers of this book can start their interaction with Copilot in Microsoft products.

1.1 What Is Copilot?

The term "Copilot" in English refers to a second pilot in an aircraft who assists the pilot who is in charge (1). The term was first recorded in English vocabulary during the period 1925 to 1930.

As for the first use of the word "Copilot" in the tech industry, Microsoft introduced a feature called "Copilot" in Microsoft 365 on March 16, 2023 (2), in a blog post published by Colette Stallbaumer, General Manager,

© Adeel Khan 2024
A. Khan, *Introducing Microsoft Copilot for Managers*, Inside Copilot,
https://doi.org/10.1007/979-8-8688-0419-9_1

Microsoft 365 and Future of Work (2). In the blog post, Colette introduced Copilot in these words:

> *Today, we announced Microsoft 365 Copilot—your Copilot for work. Copilot combines the power of large language models (LLMs) with your data in the Microsoft Graph—your calendar, emails, chats, documents, meetings, and more—and the Microsoft 365 apps to turn your words into the most powerful productivity tool on the planet. And it does so within our existing commitments to data security and privacy in the enterprise. Right now, we spend too much time on the drudgery of work and too little time and energy on the work that ignites our creativity and sparks joy.*

Introducing Copilot for Microsoft 365 | Microsoft 365 Blog

Colette's description of Copilot is precise, but to make it even simpler, we can think of Copilot as an assisted experience using "generative AI" and "large language models (LLMs)" to assist humans with complex cognitive tasks. Users of Copilot will be able to interact using natural language chat, partner with AI-powered Copilot to amplify creativity and accelerate results through guidance. The user will now be able to explain the action in natural language (prompts), and the product will perform the action using Copilot while still allowing the user to review, accept, or reject the outcome.

A simple example of the use of Copilot can be that a user of Outlook can leverage Copilot to help draft emails, schedule meetings, and set reminders based on their conversations and email content. For example, if you're emailing a colleague about a project deadline, Copilot could suggest a content that can be impactful and of high quality. Another example could be from CRM, where users can benefit from Copilot's ability to extract insights, help prepare for customer meetings, and importantly summarize the latest changes in customer-related engagements. There are many other use cases that you will be able to learn in this book.

With Copilot, every user can access and use technology services with productivity levels that used to be only for advanced or skilled users.

However, we should not forget and we will try to emphasize throughout this book that Copilot does not mean Autopilot. When we understand the features or capabilities of Copilot, you should always keep in mind the meaning of the word. It is a second pilot, supporting the first one. While Copilot will offer an amazing opportunity to enhance, speed up, and improve productivity, the outcome will depend on the first pilot, which is "us," the users of Copilot. This careful understanding is particularly important when it comes to using and learning the Copilot features.

1.2 Understanding Prompts

In your interaction with Copilots, prompts hold critical importance. A "prompt" refers to the initial instruction or information given to Copilot to guide its response. It sets the context and provides necessary details for Copilot to generate an appropriate output. Based on the prompt, you will guide Copilot to articulate the output targeted. The prompt can be a question, a statement, or a request. Here are a few examples:

- **Question Prompt**: "What is the capital of France?" – Copilot would respond with "The capital of France is Paris."

- **Statement Prompt**: "Translate the following English text to French: 'Hello, how are you?'" – Copilot would respond with "Bonjour, comment ça va?"

- **Request Prompt**: "Generate a Python function to calculate the factorial of a number." – The Copilot would respond with a Python function for calculating the factorial of a number.

It is critical to remember that the quality and relevance of Copilot's response heavily depend on the clarity and specificity of the prompt. The more specific and clear the prompt, the more accurate and relevant the response will be. A productive prompt would have the qualities as listed in Table 1-1.

Table 1-1. *Features of quality prompts*

Feature	Example
Goal: Clarity of what you expect from Copilot.	Draft a summary to prepare me for.
Context: Scoping with why you need and who is involved.	Internal project meeting on "Project Copilot," focusing on the latest progress and challenges.
Expectations: Setting Copilot tone best to address your request.	Keep the summary short up to 100 words and respond in a professional tone.
Source: Where information is residing and samples are located.	Focus on the latest project status report, emails, and teams chat with the project team in the last three weeks.

While Table 1-1 is a simple example, throughout this book I will share sample prompts to get your work done effectively, and you can also refer to Microsoft guide on Copilot prompts to learn further: `https://support.microsoft.com/en-gb/topic/learn-about-copilot-prompts-f6c3b467-f07c-4db1-ae54-ffac96184dd5`.

1.3 How Does Copilot Work?

Copilot works by leveraging machine learning algorithms to understand the task at hand and provide relevant suggestions or actions. It operates irrespective of the solution it is integrated with, meaning it can function in a variety of environments and applications.

Microsoft Copilot uses a type of machine learning model known as a large language model (LLM). It doesn't "understand" language in the way humans do. Instead, it calculates the probability of a word following a given sequence of words. LLM uses patterns that have been acquired from a huge amount of text data with which it was trained. When you input a sentence, Copilot generates the next word by selecting the word with the highest probability. This process is repeated for each subsequent word until a complete response is formed.

The core concept behind any Copilot is to assist and augment human capabilities. As mentioned earlier, Copilot is not designed to replace humans but to collaborate with them, aiding as needed. This is achieved through a combination of **natural language processing**, **pattern recognition**, and other AI technologies. The functioning of Copilot can be broken down into three primary steps as shown in Figure 1-1.

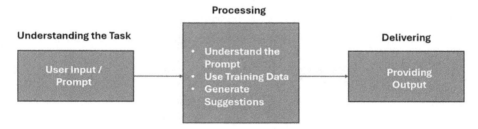

Figure 1-1. *Copilot foundational architecture*

Let's understand what happens at the steps:

- **Understanding the Task**: Copilot first needs to understand the task at hand. This involves interpreting the user's input that is called "**prompts**," which could be in the form of text, voice commands, or other types of data. Copilot uses natural language processing (NLP) techniques to parse and understand this input.

- **Processing**: Once the task is understood, Copilot processes the input prompt and generates suggestions or actions that could help the user complete the task. These suggestions are based on Copilot's training data and the specific algorithms it uses as discussed earlier.

- **Delivering**: Copilot then presents these suggestions to the user in an understandable and usable format. This could be in the form of text, code, or other types of data, depending on the task.

As illustrated in Figure 1-1, during these steps, large language models (LLMs) play a crucial role in the functioning of Copilot. An LLM is a machine learning model that has been trained on a vast amount of text data. They are trained on learning patterns and structures in the language. When LLMs are provided with a piece of text, they can predict what comes next, making them useful for tasks like drafting emails and summarization. Here's how LLMs can contribute to a Copilot scenario as illustrated in Figure 1-2.

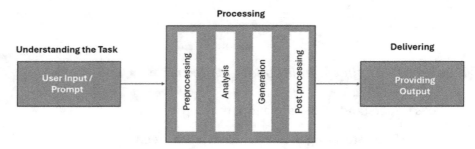

Figure 1-2. *Copilot foundational architecture expanded*

To broaden our understanding of the steps, let's understand what happens at each step with LLM in mind:

- **Understanding the User Prompt**: LLMs are used to understand the user's input. They can interpret natural language and understand the context of the task. This allows Copilot to accurately understand what the user is trying to do. For instance, you ask Copilot:

  "Can you help me draft a summary of this document?"

  Leveraging LLMs, Copilot would analyze the text, identify key points, and generate a concise summary. It doesn't understand the document's content in the human sense, but it recognizes patterns and structures in the text from its training data. This way, it assists in summarizing the document, enhancing your productivity.

- **Preprocessing the Prompt**: Copilot preprocesses the prompt to prepare it for analysis. This could involve cleaning the text, correcting spelling errors, or converting the prompt into a format that Copilot's algorithms can understand. There are various techniques used such as tokenization, stemming, and other text normalization methods for preprocessing, but we will not cover them in the context of this book as Copilot services in focus are going to perform them behind the scenes.

- **Analyzing the Prompt**: Copilot uses the LLM to analyze the prompt. The LLM interprets the natural language of the prompt and understands the context and intent of the user.

- **Generating a Response**: Based on the analysis, Copilot generates a response. This could involve providing an answer, suggesting an action, or asking for more information. The response is generated in a way that it is coherent, contextually appropriate, and in line with human language norms.

- **Postprocessing the Response**: The response is then postprocessed to ensure it is in a format that the user can understand. This could involve converting the response back into natural language, adding formatting, or performing other modifications.

- **Delivering the suggestions**: Finally, Copilot delivers the response to the user. The user can then choose to follow Copilot's suggestions, ask another question, or give feedback on Copilot's performance.

Copilot leverages the capabilities of LLM to understand tasks, generate relevant suggestions, and communicate effectively with the user. This constructive collaboration between Copilots and LLMs is what makes them so powerful and versatile. While we have now understood the Copilot skeleton or core foundations, I will explore the Copilot design further for each of the product/service in focus of this book.

1.4 Copilot in Microsoft Ecosystem

Microsoft has introduced Copilot capabilities in all of its software products and services (few pending announcements). The adoption and introduction of Copilot capabilities are at the forefront of every product and service echoing the vision of Microsoft Chairperson and CEO Satya Nadella that this is the age of Copilot (3). Users of Microsoft products and services will experience out-of-the-box Copilots (that is ready-made available off the shelf and can be enabled with on/off toggle of the feature) in various segments of products/services as well as gain the ability to build their own custom Copilots. Microsoft Copilots can be segmented into six categories as illustrated in Internet-famous Figure 1-3.

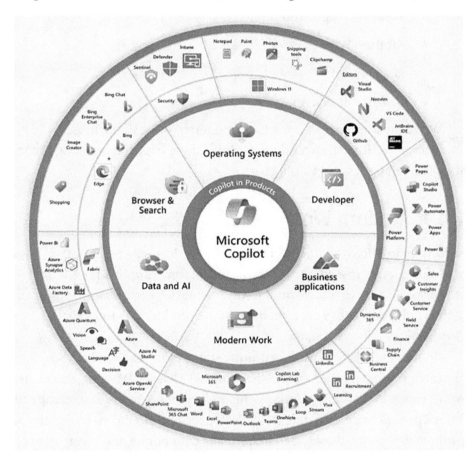

Figure 1-3. *Microsoft Copilot ecosystem*

As illustrated in Figure 1-3, the Copilot ecosystem is influencing all Microsoft products categorized in the following:

- Operating Systems

- Developers

- Business Applications

- Modern Work

- Data and AI

- Browser and Search

While the focus of this book is on modern work and business applications and I will cover them in detail, here is a brief introduction to all of the categories and Copilots.

1.4.1 Modern Work

According to Microsoft, the term "Modern Work" in the Microsoft ecosystem refers to a comprehensive suite of tools, applications, and services designed to transform the way businesses operate and empower their employees. These are a set of personal productivity tools such as Word, Office, PowerPoint, etc.

Copilot for M365 provides a unique stand-alone experience as well as in-app assistant experience for Microsoft 365 Modern Work apps such as Word, Excel, PowerPoint, Outlook, Teams, and more to unleash creativity, unlock productivity, and uplevel skills. It provides intelligent suggestions, automates repetitive tasks, and helps users collaborate and create items more effectively. We will explore Modern Work Copilot in detail in Part II of this book.

1.4.2 Operating Systems

Copilot in Windows 11 is an intelligent assistant that helps users get answers and inspirations from across the Web, supports creativity and collaboration, and helps users focus on the task at hand. Intune, Sentinel, and Defender for Endpoint also leverage Copilot's capabilities to provide enhanced security and device management features. This is specialized Copilot designed to help administrators and security professionals.

1.4.3 Developer

Microsoft Developer Tools such as GitHub, Visual Studio, and Power Platform have been integrated with specialized Copilots in specific solution areas. These Copilots aim to simplify the code generation experience and also help developers (pro or citizen) accelerate automation. As the target audience of this book is business users, we will cover Copilot for citizen developers under Part III, whereas Copilot for GitHub and Visual Studio will not be covered.

1.4.4 Business Applications

With Microsoft 365 Copilot for Business Applications, you can leverage the strength of big language models and your organization's data to transform your prompts into a great productivity tool. It integrates with the CRM solutions of your organization (Dynamics 365, Salesforce, ServiceNow, Zendesk) to provide intelligent insights and automate tasks. Part IV of this book is dedicated to Copilot for Sales and Service with a detailed discussion on how to use these Copilots with Dynamics 365 and Salesforce and also learn about Dynamics 365 in-app Copilot features for Sales and Services.

1.4.5 Data and AI

Copilot for Data Science and Data Engineering is integrated with Microsoft Data and AI solutions (such as Azure AI Studio and Fabric) to provide an assistant that can accelerate the interaction with data. With Copilot for Data Science and Data Engineering, AI engineers and data scientist are enabled to interact with data as if they are conversing with an AI assistant that can help them accelerate their daily tasks. For instance, Copilot for Data Science and Data Engineering can produce Python code that can be helpful during data preparation, transformation, or machine learning model creation. It can also help them evaluate the data and find patterns, I will discuss some of these capabilities that are introduced in Power BI under power platform section.

1.4.6 Browser and Search

Microsoft Copilot has a seamless visual identity across Bing, Edge, Microsoft 365, and Windows, being accessible through the same icon in all of them. It enhances the browsing and search experience by providing intelligent suggestions, summarizing search results, and helping users find the information they need faster.

1.5 Copilot Mapping to User Profile

As there are many Copilots available and the list will only increase in the future, here is a summary formulated in Table 1-2 for a quick understanding of typical user roles and Copilot mapping through primary Microsoft products.

Table 1-2. *Category and user mapping with services*

Category	Typical Users	Microsoft Products
Operating Systems	Windows users, IT administrators	Windows 11, Intune, Defender for Endpoint
Developers	Pro developers, programmers	GitHub, Visual Studio Code
	Citizen developers	Power Apps, Power Automate, Power BI
Business Applications	Business professionals	Dynamics 365, Salesforce, Zendesk (Service Only), ServiceNow (Service Only)
Modern Work	Professionals in various fields	Teams, Outlook, Word, Excel, PowerPoint, SharePoint
Data and AI	Data scientists, Data engineers, AI developers	Azure Synapse Analytics, Power BI, Microsoft Fabric, Azure AI Studio
Browser and Search	Internet users, researchers	Microsoft Edge, Bing Chat, Image Crawler

Note   The availability and functionality of these Copilots may vary based on the region and the specific Microsoft product version. For the most accurate and up-to-date information, please always refer to the official Microsoft website or product documentation as they are constantly updated with the latest service release or availability.

1.6 Prerequisites of Copilot

The prerequisites for Microsoft Copilot vary based on the primary product users are going to use. However, before product-based experience can be enabled, the user must have the access setup completed:

1. A Microsoft 365 E3, E5, Business Standard, or Business Premium license is required for each user.

2. IT administrators must have enabled Microsoft Search in Bing in the Microsoft 365 Admin Center.

3. Users must have Microsoft Entra ID (formerly Azure Active Directory) accounts.

4. Microsoft 365 apps for enterprise must be deployed.

5. Some features in Microsoft 365 Copilot, such as file restore and OneDrive management, require that users have a OneDrive account.

6. Customers must have access to the Internet and use Microsoft Edge as their browser.

Please note that the preceding requirements are true at the time of writing this book and may change with time. In the later part of the book, we will cover prerequisites for each of the targeted product along with potential license requirements.

1.7 Practicing Prompts

It is recommended that before we deep dive into the world of Copilots, the readers should spend some time and get familiarized with Copilot prompts. For this, I have curated a simple exercise that will use Microsoft

Bing Chat, an AI-powered chat assistant that is changing the way we access public information. Please refer to Appendix A for preparing yourself for the upcoming content in the book.

1.8 Summary

In this chapter, we discussed what Copilot is and how it works. We learned that Copilot is a system that helps users of Microsoft products and services to access and use technology with higher productivity and creativity. Copilot uses large language models (LLMs) to understand user inputs, generate suggestions, and provide outputs in various formats and applications.

We also learned about various Copilots within Microsoft products and services and categorized them under operating systems, developers, business applications, modern work, data and AI, and browser and search. We introduced each of these Copilots and explained that they have specific target audience and functionality.

Finally, we learned how to use Bing Chat Copilot to become familiar with prompts. We learned through prompts the capabilities of Copilot and how it can understand the prompt and most importantly how it can continue having conversation with generated suggestions.

The next part of the book will cover each of the focused Copilots and deep dive into their features and usage for business users.

PART II

Copilot in Microsoft Productivity Tools

In this part, we will deep dive into Microsoft 365 Copilot features and work scenarios. The part includes a discussion about Copilot extension in productivity tools, such as Word, Excel, and PowerPoint, as well as in communication and collaboration tools, such as Outlook and Teams. This part also introduces a new service in modern workspace, that is, Copilot Chat. The part includes five chapters covering the following content.

Chapter 2: This chapter delves into Microsoft 365 Copilot features for Word, focusing on creating, transforming, and chatting with Copilot. It covers the architecture of M365 Copilot, including user prompts, preprocessing, large language models, and postprocessing. The chapter provides a step-by-step guide on using Copilot to draft content, generate documents using prompts, and transform text into tables.

Chapter 3: The chapter explores Microsoft 365 Copilot features for PowerPoint, aimed at transforming presentation creation. It discusses creating presentations from files or prompts, editing existing presentations, and using Copilot to suggest design options, content, and improvements. The chapter also highlights how Copilot can answer questions about presentation content, making it a valuable tool for various industries, including education, financial services, healthcare, and retail.

Chapter 4: This chapter focuses on Microsoft 365 Copilot features for Excel, enhancing productivity and efficiency in data analysis and automation. It guides users through creating formulas, charts, pivot tables, and datasets using natural language prompts. The chapter also demonstrates how to edit data, including formatting, sorting, filtering, and data manipulation with Copilot.

Chapter 5: This chapter discusses Microsoft 365 Copilot in communication and collaboration tools like Outlook and Teams. It covers Copilot features for creating content, coaching, summarizing emails, catching up on Teams conversations, and creating new content from chat history. The chapter emphasizes Copilot's role in enhancing user experience and communication efficiency in Outlook and Teams.

Chapter 6: This chapter introduces Microsoft 365 Copilot Chat as an independent app experience, extending beyond the productivity apps like Word, Excel, Outlook, and Teams. It covers accessing Copilot through browsers, Teams, and Outlook, emphasizing the seamless integration of Bing search and M365 Copilot. The chapter discusses features available at the time of writing the book. The chapter also explores Copilot plugins, detailing their architecture and how they extend Copilot's functionality by connecting to third-party data sources.

CHAPTER 2

Microsoft Copilot in Word

In this chapter, we will start learning about Microsoft Copilot in productivity tools. Microsoft productivity tools are a suite of applications designed to enhance efficiency and productivity in various work scenarios. These productivity tools include Word, PowerPoint, Excel, Whiteboard, OneNote, Teams, OneDrive, and others.

In this chapter, we will deep dive into Microsoft 365 Copilot features and work scenarios using Microsoft Word. The objective of this chapter is to list the available Copilot features during the writing of this book. We will not cover the Microsoft Word features as it is assumed that the readers have foundational understanding of this product/service. However, we will recap on the tool's objectives. Microsoft Word is a word processing tool that lets you create, edit, and share documents. It includes features like real-time collaboration, Researcher, and Ideas.

2.1 M365 Copilot Architecture Overview

Before we dive deep into Copilot features, let's further expand on our previous explanation of how Copilot works. When we explore Microsoft Copilot, it is critical that Copilot ingests and leverages information that is available in the users organization for personalized and specific responses

© Adeel Khan 2024
A. Khan, *Introducing Microsoft Copilot for Managers*, Inside Copilot,
https://doi.org/10.1007/979-8-8688-0419-9_2

rather generic public responses and information. This brings Microsoft
Graph and Semantic Indexing into our Copilot architecture. Copilot
utilizes Microsoft Graph to search and retrieve content for the end user
executing the search. It brings more context from customer-specific data
into the prompt, such as information from emails, chats, documents, and
meetings. The other critical element is Semantic Indexing. The Semantic
Index resides on top of the Microsoft Graph, which interprets user queries
to produce sophisticated, meaningful, and multilingual responses. It
allows organizations with Microsoft 365 Copilot to search through billions
of vectors (mathematical representations of features or attributes) and
return related results. Taking the enhanced understanding of how Copilot
works, Figure 2-1 shows an updated illustration of the Copilot architecture.

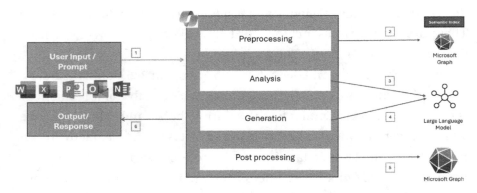

Figure 2-1. *Updated architecture for Microsoft Copilot*

The illustration in Figure 2-1 showcases what happens when a user
provides a prompt. Here's what happens step by step:

1. The user will either select a prebuilt prompt or
    provide a specific request through a prompt using
    Microsoft productivity apps.

2. Copilot then processes the prompt under preprocessing and improves the user-provided prompt by adding relevant information from the Semantic Index and Microsoft Graph. The technical term for this stage is "grounding." This stage is critical as Copilot improves and contextualizes the prompt; however, it does so by only accessing data that a user has existing access to, based on granted access. The improved prompt is then sent to the large language model.

3. The large language model receives the improved prompt and prepares the responses.

4. The large language model sends back the responses to Copilot.

5. Copilot modifies the responses from the large language model with the postprocessing step. This step includes more grounding calls to Microsoft Graph, responsible AI checks, security, compliance and privacy reviews, and command creation. This step is critical in the context of organizational information personalization and access.

6. The user receives the information in Microsoft App where they have initiated the prompt.

It is important to note that during the whole process as illustrated in Figure 2-1, organization data remains under customer tenant and Microsoft 365 service boundaries. The architecture remains the same when an input is provided from any of Microsoft 365 applications, such as Word, Excel, or PowerPoint. In the next section, we will start exploring each of the productivity apps and Copilot features within them.

2.2 M365 Copilot for Word

Copilot for Microsoft Word is a great addition to the tool that brings the transformative power of artificial intelligence to the world of document creation and editing. This innovative assistant is designed to revolutionize the way users interact with Microsoft Word, making the process of writing more efficient, intuitive, and user-friendly.

The introduction of Copilot marks a significant milestone in the evolution of Microsoft Word. It represents a paradigm shift from traditional word processing to a more dynamic, interactive, and intelligent system. By leveraging advanced AI algorithms, Copilot can draft a content from scratch, understand the context of the existing document, anticipate the needs of the user, and provide relevant suggestions and corrections.

The impact of Copilot on the user experience is profound. It not only accelerates the process of document creation but also enhances the quality of the output. Whether you are drafting a business proposal, authoring an academic paper, or crafting a personal letter, Copilot can help you articulate your thoughts more effectively.

This feature can be useful for any user irrespective of the industry or business function. To help visualize its usage, here are four examples:

- **Education**: Copilot can be a significant change in the education sector. For instance, educators can leverage it to personalize learning, saving time and energy to reinvest back into their students. Higher education students can use Copilot to draft essays, research papers, and reports, making the writing process more efficient. It can also be used to create lesson plans, grade assignments, and provide feedback to students (5).

- **Financial Services Industry (FSI):** In the financial services industry, Copilot can be used to draft, edit, and summarize complex financial reports (4). It can help in creating first drafts based on a brief prompt, rewriting and editing sections or even entire documents, and providing improved writing suggestions (4). This can lead to more accurate and efficient reporting, aiding in decision-making processes (5).

- **Healthcare:** Copilot can be a powerful tool for healthcare professionals. It can extract relevant information from various reports using natural language processing and convert it into structured data that can be imported into an Excel spreadsheet. The data can include the patient's name, age, diagnosis, treatment history, lab results, and imaging studies, among other things. This can significantly improve the efficiency of data management in healthcare settings and reduce time to convert large text block to structured information.

- **Retail Industry:** In the retail industry, Copilot can be used to create product descriptions, draft marketing content, and write customer communications. It can help in transforming existing content into more engaging and persuasive text, which can enhance the overall customer experience (5).

These are just a few examples of how Copilot for Microsoft Word can be utilized in different industries to enhance productivity and efficiency.

In essence, Copilot for Microsoft Word is more than just a feature; it's a smart assistant that works alongside you, helping you bring your ideas to life on the digital page. It's a testament to Microsoft's commitment to harnessing the power of AI to empower every person and every organization on the planet to achieve more. We will try out each of the features that are available at the time of writing this book and learn how to use them.

2.2.1 Create

The "Create" feature of Copilot allows users to draft new content. Whether you're creating a new document or working on an existing one, Copilot can help you move forward faster. Users can provide a simple sentence or a more complex request with outlines, notes, or referenced files that they want Copilot to use. Let's do an exercise to learn how to leverage this feature.

Generating Document Using Generic Prompt

In the first exercise, we will generate a proposal using a generic prompt:

1. Open Microsoft Word and select a blank document.

2. You will be greeted with a blank document and a Copilot prompt window (Figure 2-2).

Figure 2-2. *Blank Word document with the Copilot prompt*

3. Describe a prompt to generate a proposal document
    (Figure 2-3).

    *"Create a business proposal for a new product
    launch. The product is an innovative, eco-friendly
    water bottle that uses a built-in filtration system.
    The target market is health-conscious consumers in
    urban areas."*

Figure 2-3. *Generating a proposal with the prompt*

4. This prompt will create a document based on
    Copilot learnings and bring subtopics relevant
    to proposal documentation such as Executive
    Summary, Market Analysis, Product Description,
    and Marketing Strategy (Figure 2-4).

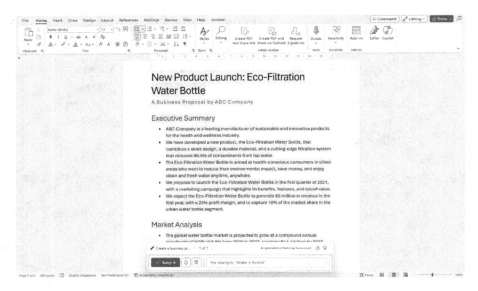

Figure 2-4. *Draft proposal generated with the provided prompt*

5. You can find the sample generated using the prompt
    at https://github.com/Apress/Introducing-
    Microsoft-Copilot-for-Managers/tree/main/
    Part-II/Word/BusinessProposal_01.docx.

6. Once the content is generated, we can perform
    the following actions. These actions are a typical
    response after every Copilot content generation
    activity:

    •   **✓ Keep it** : This will hide the prompt to let users
        continue with the next actions.

    •   ⟳ : This will advise Copilot to regenerate and
        add/revise the generated content.

- ⌑ : This will remove the generated content from the document.

- [For example, "Make it formal"   →] :
  This will allow users to add more instructions to improve the generated content.

In this example, we generated a proposal document and let Copilot decide on subsections. In the next exercise, we will experiment with a more precise prompt to demonstrate how we can control the content and guide Copilot on the content as well as structure.

Generating Document Using Structured Prompt

In the second exercise, we will generate a proposal using a more structured prompt to demonstrate the Copilot power when guided properly:

1. Open Microsoft Word and select a blank document.

2. You will be greeted with a blank document and a Copilot prompt window.

3. Improve the previous prompt to generate a new proposal document (Figure 2-5).

    "Create a business proposal for a new product launch. The product is an innovative, eco-friendly water bottle that uses a built-in filtration system. The target market is health-conscious consumers in urban areas. The proposal should include the following sections:

    1. Executive Summary: A brief overview of the product and the purpose of the proposal.

2. Product Description: Detailed information about the product, its features, and its benefits.

3. Market Analysis: An examination of the target market and competitive landscape.

4. Marketing and Sales Strategy: How the product will be promoted and sold.

5. Competition landscape and advantage: How current similar products are offered to targeted segment and what competitive advantage our product will bring.

6. Financial Projections: An estimate of the costs, revenues, and potential profits.

7. Conclusion: A final summary and call to action.

Use formal tone for the document except Conclusion where use friendly tone to demonstrate passion for eco-friendly world."

Figure 2-5. *Drafting a document with a structured prompt*

4. The sample prompt we just used is also an example of an effective prompt; it follows the guidance provided by Microsoft about prompts that we discussed in Chapter 1. The prompt provides "Goal," "Context," and "Expectations." If we were using any samples, we could have included them to tick the last box of reference as well.

5. The output of this prompt (Figure 2-6) will be more structured, organized, and specific to the prompt. Notice how Copilot has understood the assignment and, instead of generating subtopics, created content according to ask.

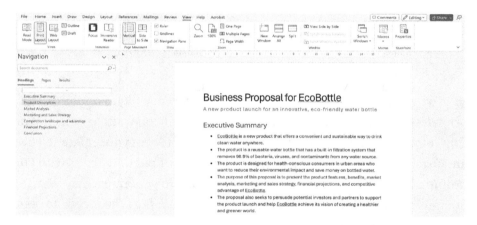

Figure 2-6. *Draft document generated using an improved prompt*

6. The sample generated using the preceding prompt can be found at `https://github.com/Apress/Introducing-Microsoft-Copilot-for-Managers/tree/main/Part-II/Word/BusinessProposal_02.docx`.

We will use the generated document for the next section, so do make sure you either download the document or save the generated one. Also, always remember these outputs are draft and may have inaccuracies; as an owner and author of the document, it is our responsibility to validate and finalize the document.

Generating Document Using Reference Files and Content

Microsoft Word Copilot allows you to leverage reference files to generate new documents as well. This feature is particularly useful when you want to

- Maintain a consistent style or format across multiple documents

- Refer an existing document and content to generate new content

To use this feature, simply upload your reference file(s) and provide a brief description or prompt of the new document you want to create. Word Copilot will analyze the structure, style, and content of your reference files and use this information to generate a new document that aligns with your prompt. Let's use our Business Proposal_02 file to generate a new Word document. In addition, we will also refer to `https://github.com/Apress/Introducing-Microsoft-Copilot-for-Managers/tree/main/Part-II/Word/BusinessProposalMeetingNotes_01.docx` that can be downloaded from the link provided. Save both files at a location you can access.

Here are the steps to experience this feature:

1. Open Microsoft Word and select a blank document.

2. You will be greeted with a blank document and a Copilot prompt window.

3. To include a file, we can either click the Reference a file ( Reference a file) button or use "/" to view the latest files.

4. Use the New Prompt to generate a summary memo based on our business proposal and Meeting Notes (Figure 2-7).

   "Draft a one-page summary Memo based on the data from [Business Proposal_02] and [BusinessProposalMeetingNotes_01]."

Figure 2-7. *Prompt with reference files for a Word document*

5. Replace the [Business Proposal_02] with the actual file by typing "/" (Figure 2-8).

Figure 2-8. *Adding document reference using "/"*

6. Replace the [BusinessProposalMeetingNotes_01] with the actual file by using the "Reference a file" button (Figure 2-9).

Figure 2-9. *Adding reference using the Reference a file button*

7. The final prompt should look like Figure 2-10 with your selected files.

Figure 2-10. *Final prompt with reference documents*

8. The prompt will initiate document content generation. You will notice that the document may go beyond one page, highlighting the need that as an owner of the document you still need to review and select the content generated

(Figure 2-11). You can download the sample generated using the prompt from `https://github.com/Apress/Introducing-Microsoft-Copilot-for-Managers/main/tree/Part-II/Word/SummaryMemoEcoBottleProject.docx`.

Figure 2-11. *Draft summary memo generated from the prompt*

In this example, we learned and practiced how to create a prompt with reference files. This is a useful feature as it helps bring the organization's own content and document as a source for generating new content. Some other sample prompts you could also use are as follows:

> *"Generate a project proposal similar to the uploaded reference file."*

> *"Create a meeting agenda in the style of the provided template."*

You can also refer to other documents such as PowerPoint, OneNote, or Sales Meeting (if you have Copilot for Sales license) for content generation.

In the next section, we will continue working with the Business Proposal_02 document and learn how to edit the document using Microsoft Word Copilot.

2.2.2 Transform

The Transform feature of Microsoft Word Copilot helps users enhance their existing content into a document. With text already in the document, users can highlight the text that they would like to rewrite or transform. Copilot provides rewritten options to choose from. Users can also adjust Copilot's response by providing instructions like "Make this more concise."

To learn about the Transform feature, let's work on some examples to understand. In Transform, we will learn

1. How to generate a new content based on the document on which we are working

2. How to rewrite the content that is already in place

3. How to transform the data from paragraph to table

To see this "Transform" feature work, we will use our previously generated Business Proposal_02 document. If you have not completed the exercise from the previous section, it is highly recommended to do so before moving forward, or you can download the sample file from `https://github.com/Apress/Introducing-Microsoft-Copilot-for-Managers/tree/main/Part-II/Word/BusinessProposal_02.docx`.

Generating New Content in Existing Document

Microsoft Word Copilot allows you to improve document content by generating a relevant content in the document. The generation of relevant content can be done by either describing what content you need to be added using the Copilot compose box or by clicking the innovative "Inspire me" button. In this exercise, we will try both of these features:

1. Open the "**business proposal_02.docx.**"

2. Notice the Copilot icon on the side of the text (⬚); click the icon to open the Copilot options (Figure 2-12).

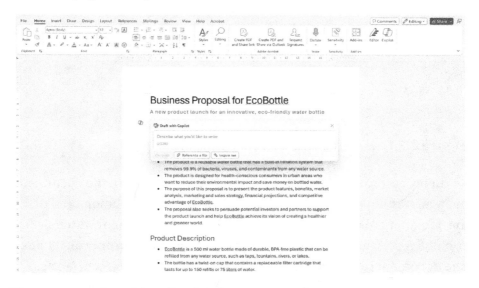

Figure 2-12. *Invoking the Copilot compose box*

3. Click Inspire me and wait for the results (Figure 2-13).

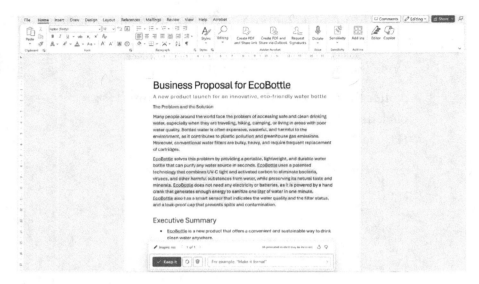

Figure 2-13. *Inspire me results in MS Word*

In my case, Microsoft Copilot generated a summary of the document in an interesting way, adding Problem Statement and Solution brief to the document. We will click Keep it to update the document with new content. Also, we will save this document as "**business proposal_03.docx**." The document can be downloaded from `https://github.com/Apress/Introducing-Microsoft-Copilot-for-Managers/tree/main/Part-II/Word/BusinessProposal_03.docx` as it will be used in the next exercises.

Rewrite the Content in Existing Document

Microsoft Word Copilot allows you to improve the text by providing alternative options. Copilot will provide three alternative sentences for users to choose from. Referring to the previous step's output "**business proposal_03.docx**," let's rewrite a few sentences in the newly generated problem and solution section:

1. Open the "**business proposal_03.docx**."

2. Select the following statement in "The Problem and the Solution" section.

3. Notice the Copilot icon on the side of the text (⌖); click the icon to open the Copilot options. This option can also be enabled by clicking "Alt+I" (Figure 2-14).

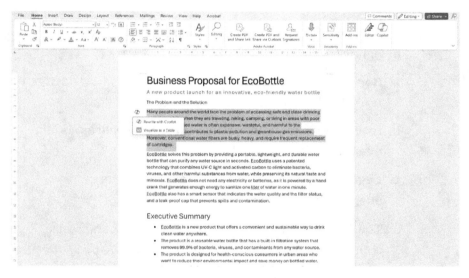

Figure 2-14. *Microsoft Copilot rewriting options*

4. Select "Rewrite with Copilot." By clicking this option, Copilot will start revising the content and provide three alternatives to choose from (Figure 2-15).

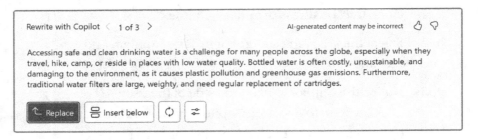

Figure 2-15. *Rewrite dialog of Microsoft Copilot for Word*

5. The user can perform a new set of actions as shown in Figure 2-15 with generated content.

   a. **Replace** will change the selected text with the selected option from the three alternatives provided by Copilot.

   b. **Insert below** will keep the existing text as well as add the newly generated text below.

   c. **Regenerate** will transform the text with some more alternatives.

   d. The **Tone** settings will allow the user to pick and revise content based on the tone options (Figure 2-16).

Figure 2-16. *Tone options with rewrite in Microsoft Copilot for Word*

6. Play with these settings and analyze the results. As for the sample document, we will keep it as is to use in the next exercise.

Transforming Text to Table in Existing Document

Microsoft Word Copilot allows you to transform text into tables. This allows the user to provide better visualization and also help in improving the user's ability to read the document. In this exercise, we will experiment with table transformation.

For this exercise, we will continue to use our "**business proposal_03. docx**." The document can be downloaded from https://github.com/ Apress/Introducing-Microsoft-Copilot-for-Managers/tree/main/ Part-II/Word/BusinessProposal_03.docx.

1. Open the "**business proposal_03.docx**."

2. Navigate to section "Financial Projections." Notice the whole section is bulleted; let's remove the bullets to make the section text simple. The final output should look like Figure 2-17 with simple text under the section.

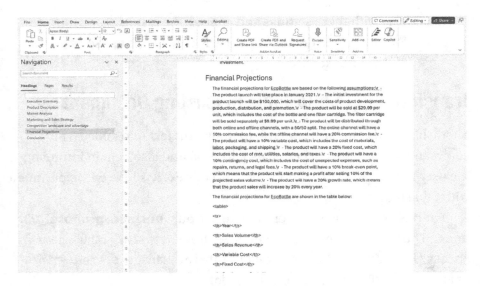

Figure 2-17. *Removing formatting from the Financial Projections section*

3. Select the first paragraph of the document. This paragraph contains information along with some financial figures about initial investment, product price, launch date, etc.

4. After selecting the paragraph, click the Copilot icon to select the "Visualize as a Table" option. The user can also use the shortcut key "Alt+I+T" to perform the same action (Figure 2-18).

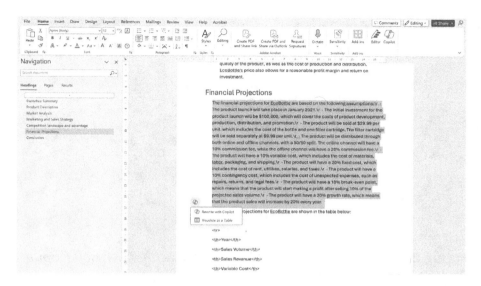

Figure 2-18. *Invoking the visualization option of Microsoft Copilot for Word*

5. The action will prompt Copilot to generate a table out of the paragraph provided as shown in Figure 2-19. The result of this action would be a table with values as explained in the paragraph.

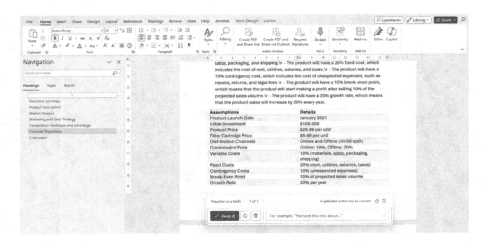

Figure 2-19. *Transforming text into a table using Microsoft Copilot for Word*

6. As discussed earlier, the user can now select any of the options provided in the Copilot compose bar and enhance or discard the generated content.

7. Repeat the same steps for the remaining HTML text in the document and save the document as "**Business_Proposal04.docx**." The sample can also be downloaded from `https://github.com/Apress/Introducing-Microsoft-Copilot-for-Managers/tree/main/Part-II/Word/BusinessProposal_04.docx`.

8. Remove the HTML text from the document to make it clean. The final document should have two tables under Financial Projections as shown in Figure 2-20.

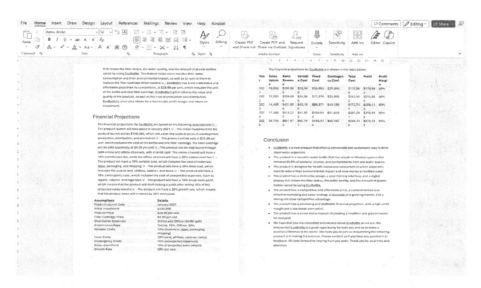

Figure 2-20. *Business Proposal 04 with tables*

2.2.3 Chat with Copilot

Microsoft Copilot for Word allows users to chat with Copilot in the context
of the document. The Copilot icon (⌬) at the home ribbon will allow users
to open the pane to access and chat with Microsoft Copilot for Word. This
useful feature gives you answers to questions, generic or detailed, about
your document. You can also have interactive conversations, get a
summary or specific information about the document content, or ask it to
create ideas, tables, or lists that you can copy and paste into your
document. The Chat features can be summarized into

1. **Change**: Perform changes to the document using
   the chat feature.

2. **Ask**: Inquire questions about the document or
   actions (how-to).

We will work with our previously saved document "**Business_Proposal04.docx**" in the following exercise. The sample can also be downloaded from https://github.com/Apress/Introducing-Microsoft-Copilot-for-Managers/tree/main/Part-II/Word/BusinessProposal_04.docx.

Changing Document Features Through Chat

Another way of changing document features is by using the chat feature. Chat allows you to ask natural language questions about your document or perform actions without using menus or commands. For example, you can ask how to change the font size, insert a table, or save a copy of your document. We will learn by trying some prompt on the previously created document "**Business_Proposal04.docx**" in the following exercise. The sample can also be downloaded from https://github.com/Apress/Introducing-Microsoft-Copilot-for-Managers/tree/main/Part-II/Word/BusinessProposal_04.docx.

1. Open the "**business proposal_04.docx**."

2. Click the Copilot (⬚) icon in the home tab of the ribbon. A chat window will open on the right side of the screen.

3. Type the following prompt to change the font color of heading 1 in the document:

   "Change Heading 1 font colour to Dark Blue and font size to 22"

4. This prompt will change the heading 1 style to a defined color and font size (Figure 2-21).

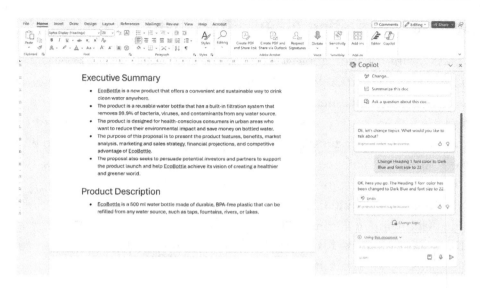

Figure 2-21. *Changes of style using chat*

5.   The user can undo the change if it is not according
     to the expectation.

Similarly, the user can perform such changes using chat. Here are
some more prompts that can be used for a learning exercise:

- *"Please change the font of the entire document to Times
  New Roman."*

- *"Can you help me replace all instances of 'EcoBottle'
  with 'EcoBottle24 in the document?"*

- *"I want to change the line spacing to double space."*

- *"Can you help me change the orientation of all pages to
  landscape?"*

Asking Information About a Document Through Chat

To ask for information about your document, you can type a question in the chat box, and Copilot will respond back based on information available in the document. Copilot will try to understand your question and provide an answer based on the data in your document. If Copilot cannot answer your question, it will suggest some alternative ways to find the information you need, such as using formulas, functions, or tools. We will learn by trying some prompt on the previously created document "**Business_Proposal04.docx**" in the following exercise. The sample can also be downloaded from `https://github.com/Apress/Introducing-Microsoft-Copilot-for-Managers/tree/main/Part-II/Word/BusinessProposal_04.docx`.

1. Open the "**business proposal_04.docx**."

2. Click the Copilot () icon in the home tab of the ribbon. A chat window will open on the right side of the screen.

3. In the Chat window, type the following question about the document:

   "what is the product price suggested and what is the initial investment required"

4. Copilot will respond back to this document-specific question and also provide a link to references; this is critical to validate the answer and ensure the information segment referred by Copilot is correct (Figure 2-22).

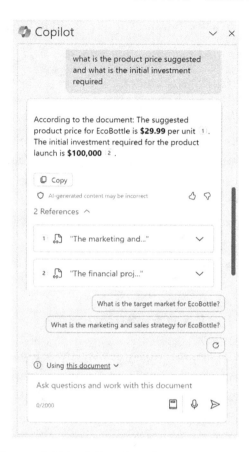

Figure 2-22. *Microsoft Word Copilot chat response to a question*

5. Also, notice that Copilot has suggested different questions that can be asked further. These questions are usually relevant to what you have asked before and provide assistance in exploring information further.

The user can also ask other questions related to the document such as

- *"What are the key points in this doc?"*

- *"Summarize this document."*

- *"Is there a call to action?"*

Apart from the preceding data-related questions, you can also use Copilot chat to get suggestions for improving your document, such as adding charts, tables, or formatting. Just type "Suggest" in the chat box along with the area of suggestion and press Enter, and Copilot will show you some options to choose from.

You can try asking the prompt "Suggest additional subsection in the document" and notice that Copilot will provide ideas of additional section relevant to business proposals.

Prompt Guide for Chat Experience

To make user experience and adoption easy, there are many sample prompts that the user can view and use. To access the sample prompts, the user can click the "View Prompt" (▢) icon. By clicking the icon, the user will be provided with prompts in various categories as shown in Figure 2-23. These prompts can be used as a guide to create your own personal prompts and chat interactions.

Figure 2-23. *Sample prompts for user guidance in Microsoft Copilot for Word*

Microsoft has also introduced a concept of Copilot Lab. If you click the View more prompts (⬛) icon as shown in Figure 2-23, Copilot chat will open "Copilot Lab," a library of prompts readily available to use (Figure 2-24).

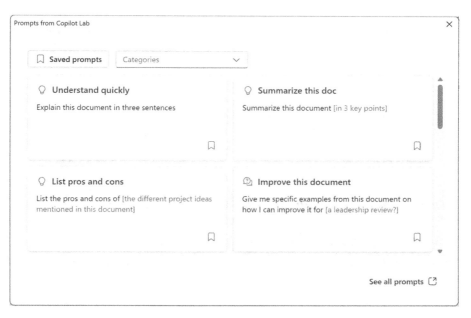

Figure 2-24. *Copilot Lab*

As shown in Figure 2-24, notice that the prompts listed are relevant to Word and Word-related content. You can save your favorite or most used prompts by clicking the save (🔖) icon and create your own personal library of prompts or as a team set few helpful prompts that can be used by your peers. You can also select Sell all prompts (See all prompts 🡥) and browse to a publicly available set of default prompts where you can choose an app, the category of action, and benefit from ready-to-use prompts (Figure 2-25).

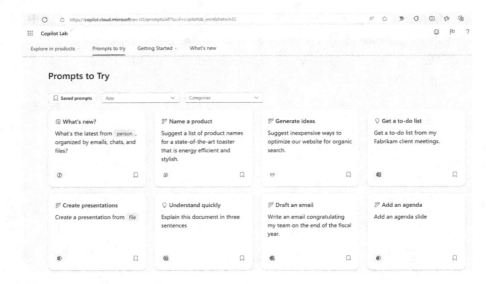

Figure 2-25. *Copilot Lab prompts by product and category*

I would highly recommend making yourself familiar with Copilot prompts and lab as you will be using many of the default prompts throughout this book.

2.3 Summary

In this chapter, we discussed and understood that Microsoft Copilot is a feature to assist in creating and editing documents in Microsoft Word. We learned by practice how it can generate content from scratch, rewrite existing text, transform data into tables, and chat with us.

We also covered the architecture of M365 Copilot that consists of four main components: the user prompt, the preprocessing, the large language model, and the postprocessing. We learned how we can leverage Copilot to provide suggestions and feedback based on the context and purpose of the document.

The chapter later discussed in detail features from Create, Transform, and Chat experience. The Create feature of Copilot allows users to draft new content based on a simple sentence or a more complex request. The Transform feature of Copilot helps users enhance their existing content by providing alternative options to rewrite or transform it. The Chat with Copilot feature allows users to chat with Copilot in the context of the document.

In the next chapter, we will continue learning the productivity tools and learn about PowerPoint Copilot.

CHAPTER 3

Microsoft Copilot in PowerPoint

In this chapter, we will continue learning about Microsoft Copilot in productivity tools and focus on PowerPoint. Microsoft productivity tools are a suite of applications designed to enhance efficiency and productivity in various work scenarios.

In this chapter, we will deep dive into Microsoft 365 Copilot features for PowerPoint. The objective of this chapter is to list the available Copilot features during the writing of this book. We will not cover the product features as it is assumed that the readers have a foundational understanding of the product/service.

However, let's just recap on each of the tool's objectives. Microsoft PowerPoint is a powerful presentation software that empowers business professionals to create compelling visual narratives. Whether you're delivering a sales pitch, training session, or boardroom presentation, PowerPoint offers a robust toolkit for crafting impactful slides. Using Microsoft PowerPoint, users can create, edit, present, and share documents. It supports real-time collaboration and has exclusive intelligent capabilities.

© Adeel Khan 2024
A. Khan, *Introducing Microsoft Copilot for Managers*, Inside Copilot,
https://doi.org/10.1007/979-8-8688-0419-9_3

Some of the key features of PowerPoint are as follows:

- **Slide Creation and Design**: PowerPoint allows you to build slides from scratch or choose from a variety of professionally designed templates. Customize layouts, fonts, colors, and graphics to align with your brand identity.

- **Content Creation**: Add text, images, charts, and multimedia elements to convey your message effectively. Leverage SmartArt for visually appealing diagrams and flowcharts.

- **Presenter View**: When presenting, use the Presenter View to see your notes, elapsed time, and upcoming slides. The audience views only the slides, while you maintain control behind the scenes.

Before beginning this chapter, it is recommended to complete Chapter 2 and its exercise as the document will be used in this chapter. Also, it is good to revise the M365 architecture as it is common across all productivity tools.

3.1 M365 Copilot for PowerPoint

Microsoft Copilot for PowerPoint is an innovative addition to Microsoft PowerPoint. It is a generative AI–powered in-app assistant that will intelligently transform the way you create presentations. It will help users of PowerPoint to boost productivity and efficiency, making it an even more valuable tool.

Microsoft Copilot for PowerPoint is a powerful feature that will help users to elevate the ability to generate impactful presentations and leverage the abundance of knowledge and power of Copilot to generate content, visualization, and even full-fledged presentation decks. Whether you need to create a new presentation from scratch or improve an existing one, Microsoft Copilot for PowerPoint can offer you various design options that suit your topic, audience, and purpose.

This feature can be useful for any user irrespective of the industry or business function. To help visualize its impact, here are some examples:

- **Education:** In the education sector, Microsoft Copilot for PowerPoint can revolutionize the way teachers and students create presentations. It can assist in structuring lesson plans, suggesting relevant content based on the topic, and even recommending engaging layouts to keep students interested. For students, it can guide them in creating presentations for projects or assignments, ensuring they communicate their ideas effectively.

- **Financial Services Industry (FSI):** In the FSI, presentations are often used for reporting financial results, forecasting trends, and proposing strategies. Microsoft Copilot for PowerPoint can assist in creating these presentations by suggesting suitable charts and graphs based on the data, recommending professional layouts, and even providing suggestions for explaining complex financial concepts in a simple and understandable manner.

- **Healthcare:** In the healthcare industry, presentations are crucial for sharing research findings, explaining medical procedures, and educating patients. Microsoft Copilot for PowerPoint can assist healthcare professionals in creating these presentations by suggesting appropriate medical imagery, recommending layouts that make complex medical information easy to understand, and providing content suggestions based on the latest medical research.

- **Retail**: In the retail industry, presentations are often used for product launches, sales meetings, and strategy discussions. Microsoft Copilot for PowerPoint can assist in creating these presentations by suggesting engaging product images, recommending layouts that highlight key sales points, and providing content suggestions that align with the latest retail trends.

The user can invoke Copilot for PowerPoint by clicking the Copilot (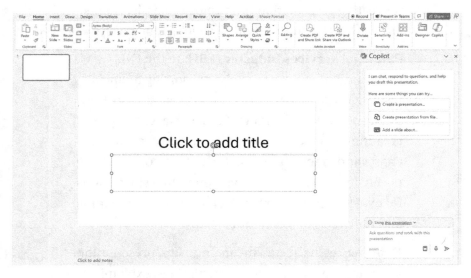) icon in the home ribbon. By clicking the Copilot icon, the system will open the Copilot pane in the PowerPoint designer screen as shown in Figure 3-1.

Figure 3-1. *Copilot for Microsoft PowerPoint*

In the next section, you will explore the various capabilities and experience these capabilities using a step-by-step guide. You will notice that Microsoft Copilot for PowerPoint has a user-friendly interface that's easy to use, even for those who are not experts in PowerPoint, making it a handy tool for improving the user's productivity and increasing PowerPoint adoption across organizations.

In a later section, we will discuss how Microsoft Copilot for PowerPoint can be used for creating a new presentation, editing an existing presentation, or understanding content and "chatting" with content present in our presentation slides.

You will be provided with a step-by-step guide to use Copilot and the Internet with an AI-powered assistant. I will also be sharing some useful prompts that you can use outside this book.

3.1.1 Create

One of the key features of Microsoft Copilot for PowerPoint is its ability to help users design attractive and effective slides from scratch. This feature allows users to start a new presentation from few available options such as Create a Presentation from a prompt or Create a Presentation from file. In this section, we will experience generating a presentation using both options.

Creating a Presentation Using a File

We will first begin with creating a presentation using a file. For this exercise, we will use the file created in the previous of the book. We will use the previously created document "**Business_Proposal04.docx**" in this exercise. The sample can also be downloaded from `https://github.com/Apress/Introducing-Microsoft-Copilot-for-Managers/tree/main/Part-II/Word/BusinessProposal_04.docx`.

1. Open a new blank PowerPoint presentation.

2. Click the Copilot (⬚) icon in the home tab of the ribbon. A chat window will open on the right side of the screen.

3. Click the Copilot prompt *"Create a Presentation from file."* This action will autotype the prompt in the Copilot chat window. Notice that you can also type a similar prompt and use "/" that will open the file selection window (Figure 3-2).

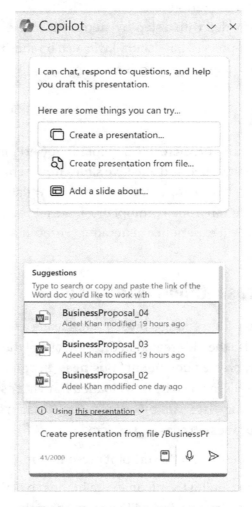

Figure 3-2. *Creating a presentation from a file using a Copilot prompt*

4. Select "**BusinessProposal_04.docx**". The final
   prompt should be like Figure 3-3.

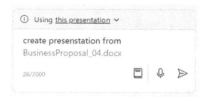

Figure 3-3. *Final Copilot prompt for creating a presentation
using a file*

5. Click the send ($\triangleright$) icon to start the Copilot action.
   Once completed, Copilot will generate a PowerPoint
   presentation relevant to our business proposal
   document (Figure 3-4).

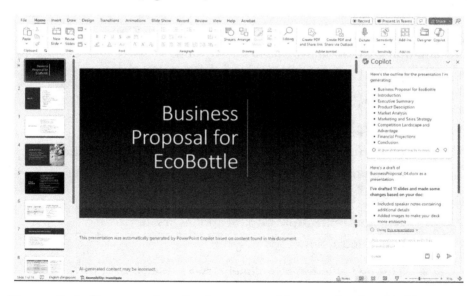

Figure 3-4. *Presentation draft generated by Copilot from a file*

6. The Copilot chat will showcase the outline of the
    presentation as well as the actions performed.
    For example, in this case, it mentions the number
    of slides drafted, the addition of speaker notes
    with details, and also the application of general
    sensitivity to the deck (Figure 3-4).

The output generated in this exercise is saved as
BusinessProposalPresentation_01.pptx and can be downloaded
from https://github.com/Apress/Introducing-Microsoft-
Copilot-for-Managers/tree/main/Part-II/PowerPoint/
BusinessProposalPresentation_01.pptx.

Let's take a moment to appreciate this feature, which is not only time
saving but also thorough in creating the draft presentation. The Microsoft
product team has done a great job in designing this feature to be very
useful for users.

Also, let us see what happened when we gave the Copilot the prompt of
presentation generation from a file step by step:

- **File Selection**: You provide Copilot with the link to
  your Word document.

- **Slide Generation**: Copilot generates slides based on
  the content of your Word document. It understands the
  structure of your document and breaks it up into slides
  of a presentation.

- **Layout Application**: Copilot applies layouts to the
  generated slides.

- **Theme Selection**: Copilot chooses a theme for your
  presentation.

- **Image Incorporation**: If your Word document contains images that are relevant to your presentation, Copilot will try to incorporate these images into your presentation.

- **Presentation Drafting**: Finally, Copilot drafts a presentation. Users can then edit the presentation to suit their needs, ask Copilot to add a slide, organize a presentation, or add images.

It's important to note that the effectiveness of Copilot in generating a presentation from a file can be enhanced by structuring your content under Titles and Headers when appropriate in your Word document. This helps Copilot better understand your document structure and how to break it up into slides of a presentation.

Creating a Presentation Using a Prompt

Creating a presentation using a prompt is similar in many ways to using a file except that the user is required to provide specifications of presentation to generate content. Microsoft Copilot for PowerPoint uses a combination of public content and content from your organization's tenant, depending on the permissions and access granted. It's designed to respect privacy and confidentiality, so it will not access or use any information that it doesn't have permission to use.

Referring to my earlier industry examples, let's try some sample prompts for generating a presentation using Microsoft Copilot for PowerPoint. Notice that we have highlighted answers to critical questions regarding any presentation. These questions are as follows:

- What is the subject of presentation?

- Who shall be the audience of this presentation?

- What would be the theme of presentation layout/design?

It is recommended you experiment with these prompts and perhaps create some of your own to be more familiar with Copilot capabilities.

- **Education**

  - Subject: "The Impact of Technology in Modern Education"

  - Audience: Education professionals and teachers attending an education technology conference

  - Theme: Modern and tech-oriented

  - Prompt: *"Create a presentation on 'The Impact of Technology in Modern Education' for an audience of education professionals and teachers. The theme should be modern and tech oriented."*

- **Financial Services Industry (FSI)**

  - Subject: "Understanding Cryptocurrency: A Guide for Financial Advisors"

  - Audience: Financial advisors in a corporate training session

  - Theme: Professional and clean

  - Prompt: *"Generate a presentation on 'Understanding Cryptocurrency: A Guide for Financial Advisors' for a corporate training session. The theme should be professional and clean."*

- **Healthcare**

  - Subject: "The Role of AI in Early Disease Detection"

  - Audience: Healthcare professionals at a medical conference

- Theme: Medical and professional

- Prompt: "*Draft a presentation on 'The Role of AI in Early Disease Detection' for healthcare professionals at a medical conference. The theme should be medical and professional.*"

- **Retail**

  - Subject: "Leveraging E-commerce for Business Growth"

  - Audience: Retail business owners at a retail industry summit

  - Theme: Business-oriented and engaging

  - Prompt: "*Create a presentation about 'Leveraging E-commerce for Business Growth' for retail business owners at a retail industry summit. The theme should be business-oriented and engaging.*"

Remember, the more specific and detailed the prompt is, the better Microsoft Copilot for PowerPoint can assist users in creating the presentation. It's always helpful to provide information about the subject, audience, and theme of the presentation. This allows Copilot to tailor the presentation to specific needs and preferences. Figure 3-5 showcases an output of a retail prompt.

Figure 3-5. *Draft presentation created using an industry prompt*

Note   Always ensure that you're following your organization's policies and guidelines when using Microsoft Copilot for PowerPoint. If you have specific concerns about data usage or privacy, it is recommended to reach out to your organization's IT department or the tool's support team for more detailed information.

In the next section, we will discuss and learn about editing the content by adding slides or changing the themes.

3.1.2 Edit

Microsoft Copilot for PowerPoint is not just for creating new presentations, but it's also a powerful tool for editing existing ones. It can analyze the content of your presentation and provide suggestions for improvement. This could include recommending changes to the layout for better readability, suggesting additional content to enhance your message, or even identifying areas where visual aids like charts or images could be beneficial. It's also capable of checking for consistency in design and formatting across all slides, ensuring a professional and cohesive look for your presentation.

Microsoft Copilot for PowerPoint can also suggest relevant icons, charts, graphs, and diagrams to enhance your data visualization and convey the message more clearly. Users can easily insert these elements into the slides with a few clicks and customize them according to the individual or organizational preferences.

Editing an Existing Presentation

We will experiment with this feature and edit previously created "**BusinessProposalPresentation_01.pptx**", which can be downloaded from `https://github.com/Apress/Introducing-Microsoft-Copilot-for-Managers/tree/main/Part-II/PowerPoint/BusinessProposalPresentation_01.pptx`.

1. Open the **BusinessProposalPresentation_01.pptx** PowerPoint Presentation.

2. Click the Copilot ( ) icon in the home tab of the ribbon. A chat window will open on the right side of the screen.

3. Click the sample prompt provided to "Organize this presentation" (Figure 3-6).

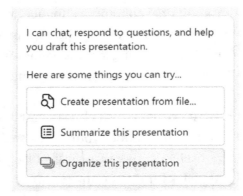

Figure 3-6. *Editing presentation using sample prompts*

4. Notice that the presentation will be updated with new slides and will be better organized with content. In our case, four additional slides were added; however, results can vary.

5. Provide another prompt to change the first slide. Type a prompt in Copilot chat "*add image on scarcity of water and natural resources, keep the theme same.*" The action will update the first slide with a relevant image (Figure 3-7).

Figure 3-7. *Editing a presentation using prompts with Copilot*

Sample Prompts for Other Experiments

Here are some sample prompts for editing an existing presentation that can be tried along with sample industry prompts shared under "Create" section of the chapter:

- *"Improve the layout of my presentation on 'The Impact of Technology in Modern Education' to make it more engaging for my students."*

- *"Suggest additional content for my presentation on 'Understanding Cryptocurrency: A Guide for Financial Advisors' to provide a more comprehensive overview of the topic."*

- *"Identify areas in my presentation on 'The Role of AI in Early Disease Detection' where visual aids could be beneficial."*

- *"Check my presentation on 'Leveraging E-commerce for Business Growth' for consistency in design and formatting."*

3.1.3 Chat with Copilot

As with Microsoft Copilot for Word, the chat feature allows you to ask natural language questions about your presentation. For example, you can ask Copilot to summarize the presentation or ask specific questions about presentation content. In addition to editing of presentation, we can perform the following actions:

- Ask Copilot to summarize the presentation.

- Ask content-related information.

We will learn these by experimenting with prompts in the following section.

Summarization of Presentation Content

We will learn by trying some prompt on previously created presentation "**BusinessProposalPresentation_01.pptx**", which can be downloaded from https://github.com/Apress/Introducing-Microsoft-Copilot-for-Managers/tree/main/Part-II/PowerPoint/BusinessProposalPresentation_01.pptx.

1. Open the **BusinessProposalPresentation_01.pptx** PowerPoint presentation.

2. Click the Copilot ($\oslash$) icon in the home tab of the ribbon. A chat window will open on the right side of the screen.

3. Click the sample prompt provided to "Summarize this presentation" (Figure 3-8).

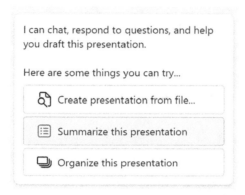

Figure 3-8. *Summarize presentation content using Copilot*

4. Copilot will summarize the presentation content and bring bulleted information that can be copied for further usage. Notice that Copilot is also providing reference details that are critical to validate the accuracy and source of information (Figure 3-9).

Here's a summary of the deck:

Main ideas:

- **EcoBottle:** EcoBottle is a reusable water bottle with a built-in filtration system that removes 99.9% of bacteria, viruses, and contaminants [1]
- **Market Analysis:** The global reusable water bottle market is valued at USD 8.1 billion in 2018 and is expected to grow at a CAGR of 3.9% from 2019 to 2025 [2]
- **Marketing Strategy:** The marketing strategy for EcoBottle includes creating awareness and interest in the product, communicating its unique value proposition, and persuading potential customers to purchase [3]
- **Competition Advantage:** EcoBottle's competitive advantage includes its advanced and comprehensive filtration system, unique and user-friendly digital display, and attractive and affordable price [4]
- **Financial Projections:** The financial projections for EcoBottle show promising results with a high profit margin and low break-even point [5]

Ask me to help with something else, or for more ideas see the prompt guide below.

☐ Copy

◯ AI-generated content may be incorrect   👍 👎

5 References ∧

1	"Reusable water bot..."	∨
2	"Target market: hea..."	∨
3	"Objectives of Mark..."	∨

Figure 3-9. *Presentation summary generated using a Copilot prompt*

Asking Information About Presentation Content

As we experienced in Microsoft Copilot for Word, we can ask questions about information in the presentation data, and Copilot can intelligently respond back with findings. We will continue to use the "**BusinessProposalPresentation_01.pptx**", which can be downloaded from https://github.com/Apress/Introducing-Microsoft-Copilot-for-Managers/tree/main/Part-II/PowerPoint/BusinessProposalPresentation_01.pptx.

1. Open the **BusinessProposalPresentation_01.pptx** PowerPoint presentation.

2. Click the Copilot (⬦) icon in the home tab of the ribbon. A chat window will open on the right side of the screen.

3. In the Copilot chat window, ask the following question:

   "what is the product price suggested and what is the initial investment required"

4. Copilot will review the presentation content and revert back with findings; in this case, it responded back with product pricing and investment requirements as stated in the document (Figure 3-10).

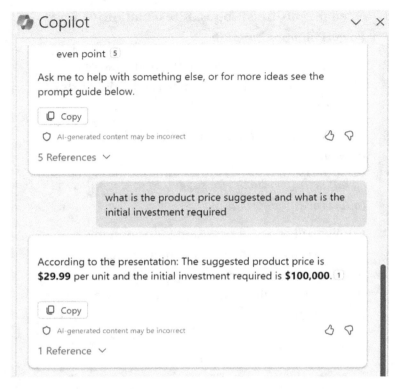

Figure 3-10. *Asking questions about information in presentation*

Users can continue to ask additional questions about the presentation content and appreciate the ease Copilot has introduced for consuming knowledge from existing presentations.

Prompt Guide for Chat Experience

Like in the case of Microsoft Word Copilot, to ensure user experience and adoption remain easy, there are many sample prompts that users can view and use. To access the sample prompts, users can click the "View Prompt" (⬜) icon. As shown in Figure 3-11, by clicking the icon, users will be provided with prompts in various categories. These prompts can be used as guides to create your own personal prompts and chat interactions.

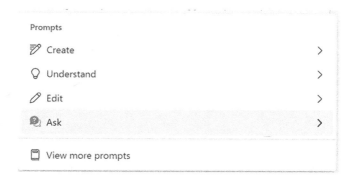

Figure 3-11. *Sample prompts available with PowerPoint Copilot*

3.2 Summary

In this chapter, we covered the features and benefits of Microsoft Copilot for PowerPoint, followed step-by-step guides for creating presentations from scratch or from a file and for editing presentations with Copilot suggestions. We discussed the benefits and use cases of Microsoft Copilot for PowerPoint.

We learned in detail that Microsoft Copilot for PowerPoint can assist users in creating presentations from scratch or from a file, suggesting relevant content and design options, and improving existing presentations with layout, content, and visual aid recommendations. It can also answer natural language questions about the presentation topic and content. It can be useful for various industries and business functions, such as education, financial services, healthcare, and retail.

This chapter has enabled us to build a PowerPoint presentation much faster and generate highly presentable content with the support of Copilot. We will continue to learn about productivity tools in the next chapter and turn our attention toward Microsoft Excel.

CHAPTER 4

Microsoft Copilot in Excel

In this chapter, we will continue learning about Microsoft Copilot in productivity tools and focus on Microsoft Excel. Microsoft productivity tools are a suite of applications designed to enhance efficiency and productivity in various work scenarios. I have discussed briefly about the suite in Chapter 1 and would recommend to quickly recap the chapter.

In this chapter, we will deep dive into Microsoft 365 Copilot features for Excel. The objective of this chapter is to list the Copilot features available during the time of writing this book. We will not cover the product features as it is assumed that the readers have a foundational understanding of the product/service.

However, let's just recap on each of the tool's objectives. Microsoft Excel is a fundamental tool in the business world – a digital platform where data performs its complex movements. Whether you're a financial analyst, project manager, or marketing strategist, Excel provides a variety of tools to coordinate your numerical tasks. Microsoft Excel has become a go-to tool for any kind of business number crunching, data analysis, and even to some extent visualization.

© Adeel Khan 2024
A. Khan, *Introducing Microsoft Copilot for Managers*, Inside Copilot,
https://doi.org/10.1007/979-8-8688-0419-9_4

Some of the key features of Microsoft Excel that make the tool so powerful are as follows:

- **Spreadsheet Creation**: Begin your journey by creating spreadsheets, a virtual table where numbers and text converge. You can define rows and columns and organize content such as budgets, inventories, and forecasts.

- **Formulas and Functions**: Excel's heart lies in its formulas. You can use them to perform calculations, manipulate data, and identify patterns. From basic arithmetic (like SUM and AVERAGE) to complex statistical analyses, Excel offers a vast library of functions for users.

- **Data Visualization**: Charts and graphs breathe life into raw numbers. Bar charts, line graphs, and pie charts help bring numbers to the visual canvas and help users share data story with ease. Excel offers users the ability to create PivotTables, transforming tangled data into meaningful summaries.

- **Cell Formatting**: A vast set of styling and formatting options are available at Excel where you can format cells for text or for types such as currency symbols, percentage signs, and date formats, tailoring your content for more clarity.

- **Collaboration and Sharing**: You can share your workbook with colleagues. Collaborate in real time and enhance productivity.

Before beginning this chapter, it is recommended to complete Chapter 2 and its exercise as the document will be used in this chapter. Also, it is good to revise the M365 architecture as it is common across all productivity tools discussed previously.

4.1 M365 Copilot for Excel

Microsoft Copilot for Excel is designed to enhance user productivity and efficiency while working with Excel. It's an intelligent assistant that understands user data, provides insights, automates tasks, and even learns from user's patterns to predict needs.

Microsoft Copilot for Excel can handle routine tasks for users, so they can save time while repeating actions. The ability to examine data allows Copilot to provide useful insights to further improve understanding of content as well as improve data within Excel. Just like Word and PowerPoint Copilot, the simplicity and user-friendly experience makes it easy to adopt and utilize in daily operations.

Like other Copilots we have discussed so far, Microsoft Copilot for Excel is designed to be helpful across a wide range of industries. Here are some examples:

- **Education:** Educators can use Copilot to track and analyze student performance data. For example, it can automate the process of calculating grades, identify trends in student performance, and even predict future performance based on historical data.

- **Financial Services Industry (FSI):** In the FSI, Copilot can be used to automate financial modeling and analysis. For example, it can help in generating financial reports, analyzing investment portfolios, and predicting market trends.

- **Healthcare:** Healthcare professionals can use Copilot to manage and analyze patient data. For example, it can help in tracking patient health metrics, identifying patterns in patient health, and predicting patient health outcomes based on historical data.

- **Retail:** In the retail industry, Copilot can help in managing inventory, sales, and customer data. For example, it can automate the process of tracking inventory levels, analyzing sales data to identify trends, and predicting future sales based on historical data.

Microsoft Copilot for Excel is going to enhance productivity and efficiency across a wide range of industries. Mastering interaction with Copilot will allow users to improve their handling of daily operations and elevate their experience further with Microsoft Excel.

In the next section, we will experiment with Microsoft Copilot for Excel and learn its features.

Note   Microsoft Copilot for Excel only works with Excel files stored in OneDrive or SharePoint. Also, Copilot works with Excel having data already.

4.1.1 Enabling

Before we begin with the exercise, it is recommended to download the sample Excel file (that is also generated using Copilot) "**MarketingCampaignExcel01.xlsx**" from https://github.com/Apress/ Introducing-Microsoft-Copilot-for-Managers/tree/main/Part-II/ Excel/MarketingCampaignExcel01.xlsx.

This will allow you a near similar experience during the rest of the exercise. Also, make sure you save this file in OneDrive or SharePoint.

1.   Open "**MarketingCampaignExcel01.xlsx**".

2.   At the home ribbon, click the Copilot for Excel (⬡) icon.

3.   This will launch and open the Copilot for Excel chat pane in Excel (Figure 4-1).

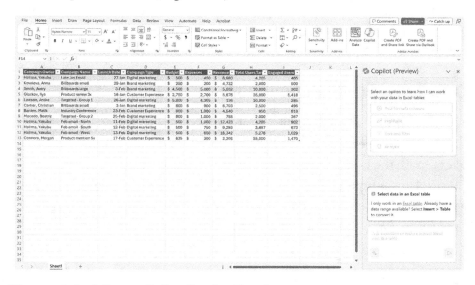

Figure 4-1. *Microsoft Copilot for Excel*

4.   Notice the reminder Copilot is highlighting. "**I only work in an Excel table**" as shown in Figure 4-1. At the time this book is written, the Copilot feature is limited to work with tables.

5.   Select Table1 in the Excel sheet and notice the change in the chat pane.

6.   The features and auto prompt will be enabled.

These limitations and prerequisites are good to remember as they will impact how we engage with Copilot in Excel.

4.1.2 Create

Microsoft Copilot for Excel can generate new content based on user requirements and existing data in Excel. It can create complex formulas, charts, pivot tables, and even entire datasets.

This capability is particularly useful when the user needs to quickly generate data for analysis or reporting. As per the format of the book, we will learn by experimenting with the Create features of Copilot.

Creating a Formula Column

We will continue to work on the same Excel sample referred to in the previous section. In this exercise, we will create a column to compare the budget and expenses. The sample Excel file "**MarketingCampaignExcel01.xlsx**" can be downloaded from https:// github.com/Apress/Introducing-Microsoft-Copilot-for-Managers/ tree/main/Part-II/Excel/MarketingCampaignExcel01.xlsx.

1. Open "**MarketingCampaignExcel01.xlsx**".

2. Select Table1 in Sheet1.

3. In the home ribbon, click the Copilot for Excel (⬭) icon.

4. This will launch and open the Copilot for Excel chat pane in Excel.

5. Type the following prompt in the chat window:

    "*Add a column to compare 'Budget' and 'Revenue'*"

6. This prompt will advise Copilot for the creation of a new column. Copilot will process the prompt and revert back with a suggestion including a formula (Figure 4-2).

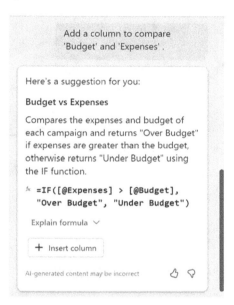

Figure 4-2. *Creating a column using Copilot for Excel*

7. Notice the intelligent suggestion, not only creating a comparison formula script but also making it business user-friendly with labeling.

8. The Explain formula section provides descriptive details of the suggested formula. This feature is extremely in validating formula, especially if complex calculations or conditions are applied (Figure 4-3).

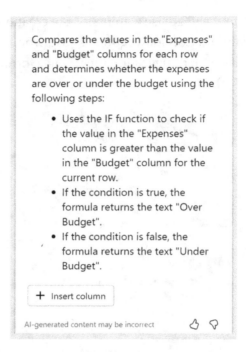

Figure 4-3. *Microsoft Copilot for Excel formula explanation*

9. If the user is okay with the suggestion, click the
    Insert column (+ insert column) button to update the
    selected Table1 with the new column (Figure 4-4).

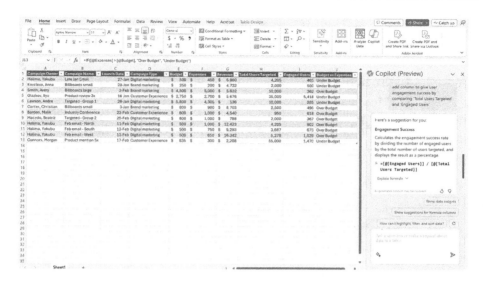

Figure 4-4. *New created column with Microsoft Copilot for Excel*

Similarly, let's add another column to further improve the dataset. Here's a prompt need to type:

"Add column to give user engagement success by comparing 'Total Users Targeted' and 'Engaged Users.'"

The final output is saved as "**MarketingCampaignExcel02.xlsx**" and can be downloaded from https://github.com/Apress/Introducing-Microsoft-Copilot-for-Managers/tree/main/Part-II/Excel/MarketingCampaignExcel02.xlsx. We will be using this file for the next exercise.

Creating a Pivot Table

We will continue to work on the "**MarketingCampaignExcel02.xlsx**" Excel sample referred to in the previous section. In this exercise, we will create a pivot table to summarize the data in Table1:

1. Open "**MarketingCampaignExcel02.xlsx**".

2. Select Table1 in Sheet1.

3. In the home ribbon, click the Copilot for Excel
    (⬭) icon.

4. This will launch and open the Copilot for Excel chat
    pane in Excel.

5. Type the following prompt in the chat window:

    "*Create a pivot table showing the total revenue and
    average engagement success per Campaign type for
    the given data.*"

6. Based on the prompt, Copilot will suggest a pivot
    table. We will be asked by Copilot to review the
    output. If it is aligned to our requirements, we can
    add the pivot table in the Excel file by clicking the
    "Add a new sheet" (+ Add to a new sheet) button (Figure 4-5).

Figure 4-5. *Adding a pivot table using a prompt in Microsoft Copilot
for Excel*

7. The add action will result in a new pivot table added in Sheet2 (Figure 4-6).

Figure 4-6. *Added sheet with the pivot table using Microsoft Copilot*

These are prompt examples that can help us create new content and generate even charts. For example, you can use the following prompt to create a bar chart:

> *"Create a bar chart using table1 data. The data includes 'Campaign Name', 'Budget', 'Expenses', and 'Revenue.' The chart should compare the budget, expenses, and revenue for each campaign."*

The outcome of this exercise is saved as **"MarketingCampaignExcel03.xlsx"**. The file can be downloaded from `https://github.com/Apress/Introducing-Microsoft-Copilot-for-Managers/tree/main/Part-II/Excel/MarketingCampaignExcel03.xlsx`. The file also includes the bar chart mentioned earlier.

4.1.3 Edit

Microsoft Copilot for Excel can assist you in editing and managing your data in Excel. It can automate tasks such as finding and replacing values, sorting, and filtering data and even more advanced operations like applying macros. By providing Copilot with clear and specific prompts, you can effectively automate many of the repetitive tasks involved in data editing. This not only saves time but also reduces the risk of manual errors. With Microsoft Copilot for Excel, editing and organizing your data becomes a more efficient and error-free process.

Sorting and Filtering Using Copilot

Users can work with datasets using prompts in Microsoft Copilot for Excel. In this example, we will experiment with Copilot's ability to sort, filter, and format data using easy natural language prompts. We will be using the Excel sample file "**MarketingCampaignExcel03.xlsx**". The file can be downloaded from https://github.com/Apress/Introducing-Microsoft-Copilot-for-Managers/tree/main/Part-II/Excel/MarketingCampaignExcel03.xlsx.

1. Open "**MarketingCampaignExcel03.xlsx**".

2. Select Table1 in Sheet1.

3. In the home ribbon, click the Copilot for Excel (⬭) icon.

4. This will launch and open the Copilot for Excel chat pane in Excel.

5. Type the following prompt in the chat window:

   "*Bold the top 5 values in 'Revenue'.*"

6. This will result in Copilot formatting the top five values in Table1 (Figure 4-7).

Figure 4-7. *Formatting through a prompt using Microsoft Copilot for Excel*

7. The next prompt we want to type is the following:

   "Sort 'Engagement Success' from largest to smallest."

8. This will sort the rows as per the provided prompt (Figure 4-8).

Figure 4-8. *Sorting through a prompt using Microsoft Copilot for Excel*

9. The last prompt we want to experience is related to the filtering of data. Let's type the following prompt:

   "Show only over budget."

10. This will sort the records according to our prompt. Observe how precise we were in our prompt and how smartly Copilot comprehended the task. This shows how simple and convenient Microsoft Copilot for Excel is for users (Figure 4-9).

Figure 4-9. *Filtering using a prompt in Microsoft Copilot for Excel*

In this example, we learned how to use prompts to perform formatting, sorting, and filtering. Copilot has made these activities easy and fast for any level of users to improve the output or work with datasets in Excel.

Data Manipulation Using Copilot

Users can perform data manipulation tasks using Copilot as well. For example, we can use prompts to update specific values in spreadsheets using easy natural language. These prompts can be useful when handling large data and improving the data quality.

For example, if we want to update certain information across the Excel spreadsheet, we can simply ask Copilot to perform the action. Let's try this feature:

1. Open "**MarketingCampaignExcel03.xlsx**".

2. Select Table1 in Sheet1.

3. In the home ribbon, click the Copilot for Excel (🖉) icon.

4. This will launch and open the Copilot for Excel chat pane in Excel.

5. Type the following prompt in the chat window:

    "find and replace all occurrences of 'Customer Experience' with 'New Customer Experience' in an Excel worksheet."

6. This will result in Copilot updating all the instances of "Customer Experience" with a new provided replacement (Figure 4-10).

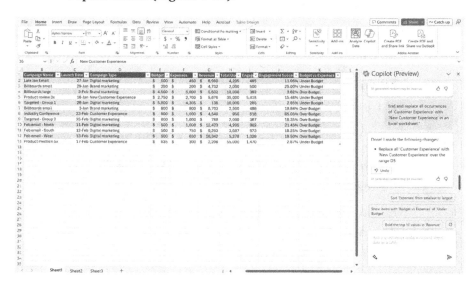

Figure 4-10. *Find and replace using Microsoft Copilot for Excel*

This is a simple example, but imagine updating a large dataset with many numerical values having "N/A" instead of "0." As suggested earlier, this feature of Copilot can be super useful for improving data quality and reducing human error.

4.1.4 Understand

As with Copilot for Word and PowerPoint, we can chat with Copilot for Microsoft Excel and understand our dataset better. In this example, we will work with "**MarketingCampaignExcel03.xlsx**" and inquire about data using Copilot chat.

Analyze and Summarize Using Copilot

In this example, we will leverage Copilot's analyze and summarize capabilities to generate insights for better understanding:

1. Open "**MarketingCampaignExcel03.xlsx**".

2. Select Table1 in Sheet1.

3. In the home ribbon, click the Copilot for Excel (⊘) icon.

4. This will launch and open the Copilot for Excel chat pane in Excel.

5. Type the following prompt in the chat window:

   "*Identify best performing campaign type, based on Engagement Success and Budget.*"

6. This prompt will result in Copilot creating a pivot table to list the campaign types based on the preceding criteria (Figure 4-11).

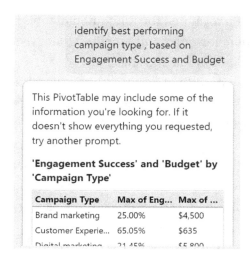

Figure 4-11. *Analyzing through a prompt using Microsoft Copilot*

Similarly, Copilot will also suggest many other prompts to users that can give valuable insights on the dataset. It is highly recommended to experiment with these prompts and identify trends and insights not known otherwise or take an expert eye to catch.

4.2 Summary

In this chapter, we introduced the features and benefits of Microsoft Copilot for Excel, the intelligent experience that can help us with data analysis and automation. The chapter demonstrated how to use Copilot to create new content in Excel, such as formulas, charts, pivot tables, and datasets, by using natural language prompts.

The chapter began with a general introduction to Microsoft Copilot within the suite of Microsoft productivity tools, emphasizing its role in enhancing efficiency and productivity in Excel. It listed the available Copilot features at the time of writing this book and assumed the readers have a foundational understanding of Excel.

The chapter then recapped the fundamental tools in Excel, such as spreadsheet creation, formulas and functions, data visualization, cell formatting, and collaboration and sharing.

The chapter also described how Copilot for Excel serves as an intelligent assistant that automates tasks, provides insights, and learns from user patterns to predict needs. It detailed how Copilot can handle routine tasks, examine data, and offer a user-friendly experience across various industries like education, financial services, healthcare, and retail.

The chapter covered the instructions on how to enable Copilot for Excel, including downloading a sample file and saving it in OneDrive or SharePoint.

The chapter also demonstrated how to use Copilot to create formulas, charts, pivot tables, and datasets in Excel. It included exercises for creating a formula column and a pivot table, with detailed steps and figures illustrating the process. It discussed the editing tasks such as formatting, sorting, filtering, and data manipulation. It provided examples of using natural language prompts to perform these tasks efficiently.

The final section discussed how to use Copilot to analyze and summarize data; identify trends, patterns, and outliers; and generate insights for better understanding.

In the next chapter, we will explore the communication and collaboration tools enhancements with the introduction of Microsoft Copilot.

CHAPTER 5

Microsoft Copilot in Communication and Collaboration

In this chapter, we will learn about Microsoft Copilot in communication and collaboration. These solutions are part of the Microsoft productivity tool suite designed to enhance efficiency in various settings.

In this chapter, we will deep dive into Microsoft 365 Copilot features and work scenarios for products like Outlook and Teams. The objective of this chapter is to list the Copilot features available during the writing of this book. We will not cover the product features as it is assumed that the readers have a foundational understanding of the product/service. However, let's just recap on each of these tools' objectives:

- **Microsoft Outlook**: An email and calendar tool that helps manage mail, schedule, contacts, and tasks. It's part of the Microsoft 365 suite and can be accessed from anywhere.

- **Microsoft Teams**: A collaboration platform that enables team members to work together seamlessly, irrespective of their locations. It offers a range of powerful tools for communication and collaboration,

© Adeel Khan 2024
A. Khan, *Introducing Microsoft Copilot for Managers*, Inside Copilot,
https://doi.org/10.1007/979-8-8688-0419-9_5

> including channels, chat, file management, meetings,
> and native and third-party app integrations. It can
> also act as a master app, as it can host a wide variety of
> applications and solutions.

Microsoft Outlook and Microsoft Teams are powerful tools that address different aspects of business operations. By enhancing communication and collaboration, these tools empower corporate employees to work more efficiently and effectively, thereby driving business success. With the addition of Copilot, your team experience and efficiency are going to be enhanced further.

In the next section, we will discuss these products' Copilot and available features.

5.1 M365 Copilot for Outlook

Copilot for Microsoft Outlook is a remarkable addition to the tool that brings the transformative power of artificial intelligence to the world of email management and scheduling. This innovative assistant is designed to revolutionize the way users interact with Microsoft Outlook, making the process of managing emails and scheduling meetings more efficient, intuitive, and user-friendly.

The impact of Copilot on the user experience is profound. It speeds up the email management process and improves the output quality. Whether you or your team is drafting a business email, scheduling a meeting, or managing your inbox, Copilot can help you achieve your goals more effectively.

In the following section, we will experience the various features available and learn about their usage.

5.1.1 Create

The "Create" feature of Copilot for Outlook brings content creation experience to emailing. As a user, you will be able to define the scope of email content using prompts within the email body and let Copilot return with suggested content. It is important to understand that Microsoft Copilot for Outlook will leverage and suggest content based on generic information. For customer-specific content suggestions, we will explore Microsoft Copilot for Sales, which has permission and access to an organization's CRM (Dynamics 365 or Salesforce). We will cover that from Sales and Service point of view in detail under Part V.

Let's continue learning about the content creation feature of Outlook using the following examples.

Creating a New Content

In the first exercise, we will generate a content using a foundational Copilot capability using a generic prompt:

1. Open the Microsoft Outlook Windows 11 application or browser app.

2. From the home ribbon, select New Email.

3. Once the New email is open, notice a Copilot (🌀) icon in the ribbon. Click the option and choose "Draft with Copilot" (Figure 5-1).

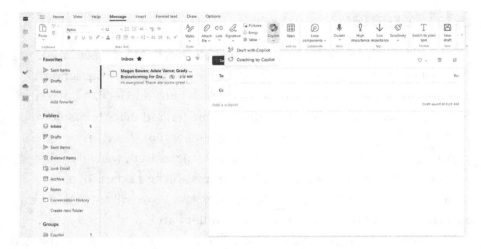

Figure 5-1. *Microsoft Copilot for Outlook, drafting a new content*

4. This will enable the Copilot compose window,
    similar to what we have experienced in Microsoft
    Word. Shown in Figure 5-2, this is a compose
    window where you will be typing the prompt.

Figure 5-2. *Microsoft Copilot for Outlook compose window*

5. We will use the following prompt to generate a
    content of our new email:

    "*draft an email for investors, thanking them for
    taking time and sharing valuable insights during
    last product launch meeting. Also provide actions*

that product team will be taking such as reviewing target market audience again, improve on market competition landscape analysis, perform SWOT analysis on new product theme. Keep the tone formal and friendly."

6. We can also set the tone using the setting (⚬) icon in the compose window; however, since we are hoping for a combination of two tones, we have chosen to define within the prompt.

7. The setting option also offers some interesting options beyond setting up of tone. We can choose the length of the response as well. Choose "Medium" from the option (Figure 5-3).

Figure 5-3. Microsoft Copilot for Outlook and settings

8. Now that we are all set to generate the content, click the Generate (Generate →) button to let Copilot curate and suggest. The output of this action would be a drafted content that we can keep, discard, or further improve by providing change details based on our personal liking and regenerate (Figure 5-4).

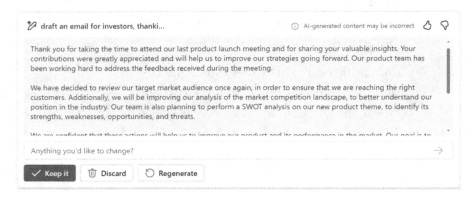

Figure 5-4. *Microsoft Copilot for Outlook, suggested email draft*

This simple exercise demonstrates the Copilot ability to generate email content and provide you with the draft that can be further fine-tuned for usage. Play around with a few prompts and features, especially the one to generate a poem. You will be surprised by the creativity of the tool.

Drafting a Reply

The next exercise is to learn and practice how to use Copilot for replying to a specific email. It is difficult to simulate the same example, so we will discuss the feature actions more than the content in the example.

1. Open the Microsoft Outlook Windows 11 application or browser app.

2. Choose any existing email and click Reply or Reply all.

3. Please ensure that you are in the safe environment, and you will not end up sending this email to any business or internal contact.

4. Once the email is open, notice a Copilot ( ) icon in the ribbon. Click the option and choose "Draft with Copilot."

5. Similar to the preceding example, the compose window will appear, and we will type our prompt in the window.

6. When replying, we can provide the prompt the context that we want to achieve. A simple and generic prompt may look like the following:

   "Acknowledge the email, thanks for partnership and suggest more interaction in future."

7. Click the Generate (Generate →) button and review the generated draft.

These are simple examples to leverage the Copilot features in Microsoft Outlook to generate the content. In the next exercise, we will learn about the Coaching feature of Copilot.

5.1.2 Coach

For users who like to draft their own emails, Coaching is an exciting feature to get reviews and suggestions on their email content. Microsoft Copilot for Outlook can coach you to deliver your message in the right tone and clarity to communicate more effectively. To perform this exercise, we will need a draft email with content as coaching can be only applied if the email contains more than 100 words. First, complete or repeat the steps in the section "Creating a New Content" before beginning this exercise:

1. Complete the actions listed in the "Creating a New Content" exercise.

2. Click the Copilot (⬙) icon in the ribbon. Choose "Coaching by Copilot" (Figure 5-5).

✐ Draft with Copilot

🎓 Coaching by Copilot

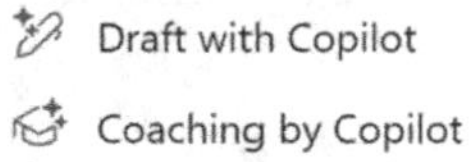

Figure 5-5. *Microsoft Copilot for Outlook, Copliot options with email*

3. This will initiate the review process using Copilot. After the assessment of content, Copilot will provide a comprehensive review with insights on the content as well as opportunities to improve the content further (Figure 5-6).

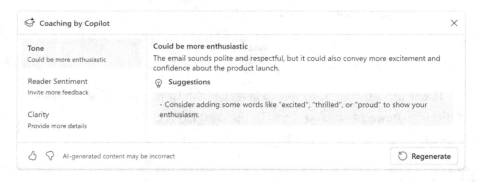

Figure 5-6. *Microsoft Copilot for Outlook, Coaching feature*

4. As visible in Figure 5-6, the review will be helpful in improving the content, tone, or context of the email.

This feature can self-help users and help them identify areas of communication they need to improve while providing them a drafting ability to create content. In the next section, we will discuss the summarization capability of Microsoft Copilot for Outlook.

5.1.3 Summarize

Another feature of Microsoft Copilot for Outlook is the ability to summarize long emails or attachments into concise bullet points. This can save time and effort for busy professionals who need to quickly grasp the main points of a message without reading lengthy paragraphs. The summarization feature can also help users compose clear and succinct replies or follow-ups based on the summary.

To use the summarization feature, you can select a conversation in the inbox and click the summarize (⏱) icon. This will trigger a summarization action where Copilot will prepare a concise summary with key takeaways of the conversations. In Figure 5-7, a long email discussing distinct options for a new office location has been summarized in a few short easy-to-read bullet points.

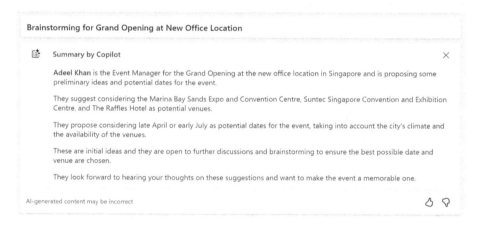

Figure 5-7. *Microsoft Copilot for Outlook, summarize feature*

This feature will enhance user experience and improve their ability to communicate and extract better information while using Microsoft Outlook. In later chapters, we will further explore how the summary feature can be used in combination with Microsoft Sales Copilot to enhance customer or stakeholder information.

5.2 M365 Copilot for Teams

M365 Copilot for Teams helps you get the most out of your meetings and conversations on Microsoft Teams. It integrates seamlessly the Microsoft Office ecosystem and drives productivity to the next level for you and your team. Copilot for Teams can assist in preparing for your upcoming meetings with personalized briefings, help you engage effectively during the meetings and follow up after the meeting with automated summaries. Copilot for teams is going to change the way we interact with MS teams and going to offload the pain of making sense out of fragmented conversations.

In this section, together we will learn how to use M365 Copilot for Teams to catch up, create, and chat with our meetings and conversations.

5.2.1 Catch Up

The catch-up feature helps you and your team connect to long conversations with much ease. We all have had a situation where the Teams channel conversations or group conversations are updated by many peers, and to track who said what and what changed since the last time you were participating in the conversation becomes quite challenging. Similarly, if you are working remotely, staying on top of the updates and information shared by your team members is a challenging task. Copilot for Teams helps you catch up with your meetings and conversations by providing you with personalized briefings, reminders, and insights.

We can now begin learning on how to leverage this feature by going through the following steps (assuming teams is already enabled with Copilot):

1. Log in to your MS Teams.

2. Choose any specific conversation.

3. You will find the Copilot (⬭) icon at the top right along with the title of the conversation. Click to open the Copilot interface in teams.

4. Like other experiences, you will find the Copilot interface with the chat box enabled (Figure 5-8).

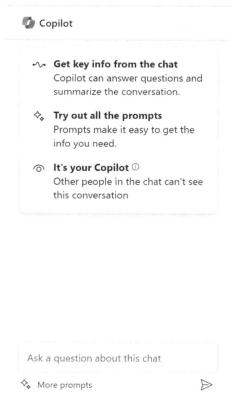

Figure 5-8. *Copilot chat interface for Teams*

5. Let's try prompts like

   "summarize the conversation."

6. This will summarize the selected conversation and provide you a bulleted response.

7. Similarly, you can ask other questions to understand the details of the conversation or if this is a meeting as prompts like *"show me the meeting notes."*

8. A detailed meeting note will be generated (Figure 5-9).

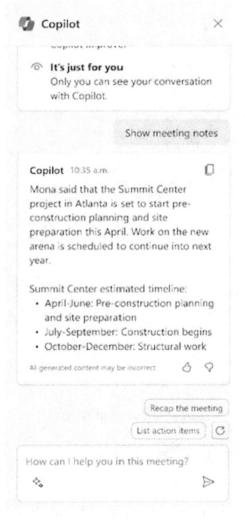

Figure 5-9. *Teams Copilot catch-up feature (6)*

This feature helps in truly catching up and becoming up to speed with conversations that are happening around us.

5.2.2 Create and Chat

Copilot for teams can also help in generating new content out of the conversation history via chat experience. Using generative AI capabilities, Copilot understands, analyzes, and helps you generate a new content. We can now do a short exercise to experience the content generation feature:

1. Log in to your MS Teams.

2. Choose any specific conversation.

3. You will find the Copilot (⌇) icon at the top right along with the title of the conversation. Click to open the Copilot interface in teams.

4. Choose any conversation that has many items discussed.

5. Like other experiences, you will find the Copilot interface with the chat box enabled.

6. In the chat box, type the following prompt:

   "Create a table of all recommendations in this conversation."

7. As in my experience, I picked up one such conversation, and Copilot generated a list of recommendations made by various participants (Figure 5-10).

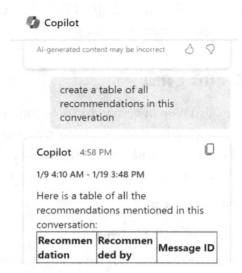

Figure 5-10. *Generating content using Teams Copilot*

8. Similarly, you can experiment with many other content creation prompts such as "list action items," "draft a pending item list," etc., to create new content.

9. You can also converse with data in chat and ask questions like *"who are most active participants,"* and Copilot will provide you with answers.

Teams indeed is becoming a master app of the future where you will experience various generic and specialized Copilots to address various business problems. These features are super useful on an individual basis; we will also discuss in later chapters how we can further elevate the conversation experience using Microsoft Copilot, Copilot for Sales, and custom Copilot via teams.

5.3 Summary

In this chapter, we discussed the features of Microsoft Copilot for Outlook and Teams. We learned how best we can use Copilot to respond to various internal and external communications and leverage the summarization feature to keep up with changes as well as content irrespective of the volume and size of interaction.

We learned with hands-on exercises on both the tools. We practiced a few prompts and learned how best to interact with Copilots for Outlook and Teams.

In the next chapter, we will cover the Microsoft Copilot Chat feature that brings the rich in-app experience to chat-like experience.

CHAPTER 6

Microsoft Copilot Chat

So far, we have discussed Microsoft Copilot in various productivity apps, such as Word, Excel, Outlook, and Teams.

I am glad to share that we can access Microsoft Copilot as an independent experience as well and infuse experience from various Microsoft productivity solutions with the help of connectors (in teams) to data that reside in third-party applications.

In this chapter, we will turn our focus on Microsoft Copilot Chat as outside app experience. We will deep dive into Microsoft 365 Copilot Chat features and work scenarios independent of product scope. The objective of this chapter is to list the Copilot features available during the time of writing this book. There are two ways we can interact with "Master Copilot":

- **M365 Copilot Chat in Browser**: This experience merges (not in data sense but in experience) Bing search and M365 Copilot. The M365 Copilot supports both Chrome and Edge browsers.

- **M365 Copilot Chat in Teams**: This experience is Microsoft Teams based and provides feature access from the Teams interface along with additional support for out-of-the-box plugins that allow users to leverage data from other solutions.

© Adeel Khan 2024
A. Khan, *Introducing Microsoft Copilot for Managers*, Inside Copilot,
https://doi.org/10.1007/979-8-8688-0419-9_6

- **M365 Copilot Chat in Outlook**: This experience is Microsoft Outlook based and provides feature access from the Outlook interface. The teams' plugins are not available using chat experience for the Outlook interface.

Microsoft 365 combines many powerful features we have discussed before and brings our organization data into conversation with much ease. While the data is made accessible, the security and privacy of the data remain at the core, and only data to allowed profiles is provided. In a simple term, if your or your team does not have access to a dataset, Copilot will not let you access the dataset. So, access matrix and privacy will remain consistent with your organization policies.

In the next section, we will discuss features available by the time this book was written.

6.1 Working with M365 Copilot

In this section, we will explore M365 Copilot and learn to use the Copilot to solve our problems. We will learn how we can merge multiple information sets and make Copilot draft outputs in faster pace. We will first begin with learning how to access and then progressively move into experiments.

6.1.1 Accessing M365 Copilot

To access M365 Copilot, we have two options. First, in the browser, we can open Bing search and click the Copilot ( ) icon and select the work (Work) tab, or you can browse to `https:/copilot.microsoft.com` (Figure 6-1). It is important to ensure that you are in a work profile of search as this tab will determine if your prompt will be responded based on your organization's data or through publicly available data.

Figure 6-1. *Copilot for M365 in Bing*

The second way to access M365 Copilot is through MS teams as shown in Figure 6-2. To experience, you can open Microsoft Teams and look for Copilot (🔵 Copilot) in the chat section. This will open similar to browser experience with similar default prompts as shown in Figure 6-2.

Figure 6-2. *M365 Copilot experience in Teams*

Note   For privacy, we have removed the chat list, so do not get confused with that section. In your environment, you would see the chat interactions as well as Copilot.

The third way of accessing Microsoft Copilot for chat is through the Outlook app as shown in Figure 6-3. From the left menu of the latest Outlook app, you can find the Copilot ( ) icon. Clicking the icon will open up the chat experience.

Figure 6-3. *M365 Copilot chat experience in Outlook*

Please note that plugins enabled for the MS Teams environment will not be available at Outlook experience by default. We will discuss plugins in this chapter briefly and in comprehensive details under Part V.

A similar experience can also be accessed by typing `www.office.com/chat` in the browser.

In the next section, we will explore features of Copilot from catching up, drafting, and exploring points of view. You will notice many of the in-app prompts (that are part of Copilot lab) are still valid, but the prompt response can now leverage larger organization data that is critical for any personalized preparation.

6.1.2 Catching Up

In the first exercise, we will use a prompt to catch up on interactions, activities, and even on persons. This feature merges information from various datasets (emails, documents, etc.) and provides easy-to-absorb summary information with the intention to keep you and your team up to speed and ready for any related activity. We will begin our experimentation with this feature in the following steps:

1. Open M365 Copilot Chat in an interface of your choice (browser or teams); I will choose the browser.

2. Type the following prompt in the chat box:

    "what's the latest from /"

3. Notice that once you end the prompt with a "/", the chat box will open up a selection box where you can select from People, Files, Meetings, or Emails. Each of these will help us summarize the activities associated with our selection and provide an easy-to-read summary (Figure 6-4).

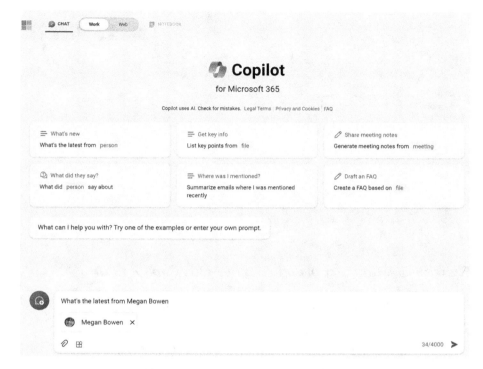

Figure 6-4. *Selecting interest for catching up using M365 Copilot Chat*

4. We can start with selecting someone from our colleagues (I have chosen Megan Bowen) and observe the results (Figure 6-5).

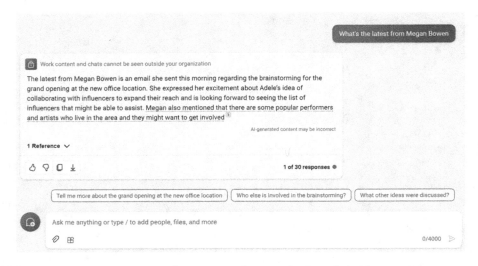

Figure 6-5. *Summary of activities by M365 Copilot Chat*

5. In this simple example, the Copilot Chat looked at all the activities happening with my colleague and provided me a summary as expected. What is interesting here is the set of next prompts; Copilot is recommending more insights that you can learn about the activity summary.

6. Now you will learn to get a summary from meetings; you will use a similar prompt only to select the latest meeting instead of people. The results will be similar where Copilot will process the information and provide us a summary from various activities associated with the meeting.

The next exercise is also interesting to catch up email threads and find out our desired results. Begin experimenting with this cool feature:

1. Open M365 Copilot Chat in an interface of your choice (browser or teams); I will choose the browser.

2. Type the following prompt in the chat box:

    "Summarize emails where I was mentioned recently"

3. This will list all the email messages where you were mentioned and with a summary of context/content.

There are many out-of-the-box prompts available that would advise you to play with them and find what works well for you. The catch-up capability really simplifies our ability to collate and absorb information from various sources and remain up to speed. In the next section, we will learn about using Copilot Chat to generate content.

6.1.3 Creating

In this section, we will use a prompt to generate content based on interactions and activities. This feature merges information from various datasets (emails, documents, etc.) and provides a draft for our consumption. We will begin our experimentation with this feature in the following steps:

1. Open M365 Copilot Chat in an interface of your choice (browser or teams); I will choose the browser.

2. Type the following prompt in the chat box:

    "Generate meeting notes from /"

3. This will open up the same content selection box; choose Meetings and then the meeting that you want to generate notes for (Figure 6-6).

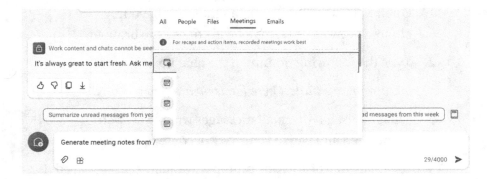

Figure 6-6. *Generating meeting notes with Microsoft Copilot Chat*

4. This prompt will generate a summary of the meeting
    for your consumption and enhancements.

Similar to this exercise, you can now also generate a summary from
multiple documents. Let's try this exercise. I will access our documents
created in previous chapters; you can refer to any other documents
you like.

1. Open M365 Copilot Chat in an interface of your
    choice (browser or teams); I will choose the browser.

2. Type the following prompt in the chat box:

    *"Generate summary from BusinessProposal_04.
    docx and BusinessProposalPresentation_02.pptx. list
    similarities and suggest improvements"* (Figure 6-7).

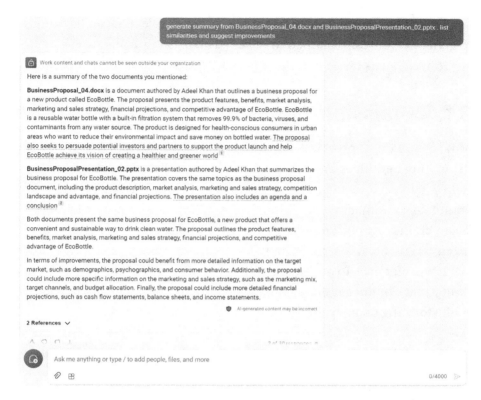

Figure 6-7. *Generating a summary of multiple documents and recommendations using M365 Copilot Chat*

3. This will generate a summary from both the documents and, as requested in the prompt, provide the improvement recommendations.

One other business use case I have seen commonly practiced is finding differences or even finding suitable candidates for a job post; the process remains the same where you will upload the two resumes along with a job description and prompt the Copilot chat to generate a summary on the candidate's suitability.

There are many out-of-the-box prompts available that can be used to generate new content or content based on existing artifacts. The next section will focus on discovering or brainstorming using M365 Copilot.

6.1.4 Brainstorming

Most of us would agree that brainstorming is a creative process of generating new ideas or solutions for a problem. Brainstorming can help you to explore different perspectives, overcome mental blocks, and stimulate your imagination. With Microsoft Copilot chat, you can now begin brainstorming, and in the process, it would suggest you relevant prompts and feedback based on your input and context.

If we refer back to our example in the "Catching Up" section, notice that Copilot suggested the next set of prompts that can help in brainstorming or analyzing the context further (Figure 6-8).

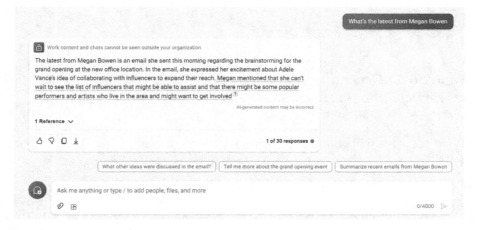

Figure 6-8. *Brainstorming with Microsoft Copilot Chat*

One of the benefits of using Microsoft Copilot for brainstorming is that it can help you to generate diverse and original ideas without being influenced by your own biases or assumptions. You can use Copilot to ask questions, challenge your assumptions, or generate alternatives. Let us experiment with brainstorming and experience this feature:

1. Open M365 Copilot Chat in an interface of your choice (browser or teams); I will choose the browser.

2. Type the following prompt in the chat box.

   "*List ideas for a fun remote team building event*"

3. As expected, this will generate a list of ideas that we can start leveraging (Figure 6-9).

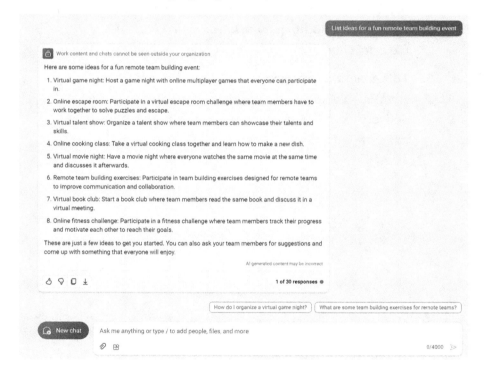

Figure 6-9. *Ideas generated using M365 Copilot Chat*

4. However, we want to use brainstorming on existing documents. This is where we can request Copilot to leverage the context and suggest accordingly. We will use our previously created presentation to request for improvements using the following prompt:

   "I need to turn BusinessProposalPresentation_02. pptx into a 15-minute presentation for a non-technical audience. Create an agenda. For each item in the agenda, include a duration, an objective, and a key talking point. Assume the intended audience is CxOs to whom we're introducing our product."

5. This generated an agenda with time duration that can not only help users improve the content but delivery as well. A pretty impressive output is shown in Figure 6-10.

Figure 6-10. *Presentation improvement as brainstorming using M365 Copilot Chat*

6.2 M365 Copilot Plugins

In this section, we briefly discuss the Copilot plugins. This subject will be discussed in detail under Part V; however, we will understand the concept and out-of-the-box offerings.

So far, we have experienced and learned that M365 Copilot leverages data that is available through a productivity app, be it a document, an email, or a meeting. But in real world, we will need data from many other sources, where either transactional data or interaction data is going to be captured. Plugins solve this problem for us where they enable Copilot to access the data into third-party sources and make it available just like Microsoft Graph data and in the process enable users to interact with data in conversational style. So, to summarize, plugins extend Copilot's functionality by connecting it to your own application data and APIs.

Note   At the time of writing this book, the plugins are only available at MS Teams.

There are two types of plugins available currently:

- **Teams Message Extensions**: Message extensions enable users to engage with your app directly from Teams. You can create custom message extensions that provide additional functionality or integrate with external services.

- **Microsoft Power Platform Connectors**: These connectors allow you to leverage existing software and tooling investments. You can integrate Power Platform connectors with Copilot to automate workflows, retrieve data, and perform various actions.

We will cover the Teams message extension in this chapter and Power Platform connectors in a later part of this book.

6.2.1 Architecture Update with Plugins

It is important to understand how plugins are going to become part of the overall Copilot experience from chat usage. If you recall the architecture (or rather soft architecture) of Copilot, let's see how it improves the same. I have updated the architecture figure and created an updated version as illustrated in Figure 6-11.

Notice the change in the Figure 6-11 architecture where now preprocessing is not only leveraging the semantic index and graph but also identifying through intent if the plugin is required. If so, it will execute the plugin and fall back to the same set of actions.

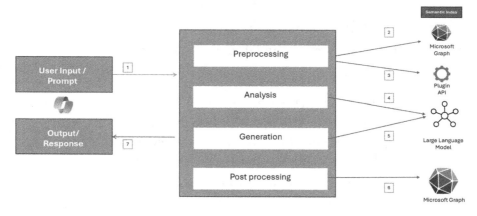

Figure 6-11. *Copilot plugin in architecture*

Here is the description of each step revised:

1. The user will either select a prebuilt prompt or provide a specific request through a prompt using Microsoft Copilot Chat.

2. Copilot then processes the prompt under preprocessing and improves the user-provided prompt by adding relevant information from the

semantic index and Microsoft Graph. The technical term for this stage is "grounding." This stage is critical as Copilot improves and contextualizes the prompt; however, it does so by only accessing data that a user has existing access to, based on granted access.

3. Based on grounding results and plugin descriptions, Copilot decides to invoke the plugin and collate responses along with graph outputs. The improved prompt is then sent to the large language model.

4. The large language model receives the improved prompt and prepares responses.

5. The large language model sends back the responses to Copilot.

6. Copilot modifies the response from the large language model with the post-processing step. This step includes more grounding calls to Microsoft Graph, responsible AI checks, security, compliance and privacy reviews, and command creation. This step is critical in the context of organizational information personalization and access.

7. Thes user receives the information in Copilot Chat.

6.2.2 Teams Message Extensions

Message extensions in Microsoft Teams are a powerful way for users to engage with apps directly from within Teams. These extensions allow you and your team to query information or post data to and from a service, seamlessly integrating it into their chat conversations.

To enable the plugins, we need to perform the following actions:

1. Open M365 Copilot chat in MS Teams.

2. In the chat box, click the Plugins (⊞) icon.

3. This will open up the selection window where you can choose the plugin you wish to switch on.

4. Choose More plugins (More plugins) from the window.

5. This will open up the list of available out-of-the-box plugins (Figure 6-12).

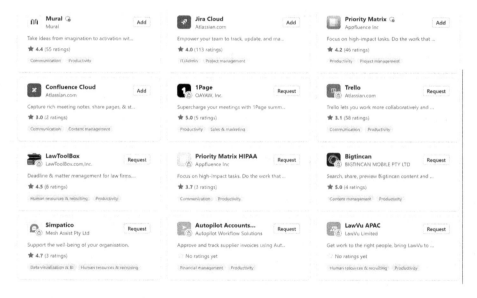

Figure 6-12. *Out-of-the-box plugins for Microsoft Copilot Chat*

6. Based on your access, you can choose the plugin and start interacting with the data using natural language.

Since this section depends on what is installed or available in your environment, it is difficult to simulate the example; however, I would highly recommend the example Microsoft has provided in their YouTube video titled "Get more from M365 Chat with external plugins" (`www.youtube.com/watch?v=gNF2pOTxO_Q`) to understand the concept.

6.3 Summary

This chapter was all about Microsoft Copilot Chat, a feature that allows users to access the Copilot AI assistant from various Microsoft 365 applications and get help with tasks such as catching up, creating, and brainstorming.

We learned that Copilot Chat can help users to catch up on interactions, activities, and events by summarizing information from different sources such as emails, files, meetings, and people. We also learned that Copilot could help users to generate content based on their inputs and context. Users can use prompts to ask Copilot to create meeting notes, summaries, agendas, or other types of documents.

The chapter concluded the working with M365 Copilot chat with exercises regarding the brainstorming feature where we learned how to engage Copilot in generating new ideas or improving existing ones.

The last part of the chapter briefly covered the plugins and introduced the concept to the readers. The discussion was intentionally kept brief as the subject is covered in detail under Part V.

This chapter also concluded Part II of the book where we learned about various Copilots in Modern Work sides of things. The next part, Part III, will take us into the world of development with a focus on the citizen development platform, "Power Platform."

PART III

Copilot in Microsoft Power Platform

In this part of the book, we delve into the features of Microsoft Power Platform Copilot. The chapters in this part encompass Power services such as Power Apps, Power Automate, Power Pages, and Power BI. This part comprises four chapters, each of which covers the following content in detail.

Chapter 7: The chapter discusses Microsoft Copilot for Power Apps, a tool that enables users to build low-code apps using conversational AI. The chapter covers the prerequisites for using Microsoft Copilot for Power Apps as well as firsthand practice to use Copilot as a Power Apps developer.

Chapter 8: The chapter introduces the features and benefits of Microsoft Copilot for Power Automate, which enables users to create and edit workflows using natural language. The chapter also demonstrates how to use Copilot to create and edit cloud flows using natural language prompts.

Chapter 9: The chapter explores Power Pages, a low-code platform for creating, hosting, and managing websites for external audiences. The chapter discusses the service offerings such as ready-made templates, a design studio, and a learning hub. The chapter also explains through hands-on exercises how to use Copilot for website creation and how to incorporate a generative AI chatbot into the website.

Chapter 10: The chapter discusses Microsoft Copilot for Power BI, a generative AI feature that aids users in creating and analyzing data visualizations. The chapter begins with a brief introduction to Power BI and expands on discussion about the use of Copilot in Power BI. The chapter uses business data from Walmart to learn about the dataset, generate reports, and generate narratives using default or custom prompts.

The aim of this part is to provide a working knowledge of the Copilot features that are either generally available or in preview at the time of writing this book. By the end of this part, the reader can become a better citizen developer and empowered to use generative AI to accelerate the hyperautomation using Power Platform services.

CHAPTER 7

Microsoft Copilot for Power Apps

The first chapter in Part III is dedicated to Power Apps. Microsoft Power Apps is a SaaS (software as a service) platform to build and manage data in a low-code/no-code environment. It provides a rapid development environment to build custom apps for your various business needs. It allows you to quickly build custom business apps that connect to your data stored either in the underlying data platform (Microsoft Dataverse) or in various online and on-premises data sources, such as SharePoint, Microsoft 365, Dynamics 365, SQL Server, and so on.

In this chapter, we will learn about Microsoft Copilot Power Apps and how using Copilot the pace of developing mobile-first and process-first apps is going to change forever.

My focus will be on Copilot, and it is assumed that you understand how Power Apps or Power Platform works. I will briefly cover the details of Power Apps to bring our conversation up to speed.

7.1 Introduction to Power Apps

Power Apps is a SaaS platform to build low-code/no-code applications that can be consumed by you, your team, or your organization. Apps built using Power Apps provide rich business logic and workflow capabilities

© Adeel Khan 2024
A. Khan, *Introducing Microsoft Copilot for Managers*, Inside Copilot,
https://doi.org/10.1007/979-8-8688-0419-9_7

to transform your manual business operations into digital, automated processes. What's more, apps built using Power Apps have a responsive design and can run seamlessly in a browser and on mobile devices (phone or tablet).

What sets Power Apps apart is the ability to truly "democratize" the business app building experience by enabling users to create feature-rich, custom business apps without writing traditional code. Power Apps also provides an extensible platform that lets pro developers programmatically interact with data and metadata, apply business logic, create custom connectors, and integrate with external data. However, I will restrict the discussion to business user experience.

Using Power Apps, you can create two types of apps: canvas and model driven.

- **Canvas Apps**: These apps start with a blank screen, like an artist's canvas, and the creator manually lays out each screen. This gives the creator complete control over the placement of each element on the canvas.

- **Model-Driven Apps**: These apps require a Microsoft Dataverse database. They're built on top of the data modeled in that database environment. Views and detail screens for model-driven apps are based on the data structure.

In summary, Power Apps is a powerful tool that enables both citizen developers and pro developers to build custom business apps that can transform manual business operations into digital, automated processes. It's a key component of Microsoft's Power Platform, which aims to empower every individual and every organization to achieve more.

In the next section, we will deep dive more on the Copilot features of Power Apps and how we can build end-to-end apps using conversational experience.

Note If you are new to Power Platform and Power Apps, I would highly recommend spending some time at `http://aka.ms/powerplatformresources` and browse through the content curated based on your experience with the platform.

7.2 Prerequisites

7.2.1 Setting and Validating

As discussed in the opening of the chapter, Power Apps is a SaaS platform that allows users to build canvas apps (mobile and tablet first) or model-driven apps (process and data first). To begin building apps, the user needs to access the Power Apps services. This can be done by browsing to `https://make.powerapps.com` or by clicking the App launcher at `https://office.com` and choosing the Power Apps (◆) icon.

Please remember that it is assumed that you are already logged in using user credentials having a Power Apps Premium license. Some of the following features discussed can be practiced through M365 E3/E5 licenses as well, but it is recommended to have a Premium license as we will work with Dataverse and premium connectors.

Note You can also sign up for a trial license that would allow you to experiment with Power Apps Premium capabilities; please refer to `https://powerapps.microsoft.com/` to learn about licensing and trial sign-up procedures.

Another important aspect is to validate the regional availability of Copilot. At the time of writing this book, the availability was limited to specific regions; however, it is best to validate with a refresh list at `https://learn.microsoft.com/en-us/power-platform/admin/geographical-availability-copilot`.

Now that both important aspects of setup are checked, let's go through the remaining prerequisites as provided by Microsoft:

- Microsoft Dataverse is required in the environment where you would leverage Copilot and AI features.

- AI Builder is required for use cases leveraging AI capabilities; this can be done by the admin of Power Platform by enabling "**AI Builder preview models**" under Environment ➤ [Name of Environment] ➤ Settings ➤ Features ➤ AI builder.

Once our initial setup is complete and validated, we can embark on our first Power Apps Copilot exercise and build an app using generative AI. As shown in Figure 7-1, you will experience a Power Apps landing page with Copilot chat enabled.

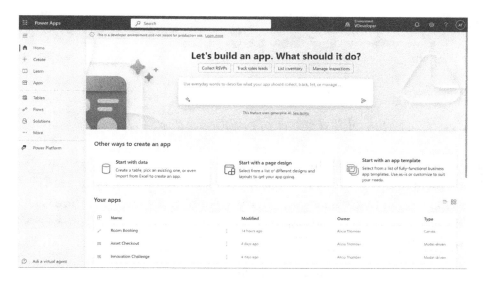

Figure 7-1. *Power Apps landing page with Copilot chat enabled*

Note   The Copilot features are in preview at the time of writing this book. Please refer to Power Platform documentation and product road map to track the availability of features.

7.2.2 Understanding the Process

It is also important to spend some time understanding the concepts of building an app as this will help you appreciate the Copilot experience much more. Whenever we start the process of solving or digitalizing data related process, there are a few common steps or stages that cannot be missed. I have illustrated the simplified life cycle in Figure 7-2.

Figure 7-2. *Simplified stages of building a data-driven app*

One could and rightfully so argue that there are many steps or stages and all of them are critical, but as this book is intended for business users like you, I have taken the liberty to simplify these stages. Here is a brief description of what happens at each stage or gate, as illustrated in Figure 7-2:

- **Identifying the Problem Statement**: This is where you would define the problem and call out what exactly you would want to do.

- **Detailing the Problem Further**: This is the stage where you improve your understanding about the subject in focus; it could be the customer, asset, application, etc.

- **Identifying the Storage Option**: Information captured must be stored somewhere; this is where you would identify where to store the information about the subject in focus.

- **Creating an Interface to Capture, Manage, and Display Information**: In this stage, you will start building an interface to perform four operations (**C**reate, **R**ead, **U**pdate, and **D**elete).

- **Extend to Personas Who Would Capture, Manage, or Use**: To make sure your solution is used and helping users automate the interaction with subject.

The reason I have illustrated this experience here is to make sure that you and your team understand the thought process or design process. Once understood, it will become easier for you to map the process with the Copilot journey. Also, you would understand where Copilot is going to help and where you would still need to drive the process.

7.3 Copilot in Canvas Apps

In the first exercise, we will leverage the build feature of Power Apps with a focus on Copilot. As mentioned in the earlier section, you can land to the Power Apps development studio by reaching to `https://make.powerapps.com`. Once you land to the Power Apps landing page, you are greeted with many options to continue your journey. We will begin with a quick review of important aspects.

The first and foremost is the environment that is mentioned at the top right. The Environment is a service container that keeps resources and data under one virtual container, helping in managing access, usage, and governance with ease. The concept of Environment is explained in detail in various Power Platform books and at Microsoft Learn (`https://learn.microsoft.com/en-us/power-platform/admin/environments-overview`), so we will not discuss it here; however, I would highly recommend to review if you are new to the Power Platform environment. Also, before moving forward with the exercise in this section, I would also recommend using the "Developer" environment so that you and your team can experiment without fear or impacting any production/critical data or process.

Referring to Figure 7-1, notice that you have many options to begin building an app. We can briefly discuss them as well:

- **Start with Copilot**: This is a latest feature added where you can describe an app you would like to build, and Power Apps will begin a guided experience to generate the draft app.

- **Start with Data**: This feature enables you to leverage existing data stored in supported data stores (Dataverse, Excel, SQL Server, SharePoint). This feature also leverages generative AI to help you explain what sort of information you would like to capture using your app.

- **Start with Template**: This feature allows you to pick from any of the ready templates, or you can also access the data sources as in "Start with Data."

- **Start with Page Design**: This is also a newly added feature, expanding offerings to start from a specific design layout, including supporting design tools like Figma to help draft an app using design features.

In this section, we will discuss Start with Data and Start with Copilot. You can learn about other features and options at the Microsoft Learn site.

7.3.1 Start with Copilot

Let us start the new way of building applications using Copilot for Power Apps. In this section, we will experience the power of generative AI and its impact on automation, especially on creating experiences where we either need users to provide data or create an experience where user data can be captured through our frontline or human agent. To begin this exercise, you must have an environment setup as discussed in the preceding prerequisites. Here are the steps to execute:

1. Log in to `https://make.powerapps.com`.

2. This will bring you to the Power Apps landing page.

3. Choose the environment you would want to use for
    the creation of this experiment. This is critical as
    you need Microsoft Dataverse enabled for Copilot
    experience.

4. At the home landing page, you would have by
    now noticed the chat box that is like other Copilot
    experiences. This is the box where we will provide
    our "prompt," a clear outline of what sort of
    experience or solution we want to build (Figure 7-3).

Figure 7-3. *Copilot chat/prompt box at the landing screen*

5. The following prompt is what we will use to create
    our first app experience with Copilot, but you
    can also pick any of the sample prompts that you
    see under the title, and they will also be good for
    learning. I have used this and two other prompts
    often in many of my customer meetings, and this
    one is the most popular choice by the attendees for
    no specific reason. We will proceed and type this:

    *"Build a room booking app for visiting guests, the
    check in and checkout date to be captured along with
    visitor information. contact details such as email and
    handphone. Also, each request will be tracked with
    status liked, booked/cancelled/completed"*

6. Click the send (▷) icon and begin the generative
    AI action.

7. The next screen you will see is the data model
    screen (Figure 7-4). If you are not clear why you
    have been presented with this screen, please revise
    or reread Section 7.2.2.

8. The data screen (Figure 7-4) will begin with
    creating a data model, suitable for such business
    requirements. Notice the fields Copilot has
    recommended; few of them are the ones we
    specifically called out, such as "Check-in Date" and
    "Check-out Date," and some Copilot added without
    asking, such as "Booking ID," "Email," and "Phone."

Figure 7-4. *Building a data model while creating an app*

9. You can further improve the data model or "table" that is going to be created in Microsoft Dataverse and will work as data storage for our booking's records.

10. You can either give a clear instruction in the chat box, such as "add note column," or seek suggestions from Copilot on what else you should add to improve your information capture. First, we will add the note column using the following prompt: "*add Note column to capture long details*" (Figure 7-5).

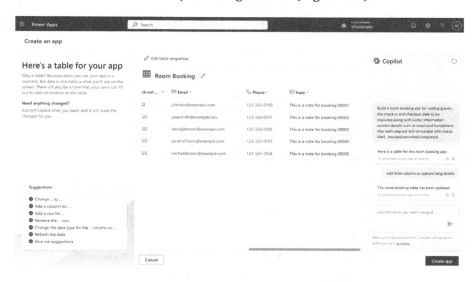

Figure 7-5. *Revising or editing the data model using Copilot*

11. This will add a note column to our data model as shown in Figure 7-5. You will use the next prompt from suggestions, that is, "Give me suggestions." The result of this prompt may vary from case to case; however, when I tried during the writing of this chapter, the suggestions were as shown in Figure 7-6.

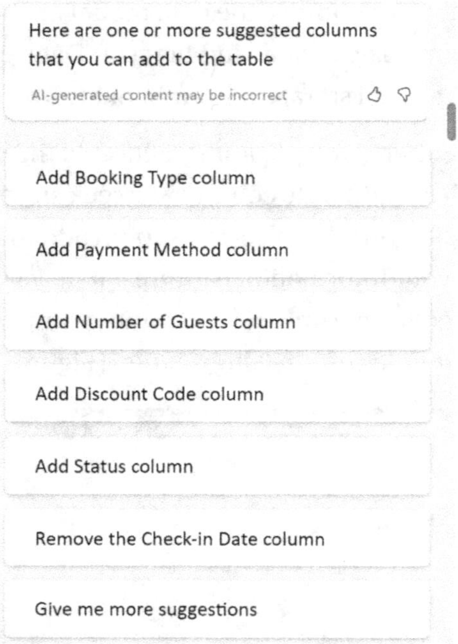

Here are one or more suggested columns
that you can add to the table

AI-generated content may be incorrect

Add Booking Type column

Add Payment Method column

Add Number of Guests column

Add Discount Code column

Add Status column

Remove the Check-in Date column

Give me more suggestions

Figure 7-6. *Column suggestions by Copilot*

12.   While some of the suggestions are really good,
        such as Booking Type and Number of Guests, the
        suggestion to remove the Check-in Date column is
        not something that qualifies as good. This is a great
        example that we as humans have to drive and assess
        generative AI recommendations before executing.
        We will choose the suggestion of adding the number
        of guests column.

13.   Now that we have a table model that is suitable
        for our business requirements, we can proceed to
        the next stage by clicking the Create App
        ( Create app) button.

14. This will begin the process of creating a table based on our model and creating a canvas app with CRUD operations as discussed in Section 7.2.2 (Figure 7-7).

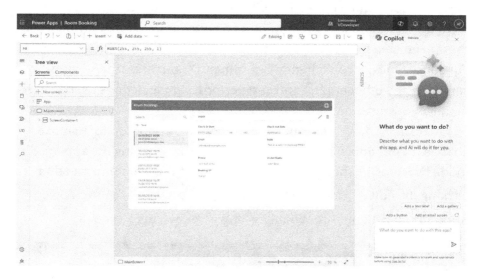

Figure 7-7. *Canvas app generated by Copilot*

15. At the canvas app developer studio, you can perform the next app editing features that will be covered in the next section.

At this stage, it is recommended to save this app first by clicking the save (⊟) icon. Name the app something that you can relate and easily find for the next set of exercise; I will be naming this app "*RoomBookingExperience*."

In the exercise, you have learned how you can use conversations to build a data model and associated app using Power Apps Maker Copilot. If you play the created app, you will be surprised how complete it is and how ready it is to be deployed for user testing.

In the next section, we will use the same app and edit it using Copilot chat in the Power Apps development studio.

7.3.2 Edit with Copilot

In this section, we will begin experimenting with the Copilot panel in Power Apps Studio. The section will focus on the actions we can perform using conversational experience and edit our canvas app. We will be using the app created in the previous section named "RoomBookingExperience." For consistency, I would highly recommend completing the section, or you can open any other application and perform similar actions as suggested in the following exercise.

We can provide various prompts or commands to Copilot to make changes in our app. We will begin the journey by opening the app in edit mode by choosing the App (⊞ Apps) icon from the left menu and then clicking the edit (✎) icon in front of the app. This will take us to Power Apps Studio with our room booking app as shown in Figure 7-8.

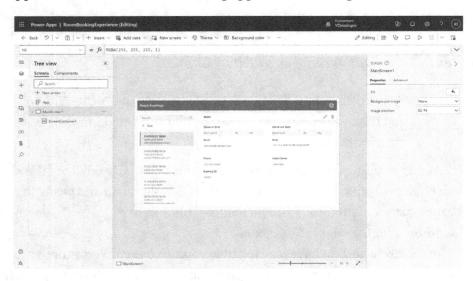

Figure 7-8. *Editing the room booking app*

To start the Copilot experience, we will click the Copilot (🔲) icon at the top right. This will open a familiar Copilot panel as shown in Figure 7-9, where we can use conversations to perform actions.

146

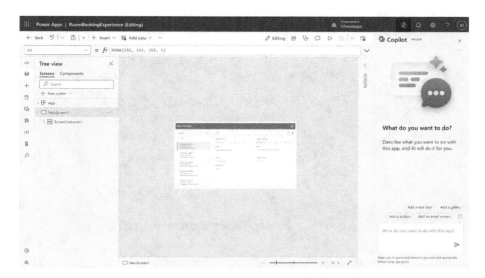

Figure 7-9. *Editing the room booking app with Copilot*

Notice that there are a few suggestions (like in all other experiences) already there to give us guidance on how to use the Copilot (Figure 7-9). We will experience the edit feature in two contexts, user interface–related actions and script-related actions, to give better understanding of how powerful the Copilot help is.

User Interface–Related Actions

User interface–related actions will help us in performing actions to improve our app interface and add new screens or controls; let's learn by experimenting with some of these prompts:

1. In the Copilot panel, let us first begin with asking to add a new screen with a prompt like *"add new blank screen."* This will create a new screen to our app; we refer to the blank screen, but you can also refer to other templates available (Figure 7-10).

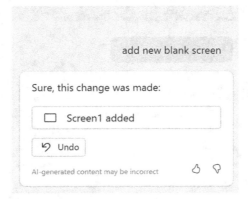

Figure 7-10. *Adding a screen to Power Apps using Copilot*

2. If the result is not according to our expectations, we can always undo the action to return to a previous state.

3. Next, we will add a label in the new screen using the prompt "*Add a text label.*" This will create a new label "Label1" in the "screen1".

4. We will change the label1 text to welcome using the prompt "change the Label1 text to Welcome."

5. I want to change our label as the header label; we can do so by prompting "*can you make label1 a header label.*" This will change the header settings similar to the header label in templates (Figure 7-11).

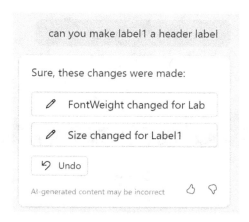

Figure 7-11. *Editing label properties using Copilot*

6.   We will make a little bit more changes to our Label1
     with a prompt "*change label1 background colour to
     dark-blue and font colour to white.*"

7.   We will now add a button on the screen, and I am
     sure you can now do the prompt yourself, but here
     we are to help, not to test, so here is the prompt we
     can use: "*add a button.*"

8.   Move these two controls to the center of the screen
     and place them as shown in Figure 7-12.

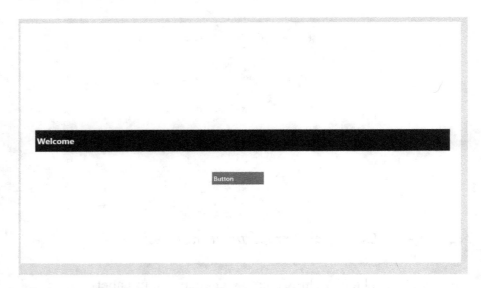

Figure 7-12. *Alignment of our two controls in Power Apps*

We will pause our experimentation with prompts in editing mode for the user interface here as by now you would have got the idea of how to use Copilot. We can also perform other user interface–related actions such as

- **Delete Components**: "Delete the label from the screen."

- **Reorder Components**: "Move the image behind the text box."

- **Resize and Reposition Components**: "Make the button wider and move it to the right."

- **Bind Data to Components**: "Bind the 'Orders' SharePoint list to the gallery."

- **Preview Changes**: "Let's preview the app to see our changes."

It is highly recommended to save this app with the work performed so far as we will continue to use the same app in the next section.

Note   One feature that I am looking forward to be added in Copilot capabilities is to reorder the screens in Power Apps. Currently, it is not available, and hopefully the product team will bring this feature to Copilot experience soon.

Script-Related Actions

In this section, we will experiment with prompts that can be used to set scripts in Copilot experience. We will continue to edit our "RoomBookingExperience." If you have not completed the preceding section, it is recommended to do so before moving forward with this section.

1. Open the "RoomBookingExperience" app in edit mode.

2. Open the Copilot panel.

3. Select "Screen1" from the screen's tree view.

4. The first prompt we want to use is to make our button1 title as "Proceed" and at click to move our user to MainScreen1. This can be achieved by *"Make Button1 Text as Proceed and when button1 is clicked, navigate to MainScreen1."*

5. The prompt will successfully perform both the actions (Figure 7-13).

Figure 7-13. *Adding a script using Power Apps Copilot*

6. If we choose button1 and select the "OnSelect," we
    will see the script added successfully as shown in
    Figure 7-14.

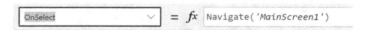

Figure 7-14. *Script added to the property of the button using Copilot*

7. Try to update the Label1 text to have the current
    logged-in username. Traditionally, if we don't know
    this, we will switch context to any search engine and
    try to find answers; here, we can actually ask the
    same question to Copilot, and it can help us learn
    and execute. Use this prompt to learn about user
    details: *"how to read User Full name in PowerApps"*
    (Figure 7-15).

how to read User Full name in powerapps

You can read the user's Full name in a Canvas app by following these steps:
1. On the Insert tab, click or tap Media, and then click or tap Image.
2. Set the Image property to this formula: User().Image
3. On the Insert tab, click or tap Text, and then click or tap Label.
4. Set the Text property to this formula: User().FullName
5. Add ...

Show more

AI-generated content may be incorrect

Figure 7-15. *Getting help in the studio using Copilot*

8. Now that we know User().FullName can be used, you will improve the Label1 text as shown in Figure 7-16.

Text   = *fx*   "Welcome " & User().FullName

Figure 7-16. *Adding the user full name to the label*

9. Move to the main screen to learn one more Copilot feature. Select MainScreen1 from the tree view.

10. In the MainScreen1, select the Label Title1. You will notice a Copilot icon appearing on top of the label as shown in Figure 7-17.

Figure 7-17. *Formatting using Copilot in Power Apps*

11. This Copilot as shown in Figure 7-17 can help us format the text in the label. Click the Copilot icon to see text formatting as the option and select that.

12. This will open up a new screen with formatting suggestions as well as other recommendations from Copilot (Figure 7-18).

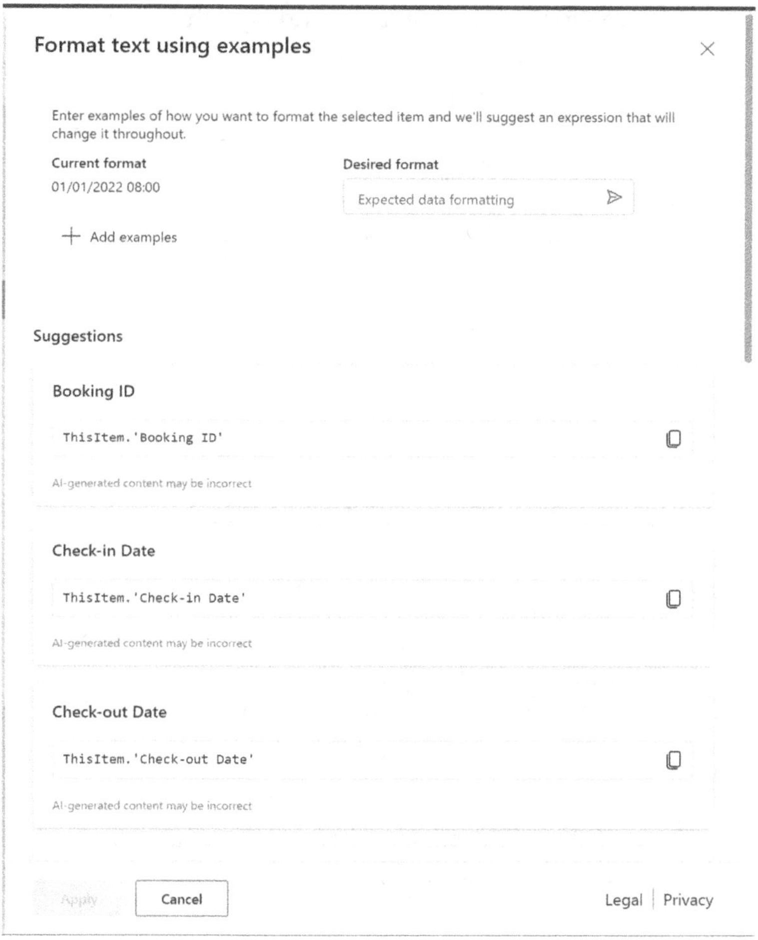

Format text using examples   ✕

Enter examples of how you want to format the selected item and we'll suggest an expression that will change it throughout.

Current format   Desired format

01/01/2022 08:00

                                        ┌─────────────────────────────┐
                                        │ Expected data formatting   ▷ │
                                        └─────────────────────────────┘

    ＋ Add examples

Suggestions

    Booking ID

        ThisItem.'Booking ID'   ▢

    AI-generated content may be incorrect

    Check-in Date

        ThisItem.'Check-in Date'   ▢

    AI-generated content may be incorrect

    Check-out Date

        ThisItem.'Check-out Date'   ▢

    AI-generated content may be incorrect

    Apply   ┌─────────┐   Legal │ Privacy
               │ Cancel │
               └─────────┘

Figure 7-18. Formatting suggestions by Copilot in Power Apps

13.   While there are other suggestions to replace the
      current data binding of our Title1 label to other
      fields, we will use this feature to change the date
      display format.

14. At desired format, we can click and type the format
     we want or choose one from the recommended
     formats (Figure 7-19).

Format text using examples   ✕

Enter examples of how you want to format the selected item and we'll suggest an expression that will
change it throughout.

Current format	Desired format
01/01/2022 08:00	Expected data formatting ▷

+ Add examples

1/1/2022

1/1/2022 8:00 AM

January 1, 2022

Saturday, January 1, 2022

Saturday, January 1, 2022 8:00 AM

Not enough information

Try rewording your question.

Tip: Use the autocomplete menus that appear as you type.

Figure 7-19. *Desired format recommendations by Copilot*

15. We will choose one of the recommendations and
     ask Copilot to generate us a formula to format the
     Check-in Date accordingly (Figure 7-20).

Format text using examples   ✕

Enter examples of how you want to format the selected item and we'll suggest an expression that will change it throughout.

Current format   Desired format
01/01/2022 08:00   Saturday, January 1, 2022 8:00 AM   ▷

     ＋ Add examples

Suggestions

Check-in Date

Text(ThisItem.'Check-in Date', "dddd, mmmm d, yyyy h:mm AM/PM", "en-GB")   ▢

AI-generated content may be incorrect

Figure 7-20. *Formatting formula creation using Copilot in Power Apps*

16. We can confidently copy the suggestion and choose Apply ( Apply) to reflect the formatting changes in the Title1 label (Figure 7-21).

Figure 7-21. *Formatting updates to control using Copilot of Power Apps*

This exercise illustrates the ease developers' Copilot will bring for citizen developers, and importantly your team can learn as they use Power Apps with much more ease and potentially build great apps much faster.

At the time of writing this book, users can perform actions such as add a screen using preexisting templates; add and modify properties of a single control, limited to classic controls only; update multiple controls; work with containers; or use formulas such as Navigate() or SubmitForm(). Also, it is worth noting that the controls supported currently are the following:

- Screen
- Container
- Gallery
- Form
- Button

- Label

- TextInput

Microsoft is committed to Copilot infusing and reviewing the Power Platform release; it is clear that this feature list will only grow further.

7.4 Copilot in Model-Driven Apps

One of the exciting features of Copilot that can really elevate the end-user experience is the Copilot infusion in model-driven apps. As discussed in the introduction, model-driven apps are data-specific apps that are built on top of the data modeled in that Dataverse, or simply they are tightly integrated with tables in Dataverse. While canvas apps allow us to be super creative and build experiences that may or may not require data integration, model-driven apps ease our way of managing data in various stages with the ability to build dashboards and reports.

Most of business applications that require various teams' input or collaboration, real-time monitoring, and dedicated dashboards will eventually choose model-driven apps to automate and solve the business problem.

Copilot experience in model-driven apps is a bit different than what we learned in canvas apps. While canvas app experience is targeted to help your citizen developers in building solutions at accelerated speed, Copilot in model-driven apps is targeted to application users and enables a conversational experience to interact with the data captured or in focus of the application. This will become clear in the following section when we enable the experience.

7.4.1 Additional Settings

We discussed in the previous section about the initial setup of Copilot; there are a few additional steps or validations required to enable Copilot with model-driven apps. There are two specific settings that require confirmation of feature availability. As an app maker, you may not have access to set up these features; hence, a user with a system administrator, system customizer, or environment maker role is required to change.

1. Browse to `https://admin.powerplatform.com`.

2. Choose the environment in which you want to enable this experience.

3. Select settings (⚙ Settings) from the top menu.

4. Under Product, select Features (Figure 7-22).

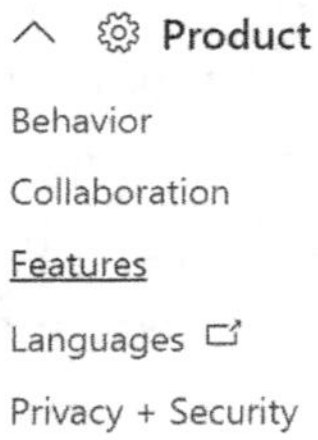

       ∧ ⚙ **Product**

       Behavior

       Collaboration

       Features

       Languages ⌁

       Privacy + Security

Figure 7-22. *Features settings in Environment*

5. In the Features section, search for Copilot; ensure it is on and the user's ability to analyze data is switched on as well (Figure 7-23).

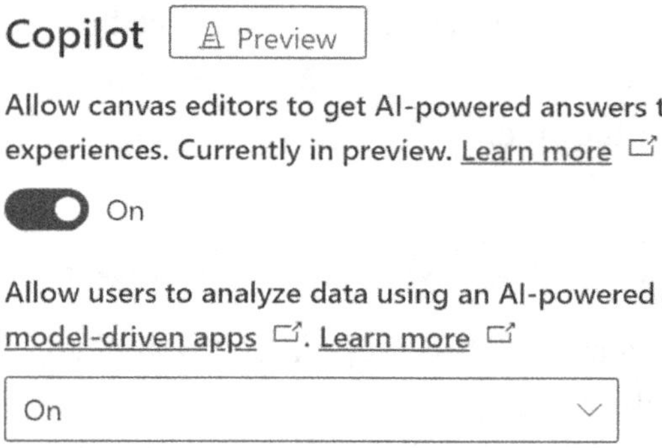

Copilot   ☐ Preview

Allow canvas editors to get AI-powered answers to how-to questions and AI Builder GPT experiences. Currently in preview. Learn more ☐

⬤○ On

Allow users to analyze data using an AI-powered chat experience in canvas ☐ and model-driven apps ☐. Learn more ☐

On	⌄

Figure 7-23. *Copilot feature enablement in the environment*

6.   Ensure you save the settings.

7.   Next is to select the "Behavior" from the feature list (Figure 7-24).

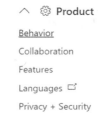

Figure 7-24. *Behavior settings for the environment*

8.   Select "Monthly Channel" as shown in Figure 7-25.

Figure 7-25. *Release channel settings for the environment*

9.   This setting will ensure monthly updates for model-driven apps. Save the settings.

These settings will ensure that we can add Copilot experience for our end users. In the next section, we will use our room booking app and experience a model-driven app with Copilot.

7.4.2 Enabling Copilot in a Model-Driven App

In this section, we will experience a model-driven app with Copilot. For this, we first need to build a model-driven app using the "room booking" table created in the previous section. If you have not completed Copilot with canvas apps, I would highly recommend doing so, or you can also download the ready solution to begin with the output of the previous section from `https://github.com/Apress/Introducing-Microsoft-Copilot-for-Managers/tree/main/Part-III/PowerApps/Copliot_Chapter7Output_1_0_0_1.zip`.

This is a solution file, and you need to import this file in your environment where you intend to perform this section's exercise. If you are new to the solution file import, please refer to `https://learn.microsoft.com/en-us/power-apps/maker/data-platform/import-update-export-solutions`.

We will perform the following steps to create a model-driven app using the "room booking" table:

1. Log in to `https://make.powerapps.com`.

2. This will bring you to the Power Apps landing page.

3. Choose the environment where you have either performed the previous experiment and created the "room booking" table or imported the solution file.

4. On the landing page, select "Start with a page design" (Figure 7-26).

Figure 7-26. *Building a model-driven app with a page design*

5. Choose "Views and forms" as the design template from the options (Figure 7-27).

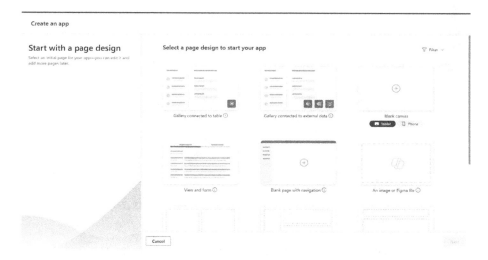

Figure 7-27. *Choosing a page design while building a model-driven app*

6. This will browse to the model-driven app studio, where we will start building our experience.

7. The first step is to name the model-driven app; we can name it "Room Booking MDA." Add a description that can make it easy to understand the purpose of this app.

8. The next step is critical as we will choose the table or tables of interest. In this example, we will only select the room booking table (Figure 7-28).

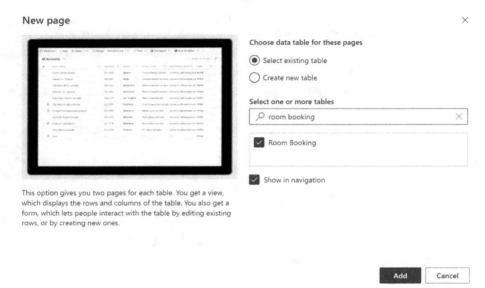

Figure 7-28. *Selecting a table for the model-driven app*

9. This will create a model-driven app with a room booking table record view. Now we can further improve and learn about the model-driven app at `https://learn.microsoft.com/en-us/power-apps/maker/model-driven-apps/model-driven-app-overview`. However, we will not cover the details in this book (Figure 7-29).

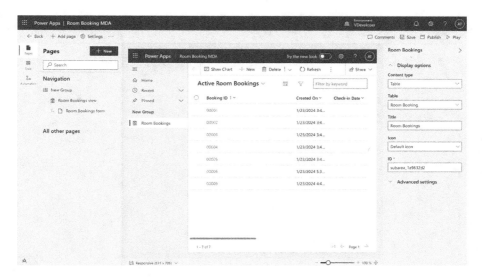

Figure 7-29. *Ready to test the model-driven app*

10. We can now test the app. Save and publish the app and click Play (▷ Play); this will launch the model-driven app in the new tab (sometimes, you need to allow the pop-up to launch the app).

11. You will notice that this is a ready app to manage all the bookings, and at the right-side pane, you can find the Copilot (⊛) icon. Clicking the icon will open the Copilot pane where we can now engage with room booking data in a conversation style (Figure 7-30).

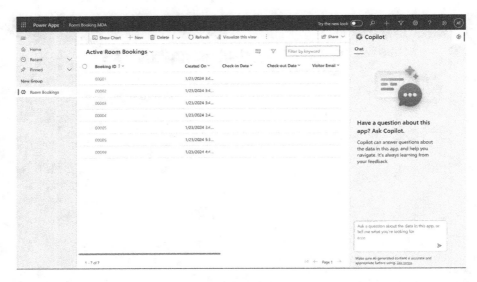

Figure 7-30. *Copilot pane in the model-driven app*

12. We can ask questions about bookings, inquire, or summarize the details using a conversational prompt; you can try the following and expand further:

    "What is the status of booking id 0001."
    "What is that status of booking for visitor John."

13. As expected, Copilot will start bringing the results as well as the link to the records (Figure 7-31).

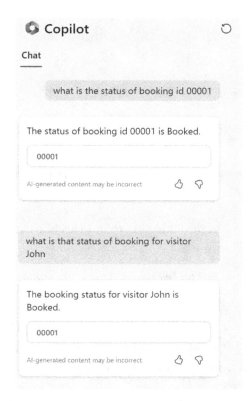

Figure 7-31. *Copilot output for a custom prompt in the model-driven app*

14. Apart from searching records, we can prompt to get summaries as well, as shown in Figure 7-32, such as the following prompt:

"How many bookings have status as cancelled"

Figure 7-32. *Summary of records using a prompt in Copilot for the model-driven app*

15.   Lastly, we can find answers to queries like the following prompt:

"what is the latest check-in date and for which visitor"

16.   Copilot will bring the information from our dataset and provide us an interactive way of finding details about our room booking data (Figure 7-33).

Figure 7-33. *Finding insights using Copilot in the model-driven app*

This feature opens up worlds of possibilities as well as a new generative AI experience for our teams to explore data and find answers in a natural, conversational, and intuitive way. The possibilities are endless, and I am sure we will see many great examples from the industry coming forth in the near future.

7.5 Summary

The chapter introduced the features and benefits of Microsoft Copilot for Power Apps, a tool that enables users to build low-code apps using conversational AI. We discussed the prerequisites for using Microsoft Copilot for Power Apps, such as having a Power Apps Premium license, a Microsoft Dataverse database, and AI Builder enabled in the environment. The chapter also provided links to resources for learning more about Power Apps and its geographical availability.

We discussed and demonstrated how to use Copilot to build and edit a room booking app for visiting guests. The chapter showed how to use natural language prompts to create a data model, a canvas app, and a user interface. We also covered how to use Copilot to add scripts and format the app.

We finally covered the Copilot pane experience that can be enabled in model-driven apps. We built an app using our room booking table and learned how to include Copilot in our apps. These Copilots are auto-enabled on app data and provide responses to our prompts using generative AI.

Before we conclude, let's revisit the app building process and the stages Copilot is impacting. As illustrated in Figure 7-34, with the support of Copilot, you and your team can expedite the manual work required in each stage and improve our ability to digitalize the actions required.

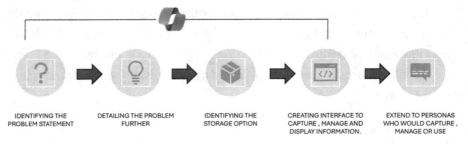

IDENTIFYING THE PROBLEM STATEMENT → **DETAILING THE PROBLEM FURTHER** → **IDENTIFYING THE STORAGE OPTION** → **CREATING INTERFACE TO CAPTURE , MANAGE AND DISPLAY INFORMATION.** → **EXTEND TO PERSONAS WHO WOULD CAPTURE , MANAGE OR USE**

***Figure 7-34.** Copilot impact on the app building process*

The features of Copilot are going to be improved further and further and with that our ability to optimize and accelerate digitalization of process – exciting times ahead.

CHAPTER 8

Microsoft Copilot for Power Automate

The first chapter in Part III discussed and prepared us to use Copilot in Power Apps. In this chapter, we will discuss and learn the Copilot usage in Microsoft Power Automate. Microsoft Power Automate is a component of the Power Platform SaaS (software as a service) platform that allows users to create, manage, and automate workflows using a low-code/no-code environment.

Just like Power Apps, Power Automate provides a rapid development environment to build business workflows to streamline various business processes. It allows you to quickly build the processes using connectors to perform actions at Microsoft solutions or third-party solutions (such as Adobe Sign, ServiceNow, Salesforce, etc.) or retrieve information from data stores (Microsoft Dataverse, SharePoint, SQL Server, Azure Blob Storage, Oracle, etc.).

In this chapter, you will learn about Microsoft Copilot for Power Automate and leverage the conversational method to automate the business processes.

My focus will be on Copilot, and it is assumed that you understand how Power Automate or Power Platform works; I will briefly cover the details of Power Automate to bring our understanding up to speed.

© Adeel Khan 2024
A. Khan, *Introducing Microsoft Copilot for Managers*, Inside Copilot,
https://doi.org/10.1007/979-8-8688-0419-9_8

8.1 Introduction to Power Automate

Power Automate is a cloud-based service that allows you to create automated workflows across different applications and services. With Power Automate, you can automate simple tasks such as sending email notifications or complex multisystem/touchpoint actions such as updating data in databases, generating reports, and initiating business condition–based approvals.

One of the key features of Power Automate is the use of triggers and actions. Triggers are events that start a workflow, such as a new email, a button click, or a scheduled time. Actions are the steps that follow a trigger, such as sending an email, creating a file, or calling an API. You can combine multiple triggers and actions to create complex workflows that suit your business needs.

Power Automate allows you to automate repetitive tasks and streamline processes within your organization with different types of flows and automation methods. Power Automate offers both connector-based digital process automation (DPA) and UI-based robotic process automation (RPA), catering to a wide range of automation needs (7). Here is a short introduction to various flows:

Cloud Flows

- **Automated Flows:** These are triggered by specific events, such as receiving an email from a particular sender or a mention of your company on social media. You can connect various cloud or on-premises services using connectors to create these automated flows.

- **Instant Flows:** With a simple click of a button, you can start an automation. Instant flows are useful for repetitive tasks, whether you're working from your desktop or mobile device. For example, you could instantly send reminders to your team or perform actions in Teams or SharePoint.

- **Scheduled Flows**: Use scheduled flows to automate tasks on a regular basis. For instance, you can schedule daily data uploads to SharePoint or a database.

Desktop Flows – RPA

- **Desktop Flows**: RPA offering of Power Automate that allows you to automate tasks both on the Web and your local desktop environment. They're particularly handy for automating actions within specific applications or websites.

Business Process Flows

- **Business Process Flows**: These flows provide a guided experience for users, leading them through predefined processes within your organization. Business process flows ensure consistency and efficiency by tailoring the user experience based on different security roles.

To create workflows in Power Automate, you can use either the graphical user interface (GUI) or the Copilot-based conversational user interface (CUI). The GUI allows you to drag and drop triggers and actions from a library of connectors and templates. The CUI allows you to describe your workflow in natural language and get suggestions from Microsoft Copilot, a smart assistant that helps you build workflows faster and easier.

Note   If you are new to Power Platform and Power Apps, I would highly recommend spending some time at http://aka.ms/powerplatformresources and browse through the content curated based on your experience with the platform.

8.2 Prerequisites

8.2.1 Setting and Validating

As discussed in the previous section, Power Automate is a SaaS platform. To access the service, users can either browse to `https://make.powerautomate.com` or click the App Launcher at `https://office.com` and choose the Power Automate () icon. Please remember that it is assumed that you are already logged in using user credentials having a Power Automate or Power Apps Premium license. Some of the following features discussed can be practiced through M365 E3/E5 licenses as well, but it is recommended to have a Premium license as we will work with Dataverse and premium connectors.

Note   You can also sign up for a trial license that would allow you to experiment with Power Apps Premium capabilities; please refer to `https://powerautomate.microsoft.com/` to learn about licensing and trial sign-up procedures.

Another important aspect is to validate the regional availability to Copilot. At the time of writing this book, the availability was limited to specific regions; however, it is best to validate with a refresh list at `https://learn.microsoft.com/en-us/power-platform/admin/geographical-availability-copilot`.

If you are following along with the exercises in this book in a sequence, then you should have an environment ready as we covered the prerequisites in the previous chapter. If you are starting fresh, I would recommend you to complete Chapter 7 before starting this chapter as it will help you set up the environment as well as the example. For better understanding and clarity we will be using the outputs generated in Chapter 7.

We will need an additional setup step for the desktop cloud, which I will cover later in the chapter.

8.2.2 Setting Up with Power Apps Output

If you have not performed the learning activities mentioned in Chapter 7 or may have left it in between or start this section after some time and need those outputs, don't worry; we got you covered. You can download the output of our "RoomBookingExperience" from **https://github.com/ Apress/Introducing-Microsoft-Copilot-for-Managers/blob/main/ Part-III/PowerApps/Copliot_Chapter7Output_1_0_0_1.zip**. This is a solution file, and you need to import this file in your environment where you intend to perform this chapter's exercise. If you are new to the solution file import, please refer to https://learn.microsoft.com/en-us/ power-apps/maker/data-platform/import-update-export-solutions. However, here are easy steps to remember:

1. Download the solution file from the provided link earlier.

2. Go to https://make.powerapps.com and select the preferred environment.

3. From the side menu, select the Solutions (🗒) icon.

4. Click the Import solution (← Import solution) icon and browse to the location where you have downloaded the file "**Copliot_Chapter7Output_1_0_0_1**".

5. Follow the instructions.

Once the import of the solution is completed, validate that you have the table "room booking" available. You can validate this by selecting the Tables (▦) icon from the side navigation, then selecting Custom (🔲 Custom) from the Filter tab as shown in Figure 8-1.

| Room Booking | ⋮ | cr34c_roombooking1 | Standard | No | Yes | Custom |

Figure 8-1. *Room booking table under the Custom tab*

This setup prepares your environment for the next section, where we will begin experimenting with Copilot in Power Automate.

8.3 Copilot with Cloud Flows

In this section, we will discuss and experience Copilot in Power Automate for cloud flows. To begin, we will browse to `https://make.powerautomate.com/` to start using Power Automate with Copilot for cloud flows.

Just like Power Apps, at the landing page you will see the Copilot chat box, as shown in Figure 8-2, where you can explain the automation scenario.

Figure 8-2. *Power Automate landing page*

8.3.1 Start with Copilot

We will begin the new approach to automation using Copilot for Power Automate. In this section, we will see the power of generative AI and its effect on automation, especially in changing actions and activities and lowering manual work.

Using Out-of-the-Box Prompt

To start this exercise, you need to have an environment setup as mentioned in the prerequisites in the previous chapter and in this chapter. Here are the steps to follow:

1. Log in to `https://make.powerautomate.com`.

2. This will bring you to the Power Automate landing page.

3. Choose the environment where you want to experiment with this example.

4. In the first example, we will create a cloud flow using an out-of-the-box prompt to begin understanding the process.

5. We will use the following prompt which is part of the recommended prompts by the platform:

   "Every week, post a message to a team's chats or channel" (Figure 8-3).

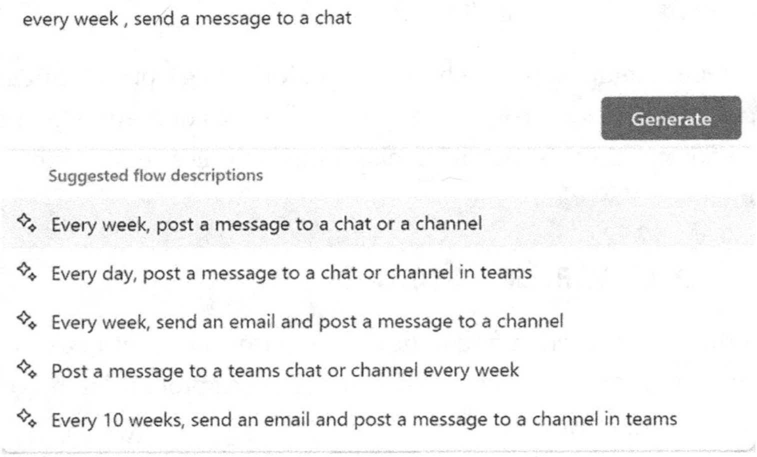

every week , send a message to a chat

Generate

Suggested flow descriptions

✦ Every week, post a message to a chat or a channel

✦ Every day, post a message to a chat or channel in teams

✦ Every week, send an email and post a message to a channel

✦ Post a message to a teams chat or channel every week

✦ Every 10 weeks, send an email and post a message to a channel in teams

Figure 8-3. *Choosing a recommended prompt for Power Automate Copilot*

6. Once you choose the prompt, it will begin the process of creation.

7. At the first screen, you will see the transformation of our prompt into a flow, where based on generative AI, Copilot will suggest the connectors and flow based on our prompt (Figure 8-4).

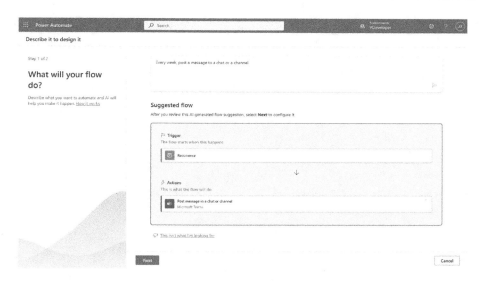

Figure 8-4. *Describe it with Power Automate Copilot*

8. The output is not according to our expectations; we can choose 🗩 This isn't what I'm looking for. This is an important feedback as the module will only improve from these types of feedback; hence, it is recommended to always provide feedback.

9. You will proceed forward and select Next; this will open a configuration screen where we may or may not have to sign in to use the connectors. This screen can be potentially different based on your existing connections (Figure 8-5).

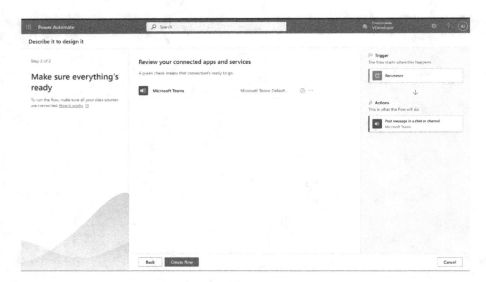

Figure 8-5. *Configuring connections using Power Automate Copilot*

10. Since there is only one connector needed, once the connection is okay, we can safely create a flow by clicking the "Create flow" button.

11. This will create a flow and open a flow studio. This is a new look studio that is more suitable to Copilot (Figure 8-6).

Figure 8-6. *Power Automate flow studio with Copilot*

12. The next step is to click the team's connector to start
     configurations.

13. Configure with the details shown in Figure 8-7; you
     can choose the relevant information based on your
     environment.

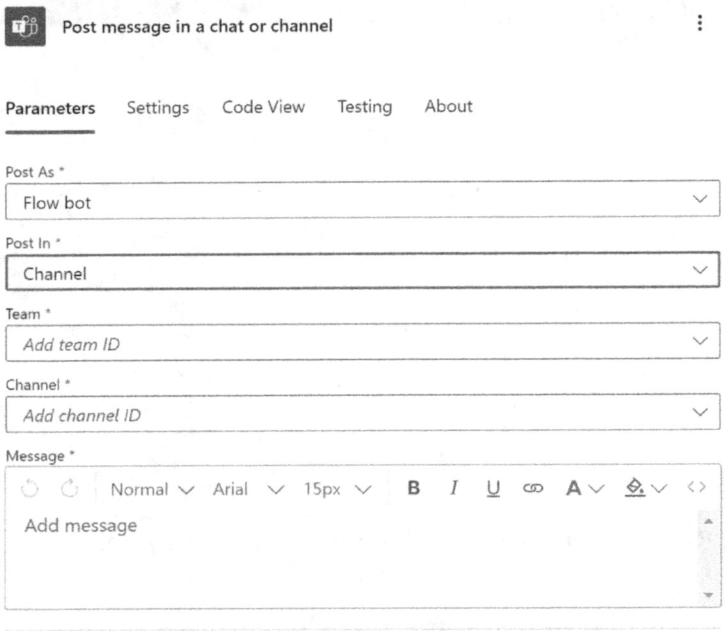

Figure 8-7. *Connector configuration for the first Power Automate use case*

14. The team ID and channel ID will be from your own environment; select a drop-down and choose the testing team and channel where you would like to test the message posting.

15. We will configure a simple message as follows:

    "This message is created by flow bot."

16. The last part of this exercise is to configure the recurrence and save it. Configure it as your need and save the flow for the test.

This marks the completion of the first use case; we will now create a bit complex flow and use the table created in "RoomBookingApp."

Custom Prompt with Custom Table

In this example, we will use a custom prompt to use the "room booking" table. In this example, we want to address a common business problem of approval. Like any other business use case, at times we need the approval process to start as soon as a new record, a new expense, or a new leave request is created; all such request will require an approval process. We will simulate the same process using the room booking scenario.

Every time a new room booking request is created, we want to initiate an approval, and if the approval is successful, we want to notify the owner of the request. Let's deliver this use case with Copilot:

1. Log in to https://make.powerautomate.com.

2. This will bring you to the Power Automate landing page.

3. Choose the environment where you have deployed the solution file and with that created "room booking" table.

4. We will use the following prompt, this time to create a flow:

   "Start an approval process for a new item in dataverse room booking table and wait for approval. upon successful approval, send email to owner of item."

5. Notice this prompt is specific and clearly instructing what is expected of Copilot. This is critical to the successful usage of Copilot in any scenario.

6. Copilot will interpret our prompt just like it did in the first example and create a suggestion (Figure 8-8).

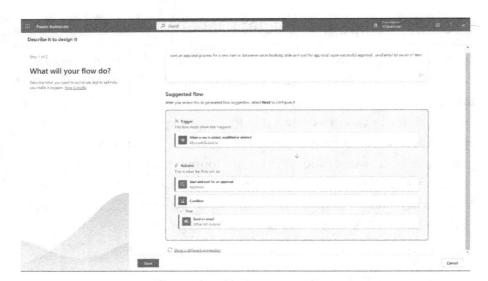

Figure 8-8. *Room booking approval using Copilot in Power Automate*

1. This flow looks exactly what we want to do, that is, at the creation of the new room booking record, approval will start, and if the condition is met, an email will be sent. However, notice there is an additional option available below "Show a different suggestion" (Show a different suggestion) as shown in Figure 8-8.

2. This option will provide a different alternative of solving the same problem and even improvements that would be beneficial to the use case. We will click the option to observe the results (Figure 8-9).

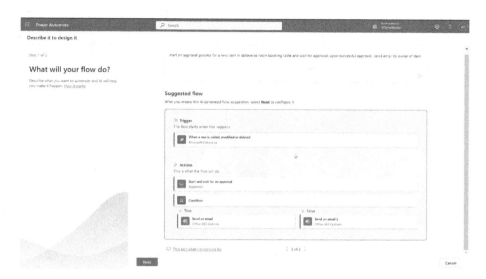

Figure 8-9. *Suggestions by Copilot during flow creation*

3. Notice that the second flow created has an email
    notification in false condition as well. That is if our
    room booking has been rejected, we can also inform
    the owner that the transaction was not successful.
    This suggestion is practical and useful for the
    improvement of our initial requirements. We will
    choose this option and click Next.

4. Similar to the previous example, the next screen will
    validate our connections.

5. Once connections are established or verified, we
    can create a flow (Figure 8-10).

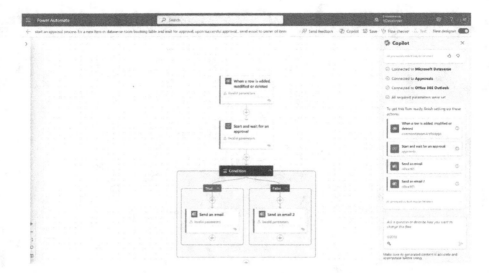

Figure 8-10. *Complex flow creation using Copilot in Power Automate*

6. This will create a flow based on our requirements; now we can perform configurations of the flow.

7. I will not cover the flow configuration here; however, I would recommend saving this flow as "FlowwithCopilot-RoomBookingApproval."

The last step completes the flow creation using Copilot. To complete the configuration, please refer to Appendix B or download the ready flow as part of the solution "**Copilot_Chapter8StartOutput_1_0_0_1**" from https://github.com/Apress/Introducing-Microsoft-Copilot-for-Managers/blob/main/Part-III/PowerAutomate/Copilot_Chapter8StartOutput_1_0_0_1.zip.

8.3.2 Edit with Copilot

In this exercise, you will use prompts to make changes in our flow. The flow we created in the previous section will be used; it is recommended to complete the exercise. The business case we want to address is minimizing the need for approvals.

We will restrict approvals only in case the duration of stay is more than three days. We will begin our exercise by logging in to the Power Automate environment (the same as the one used for the previous exercise).

In the environment, you can access your flows by selecting My flows (My flows). In the My flows page, select "FlowwithCopilot-RoomBooking Approval." Click Edit (Edit) to start the editing process. This will take you to the Power Automate cloud flow studio. If the Copilot pane is not opened automatically, you can always enable it by clicking the Copilot (Copilot) icon at the top left as shown in Figure 8-11.

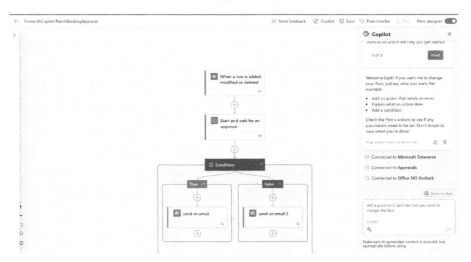

Figure 8-11. *Copilot in Power Automate cloud flow*

We will now begin our exercise with the following steps:

1. The first prompt we want to use is to understand what a specific action is doing; this is a quick guide on actions already configured in the flow. We can type the following prompt to understand the condition:

   "*explain the condition action in this flow*"

187

2. Copilot with its simplicity explains the action in business language (Figure 8-12).

Figure 8-12. *Understanding actions using Copilot in Power Automate*

3. We will proceed to solve our business problem. We are taking a longer route to solve this problem just to experiment with the Copilot prompt. You will ask Copilot to convert the Check-in and Check-out dates to Day of Year and then find the difference between them. We can use following prompt:

    "calculate check-in date and check-out date to day of year and find difference between them"

4. This will add these requested actions in the flow (Figure 8-13).

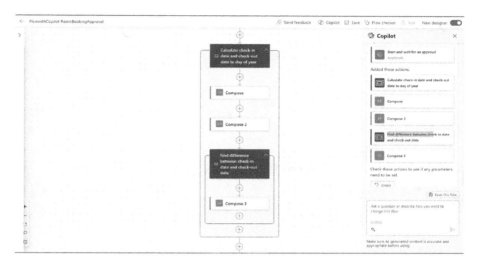

Figure 8-13. *Adding multiple actions using Copilot in Power Automate*

5. Note that these actions still require validation; we will validate the formulas and save the flow using the Copilot action.

6. Add a prompt to include the condition control. This can be done using the following:

   "add condition before Start and wait for an approval"

7. This will add condition control and move the approval flow in true condition, as expected (Figure 8-14).

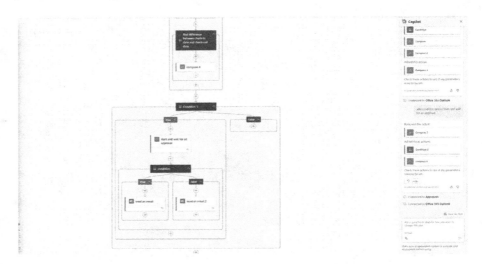

Figure 8-14. *Adding conditional control using Copilot in Power Automate*

8. Notice in Figure 8-14, it also made a few changes that were not required, like removing compose 3 and adding compose 4. That is why it is important to validate all the changes and observe closely the changes made. We will fix the formulas and ensure our flow remains intact.

9. As per our business requirement, we will set the condition to check if the duration is more than three days. Also, change the name from "Condition 3" to "Check Duration." If so, approval will start; if not, the flow will execute the action in a false path (Figure 8-15).

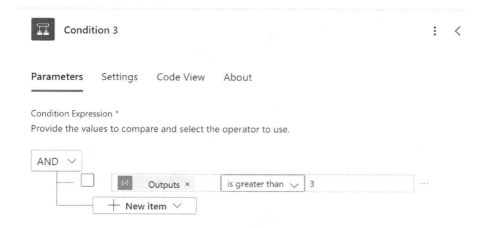

Figure 8-15. *Validating and configuring condition in Power Automate*

10. The last action of this flow we want to perform is to add a new action under false. For that, we can click the false path of "Check Duration" and type the following prompt:

    "send mobile notification if "Check Duration" is false"

11. This will add the notification action in our flow that we can configure to work and send notification in case no approval is required (Figure 8-16).

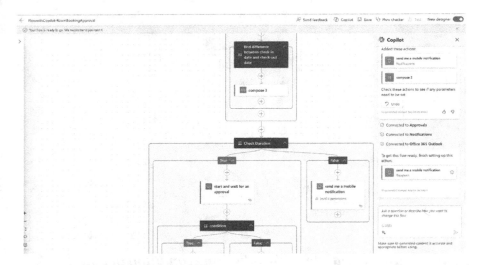

Figure 8-16. *Adding connections and actions using Copilot in Power Automate*

Save this flow and "test" it with the room booking experience canvas or model-driven app. The flow will successfully run and execute the steps as defined. This assistance is definitely going to help citizen developers learn fast and automate fast.

We have covered a few basic examples, but it is recommended to experiment more with new actions. At the time of writing this book, the edit with Copilot was not fully mature and made few mistakes here and there, but hopefully by the time it reaches general availability, the Copilot feature will be mature.

8.4 Copilot with Desktop Flow

Power Automate Desktop flows allow you to automate repetitive tasks on your desktop. Whether you're a home user, a small business owner, or part of a large enterprise, desktop flows can significantly enhance your productivity. While it is integrated with cloud offerings, the ability to use a solution at a desktop addresses many other business use cases that require automation with legacy solutions.

The new intuitive flow designer makes creating desktop flows quicker and easier. Just like Power Automate cloud flows, you don't need to be a coding expert to automate tasks. You can use desktop flows to perform or automate business tasks such as

- Organizing documents

- Extracting data from websites

- Interacting with applications

Desktop flows work seamlessly with both legacy applications (such as terminal emulators) and modern web/desktop apps (including Excel files and folders).

Copilot will help make the product experience more streamlined and easier to use. With Copilot, you can benefit from suggestions on how to choose the best actions and logic for faster flows, create code snippets for different tasks, saving time and effort, and improve documentation and communication for desktop flows.

In summary, Power Automate Desktop flows empower users to automate repetitive desktop tasks, and with Copilot's assistance, the possibilities are endless. In this section, we will learn about using Copilot; however, if you are not familiar with Power Automate Desktop, I would encourage you to spend some time learning and experimenting with the service. You can refer to a great learning source at `https://learn.microsoft.com/en-us/training/paths/pad-get-started/`.

In this section, we will begin with understanding briefly how to set up the desktop flow and perform hands-on to learn about the Copilot features in Power Automate Desktop.

8.4.1 Setting Up

To set up Power Automate Desktop, we can simply begin with downloading the solution from `https://make.powerautomate.com`. To download, you can browse to the Power Automate landing page, select My flows, and look for the Install (Install ∨) button. Once you click the button, the option to download Power Automate for Desktop will be presented.

You can select the option to start the solution package download. Once the package is downloaded, begin the installation process. You can learn more about installation features at `https://learn.microsoft.com/en-us/power-automate/desktop-flows/install`.

Once installation is completed, you will be required to sign in to the Power Automate Desktop app (⚡). Once sign-in is complete, you will be in the Power Automate Desktop app where you can begin the experiment as shown in Figure 8-17.

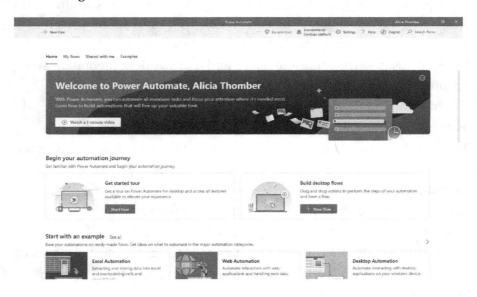

Figure 8-17. *Power Automate Desktop app*

In the next section, we will begin with a simple exercise to learn about Copilot features in Power Automate Desktop.

8.4.2 Working with Copilot

In this section, we will explore how to use Copilot with Power Automate Desktop. We will learn how to create a simple flow that opens a web browser and navigates to a website. We will also see how Copilot suggests actions and parameters based on the user's input and the context of the flow.

Getting Help from Copilot

To begin our experiment, we will first start with a click on the Copilot (Copilot) icon. This will open a familiar chat pane of Copilot with suggestions on how Copilot can help in the scope of Power Automate Desktop as shown in Figure 8-18.

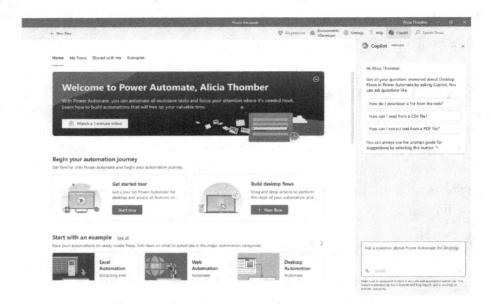

Figure 8-18. *Copilot experience in Power Automate Desktop*

Copilot chat can provide help to our questions in a conversational style, just like we have experienced in the previous examples throughout the chapter. We will begin step by step to create a new flow and use Copilot experience in drafting.

1. We will start this exercise by clicking the New flow
    ($+$ New flow) icon.

2. The system will prompt you to provide the flow
    name; we will use "Chapter8-PDA-01" (Figure 8-19).

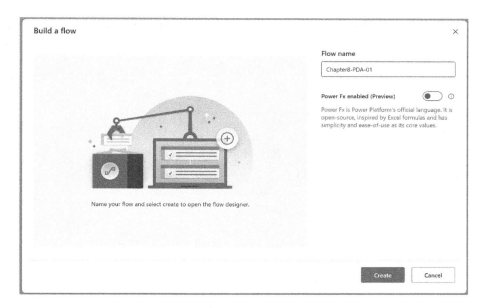

Figure 8-19. Naming a PDA

3. This will open a Power Automate Desktop designer
    with the Copilot side pane (Figure 8-20).

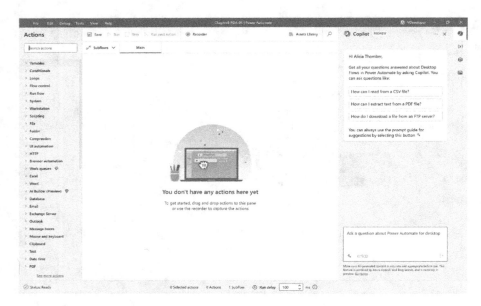

Figure 8-20. *Power Automate Desktop designer*

4.   To perform the preceding stated action, we need to
     open a web browser as a first step. If you are new to
     a designer, you will need to learn the steps outside,
     but with Copilot we can inquire and learn the action
     here. We will question Copilot as follows:

     "*How can I open a browser*"

5.   Copilot has now provided us step-by-step actions
     to address the need. We will follow these steps to
     launch a browser (Figure 8-21).

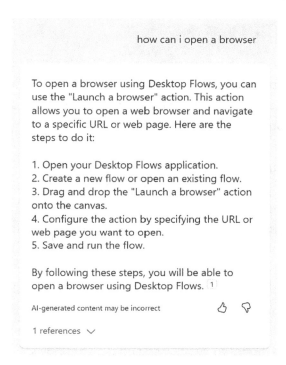

how can i open a browser

To open a browser using Desktop Flows, you can use the "Launch a browser" action. This action allows you to open a web browser and navigate to a specific URL or web page. Here are the steps to do it:

1. Open your Desktop Flows application.
2. Create a new flow or open an existing flow.
3. Drag and drop the "Launch a browser" action onto the canvas.
4. Configure the action by specifying the URL or web page you want to open.
5. Save and run the flow.

By following these steps, you will be able to open a browser using Desktop Flows. [1]

AI-generated content may be incorrect

1 references ∨

Figure 8-21. *Copilot guide on opening a browser*

6. In the next action, we can inquire how to read an Excel file and save results in a variable. We will inquire the same question as a prompt:

    "how to read from excel file and read result in variable"

7. This will again guide us and help us create the action in Power Automate Desktop.

Similar to the discussed exercise, we can ask questions and get help to perform the actions in Power Automate Desktop. The Copilot experience in Power Automate Desktop is limited to help only; however, it is assumed that in the future more features such as editing the flow will be made available.

8.5 Summary

In this chapter, we learned about Microsoft Copilot for Power Automate. The chapter introduced the features and benefits of Microsoft Copilot for Power Automate and how it enables users to create and edit workflows using natural language.

The chapter also covered the prerequisites for using Copilot in cloud flows, such as having a Power Automate Premium license, a Microsoft Dataverse database, and a supported region. We then discussed and demonstrated how to use Copilot to create and edit cloud flows using natural language prompts. We learned how to use scenario prompts, connect to various services, add conditions and actions, and handle changes and feedback.

We discussed Copilot with desktop flows. We briefly discussed the concept of desktop flows and learned about how to install and use Power Automate Desktop, how to use Copilot to get guidance and suggestions, and how to use Copilot to create and edit desktop flows.

The next chapter will cover Copilot in Power Pages, another Power Platform service to solve our web/portal-related use cases.

CHAPTER 9

Microsoft Copilot for Power Pages

In this chapter, we will explore Power Pages, a SaaS platform that is secure, enterprise-grade, and low-code for making, hosting, and managing modern websites for external business use. You can easily create and launch websites that are compatible with web browsers and devices, whether you're a low-code maker or a professional developer. It offers adaptable, ready-made templates, a smooth visual experience through the design studio, and a built-in learning hub to help you develop sites for your specific business requirements.

Until recently, Power Pages was part of the overall Power Apps experience. However, in recent years, Microsoft has separated Power Pages (rightfully), and even the investments in the product have increased considerably.

I had the pleasure of meeting and presenting customer sessions with Sangya Singh, the Vice President of Power Pages. It was great to learn about the investment, future roadmap of product, and how excited product leadership is with the potential.

In this chapter, you will learn about Microsoft Copilot for Power Pages and expand your knowledge of working with Power Pages in natural and conversational style.

© Adeel Khan 2024
A. Khan, *Introducing Microsoft Copilot for Managers*, Inside Copilot,
https://doi.org/10.1007/979-8-8688-0419-9_9

Just like in previous chapters, the focus will be on Copilot, and it is assumed that you understand how and why Power Pages are used. I will briefly cover the details of Power Pages to bring our conversation up to speed, but I recommend you to go through the learning site of Power Pages (`https://learn.microsoft.com/en-us/training/paths/power-pages-get-started/`).

9.1 Introduction to Power Pages

Power Pages is a new service of Power Platform that was rebranded recently. It is a secure, enterprise-grade, low-code SaaS platform that lets you create, host, and manage modern websites for external audiences.

You can instantly design, configure, and publish websites that are compatible with different web browsers and devices, whether you are a low-code maker or a professional developer. There have been many use cases where Power Pages can be applied. We can categorize them based on the audience, which is the internal audience or the external/public audience. Let's discuss some of the common examples:

Internal Audience (Intranet Sites)

- **Community Portals**: These sites are meant for internal teams, departments, or company-wide collaboration. They facilitate communication, document sharing, and knowledge exchange among employees.

- **Employee Dashboards**: Create personalized dashboards for employees to access company news, announcements, HR information, and performance metrics.

- **Training and Onboarding Sites**: Develop sites for employee training, onboarding, and continuous learning. Share resources, policies, and training materials.

- **Project Management Sites**: Use Power Pages to build project-specific sites where team members can collaborate, track progress, and manage tasks.

External or Public-Facing Sites

- **Business Websites**: These are public-facing sites that showcase your company's products, services, and brand. They provide information to potential customers, partners, and investors.

- **Marketing Landing Pages**: Create attention-grabbing landing pages for marketing campaigns, promotions, or product launches. These are accessible to external audiences.

- **Event Websites**: When organizing conferences, webinars, or events, use Power Pages to create event-specific sites with registration forms, schedules, and speaker details.

- **Product Showcases**: Highlight your products or services to external audiences. Include features, benefits, and customer testimonials.

- **Nonprofit Websites**: If you're part of a nonprofit organization, build sites to raise awareness, share stories, and collect donations from the public.

These are some of the common examples but not limited to. While Power Pages offer many features and functionalities, a few noticeable are the following:

- **Simplified Authoring Experience for Makers**: The enhanced design studio allows you to build powerful and engaging sites without writing code. It includes workspaces for creating, designing, styling, and managing data-driven web applications.

- **Responsive Rendering**: Power Pages is based on Bootstrap, which inherently supports responsive design. Your websites will be mobile-friendly, adapting seamlessly to various screen sizes and form factors.

- **Pro Developers' Features**: Work with pro developers in fusion teams and add more functionality using Visual Studio Code and the Microsoft Power Platform CLI. Build effective business application websites by using custom code components.

- **Security and Governance**: Provide built-in security that ensures safe access to business data. Define authorization rules for users (internal or external) securely. Hosted on Azure App Service with ISO, SOC, and PCI DSS compliance.

At the time of writing the book, there are only two prerequisites for enabling Power Pages Copilot experience:

- The environment must be located in the United States or Europe regions.

- The browser language must be set to US-English.

This may change in the future, as the product and Copilot experience are still going through an evolution process. It is recommended to keep reviewing the documentation at `https://learn.microsoft.com/en-us/power-pages/` for latest updates.

9.2 Copilot for Power Pages in Action

In this section, we will experience the Copilot feature in Power Pages. As we have learned in the book so far, we will build a simple use case to visualize a business problem and leverage Copilot for Power Pages to smoothen our journey of solution creation.

In this section, we will build a web portal for our persona "TechCo." TechCo is a small startup that sells handmade crafts online. They have been doing well, but they want to make their website better and improve how they talk to their customers. In the section, we will build a portal and learn how various features of Power Pages Copilot can help us generate an end-to-end solution.

9.2.1 Setting Up Power Pages

The first action as a project leader would be to define the scope of the project; you would perform this action outside the scope of Power Pages, but I wanted to highlight the need to ensure that you understand that what we are solving here is the execution process; the planning phase, testing phase, or rollout phase will be outside of this exercise scope.

Now that we know that our objective is to create a better website and improve the connection with customers, we will start with logging in to the Power Pages site using `https://make.powerpages.microsoft.com/`, as shown in Figure 9-1.

As with all other Power Platform services, be mindful of the environment you are choosing, and for all experiments in this book, I recommend using sandbox or development environments.

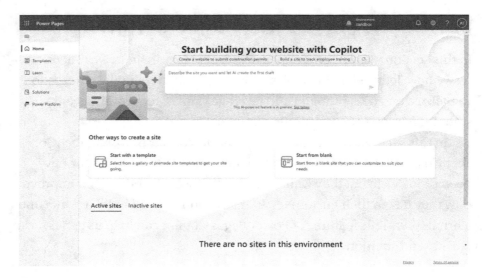

Figure 9-1. *Landing page of Power Pages with Copilot experience*

I can also choose from one of the templates available out of the box, but since we want to experience Copilot, we will choose the route of Copilot to set up our website. Here is the set of actions we need to perform:

1. Log in to the Power Pages environment.

2. Choose the right environment.

3. In the Copilot prompt box, we will provide the following prompt:

   "Create a new project named "Crafty Creations" with a simple template."

4. This will initiate the process of building the project, and Copilot will take us to step 1 of creation (Figure 9-2).

Figure 9-2. *Using a prompt to set up the project in Power Pages*

5. In this step, we will be asked to verify the name
    of the project and site link. Notice that the site
    link will be globally unique, which means the
    recommendation I may get would be different from
    yours (Figure 9-3).

Figure 9-3. *Step 1 of project creation using Power Pages*

6. Click Next if you are okay with the default web address or try a few with the system validating their availability globally.

7. The next step is about choosing the template. Notice that we requested for a simple template in our prompt that is already applied; however, we can choose any other template here as well if needed. For the sake of simplicity, we will continue with the default selection (Figure 9-4).

Figure 9-4. *Step 2 of project creation using Power Pages*

8. Based on our prompt, the system has intelligently identified a gap; we have not explicitly identified what website will entail. Here, the system is recommending the pages we should consider adding in the website (Figure 9-5).

Figure 9-5. *Step 3, common page addition in Power Pages project*

9. You will choose all four recommendations and click Done to begin the site creation.

10. This will take some time; if you were waiting for a coffee break, now is the good time.

Once the setup is complete, you can view the new project at the Power Pages landing page as shown in Figure 9-6.

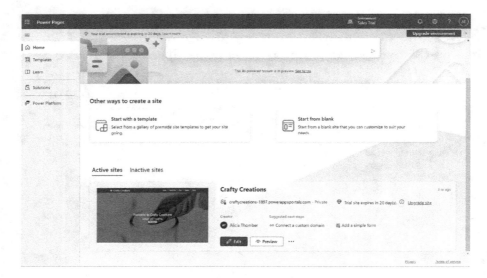

Figure 9-6. *Project created using Copilot in Power Pages*

In the next section, we will use Copilot to start editing the website we have just created.

9.2.2 AI-Generated Page and Form

In this section, we will experience Copilot under the project site. We will use the "Crafty Creations" project for the experiment and attempt to add a new page as well as make changes in the created page.

We will be adding a contact page, and along with that, we will include a customer request form. The form will include fields for name, email, inquiry type (custom order, shipping, or general), and a message box.

When visitors submit the form, we need Copilot to help categorize the inquiry and send it to the appropriate department for a timely response.

1. Log in to the Power Pages environment.

2. Choose the environment where the "Crafty Creations" project is created.

3. The project will be listed under Active Sites
    (Figure 9-7).

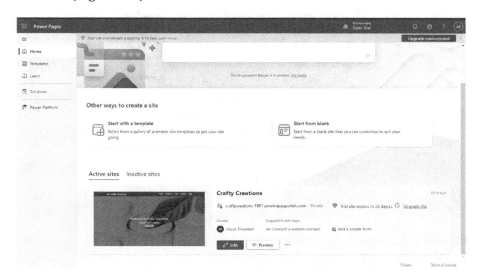

Figure 9-7. *Project "Crafty Creations" ready for edit in Power Pages*

4. Click Edit to open the project design studio. You will
    notice a similar right pane of Copilot chat enabled in
    the design studio environment (Figure 9-8).

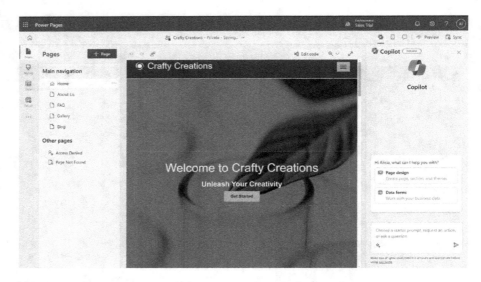

Figure 9-8. *Power Pages design studio with Copilot pane*

5. We will create a Contact Us page with the following prompt:

    "Create a new Contact Us Page for Crafty Creations"

6. This will create a new Contact Us page and incorporate the design of the website automatically (Figure 9-9).

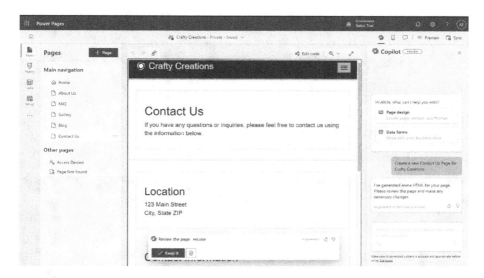

Figure 9-9. *Page creation with Copilot in Power Pages*

7. Notice that you have to keep the recommendations
    by clicking Keep it (✓ Keep it) or click Delete (🗑) to
    ask for new changes. In this case, we will continue
    with the recommendations.

Note   As with previous experiences, you can get different responses
than what is shown in images; please review and use these steps as
guidance and expect some changes in your execution.

---

8. Now that we have a Contact page setup, we will
    include a form with certain fields so that customers
    of Crafty Creations can reach out to them. For that,
    we will use the following prompt:

"Generate a form with fields for name, email, inquiry type (custom order, shipping, or general), and a message box"

9. This will start a form creation process with AI-powered form designer screen. The Copilot will display the form with requested fields and with option to additional changes (Figure 9-10).

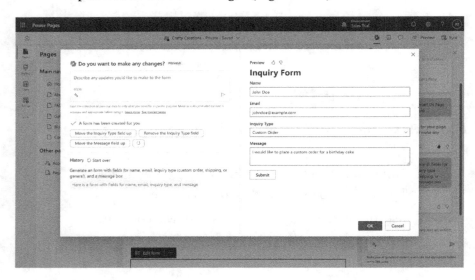

Figure 9-10. *AI-powered form designer in Power Pages*

10. You can now perform additional actions, such as sorting of fields, addition of new information, or removal of field that was initially requested. While we will accept the form as is, we highly recommend you play with features and try introducing some changes (Figure 9-11).

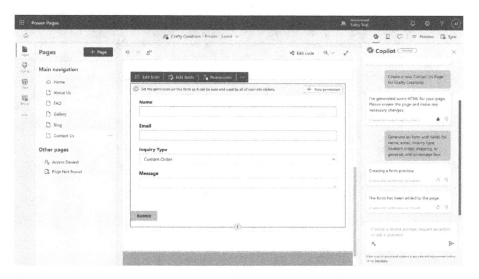

Figure 9-11. *Contact Us page with form created through Copilot experience in Power Pages*

The form addition can take a bit of time, but as soon as it is created, you can appreciate the ease Copilot has introduced to create such data-driven forms in the website experience. To test the website at any point, you need to perform the following actions:

1. Click the Sync (🖥 Sync) button at the top bar.

2. Click the Preview (⊙ Preview) button.

3. This will present a couple of options, where you can choose the desktop to experience the browser-based experience or scan the QR code for mobile experience.

As a final output, now we have a Contact Us page with a form where customers of Crafty Creations can submit various types of inquiries (Figure 9-12).

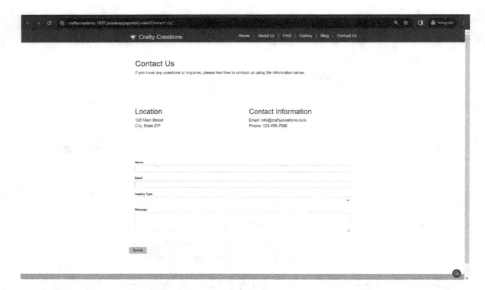

Figure 9-12. *Contact Us form in preview*

9.2.3 AI-Powered Chat Support

In this section, we will experience Copilot to enable a true generative AI experience for our end users as well. We will use the "Crafty Creations" project for the experiment and attempt to add a friend bot. The bot provides brief descriptions of featured products, enticing visitors to explore further.

1. Log in to the Power Pages environment.

2. Choose the environment where the "Crafty Creations" project is created.

3. The project will be listed under Active Sites.

4. Click Edit to open the project design studio. You will notice a similar right pane of Copilot chat enabled in the design studio environment.

5. To enable the bot, we can use the following prompt:

    "*Add a chatbot widget with the greeting: " Hi , I'm Crafty Creations bot! How can I help you today?*"

6. This will create a chatbot that can start answering questions regarding the products and content that is available at the website (Figure 9-13).

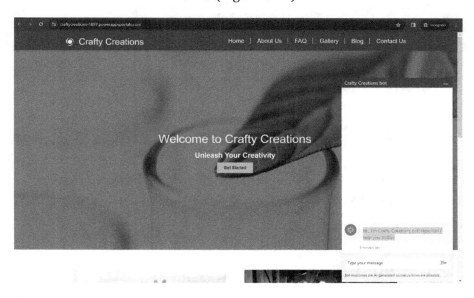

Figure 9-13. *Chatbot created using Copilot in Power Pages*

This bot will be able to use generative AI to answer questions, best part without spending time to train the FAQ bot. For example, if we inquire about the products Crafty Creations offer, the bot will be able to answer as well as guide users to links. Such experience can benefit organizations by reducing time to market and for users to have easy and fast access to information through regular conversations (Figure 9-14).

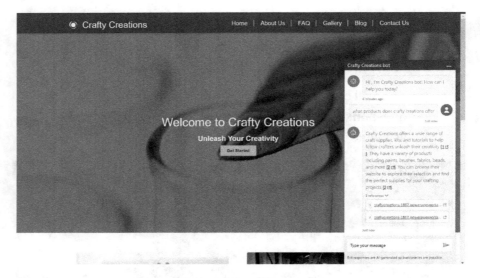

Figure 9-14. *Generative AI-enabled bot in Power Pages*

The bot created can be further maintained and enhanced using Copilot Studio. We will discuss Copilot Studio in detail in the upcoming chapters.

9.2.4 Dynamic Text Using Copilot

In this section, we will learn to use Copilot in Power Pages to generate content. In this exercise, we will continue using the "Crafty Creations" website and improve content in one of the pages. In case your experience of Copilot has generated some other page, you can understand the concept using the following exercise and replicate the same in your project. Let's begin this experience with the following steps:

1. Log in to the Power Pages environment.

2. Choose the environment where the "Crafty Creations" project is created.

3. The project will be listed under Active Sites.

4. Click Edit to open the project design studio.

5. In the main navigation pane, select the Gallery page
    (Figure 9-15).

Figure 9-15. *Design studio with the main navigation in Power Pages*

6. Click the Add icon under the first image to open a
    new component addition experience (Figure 9-16).

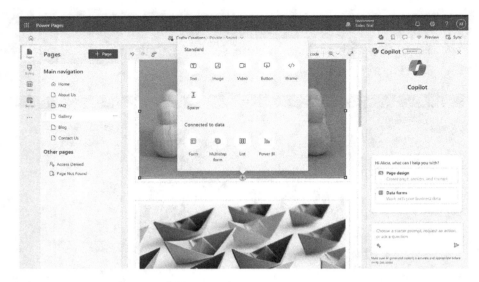

Figure 9-16. *Adding a new component in Power Pages*

7. Select Text (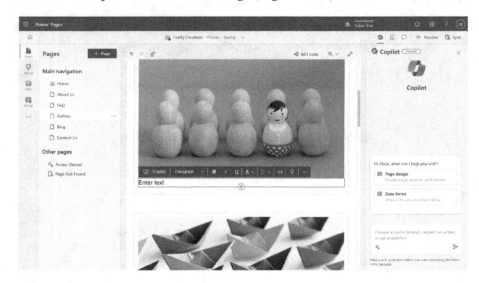) from the option to add a text

    component under the image (Figure 9-17).

Figure 9-17. *Adding a text component in Power Pages*

8. Notice the Copilot (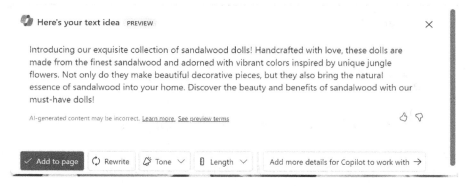) icon in the experience that can enable the text draft experience. We will provide the following prompt to generate the text:

   "*draft a catchy discription about dolls made out of sandal wood and painted with natural colours of unique jungle flowers, explain the benefits of sandal wood and why these dolls are must buy items. keep description under 50 words*"

9. This will generate a draft text (just like we have previously experienced in productivity experiences); along with the draft, Copilot will allow you to further improve, change the tone, or generate more ideas (Figure 9-18).

Here's your text idea PREVIEW   ✕

Introducing our exquisite collection of sandalwood dolls! Handcrafted with love, these dolls are made from the finest sandalwood and adorned with vibrant colors inspired by unique jungle flowers. Not only do they make beautiful decorative pieces, but they also bring the natural essence of sandalwood into your home. Discover the beauty and benefits of sandalwood with our must-have dolls!

AI-generated content may be incorrect. Learn more. See preview terms   👍 👎

✓ Add to page   ↻ Rewrite   ✎ Tone ∨   ▤ Length ∨   Add more details for Copilot to work with →

Figure 9-18. *Draft generated for the web page using Copilot in Power Pages*

10. We can now experiment with tone or length or completely rewrite the draft. I have chosen to improve the text to add a name of the flower using the "Add More details" option and the following prompt:

   "add some famous jungle flower name that is used for colouring and also provide natural fragrance"

11. The final draft output is ready for my use, and I can add the text to my page (Figure 9-19).

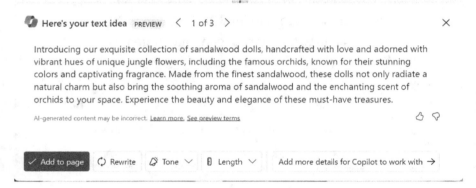

Figure 9-19. *Final draft generated using Copilot in Power Pages*

12. Click the Add to page (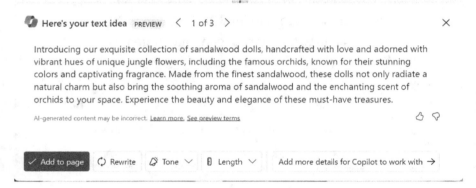) button to incorporate the text under the product image as shown in Figure 9-19. The output would reflect as shown in Figure 9-20.

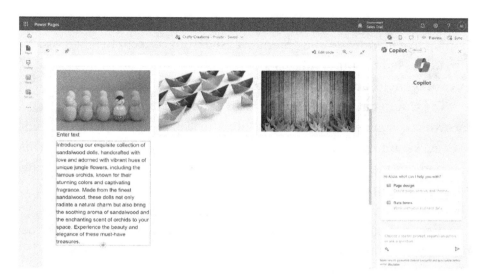

Figure 9-20. *Text added under the product using Copilot in Power Pages*

13. You can repeat the same steps to add descriptions or titles as required at the page as shown in Figure 9-20.

In this exercise, we learned how to use the Copilot text generation feature under Power Pages. This will help content creators to generate drafts with much faster pace and ultimately improve the overall time to market.

9.3 Summary

In this chapter, we discussed Copilot features in Power Pages, a low-code platform for creating, hosting, and managing websites for external audiences. We learned about the service offerings such as ready-made templates, a design studio, and a learning hub.

We experimented with Copilot for Power Pages features. We used Copilot to generate the end-to-end website from concept to first draft. We also discussed the prerequisites and limitations for Copilot such as the environment location and language.

The chapter also explained through hands-on exercise how to incorporate a generative AI chatbot into the website that can help the end user access information available at the website in natural language. This was perhaps the first experience we created where the benefit is expanded beyond our employees to our customers or citizens.

The next chapter will discuss Copilot experience in Power BI. The experience is critical for business managers to learn as it opens doors to a new way of interacting with data and insights.

CHAPTER 10

Microsoft Copilot for Power BI

In this chapter, we will look at Copilot in Power BI. I think Power BI is the easiest Power Platform service to talk about with business users, as it is one of the most popular business visualization tools.

Power BI, Microsoft's robust business intelligence platform, empowers organizations to transform data into actionable insight. Whether you're an expert data analyst or a business user, Power BI offers a set of tools that let you analyze, visualize, and share data efficiently.

Power BI evolved from Microsoft's SQL Server, where it started as a set of Excel add-ins – specifically, Power Query, Power Pivot, and Power View. Gradually, these components became a complete platform that goes beyond conventional spreadsheet analytics. Now, Power BI is a flexible ecosystem that works well with other Microsoft services and integral to business decision-making.

This chapter will teach you on how to use Microsoft Copilot for Power BI and enhance your skills of creating effective reports and visualization using natural and conversational style.

As practiced in previous chapters, my focus will remain on including practices to learn about Copilot, and it is assumed that you have acquired essential skills of creating reports using Power BI. However, I will briefly

© Adeel Khan 2024
A. Khan, *Introducing Microsoft Copilot for Managers*, Inside Copilot,
https://doi.org/10.1007/979-8-8688-0419-9_10

discuss the features of Power BI and recommend you go through the learning site of Power BI (`https://learn.microsoft.com/en-us/training/paths/get-started-power-bi/`).

10.1 Introduction to Power BI

As mentioned in the introduction, Power BI is the most popular Power Platform service. The goal of Power BI is to make data visualization easy and powerful for users with different levels of experience as data analysts or business operations leaders. With Power BI, you can create and share informative reports and dashboards for a large audience using default or custom visualization controls and data from various business sources. Some of the main features of Power BI are as follows:

- **Data Connectivity**: It connects to a wide range of data sources, including databases, cloud services, APIs, and flat files. Whether you're pulling data from an Excel spreadsheet, a SQL database, or an online service, Power BI simplifies the process.

- **Data Transformation**: With Power Query, you can clean, reshape, and transform data before loading it into your reports. This step is crucial for ensuring data accuracy and consistency.

- **Data Modeling**: Power Pivot allows you to create relationships between tables, define calculated columns, and build data models. These models serve as the foundation for your visualizations.

- **Visualizations and Dashboards**: Power BI's strength lies in its ability to create compelling visualizations. From bar charts and line graphs to maps and gauges, you can convey complex information in an easily digestible format. Dashboards provide at-a-glance views of key performance indicators (KPIs) and metrics.

- **Reports**: Reports offer more detailed insights than dashboards. Users can explore data, apply filters, and drill down into specific aspects. Reports are multipage documents that allow for in-depth analysis.

There are a wide variety of business use cases where you can use Power BI; here are a few examples just to give you an idea of Power BI's impact or usage:

- **Sales and Marketing**: Analyze sales trends, monitor marketing campaign performance, and track customer behavior.

- **Financial Reporting**: Create financial dashboards, income statements, balance sheets, and cash flow analyses.

- **Supply Chain Management**: Monitor inventory levels, supplier performance, and planning efficiency.

- **Human Resources**: Visualize employee data, track workforce metrics, and identify talent gaps.

- **Healthcare and Life Sciences**: Explore patient outcomes, clinical data, and research findings.

- **Education and Academia**: Generate educational dashboards, student performance reports, and enrollment analytics.

As we have seen, these are the few examples to inspire creativity. Power BI can help businesses visualize their data and empower users from different levels to examine, comprehend, and consume vital information. With built-in AI features, Power BI can easily tackle important questions that rely on data.

With a variety of out-of-the-box templates and examples available at Microsoft App Store as shown in Figure 10-1, you can learn about the Power BI application and prebuild samples. I would encourage the readers of this book who are new to Power BI to spend time learning Power BI apps and play with sample reports and dashboards to get familiar with the platform.

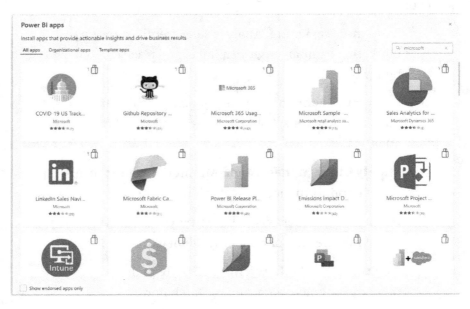

Figure 10-1. Power BI apps with sample data and reports

10.2 Setting Up Copilot for Power BI

In this section, we will first learn how to set up our environment for the Copilot feature in Power BI. At the time of writing this chapter, the feature was still in preview. The feature is not by default available to every user in the organization and cannot be experienced using a trial license. In addition, there are some considerations about geo data residency that administrators should review before enabling the feature. We will discuss how to enable as well as how to set up the data required in this chapter.

We will continue our learning method of the book and use real-life business use cases and apply Copilot to deliver the output.

We have discussed the concept of Copilot in detail; if in case you are starting from this chapter, which is not ideal but can be done, I would encourage you to spend some time at reading Chapter 1.

10.2.1 Enabling Power BI Copilot

Power BI Copilot requires administrators' actions to become available for users. We will discuss this section from two access paths.

Tenant with Power BI

For organizations having Power BI reporting services deployed or organizations only interested in Power BI reporting services with any data estate management tool, any user that requires Copilot experience to be enabled must have a Premium license assigned. This will allow users to have Copilot experience available at Power BI web experience. Premium licenses will unlock the Copilot feature, making data exploration and insights even more accessible and exciting.

Tenant with Microsoft Fabric

For organizations where Microsoft Fabric is enabled, Fabric Capacity starting from F64 and onward will inherently allow users to experience Copilot features for Power BI users, data analysts, or even data scientists.

If you don't know about Microsoft Fabric, I suggest you learn about the exciting new SaaS solution that promises to democratize data engineering and data sciences.

Once we have sorted the license requirements, there are still a few common actions required for the usage of Copilot. The administrator needs to log in to the Power BI environment; under Admin Portal settings (Figure 10-2), search for the new group "Copilot and Azure OpenAI Service (preview)."

Figure 10-2. *Admin portal settings for enabling the Copilot feature*

These two settings need to be enabled for either all organization users or selected security groups. The first feature to enable user accessing Copilot is required for all users. However, the second setting about data in transit is required if your tenant is in the region where Azure OpenAI is not enabled.

As these settings are still in preview, there can be evolving requirements, and it is recommended to review them at `https://learn.` `microsoft.com/en-us/fabric/admin/service-admin-portal-copilot` (Figure 10-3).

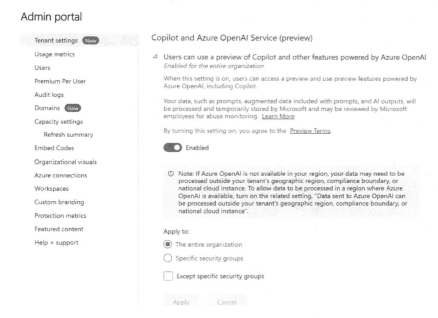

Figure 10-3. *Copilot and Azure OpenAI service settings for Power BI*

After finishing our setup, we can start our process of creating the report. We will first upload the data.

10.2.2 Bringing Data to Power BI Environment

To learn the usage of Copilot in Power BI, we will try to solve the data visualization problem using Walmart sales invoice data, which is available for learning usage at Kaggle (`www.kaggle.com/datasets/antaesterlin/` `walmart-commerce-data?resource=download`).

This dataset provides various invoice attributes such as ID, Branch, City, Customer Type, Gender, Product Line, Unit Price, Quantity, Tax (5%), Total Price, Date, Time, Payment Method, Cost of Goods Sold (COGS), Gross Margin Percentage, Gross Income, and Rating. The dataset can be used for detailed analysis and insights into sales patterns, customer preferences, revenue generation, and performance evaluation. We will use this dataset to generate reports that can help us unearth unknown facts about the Walmart business.

I have created a simplified version of a similar dataset that can be downloaded from `https://github.com/Apress/Introducing-Microsoft-Copilot-for-Managers/tree/main/Part-III/PowerBI/WallMartInvoiceDetails.csv`.

Here are the steps to upload data for the next experiment:

User with P1 License (No Fabric Environment)

1. Open Power BI Desktop.

2. Click Get Data.

3. Select the downloaded CSV file (WallMartInvoiceDetails.csv).

4. Provide connection details.

5. Click Load as shown in Figure 10-4.

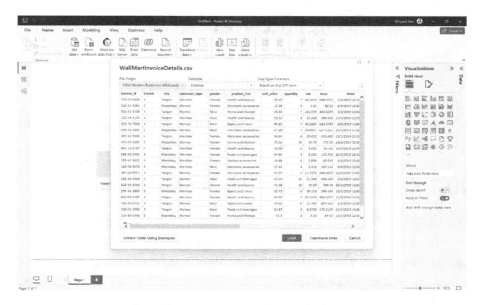

Figure 10-4. *Loading data using Power BI desktop*

User with Fabric Capacity

The fabric users need the data analyst to upload the downloaded file into the data lake or data warehouse. There are several steps required to upload the CSV file and convert the file into a table. These steps can be found in detail at `https://learn.microsoft.com/en-us/fabric/data-engineering/tutorial-build-lakehouse`.

Once the data is uploaded, it will be available to Power BI users as a semantic model. We will assume that the semantic model is now available, and users can access the Power BI browser environment to further perform actions mentioned in the next section.

10.3 Copilot in Power BI

In this section, we will experience the Copilot feature in Power BI. We will
continue our practice of this the book and use real-life business use cases
and apply Copilot to deliver the output.

In the previous section, we uploaded data and prepared the semantic
model. Now we can explore the features of Copilot.

10.3.1 Copilot to Understand the Dataset

The first experience we want to learn is how we can use generative AI
to help us understand the dataset better. Before beginning this exercise,
please ensure that Copilot setup is complete from both enablement and
data availability perspectives.

1. Log in to the Power BI browser environment.

2. Choose the workspace that has P1 or Fabric Capacity
    enabled. You can validate by selecting Workspace
    settings ➤ Premium as shown in Figure 10-5.

Figure 10-5. *Validating the license settings for Power BI Copilot*

3. Choose the environment where the "Crafty Creation" project is created.

4. Back at the main workspace, click the New (+ New ∨) button and choose the Report (Report) icon to create a new report.

5. The next step can vary between P1 users and fabric users, where you need to select the data model or semantic model.

6. Choose to create a blank report to give ourselves more chance of playing with the dataset.

7. Once a model is selected, you will be presented with the Copilot report creation interface called Power BI service with Copilot (Figure 10-6).

Figure 10-6. *Power BI service with Copilot*

8. Click Get started ( Get started) to bring the Copilot usage on the dataset.

9. The first action we want to learn about our dataset. While we have a simple dataset here, but imagine a dataset generated by your data analyst team, comprising of data from various sources and with many attributes, this feature can help us get up to speed and have better clarity about our dataset.

10. You will click the ✦ icon at the Copilot chat box and choose the default prompt *"what's in my dataset?"*

11. This will prompt Copilot to analyze the dataset and provide a business explanation (Figure 10-7).

What's in my dataset?

The dataset contains information about the sales transactions of a Wallmart store in different branches and cities, as well as the characteristics of the customers, products, and payment methods. The dataset can be used to analyze the sales performance, customer behavior, product preferences, and profitability of the store across different locations, time periods, and segments. The dataset can also help to identify the factors that influence the customer satisfaction and loyalty, as measured by the rating variable.

Figure 10-7. *Analyzing dataset using Copilot in Power BI*

12. The analysis is accurate and describing the details of attributes that are good to start with. What I really like is the business analyst context where it immediately suggests how this dataset can be used.

This exercise was a simple but important start as now we have Copilot setup with data in our environment. In the next exercise, we will learn how we can generate a report using Copilot. For the remaining exercise, we will not repeat the steps to reach Copilot in Power BI services.

10.3.2 Copilot to Generate Report

In this section, we will learn to use Copilot to generate the report. We began our experiment with understanding the dataset. We will begin with the foundation that we want Copilot to suggest how best the dataset can be presented:

1. It is assumed that you are in Power BI services, and the Walmart dataset is selected in the report.

2. In the Copilot pane, we will click ✦ and choose the out-of-the-box prompt "*Suggest content for this report.*"

3. This will use generative AI power to create a few suggestions on how the data and attributes can be used for business analysis (Figure 10-8).

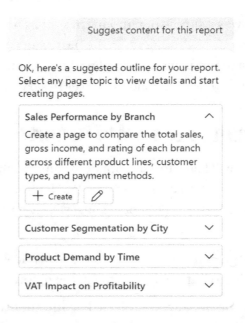

Figure 10-8. *Content suggestion by Copilot in Power BI*

4. We can iteratively select the various suggestions provided to generate the report pages.

5. We will first select "Sales Performance by Branch"; click the Create (+ Create) button (Figure 10-9).

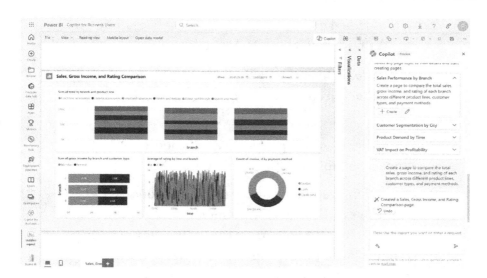

Figure 10-9. *Sales report generated using Copilot for Power BI*

6. The completion and attention to detail are
    very impressive. Review the report created and
    appreciate the work done and reporting made easy
    by Copilot.

You can continue to choose other options and generate additional
pages. In the next section, we will experiment with report creation with our
own prompt.

10.3.3 Copilot to Generate Report with Custom Prompt

In this experiment, you will create a prompt or rather enhance one of the
suggested prompts to build a unique report. We will continue working on
the dataset and report created in the preceding step:

1. It is assumed that you are in Power BI services, and the Walmart dataset is selected in the report.

2. In the Copilot pane, we will click ✦ and choose the out-of-the-box prompt "*Suggest content for this report.*"

3. From the suggested prompt, we will choose "VAT impact on profitability" and click the Edit (✐) icon.

4. If you don't get VAT as one of the suggestions, you can also use the following prompt: "Create a page to examine the effect of VAT on the profitability of each product line and city, and how it relates to the unit price, quantity, and gross margin percentage."

5. Click the Send (▷) icon after writing the preceding prompt to generate a report (Figure 10-10).

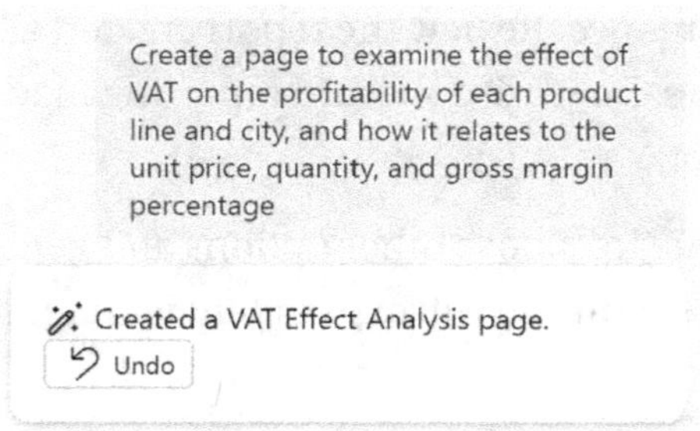

Figure 10-10. *Creating a page using a custom prompt in Power BI Copilot*

6. This will add a new page to our report as "VAT Effect Analyses" with recommended visualization. Again, the choice of charts is relevant to what is required in such scenarios (Figure 10-11).

Figure 10-11. *VAT effect page created using Copilot in Power BI*

7.   The report can then further enhance based on
     your needs.

In this experiment, you created a page with a custom prompt. In
the next section, you will learn how to improve our reports by adding a
narrative using Copilot.

10.3.4 Copilot to Add Narrative in Reports

In this example, you will continue to work with the report and learn how
to add narrative using Copilot. A narrative is a feature that provides a
quick text summary of visuals and reports. This feature offers relevant
insights that you can customize. It can summarize the visuals, customize

the language, change based on data changes, and can be interactive. Let's learn how we can combine narratives with Copilot experience:

1. It is assumed that you are in Power BI services, and the Walmart dataset is selected in the report.

2. Select the "Sales, Gross Income, and Rating Comparison" page for this experiment.

3. In the Visualizations pane, select the Narrative (🗄) icon.

4. In Choose a narrative type, select the Copilot button to use the new narrative visual (Figure 10-12).

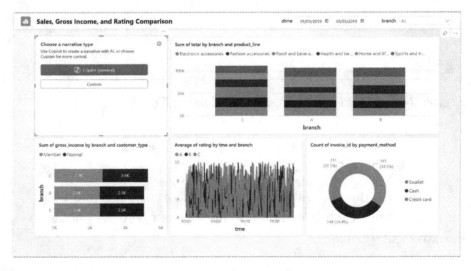

Figure 10-12. *Adding narrative visuals in Power BI*

5. You will be further provided with a prompt to select
    the type of narrative; this could be your guidance on
    how to address the needs of this report consumer
    (Figure 10-13).

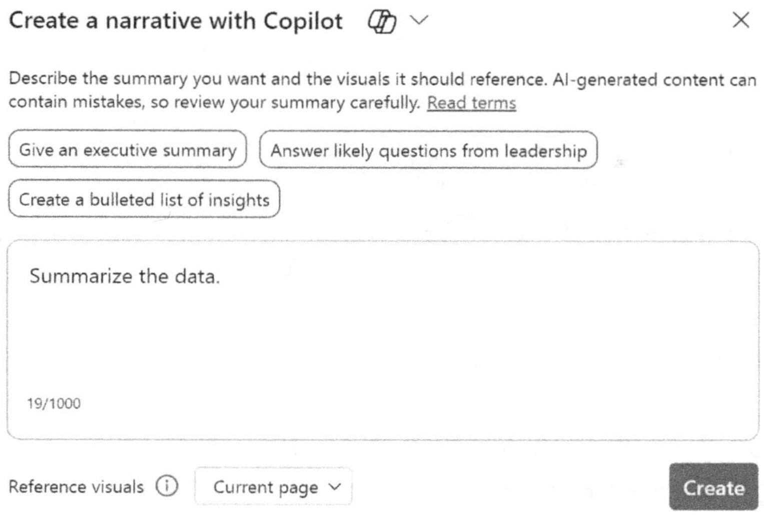

Figure 10-13. *Create a narrative with Copilot in Power BI*

6. We will add the following instructions:

    *"Summarize the data. Based on the data, what
    questions are likely to be asked by sales leadership?
    Answer these questions."*

7. In the reference visuals, you can choose to include
    or exclude any visualizations from the narrative
    summarization (Figure 10-14).

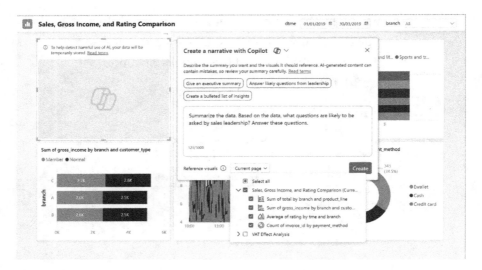

Figure 10-14. *Choosing visuals for narrative summary*

8. You will not change the default selection as all these visuals can be important for sales leadership to analyze.

9. Click Create (Create) to enable the narrative as shown in Figure 10-14. The result will generate a text summary of reports with key summaries important for sales leaders (Figure 10-15).

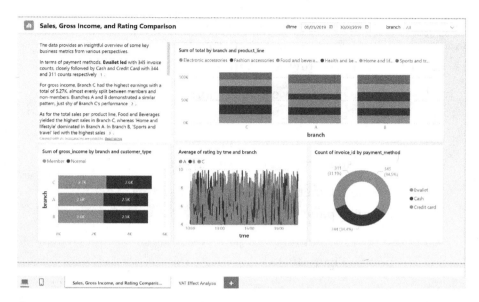

Figure 10-15. *Narrative with Copilot in Power BI*

10. If you want to change the narrative settings and add new instructions for Copilot, you can select the narrative visual and update with instructions.

11. Save this report with the report name "CopilotForBusinessReport" under the workspace you are working.

The narrative is a great feature for Power BI visuals, and with Copilot support, it can improve the experience of end users. At the moment, the experience is only available in Power BI services.

10.3.5 Summarize Report Using Copilot

In this example, we will learn to use Copilot to summarize the visuals in our report. This feature can help in the summarization of report in a business language that can help our users understand the visual in natural language. For using summarization in a Power BI report, you don't need to have permission to edit the report. You can just be a report reader and yet use generative AI for creating summaries.

1. Open the previously created report "CopilotForBusinessReport."

2. Select the "Sales, Gross Income, and Rating Comparison" page for this experiment.

3. From the top menu, choose Copilot (⌬ Copilot) to open the Copilot pane.

4. This will open the Copilot pane with default prompts (Figure 10-16).

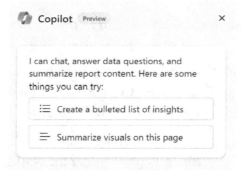

Figure 10-16. *Default Copilot prompt in a Power BI report view*

5. First, select *"Create bulleted list of insights."*

6. This will generate bulleted insights about our sales report (Figure 10-17).

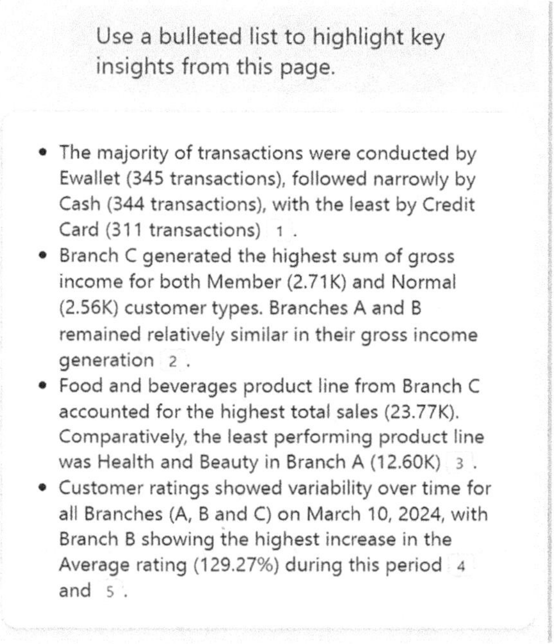

Use a bulleted list to highlight key insights from this page.

- The majority of transactions were conducted by Ewallet (345 transactions), followed narrowly by Cash (344 transactions), with the least by Credit Card (311 transactions) [1].
- Branch C generated the highest sum of gross income for both Member (2.71K) and Normal (2.56K) customer types. Branches A and B remained relatively similar in their gross income generation [2].
- Food and beverages product line from Branch C accounted for the highest total sales (23.77K). Comparatively, the least performing product line was Health and Beauty in Branch A (12.60K) [3].
- Customer ratings showed variability over time for all Branches (A, B and C) on March 10, 2024, with Branch B showing the highest increase in the Average rating (129.27%) during this period [4] and [5].

Figure 10-17. *Bulleted insights generated using Copilot in Power BI*

7. Notice the citations; if you click any, it will take us to the relevant visual. Let's click the first one (Figure 10-18).

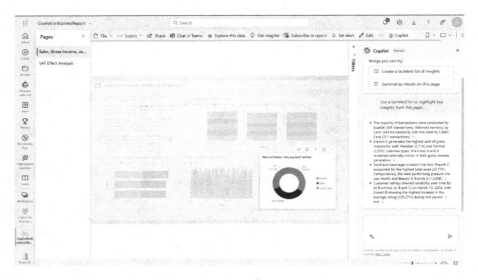

Figure 10-18. *Citation in Power BI Copilot insights*

8. We can copy the insights and add/modify based on our review and use them as needed.

9. Next is to generate the summary of the page; for this, we will select the "VAT Effect Analysis."

10. Click "VAT Effect Analysis" and select "Summarize visual on this page" in the Copilot pane.

11. This will generate a summary of the VAT Effect page, explaining the visuals. The summary generated as shown in Figure 10-19 can be copied and shared with the audience as required.

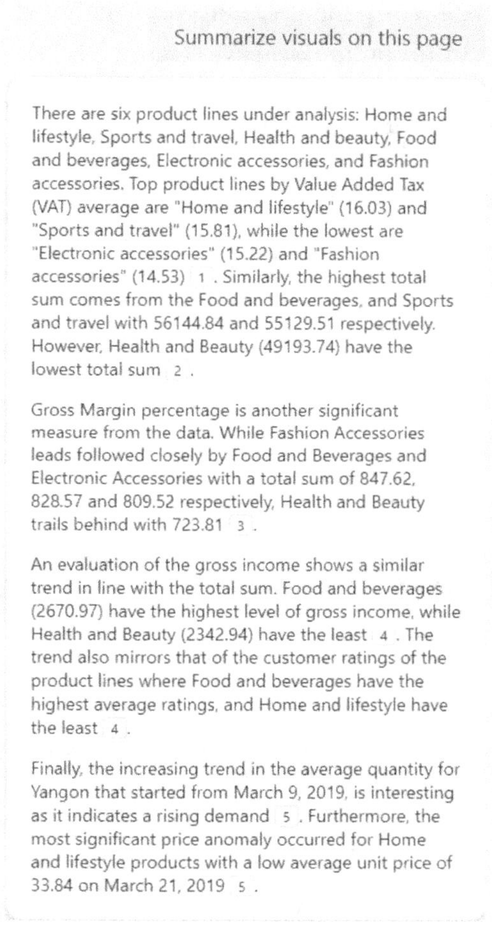

Summarize visuals on this page

There are six product lines under analysis: Home and lifestyle, Sports and travel, Health and beauty, Food and beverages, Electronic accessories, and Fashion accessories. Top product lines by Value Added Tax (VAT) average are "Home and lifestyle" (16.03) and "Sports and travel" (15.81), while the lowest are "Electronic accessories" (15.22) and "Fashion accessories" (14.53) 1 . Similarly, the highest total sum comes from the Food and beverages, and Sports and travel with 56144.84 and 55129.51 respectively. However, Health and Beauty (49193.74) have the lowest total sum 2 .

Gross Margin percentage is another significant measure from the data. While Fashion Accessories leads followed closely by Food and Beverages and Electronic Accessories with a total sum of 847.62, 828.57 and 809.52 respectively, Health and Beauty trails behind with 723.81 3 .

An evaluation of the gross income shows a similar trend in line with the total sum. Food and beverages (2670.97) have the highest level of gross income, while Health and Beauty (2342.94) have the least 4 . The trend also mirrors that of the customer ratings of the product lines where Food and beverages have the highest average ratings, and Home and lifestyle have the least 4 .

Finally, the increasing trend in the average quantity for Yangon that started from March 9, 2019, is interesting as it indicates a rising demand 5 . Furthermore, the most significant price anomaly occurred for Home and lifestyle products with a low average unit price of 33.84 on March 21, 2019 5 .

Figure 10-19. *Summary generation using Copilot in Power BI*

12.   If this summary is too detailed or long for our liking, we can also provide a prompt like the following:

"Provide an executive summary, indicating important takeaways."

13. This will help us generate a shorter version with a focus on important takeaways (Figure 10-20).

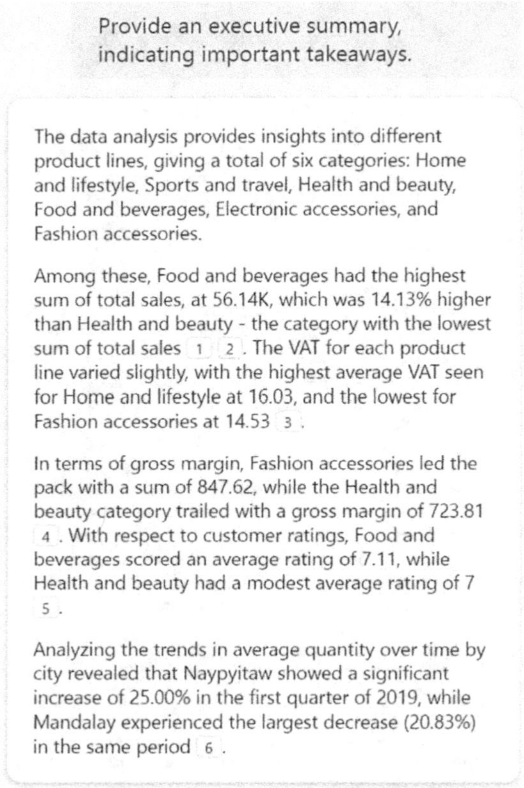

> Provide an executive summary, indicating important takeaways.
>
> The data analysis provides insights into different product lines, giving a total of six categories: Home and lifestyle, Sports and travel, Health and beauty, Food and beverages, Electronic accessories, and Fashion accessories.
>
> Among these, Food and beverages had the highest sum of total sales, at 56.14K, which was 14.13% higher than Health and beauty - the category with the lowest sum of total sales [1] [2]. The VAT for each product line varied slightly, with the highest average VAT seen for Home and lifestyle at 16.03, and the lowest for Fashion accessories at 14.53 [3].
>
> In terms of gross margin, Fashion accessories led the pack with a sum of 847.62, while the Health and beauty category trailed with a gross margin of 723.81 [4]. With respect to customer ratings, Food and beverages scored an average rating of 7.11, while Health and beauty had a modest average rating of 7 [5].
>
> Analyzing the trends in average quantity over time by city revealed that Naypyitaw showed a significant increase of 25.00% in the first quarter of 2019, while Mandalay experienced the largest decrease (20.83%) in the same period [6].

Figure 10-20. *Executive summary using Copilot in Power BI*

14. You can also create a custom summary prompt and let Copilot generate a summary of interest. One example could be the following:

"Summarize the data on this page specific to Sports and Travel."

15. This will generate a focused summary with respect
to the product we choose (Figure 10-21).

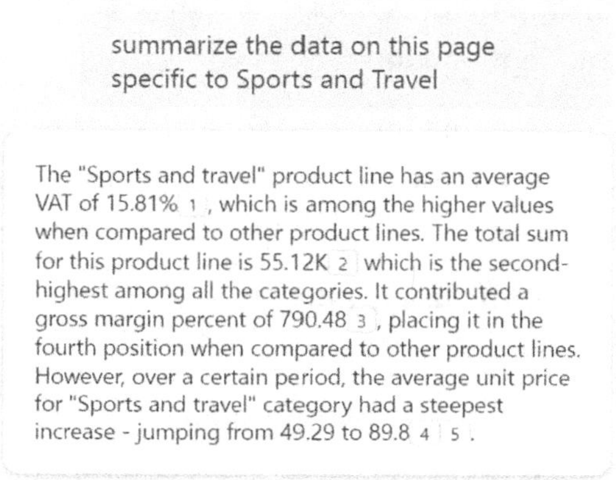

summarize the data on this page
specific to Sports and Travel

The "Sports and travel" product line has an average
VAT of 15.81% 1 , which is among the higher values
when compared to other product lines. The total sum
for this product line is 55.12K 2 which is the second-
highest among all the categories. It contributed a
gross margin percent of 790.48 3 , placing it in the
fourth position when compared to other product lines.
However, over a certain period, the average unit price
for "Sports and travel" category had a steepest
increase - jumping from 49.29 to 89.8 4 5 .

*Figure 10-21. Summary with a custom prompt using Copilot in
Power BI*

In this exercise, you learned how to use Copilot in Power BI as
an assistant and understood the report with ease. We can either use
default prompts or create our own custom prompts to get summaries of
interest. In the future, managers, directors, or CXOs will be able to get the
information of their interest with ease and without sending many emails or
reminders to analysts.

10.3.6 Answering Questions Using Copilot

In this example, we will explore how our end users can leverage Copilot
to ask questions about what and why in the report. We will use our
"CopilotForBusinessReport" report in this practice:

1. Open the previously created report
"CopilotForBusinessReport."

2. Select the "Sales, Gross Income, and Rating Comparison" page for this experiment.

3. From the top menu, choose Copilot (⊘ Copilot) to open the Copilot pane.

4. In the Copilot chat box, we will first start with asking questions about the lowest sales for sports products by branch. We can use the following question:

    "Which branch has lowest invoices for sports products"

5. This will provide an insightful summary of information that is not apparent in our report but can be useful. Copilot responds with an answer generated using generative AI as shown in Figure 10-22.

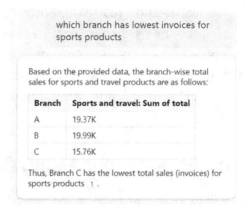

Figure 10-22. Exploratory questions on data with Copilot in Power BI

6. We can also ask "why" questions, forcing Copilot to find reasons and correlation in the dataset. We can use the following prompt to experiment with such type of questions:

   "Why is there a significant variance between the rating by branch?"

7. Copilot provides reasoning for such correlation. We always need to validate the response for accuracy, but it can always provide a good starting point (Figure 10-23).

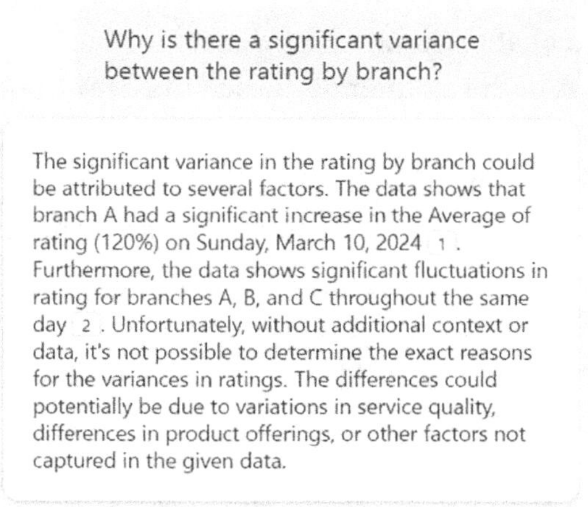

Why is there a significant variance between the rating by branch?

The significant variance in the rating by branch could be attributed to several factors. The data shows that branch A had a significant increase in the Average of rating (120%) on Sunday, March 10, 2024 1 . Furthermore, the data shows significant fluctuations in rating for branches A, B, and C throughout the same day 2 . Unfortunately, without additional context or data, it's not possible to determine the exact reasons for the variances in ratings. The differences could potentially be due to variations in service quality, differences in product offerings, or other factors not captured in the given data.

Figure 10-23. *Why questions answered with reasons by Copilot in Power BI*

This is a remarkable feature that can enable executive leadership to query data in real time and obtain relevant insights that can guide them to make better decisions. It will facilitate the executive leadership's interaction with data and reduce the workload for the team to produce results for such spontaneous and varied requests.

10.4 Summary

In this chapter, we explored Microsoft Copilot for Power BI, a generative AI feature that aids users in creating and analyzing data visualizations. We began the chapter with a brief introduction of Power BI, Microsoft's business intelligence platform that offers a range of features for easy and powerful data visualization. We learned about various capabilities of Power BI such as data connectivity, transformation, modeling, and report creation.

The next section discussed the prerequisites for setting up Copilot in your tenant. We discussed two paths to enable based on the current licensing of the organization and called out actions required by administrators to enable Copilot experience.

The latter part of the chapter discussed the use of Copilot in Power BI. We used business data of Walmart to learn about the dataset, generate report, and generate narratives using default or custom prompts. We also experienced the Copilot experience for end users to generate a summary or answer critical questions about data in our report.

There are a few more features of Copilot in Power BI such as using Copilot for measure creation (`https://learn.microsoft.com/en-us/power-bi/create-reports/copilot-introduction#descriptions-for-semantic-model-measures`) or enhancing QA experience (`https://learn.microsoft.com/en-us/power-bi/natural-language/q-and-a-copilot-enhancements`); however, due to their suitability to data analyst roles, most business users have found these features advanced for their consumption. Please refer to the provided links if you have an interest in learning these features.

This chapter also marked the completion of Part III where we covered Copilot experience in Power Platform services for our advanced business users or citizen developers. So far, we have discussed Copilot features that can be used by any user in the organization; Part IV will focus on role-specific Copilots such as Sales and Services.

The next chapter will discuss out-of-the-box Copilots that are enabled for specialized roles in the organization. We will begin with sales experience and close Part IV with Service Copilot.

PART IV

Copilot in Microsoft Business Applications

In this part, we will explore and learn Copilot in key business application solutions. The discussion includes Microsoft Copilot for sales and service and their integration in business processes. The objective of this part is to list the Copilot features available during the writing of this book. The part includes six chapters covering the following content.

Chapter 11: This chapter will delve into the innovative realm of Microsoft Sales Copilot, an innovative AI assistant designed to elevate the sales experience by seamlessly integrating with Microsoft 365 and CRM platforms like Microsoft Dynamics Sales and Salesforce. We will discover the strategic importance of sales functions, the compelling reasons for prioritizing automation, and the remarkable capabilities of Sales Copilot to enhance efficiency, lead management, and customer relationships.

Chapter 12: This chapter is an erudite composition tailored for professionals who aspire to elevate their sales methodologies through the integration of AI. It elucidates the seamless amalgamation of Microsoft 365 with Salesforce, providing a holistic view of customer engagements. From the initial configuration to the utilization of AI-facilitated CRM insights, each section is intricately designed to expand your expertise in sales automation.

Chapter 13: This chapter offers a deep dive into the user experience of Dynamics 365 Sales, enriched by the innovative features of Copilot for Sales. You will learn about the first-time login experience, the convenience of summarizing emails with CRM context, and the finesse of drafting personalized email responses directly from the Copilot sales pane. Furthermore, the chapter explores the integration of Teams with Copilot for Sales, enhancing collaboration and accelerating sales processes. As we navigate through the functionalities of Sales Copilot within Dynamics 365 Sales apps, you will gain insights into features such as asking questions, staying ahead of sales trends, and replying to emails with enriched CRM data. Chapter 13 is your comprehensive guide to mastering the sales operations of the future, where AI-driven efficiency meets the robust capabilities of Dynamics 365.

Chapter 14: This chapter serves as a foundational guide to integrating Copilot with Dynamics 365 Customer Service, providing a detailed walk-through of the setup process, licensing options, and deployment strategies. The readers will gain a thorough understanding of how Copilot for Service leverages AI to enhance service operations, offering insights across productivity platforms like Outlook and Teams, and discover the pivotal role of service functions in organizational success and how Copilot for Service redefines customer engagement through innovative AI assistance.

Chapter 15: The chapter discusses Microsoft Copilot in communication and collaboration with Outlook and Teams. We will learn the features of Copilot for Outlook and features of Teams and how they can enhance our usage of these tools.

Chapter 16: This chapter provides a comprehensive guide to enhancing service experiences through the power of generative AI. You will learn about the seamless login process and the innovative features accessible from Outlook and Teams interfaces and discover how Copilot for Service can summarize key email information with CRM context, draft email responses that are both relevant and personalized, and perform

CRM actions directly from the service pane. The chapter also delves into the Teams integration, facilitating collaboration and accelerating service processes.

The objective of this part is to enable you and your team to become more effective using Copilot in customer interaction using CRM processes and data.

CHAPTER 11

Microsoft Copilot for Sales

The significance of the sales function in a business cannot be overstated. It is the primary source of revenue, the lifeblood that sustains a company. Moreover, it is through sales that a business can establish and nurture relationships with its customers. These relationships provide invaluable feedback and insights that can guide the company's strategies and decisions. Furthermore, all business planning is anchored on the sales forecast. The sales function serves as the bridge between the business and the market, effectively communicating the value proposition of the business.

In the context of automation, the sales function is often prioritized due to several compelling reasons I mentioned earlier. The goal of automation is to enhance efficiency by reducing repetitive manual tasks, thereby freeing up the sales team to focus on their core responsibilities of selling and relationship building.

As an automation and digital transformation market leader, Microsoft has responded to sales automation needs with the announcement of the latest Copilot product, that is, Sales Copilot. It is worth mentioning that Microsoft's decision to roll out Copilot for Sales as the first among other business role-based Copilots underscores the importance of the sales function in business operations. This strategic move acknowledges

© Adeel Khan 2024
A. Khan, *Introducing Microsoft Copilot for Managers*, Inside Copilot,
https://doi.org/10.1007/979-8-8688-0419-9_11

the critical role that sales play in revenue generation and customer relationship management and the potential of automation to enhance these areas.

Microsoft Copilot for Sales is poised to play a pivotal role in the future of sales automation. This AI assistant supports sellers using Microsoft 365 by integrating with sales platforms, providing advanced AI and CRM updates, as well as insights within their productivity workflows.

It sources data from an organization's CRM platforms (Microsoft Dynamics Sales or Salesforce), large language models (LLMs), Microsoft Graph, Microsoft 365 apps, and the Internet. This integration of AI capabilities into the sales process promises to transform how sales teams operate.

The sales function is crucial for a business to stay alive and grow. Automation in sales, as a key factor, enhances efficiency, lead management, communication, and data management. Microsoft Sales Copilot, with its innovative AI abilities and smooth integration with CRM systems, is going to revolutionize the field of sales automation and help sales teams to focus more on their core tasks, driving business growth.

This chapter is a foundational chapter for the next two chapters; it will begin with Copilot for Sales prerequisites and setup-related details. The subsequent chapters will highlight and discuss the features of Copilot for Sales with respect to the CRM platform of choice (Microsoft Dynamics Sales or Salesforce). It is assumed the readers have a fair understanding of Outlook, Teams, and CRM platform of choice (Microsoft Dynamics Sales or Salesforce). It is also recommended to spend some time learning the basics of the sales module in the CRM solution deployed at your organization before deep diving into later chapters.

If you are starting the book from this chapter and new to the concept of Copilot, I would encourage you to spend some time at reading Chapter 1. Also, since Copilot for Sales works closely with M365 Copilot, I suggest reading Part II of this book to better appreciate and understand the features.

11.1 Setting Up Copilot for Sales

In this section, we begin with guidance on how to set up Sales Copilot. We will explore the licensing options available for organizations to begin Copilot for Sales procurement and the deployment options available and deep dive into the enablement of Copilot for Sales for the sales team.

11.1.1 Licensing Options

Organizations embarking on the Copilot for Sales journey require Copilot for Sales licenses for the sales teams. The license is user based, that is, each and every seller/user will require a Copilot for Sales license to benefit from this intelligent AI assistant. There are several options available for organizations to procure Copilot for Sales based on their current license scheme. I will discuss them based on the CRM solutions your organization has.

- **Dynamics 365 Sales Install Base:** If your organization has a Dynamics 365 sales **Enterprise** or **Premium** license, you can enable Copilot for Sales experience for record summarization, recent changes, meeting preparation, email assistance, news updates, etc. There is no additional cost required except when you want to take the benefit of complete Copilot experience (M365 and Copilot for Sales together). The user will benefit from the Copilot in sales module of Dynamics 365 Sales and be able to use Copilot features in Outlook and teams for sales-related activities.

- **Salesforce Install Base:** If your organization has Salesforce, there could be further two scenarios. First, if your organization does not have a Microsoft 365 license, you would need to purchase a Microsoft 365 for

Enterprise license to use Microsoft Sales Copilot. The second scenario could be where your organization uses Salesforce as the CRM system and has any Microsoft 365 license, you can use Microsoft Sales Copilot. However, you must have a Microsoft 365 for Enterprise license and an **Entra** (previously known as Azure Active Directory) account, which gives you access to Microsoft 365 apps like Outlook and Teams.

These are the licensing options available at the time of writing this book; it is always best to check the latest licensing options as they can change based on market needs.

11.1.2 Deployment Options

Once your licensing is sorted, let's discuss the deployment options. Microsoft Copilot for Sales can be deployed through two primary methods, admin deployed and user deployed. The choice between admin-deployed and user-deployed methods depends on the organization's needs and preferences. If the organization prefers centralized control and uniformity, the admin-deployed method would be more appropriate. If the organization values flexibility and individual customization, the user-deployed method would be a better choice.

Admin Deployed

The admin-deployed method allows administrators to install Copilot for Sales as an integrated app on multiple platforms or as an individual add-in on a single platform. The setup can be initiated from either the Microsoft 365 admin center or Microsoft AppSource to install it in Outlook and assign users. In the admin-deployed method, administrators have the authority to install Copilot for Sales as an integrated application across multiple platforms or as an individual add-in on a single platform.

Here are the summarized steps required for deploying using the admin-deployed method. Please note that for the admin-deployed option, you need to be a Microsoft 365 administrator to perform these actions:

1. Log in to `https://admin.microsoft.com/`.

2. From the site navigation, click the Settings (⚙ Settings) menu.

3. Under the submenu, click the Integrated apps (▮ Integrated apps) option.

4. This option allows the admin to purchase and deploy Microsoft 365 apps developed by Microsoft or Microsoft Partner.

5. At the Integrated apps page, select the Get apps (⊞ Get apps) icon to open the app source.

6. Search for "Copilot for Sales" to list the Copilot Sales apps as shown in Figure 11-1.

Figure 11-1. *AppSource "Copilot for Sales" app listing*

7. Click the Get it now (Get it now) icon under "Copilot for Sales" to begin the deployment as shown in Figure 11-1.

8. The Get it now will require a confirmation about terms of use and privacy; review if required, or you can proceed with acceptance based on your organization's policies.

9. This will take you to the admin center to complete the remaining steps. The first step is the validation of the selected app as well as "Copilot for sales Microsoft Outlook." The deployment process understands the importance of both apps and simplifies our deployment process as shown in Figure 11-2.

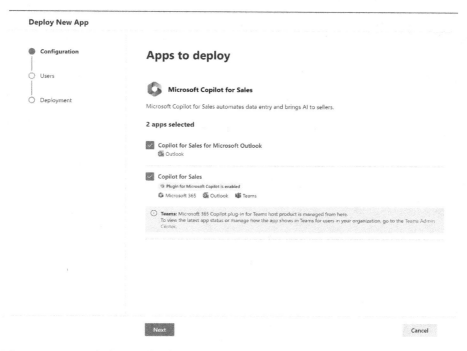

Figure 11-2. *Admin deployment configuration for Copilot for Sales*

10. The next step is to validate the user group for deployment (Figure 11-3). This is where the admin-deployed option is helpful as admins have full control over selection options. In my case, I have chosen "Entire organization" to benefit from Copilot for Sales; however, it can vary based on the number of licenses and number of sellers in your organization.

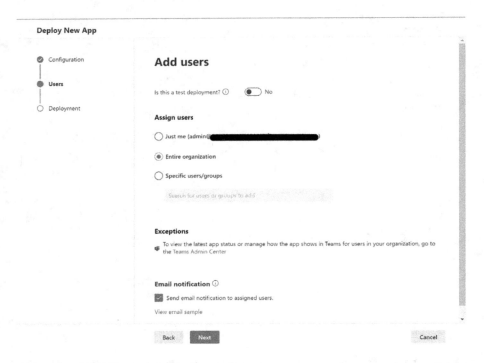

Figure 11-3. *Admin-deployed option, selecting users for Copilot for sales*

11. The final step is regarding app permissions. Copilot for sales will leverage the Internet and send data over the Internet to Microsoft-hosted Azure OpenAI services. It is critical to review this step based on the organization's policies and procedures. If Copilot for Sales is already approved by your enterprise security team, please select accept permissions for both apps and proceed (Figure 11-4).

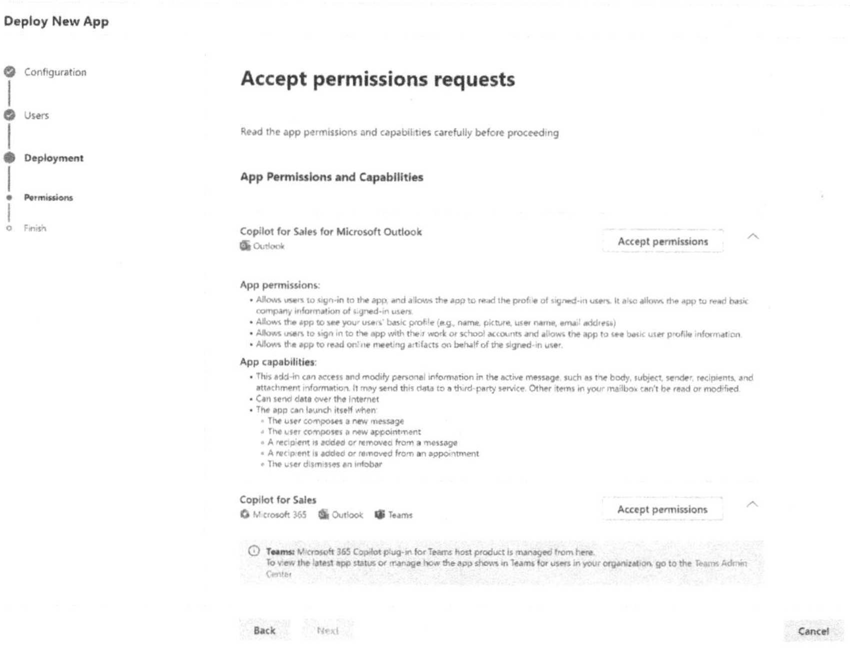

Deploy New App

Configuration

Users

Deployment

Permissions

Finish

Accept permissions requests

Read the app permissions and capabilities carefully before proceeding

App Permissions and Capabilities

Copilot for Sales for Microsoft Outlook
Outlook

Accept permissions

App permissions:

- Allows users to sign-in to the app, and allows the app to read the profile of signed-in users. It also allows the app to read basic company information of signed-in users.
- Allows the app to see your users' basic profile (e.g., name, picture, user name, email address)
- Allows users to sign in to the app with their work or school accounts and allows the app to see basic user profile information.
- Allows the app to read online meeting artifacts on behalf of the signed-in user.

App capabilities:

- This add-in can access and modify personal information in the active message, such as the body, subject, sender, recipients, and attachment information. It may send this data to a third-party service. Other items in your mailbox can't be read or modified.
- Can send data over the Internet
- The app can launch itself when:
  - The user composes a new message
  - The user composes a new appointment
  - A recipient is added or removed from a message
  - A recipient is added or removed from an appointment
  - The user dismisses an infobar

Copilot for Sales
Microsoft 365   Outlook   Teams

Accept permissions

ⓘ **Teams:** Microsoft 365 Copilot plug-in for Teams host product is managed from here.
To view the latest app status or manage how the app shows in Teams for users in your organization, go to the Teams Admin Center.

Back   Next   Cancel

Figure 11-4. *Admin-deployed option, reviewing and accepting permissions for Copilot for sales*

12. Before completing the deployment, review all the options selected and click the Finish deployment ( Finish deployment) button to proceed with the deployment (Figure 11-5).

Figure 11-5. *Admin-deployed option, reviewing and finishing deployment for Copilot for sales*

13. Notice the channels option displayed in Figure 11-5. Copilot for sales will be deployed as an add-on in Microsoft Outlook and Microsoft Teams and deployed as a plugin in Microsoft 365 Copilot Chat. I have covered the plugin concept briefly earlier in the Chapter 6 and will also be discussing it in detail in Chapter 17.

14. Once the deployment is completed, the system will provide a confirmation. Please note that it could typically take up to six hours for any app to appear in Outlook. However, for my deployment, it was available immediately (Figure 11-6).

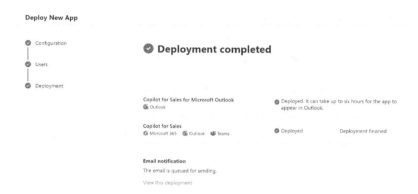

Figure 11-6. *Admin-deployed option, deployment completion for Copilot for sales*

This setup completes the admin-deployed Copilot for sales enablement for sellers. However, still the administrator needs to perform additional actions that can vary based on the CRM of your organization.

User Deployed

The user-deployed method empowers individual users to install the Copilot for Sales for Microsoft Outlook application from Microsoft AppSource. The option is suitable for organizations where flexibility is provided to choose based on individual needs. Please note that the Outlook add-in is a user-deployed installation, not an admin-deployed one, and it has limited features. User-deployed add-ins don't have the Copilot for Sales banner notifications that show up at the top of new or reply to emails (we will experience this later in the chapter). Also, the meeting invites don't automatically include the Copilot for Sales app. But you can add Copilot for Sales to the meeting yourself to get meeting summaries.

The user needs to perform the following actions to enable the Microsoft Copilot for Sales Outlook add-in, provided your tenant administrator has allowed downloading add-ins:

- Open the Outlook app or browser experience.

- Select the Apps (⊞) icon from the side menu.

- Select the Add apps (Add apps ⊞) button to search for the "Copilot for Sales" app.

- At AppSource, search for the "Copilot for Sales" app.

- Choose the Add (Add) option to add and enable the Copilot for sales.

In summary, the choice between admin-deployed and user-deployed methods depends on the organization's needs and preferences. If the organization prefers centralized control and uniformity, the admin-deployed method would be more appropriate. If the organization values flexibility and individual customization, the user-deployed method would be a better choice.

Microsoft Teams Settings

After completing the Outlook setup, the tenant admin needs to perform two actions so that you can leverage the Copilot for sales in Microsoft Teams environment. Here are the two actions required:

1. Log in to `https://admin.teams.microsoft.com/`.

2. Select the Meetings (Meetings) menu from the options and then select the Meeting policies (Meeting policies) option.

3. Choose the appropriate policy, or in case the admin wants to enable this for all organizations, choose "Global (Org-wide default)."

4. In the policy, ensure the "Transcription" option is on under "Recording & transcription" as shown in Figure 11-7.

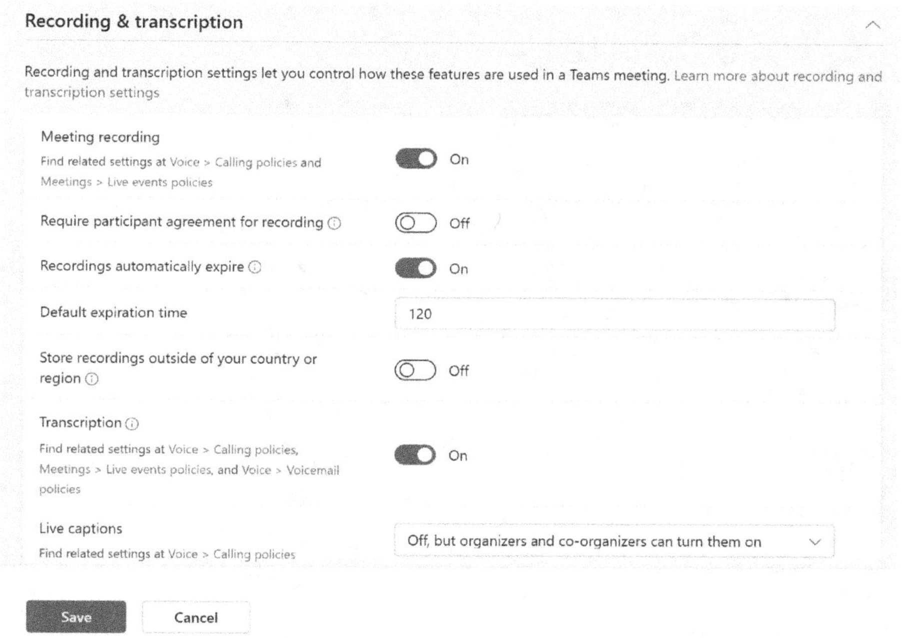

Figure 11-7. Setting Teams meeting policy for Copilot for Sales

5. Ensure to click Save (Figure 11-7) after making the change in case the transcription was not on.

6. Next, at the main menu, select the Teams apps (⊞ Teams apps) option and select Setup policies (❙ Setup policies).

7. Choose the appropriate policy, or in case the admin wants to apply this for all organizations, choose "Global (Org-wide default)."

8. Under "Pinned App," select the Add apps
   (+ Add apps) icon.

9. This will open the search box where the admin can
   search for "Copilot for Sales." Add the app to reflect
   the change in the App bar (Figure 11-8).

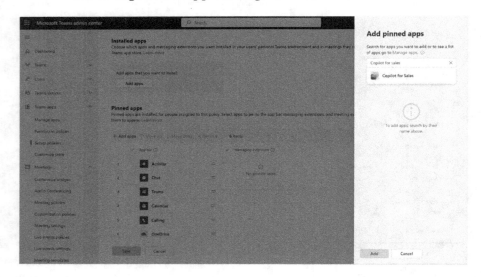

Figure 11-8. *Pinning Copilot for Sales in Teams*

10. Choose the appropriate location of the Copilot
    for sales app and click Save to reflect the change
    (Figure 11-9).

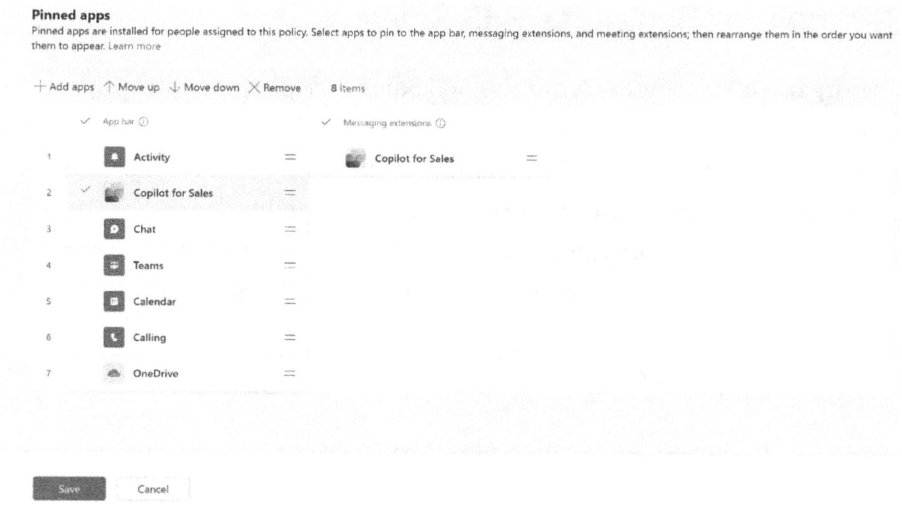

Pinned apps

Pinned apps are installed for people assigned to this policy. Select apps to pin to the app bar, messaging extensions, and meeting extensions; then rearrange them in the order you want them to appear. Learn more

+ Add apps ↑ Move up ↓ Move down ✕ Remove   8 items

	✓ App bar ⓘ		✓ Messaging extensions ⓘ	
1	🔔 Activity	=	🟦 Copilot for Sales	=
2	✓ 🟦 Copilot for Sales	=		
3	💬 Chat	=		
4	🟪 Teams	=		
5	🟦 Calendar	=		
6	📞 Calling	=		
7	☁ OneDrive	=		

Save   Cancel

Figure 11-9. Pinned app in policy for all Copilot for sales users

> 11. Confirm the changes and wait for some time to
>   reflect the change for all users.

Please note that the Outlook setup is mandatory before setting up Copilot for Sales in teams.

This marks the completion of the deployment setup. In the next section, we will finalize the setup-related activities based on the CRM deployed at your organization.

11.1.3 CRM-Based Settings

This section will discuss the remaining steps required for setting up working Copilot for sales. We will begin with discussing activities required for the Dynamics 365 Sales install base and complete with the discussion of activities required for the Salesforce install base.

Settings for Dynamics 365 Sales

The organization where Dynamics 365 Sales is deployed, following activities are required by users having system administrator roles. Tenants in North America have Copilot enabled by default; however, the tenants in other parts of the world require the following actions to enable the experience in Dynamics 365 Sales as well as Copilot for Sales. Here are the steps that need to be performed in the Dynamics 365 sales app:

1. Log in to the Sales Hub app and change to App Settings.

2. In the general settings, click Overview (▮ ⚘ Overview) or you can also select Copilot (▮ ⊛ Copilot) (Figure 11-10).

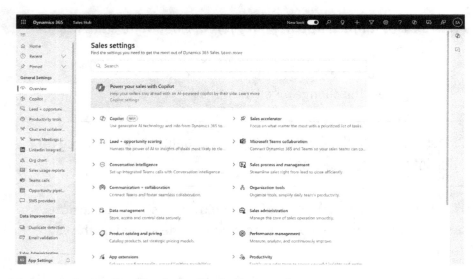

Figure 11-10. *Copilot for sales in Dynamics 365*

3. Under Setup, review "Enable Copilot For" and set globally setting for all sales app or select individual options (Figure 11-11).

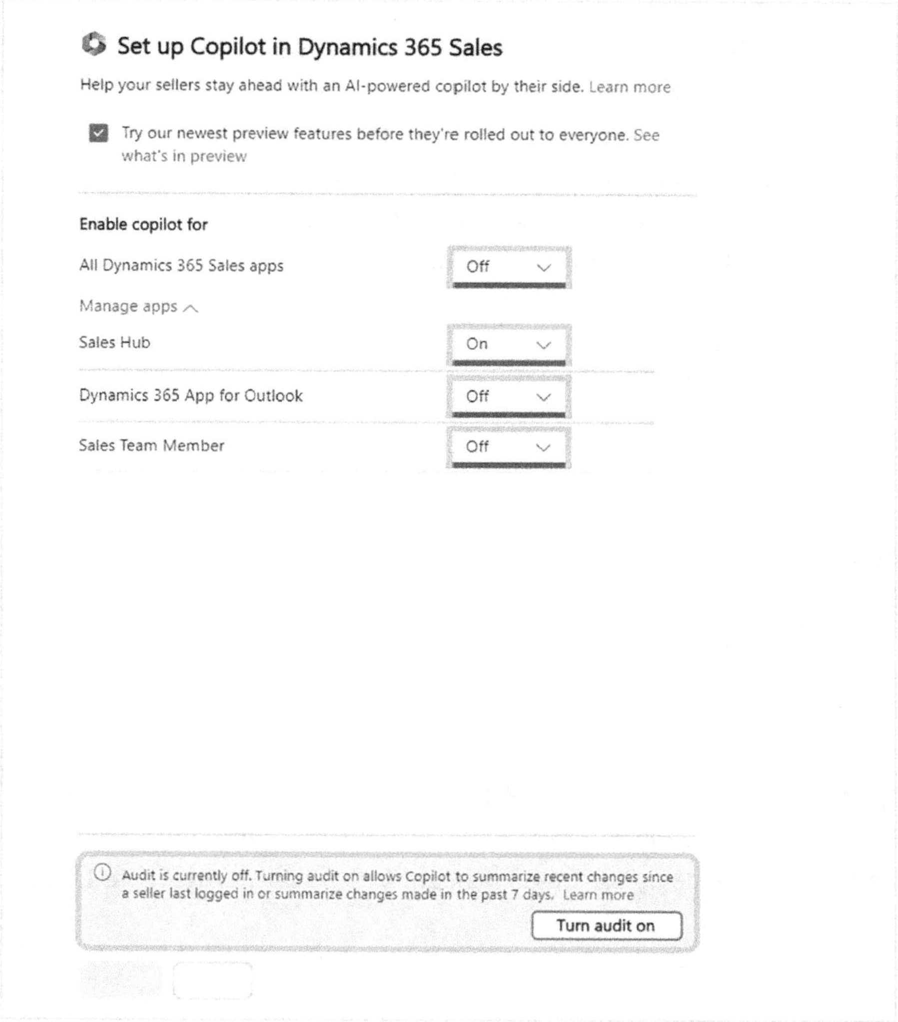

Figure 11-11. *Set up Copilot in Dynamics 365 sales*

4. As shown in Figure 11-11, notice the audit settings
    that are required for Copilot for sales; ensure to turn
    audit on.

5. The other prompt that may be visible is the permission regarding data. For tenants outside North America, Power Platform administrators require to accept the cross geo data movement (Figure 11-12). Please refer to steps at `https://` `learn.microsoft.com/en-us/power-platform/` `admin/geographical-availability-` `copilot#enable-data-movement-across-regions`.

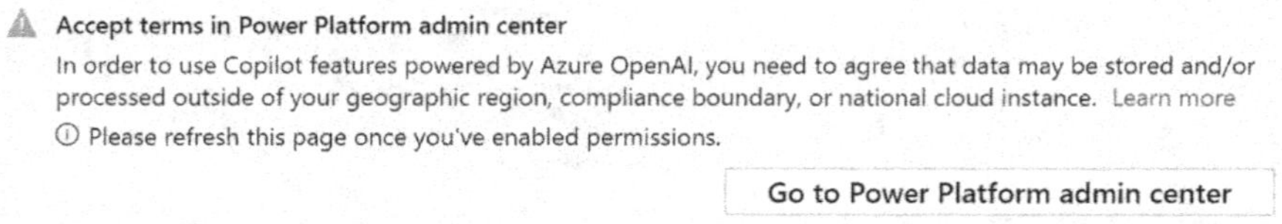

⚠ **Accept terms in Power Platform admin center**
In order to use Copilot features powered by Azure OpenAI, you need to agree that data may be stored and/or processed outside of your geographic region, compliance boundary, or national cloud instance. Learn more
ⓘ Please refresh this page once you've enabled permissions.

[Go to Power Platform admin center]

Figure 11-12. *Cross geo data movement alert*

6. Click Publish ( Publish) to reflect the changes and settings made.

The admin can then move to the remaining features such as the opportunity and lead and set the fields critical for your sells to receive updates about recent changes and to be included in the summary. You will leave it with the default features to begin with as shown in Figure 11-13.

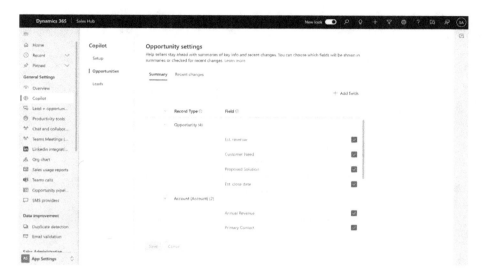

Figure 11-13. *Copilot for Sales, setting opportunity fields*

Once these settings are enabled as shown in Figure 11-13, you will notice the Copilot icon at the right pane, like other Copilot experiences we have previously discussed. Any user with a salesperson, sales manager, or administrator role will have access to Copilot features.

The next steps of settings are required at the Copilot for Sales app under Outlook. To set up further, your admin can follow these steps:

1. Log in to the Outlook client or web portal.

2. Select the App (⊞) icon from the side menu.

3. From the pop-up menu, choose the Copilot for Sales ( ) icon (Figure 11-14).

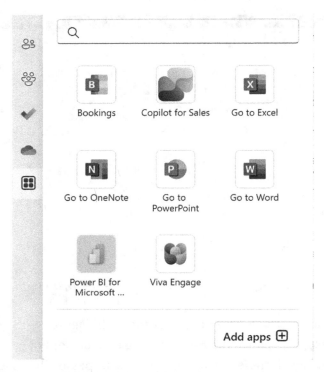

Figure 11-14. *App selection menu in Outlook for Copilot for Sales*

4. This will open the Copilot for sales app where you can access the Settings tab. Please note that you can also land to a similar app using Teams (Figure 11-15).

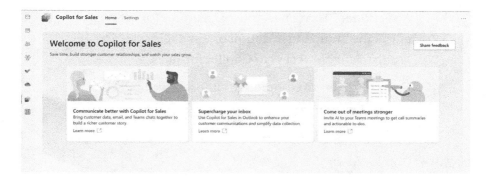

Figure 11-15. *Copilot for Sales app with Dynamics*

5.   Choose the Settings (settings) tab from the top to open
the settings page.

6.   Choose Copilot AI (✦ Copilot AI) under Tenant and
ensure Copilot AI is on as shown in Figure 11-16.

Figure 11-16. *Enabling Copilot at Tenant using the Copilot for Sales
App with Dynamics*

7. Also, under "Turn on Copilot AI features for," choose either the entire organization or a specific security group to enable access to Copilot for sales.

8. Once settings are completed, choose Save (⊙ Save) to reflect the changes.

9. Select Copilot AI (+, Copilot AI) and switch the Copilot AI on.

10. In addition, the admin needs to check the "Allow Azure OpenAI" checkbox if that is required to process the data from Salesforce for the purpose of Copilot for Sales (Figure 11-17).

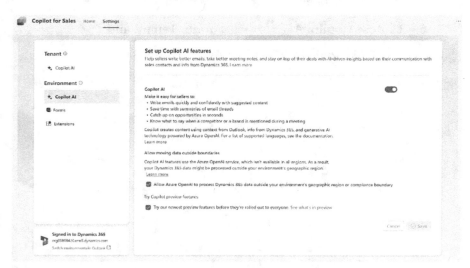

Figure 11-17. *Environment settings for Copilot for Sales with Dynamics*

11. The admin can add Dynamics 365 sales records to be available for creation and editing using Copilot for sales as shown in Figure 11-18.

Figure 11-18. *Form settings for Copilot for Sales with Dynamics*

12. The admin can set up form-level details for
     Dynamics 365 records such as contact, account, or
     opportunity. The admin can also add additional
     records if required (Figure 11-18).

13. The admin can enable each table to be either
     available for creation or edit individually
     (Figure 11-19).

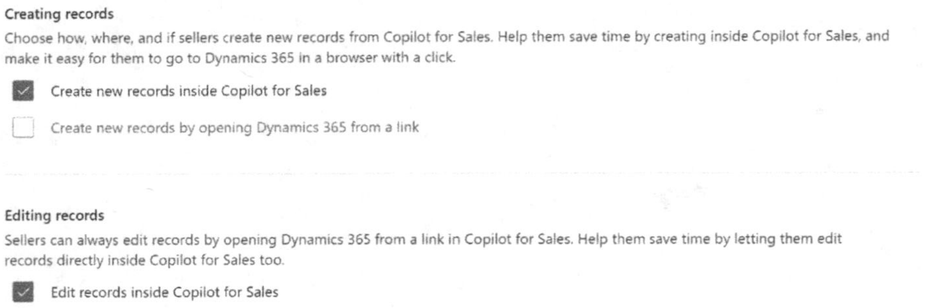

Creating records

Choose how, where, and if sellers create new records from Copilot for Sales. Help them save time by creating inside Copilot for Sales, and make it easy for them to go to Dynamics 365 in a browser with a click.

☑ Create new records inside Copilot for Sales

☐ Create new records by opening Dynamics 365 from a link

Editing records

Sellers can always edit records by opening Dynamics 365 from a link in Copilot for Sales. Help them save time by letting them edit records directly inside Copilot for Sales too.

☑ Edit records inside Copilot for Sales

Figure 11-19. *Creating and editing table records in Dynamics CRM from the Copilot sales pane*

14. Only tables with any of the Create new option selected will be available under the Create new record list.

15. The admin can choose fields that will be used for display under Copilot for sales as well as an option to edit these records. The admin can select fields allowed for editing and required as mandatory input in case of new record as shown in Figure 11-20.

+ Add fields   C Refresh data

Display name	Allow editing	Required
:: First Name	⬤◯	☐
:: Last Name	●	☑
:: Title	⬤◯	☐
:: Email	◯	☑
:: Account ID	⬤◯	☐
:: Business Phone	⬤◯	☐
:: Mobile Phone	⬤◯	☐
:: Owner ID	⬤◯	☐

Figure 11-20. *Form fields and editing features for Copilot for sales with Dynamics*

16. Lastly, the admin can also choose the key fields that are going to be displayed under the table record. Fields that are critical such as identifiers, closing dates, etc., are recommended (Figure 11-21).

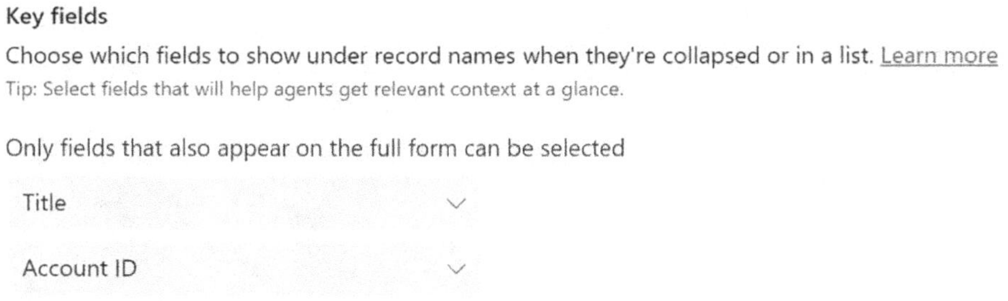

Key fields

Choose which fields to show under record names when they're collapsed or in a list. Learn more

Tip: Select fields that will help agents get relevant context at a glance.

Only fields that also appear on the full form can be selected

Title	⌄

Account ID	⌄

Figure 11-21. *Key Dynamics table fields to be displayed under the record*

17. Make sure to publish as shown in Figure 11-22. The changes will reflect in the environment only after being published.

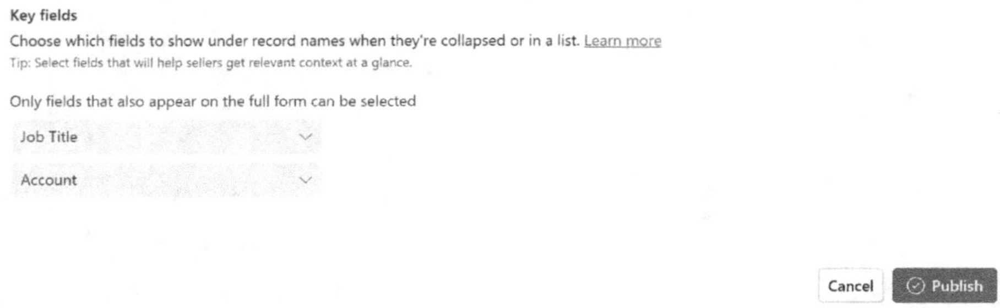

Key fields

Choose which fields to show under record names when they're collapsed or in a list. Learn more

Tip: Select fields that will help sellers get relevant context at a glance.

Only fields that also appear on the full form can be selected

| Job Title | ∨ |

| Account | ∨ |

Cancel   ⊙ Publish

Figure 11-22. Publishing the form changes

This marks the completion of our setup for Dynamics 365 Sales. You can skip the Salesforce settings and start experimenting with the Copilot for Sales.

Settings for Salesforce

The organization where Salesforce is deployed, following activities are required by users having role access to **Modify All Data** or **Manage Data Integrations** permission (Figure 11-23).

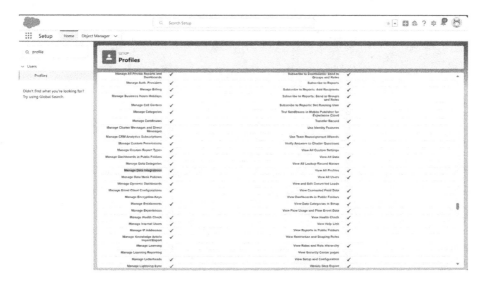

Figure 11-23. *Salesforce Manage Data Integration setting verification*

The next steps of settings are required at the Copilot for Sales app under Outlook. To set up further, your admin can follow these steps:

1. Log in to the Outlook client or web portal.

2. Select the App (▦) icon from the side menu.

3. From the pop-up menu, choose the Copilot for Sales (🔷) icon (Figure 11-24).

Figure 11-24. *App selection menu in Outlook for Copilot for Sales*

4. This will open the Copilot for sales app where you can access the Settings tab. Please note that you can also land to a similar app using Teams (Figure 11-25).

Figure 11-25. *Copilot for Sales app*

5.   Choose the Settings (Settings) tab from the top to open
     the settings page.

6.   Choose Copilot AI (✚ Copilot AI) under Tenant and
     ensure Copilot AI is on as shown in Figure 11-26.

Figure 11-26.   *Enabling Copilot at Tenant using the Copilot for*
Sales app

7.   Also, under "Turn on Copilot AI features for,"
     choose either the entire organization or a specific
     security group to enable access to Copilot for sales
     (Figure 11-26).

8.   Once settings are completed, choose Save (⊙ Save) to
     reflect the changes.

9.   Next is to select Copilot AI (✚ Copilot AI) and switch the
     Copilot AI on.

10. In addition, the admin needs to check the "Allow
     Azure OpenAI" checkbox if that is required to
     process the data from Salesforce for the purpose of
     Copilot for Sales (Figure 11-27).

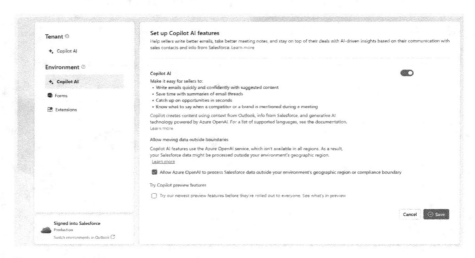

Figure 11-27. *Environment settings for Copilot for Sales*

11. The admin can set up form-level details for
     Salesforce objects such as contact, account, or
     opportunity. In Figure 11-28, I have added "Assets"
     as an additional object to the default view.

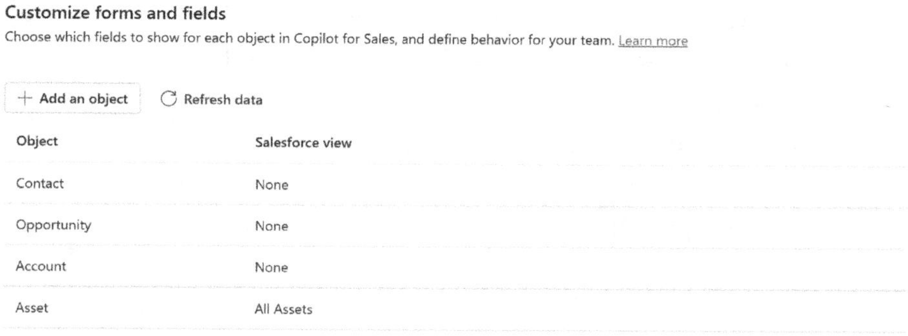

Customize forms and fields

Choose which fields to show for each object in Copilot for Sales, and define behavior for your team. Learn more

Object	Salesforce view
Contact	None
Opportunity	None
Account	None
Asset	All Assets

+ Add an object   ⟳ Refresh data

Figure 11-28. *Object list in Copilot for sales settings*

12.   The admin can also choose if the selected object is going to be created or edited using the Copilot for sales pane. These settings are similar for all the objects (Figure 11-29).

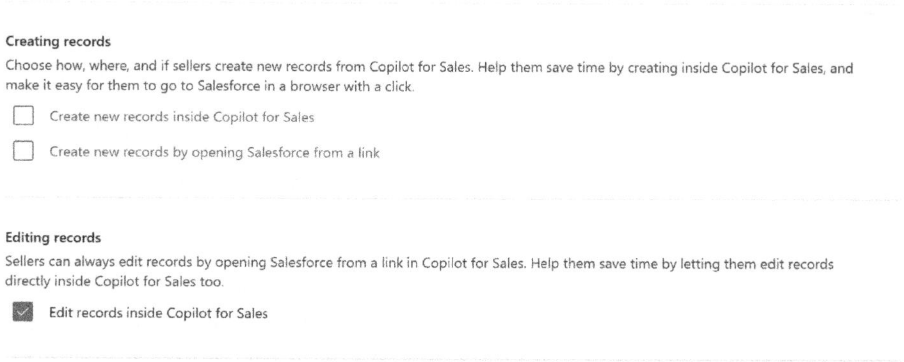

Creating records

Choose how, where, and if sellers create new records from Copilot for Sales. Help them save time by creating inside Copilot for Sales, and make it easy for them to go to Salesforce in a browser with a click.

☐   Create new records inside Copilot for Sales

☐   Create new records by opening Salesforce from a link

Editing records

Sellers can always edit records by opening Salesforce from a link in Copilot for Sales. Help them save time by letting them edit records directly inside Copilot for Sales too.

☑   Edit records inside Copilot for Sales

Figure 11-29. *Create and edit objects from the Copilot for Sales pane*

13.   Only tables with any of the Create new option selected will be available under the Create new record list.

14. The admin can choose fields that will be displayed at the respective action card and view. Default fields are listed; however, the admin can choose additional fields and define required fields as well. In the case of the new record creation, the user will be required to fill in the "Required" fields (Figure 11-30).

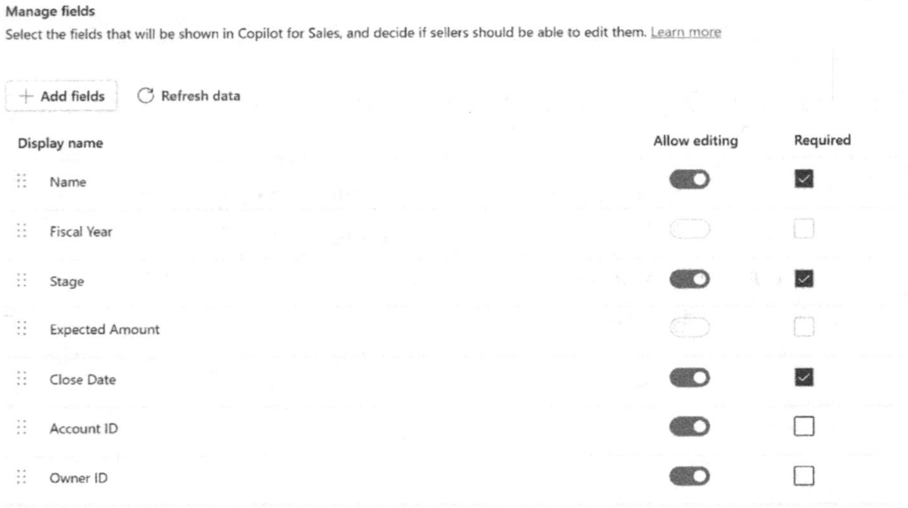

Manage fields
Select the fields that will be shown in Copilot for Sales, and decide if sellers should be able to edit them. Learn more

Display name		Allow editing	Required
⠿	Name	⬤▬	☑
⠿	Fiscal Year	▬◯	☐
⠿	Stage	⬤▬	☑
⠿	Expected Amount	▬◯	☐
⠿	Close Date	⬤▬	☑
⠿	Account ID	⬤▬	☐
⠿	Owner ID	⬤▬	☐

Figure 11-30. *Managing fields for the object form in Copilot for sales*

15. Lastly, the admin can also choose the key fields that are going to be displayed under the object record. Fields that are critical such as identifiers, closing dates, etc., are recommended (Figure 11-31).

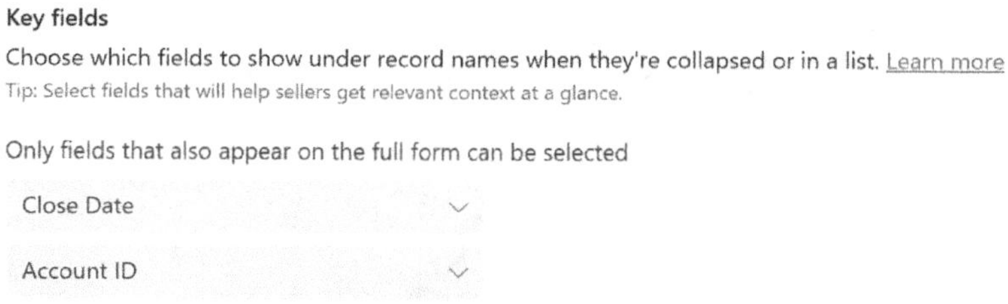

Key fields

Choose which fields to show under record names when they're collapsed or in a list. Learn more
Tip: Select fields that will help sellers get relevant context at a glance.

Only fields that also appear on the full form can be selected

Close Date   ⌄

Account ID   ⌄

Figure 11-31. *Key Salesforce object fields to be displayed under the record*

With these steps, your Copilot for Sales is ready to work with Salesforce solutions. The users having access to Copilot will now be able to use Copilot for Sales in Outlook or Teams.

11.2 Summary

In this chapter, we started our journey to explore and practice Microsoft Copilot in business applications. The chapter introduced Microsoft Copilot for Sales, an AI assistant for sellers that connects to sales solutions and provides insights across productivity platforms.

The chapter discussed the licensing and deployment options and listed the process of setting up an environment. We learned how organizations can procure Copilot for Sales licenses based on their current CRM system (Dynamics 365 Sales or Salesforce) and Microsoft 365 license scheme. We also explored how Copilot for sales can be deployed as an integrated app or an individual add-in on multiple platforms, such as Outlook and Teams.

The latter part of the chapter discussed the CRM-based settings varied between Dynamics 365 Sales and Salesforce Sales cloud.

As we move on to feature discussion in the next chapters, you can choose to read either Chapter 12 or 13 depending on the platform your organization has chosen.

CHAPTER 12

Microsoft Copilot for Sales with Salesforce

Salesforce is one of the world-leading customer relationship management (CRM) platforms that brings companies and customers together. It's an integrated CRM platform that gives all your organization's departments from marketing to sales to commerce and to service an opportunity to engage with customers effectively and with a single, shared view.

One of the key modules in Salesforce is the Sales Cloud, a sales module designed to support the sales process from acquiring a new lead through the close of a sale. The Sales Cloud provides a plethora of options for users, including account and contact management, opportunity management, lead management, sales data, and more.

As practiced in previous chapters, this chapter will highlight and discuss the features of Copilot for sales, assuming you have a fair understanding of Outlook, Teams, and Salesforce. It is recommended to spend some time learning the basic concepts of sales and the sales module of Salesforce before deep diving into the chapter further.

If you are starting the book from this chapter and new to the concept of Copilot, I would encourage you to spend time at reading Chapter 1. Also, since Copilot for sales works closely with M365 Copilot, I suggest reading Part II of this book to better appreciate and understand the features.

© Adeel Khan 2024
A. Khan, *Introducing Microsoft Copilot for Managers*, Inside Copilot,
https://doi.org/10.1007/979-8-8688-0419-9_12

It is also assumed that you have completed the setup as discussed in the previous chapter. It is recommended to read this chapter after Chapter 11 for better understanding and continuation.

12.1 Copilot for Sales Experience

This section will discuss Salesforce user experience and highlight how users of Salesforce can benefit from Copilot for sales. In this section, you will also learn the various features and experiences available from Outlook and Teams interfaces, simplifying user access to sales- and relationship-related information, powered by generative AI.

While Salesforce is one of the leaders in CRM space, Microsoft Modern Work remains the top choice for S500 and the majority of large enterprises. In this section, you will learn how using Copilot for sales brings a unique and never-before- experienced ability to bring the best of both platforms together. We will begin our experience from first time login and expand on various features available during the time of this book's writing.

12.1.1 First Login

In the first exercise, you are going to log in to Copilot for sales from Outlook experience. As discussed earlier, Outlook experience is critical and foundational to the overall Sale Copilot experience as your gateway to choose and sign in to your CRM of choice can only be done through the Outlook app.

For the experiment, I have signed up for a developer access to Salesforce sales cloud. You can either sign up for a developer account or use your own organization's Salesforce account. The following are the step-by-step guide to try your first Copilot for sales experience:

1. Log in to Outlook Office, either through app or
    browser experience.

2. Confirm the settings mentioned in Section 11.1.3 for
    Salesforce.

3. Select an email of a customer that you wish to
    review and use for this experiment.

4. At the email view, click the Apps (⊞) icon to open
    the app add-in available (Figure 12-1).

Figure 12-1. *List of apps available at Outlook*

5. Please note that the list can be different based on
    your setup; however, you can see Copilot for sales
    (🔳) that is required for the next steps as shown in
    Figure 12-1.

6. Click the Copilot for sales (🔳) icon to launch the
    Copilot side pane (Figure 12-2).

Figure 12-2. *Copilot for sales side pane in Outlook*

7. Click the "Sign in to your CRM" and select Salesforce
   for this experience (Figure 12-3).

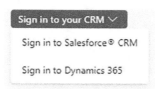

Figure 12-3. *Selecting the CRM of choice, Copilot for Sales*

8. In the next step, you will be asked to choose the correct environment of sales cloud. Choose a production, according to your organization policies (Figure 12-4).

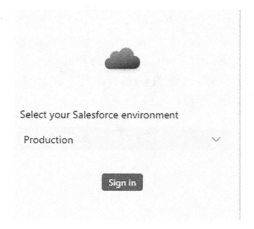

Figure 12-4. *Selecting Salesforce environment for Copilot for sales*

9. For the login process, Copilot for sales will be required to launch the Salesforce login screen. You will be required to allow the launch of a new window (Figure 12-5).

Figure 12-5. *Allow the login screen launch, Copilot for sales*

10. This will take you to the Salesforce login screen; provide credentials accordingly.

11. Microsoft will be leveraging the Power Platform Salesforce connector to fetch information from Salesforce cloud. For that, Power Platform requires confirmation for the first time only. Click Allow to proceed forward (Figure 12-6).

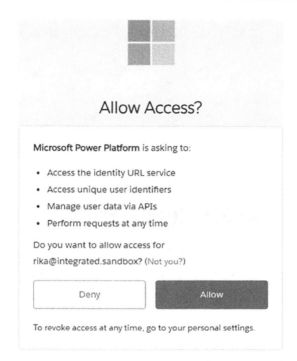

Figure 12-6. *Power Platform access for Copilot for sales*

12.   Lastly, Salesforce requires the validation of the
       access provided to the Power Platform connector.
       Select Allow access to proceed (Figure 12-7).

Figure 12-7. *Connector validation for Copilot for Sales*

13. Once completed, you will be able to see the Copilot
     for sales information pane filled in with related
     information (Figure 12-8).

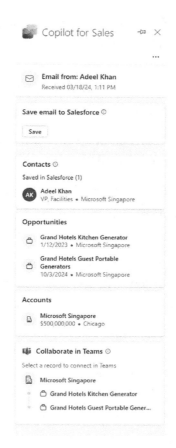

Figure 12-8. *Copilot for sales with action cards in Outlook*

Your Copilot for sales is ready for consumption; we will continue using Copilot for sales and learn the features now with ease.

12.1.2 Email Summary with CRM Context

The second experience you are going to learn is to use the summary feature. The Copilot summary you learned in Part II was generated using the content available only in the email (or in the email chain); however, now with CRM data to refer to, the summary is going to be more relevant to the current customer situation. Follow the steps to experience the context-based summarization:

1. Log in to Outlook Office, either through app or browser experience.

2. Select an email of a customer that you wish to review and use for this experiment.

3. Notice the Summary by Copilot (📝) option at the top of the selected email; click to begin the summarization.

4. It may take a few seconds to complete; once ready, you will be provided with an initial summary of the email along with an indication that this summary is generated "With sales insights added" (Figure 12-9).

Figure 12-9. *Summary generated with Sales insights added in Outlook Sales Copilot*

5. Do verify the summary and validate as it is AI generated and can be incorrect.

6. You can now expand further on the summary and assess key points with links to Salesforce objects. Click Go to Sales (📝 Go to Sales) to open the side pane (Figure 12-9).

7. The Copilot for sales pane will be launched with
    identified information. In the example I have used,
    my contact and opportunity already exist in Sales
    Cloud. Copilot for sales was able to identify and
    provide key info with sales cloud object reference as
    shown in Figure 12-10.

Figure 12-10. *Copilot for sales with key email information
in Outlook*

8. If you are comfortable with the key email info, you
    can choose either to save directly in Salesforce, copy
    the summary, or change the language of summary.
    Click More actions (⋯) to expand the options
    (Figure 12-11).

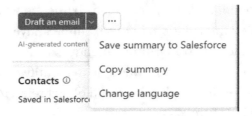

Figure 12-11. *Options with a summary in Copilot for sales in Outlook*

9. Select "Save Summary to Salesforce" first; Copilot for sales will display the object where you want to save the information at Salesforce. Choose the object suitable (Figure 12-12).

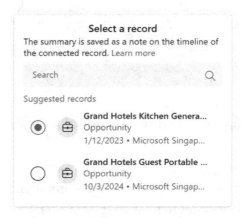

Figure 12-12. *Select an object for the summary to be saved in Copilot for sales at Outlook*

10. Click Save (Save) to reflect the changes at Salesforce.

11. Next, click the three dots (⋯) and experience the change language feature. Notice that the save summary is grayed out as you have already copied the summary at the related object (Figure 12-13).

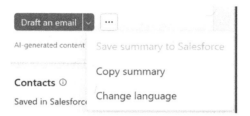

Figure 12-13. *Grayed out save summary, Copilot for sales Outlook experience*

12. Click "Change language"; this will prompt the user to select the language they need "key info summary" to be prepared. Experiment with a few languages you know and analyze the results (Figure 12-14).

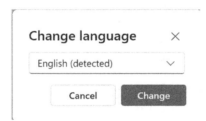

Figure 12-14. *Changing language for the key info summary, Copilot for sales in Outlook*

12.1.3 Draft an Email Response with CRM Context

In this section, you will experience generating a draft email response with CRM data. We discussed and experienced Copilot's ability to generate draft responses to emails in Part II; you will now expand the experience with CRM data. This will make your draft more aligned with customer information and activities, personalized with useful information available in CRM. Follow the steps to experience the CRM-based draft response:

1. Log in to Outlook Office, either through app or browser experience.

2. Select an email of a customer that you wish to review and use for this experiment.

3. Click the Reply button to draft the response (Figure 12-15).

Figure 12-15. *Draft options with Copilot for sales*

4. At the draft bar, you can choose any of the given default prompts or provide a custom prompt. Let's choose a custom prompt to experiment.

5. This will open a Copilot prompt box where you can provide a custom instruction to Copilot regarding the reply (Figure 12-16).

Figure 12-16. *Custom prompt using Copilot for sales in Outlook*

6. You can provide a prompt relevant to address the
    customer response. In my case, I provided the
    response as shown in Figure 12-17.

Figure 12-17. *Providing a custom prompt to draft a reply with
Copilot for sales*

7. Click Generate to view the draft; you can also set
    other features such as the tone and length like
    Outlook Copilot experience.

8. Review the draft, and if you find it relevant, select
    Keep it or Regenerate (Figure 12-18).

Figure 12-18. Draft generated by Copilot for sales in Outlook

This is one way of generating a draft reply; let's experience the other way of drafting a reply using the Copilot for sales pane.

1. Log in to Outlook Office, either through app or browser experience.

2. Select an email of a customer that you wish to review and use for this experiment.

3. At the email view, click the Apps (⊞) icon to open the app add-in available and select the Copilot for sales (⬤) icon.

4. This will launch Copilot for sales with relevant customer information and key email info as experienced in the previous section (Figure 12-19).

Figure 12-19. *Copilot for sales pane with customer information*

5. Click Draft an email (Draft an email ⌄). Like Outlook-
    based experience, you can either provide a custom
    prompt or choose from any of the default options
    (Figure 12-20).

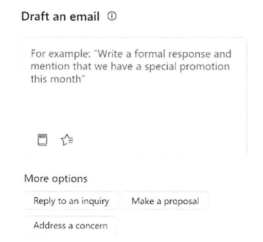

Figure 12-20. *Draft option using the Copilot for sales pane*

6. You can choose the "Reply to an inquiry" first and analyze the results. Copilot will leverage the data in Salesforce and draft a response.

7. Analyzing the response as shown in Figure 12-21, Copilot for sales has leveraged Salesforce data and prepared a lot better draft response. The response has citation as well, so you can validate reasons during the review of the draft.

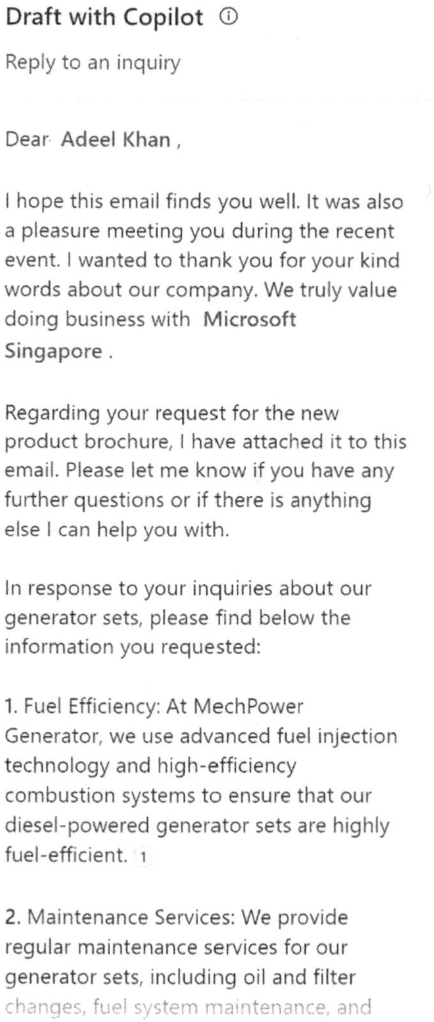

Draft with Copilot ⓘ

Reply to an inquiry

Dear Adeel Khan ,

I hope this email finds you well. It was also a pleasure meeting you during the recent event. I wanted to thank you for your kind words about our company. We truly value doing business with Microsoft Singapore .

Regarding your request for the new product brochure, I have attached it to this email. Please let me know if you have any further questions or if there is anything else I can help you with.

In response to your inquiries about our generator sets, please find below the information you requested:

1. Fuel Efficiency: At MechPower Generator, we use advanced fuel injection technology and high-efficiency combustion systems to ensure that our diesel-powered generator sets are highly fuel-efficient. 1

2. Maintenance Services: We provide regular maintenance services for our generator sets, including oil and filter changes, fuel system maintenance, and

Figure 12-21. *Draft generated using the Copilot for sales pane*

8.   The other difference I noticed was the awareness of the upcoming meeting; the draft prepared by Copilot for sales included the date of the meeting and created a related response (Figure 12-22).

Draft with Copilot ⓘ

Reply to an inquiry

implementing fuel-efficient designs, and
recycling used oil and filters. [2]

5. Warranty Coverage: Our generator
products come with a standard one-year
warranty that covers defects in materials
and workmanship. We also offer extended
warranty coverage for an additional fee.

Regarding the Grand Hotels Kitchen
Generators, I'm glad to hear that
MechPower Generator's solutions might
be a great fit for your power backup
system. I'm looking forward to discussing
more details about it during our meeting
on 3/21/24 .

Thank you for your continued interest in
our company, and I look forward to
speaking with you soon.

Best regards,

Rika Khamil

👍 👎

Figure 12-22. *Using upcoming event information in the Copilot sales email draft*

9. You can further improve the draft response; you can choose Adjust Draft (⚏) to set the additional attributes (Figure 12-23).

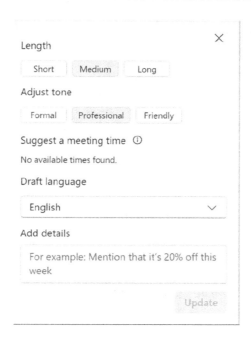

Figure 12-23. Adjust draft attributes using Copilot for sales

10. Play with the options and analyze the changes in the draft.

11. Once you are satisfied with the draft, click the Copy (🗋) icon to copy the draft that can be used to reply to the customer email at Outlook.

In this exercise, you generated a draft reply using two options. The exercise also covered various attributes and settings offered for preparing a reply to customers. To combine best of M365 and Copilot for sales, you can apply Coaching by Copilot to further improve the draft reply. Refer to Part II where I have discussed the Coaching feature (Figure 12-24).

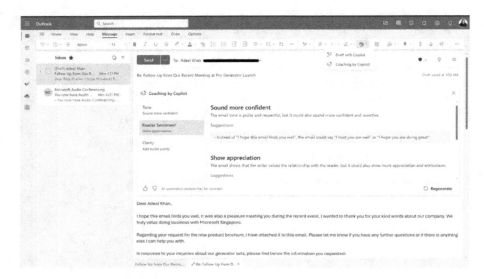

Figure 12-24. *Applying coaching at the final draft created using Sales Copilot*

12.1.4 CRM Actions from Copilot for Sales Pane

In this exercise, you will learn about how to perform CRM-related actions from the Copilot for sales pane. You will learn how to save the interaction in Salesforce, how to update object information, and how to get a summary of active associated opportunities in Sales Cloud.

Create New Record

Copilot for sales allows users to create a new object record. This feature has been recently added to the Copilot for sales pane. There are two ways to create a record available at the time of writing this book. The list of available objects depends on the form settings discussed in Chapter 11, Section 11.1.3. Admins can allow the creation of records through the Copilot for sales pane or allow the creation through a link to Salesforce. Using Settings discussed in the previous chapter, I have set the configurations for objects as listed in Table 12-1.

Table 12-1. *Object form setting summary*

Object	Create Inside Pane	Create by Opening Salesforce	Edit Inside Pane
Contact	Yes	No	Yes
Account	No	Yes	Yes
Opportunity	Yes	Yes	Yes
Asset	No	No	No

Keep Table 12-1 in mind while exploring the creation feature as the options available will vary based on those settings.

1. Log in to Outlook Office, either through app or browser experience.

2. Select an email of a customer that you wish to review and use for this experiment.

3. At the email view, click the Apps (▦) icon to open the app add-in available and select the Copilot for sales (▦) icon.

4. This will launch Copilot for sales with relevant customer information and key email info.

5. The first way is to create from the top menu. At the top menu, you will find an Add (╋) icon. Click the icon (Figure 12-25).

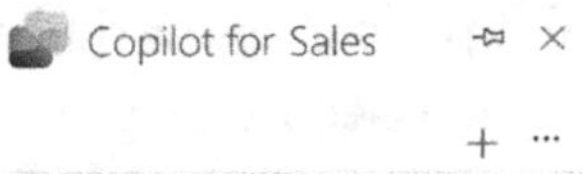

Copilot for Sales   ⊷ ✕

+ ⋯

Figure 12-25. *Create a new object icon at the menu in Copilot for sales*

6. This will open an object selector. You will find the objects allowed for creation listed. For options where only one mode of creation is allowed, you will see the Create record action, whereas for options with both inside and link selected, you will see the Create options with allowed objects to choose. Notice that the "Asset" object is not listed as we selected no creation option at the time of configuration (Figure 12-26).

Choose which type of object to create

Contact	+ Create record
Opportunity	Create ∨
Account	⬒ Create in CRM

Figure 12-26. *Choosing the object type for creation in Copilot for sales*

7. You can select the Create record (+ Create record)
   action to launch the create contact form
   (Figure 12-27). I have discussed the form field setup
   in the previous chapter.

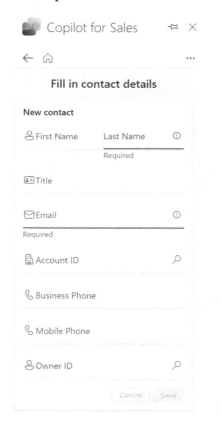

Figure 12-27. *New contact form in Copilot for sales*

8. When you select the Create in CRM (⤢ Create in CRM)
   action, you will be taken to the New Account
   creation form at Salesforce.

9. The second option is to select the Add (+) at the
    top of the action card of an object. A similar
    behavior will be experienced (Figure 12-28).

Figure 12-28. *Add new contact from the Contacts action card in
Copilot for Sales*

Add New Contact Details from Suggestions

At times, a new stakeholder, decision-maker, or influencer is introduced
via email that needs to be captured at CRM, but manual efforts and context
switching make it harder for sellers to perform such timely updates. Using
Copilot for sales, sellers will not only be advised that there is a new contact
that does not exist in Salesforce but also provided with an opportunity
to add new contacts seamlessly, without worrying about losing focus or
switching interface.

1. Select a contact from the Contacts action card. This
    is where you would notice contacts that are already
    in CRM as well as new contacts introduced through
    email. You can choose to add new contacts directly
    to Sales cloud by choosing "Add to Salesforce"
    (Figure 12-29).

Figure 12-29. *Adding a new contact in Salesforce from Copilot for sales*

2. Copilot will display a new contact form where you
    can enter the details of the new contact and save the
    object to Salesforce as shown in Figure 12-30.

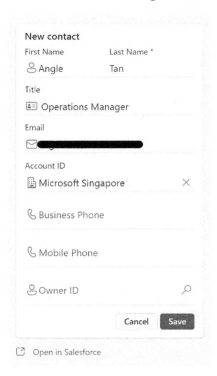

Figure 12-30. *New contact to Salesforce using Copilot for sales*

3. Click Save as shown in Figure 12-30 to reflect the
    changes to Salesforce.

This feature allows you to capture new stakeholders' information
with ease, without losing context or focus; sellers can now add new
stakeholders in Sales Cloud with ease.

Update Contact Details

Contacts need to have accurate and current information in Salesforce.
Copilot for sales lets sellers update their contact details right from Outlook,
without any hassle, following these sets of steps:

1. Click Contact that is saved in the Salesforce to open
    the Contact view.

2. You can add private notes to contacts that are saved
    only at Copilot for sales (Figure 12-31).

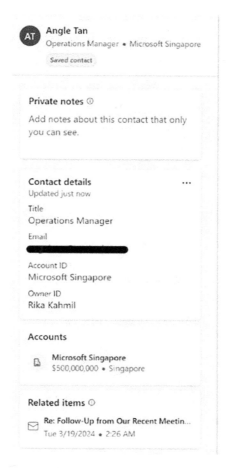

Figure 12-31. *Contact information with private notes with Salesforce information*

3. Note that you do not have to save the private notes; they will be automatically saved.

4. Review the contact's related account and related
    items to familiarize yourself with the contact
    information. Click More actions (⋯) and select
    "Edit object" to perform editing actions and Update
    (Update) to reflect changes (Figure 12-32).

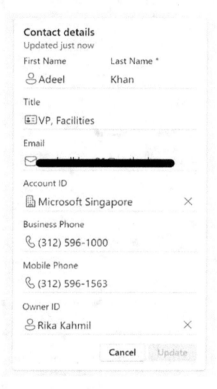

Figure 12-32. *Edit contact details in Salesforce using Copilot for sales*

Update Account Details

When it comes to email communication, important account information
often requires updates within Salesforce; however, manual work can be
hard and time-consuming for sellers. Sellers can now easily keep their

customer account details up to date and accurate right from Outlook using Copilot for sales. This smooth integration not only improves data quality but also makes it easy for sellers to perform such updates frequently.

1. Select the Account action card in Copilot for sales and click Object. This will expand the account view in Copilot for sales. You can view the account information with default fields and opportunities with the account (Figure 12-33).

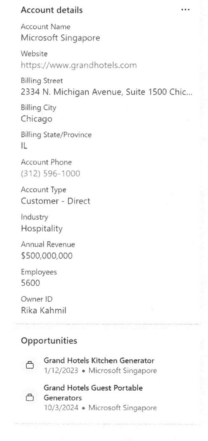

Figure 12-33. *Account view in Copilot for sales with Sales Cloud information*

2. Click More actions (⋯) and select Edit object (✐ Edit object)
    to edit the information of the account (Figure 12-34).

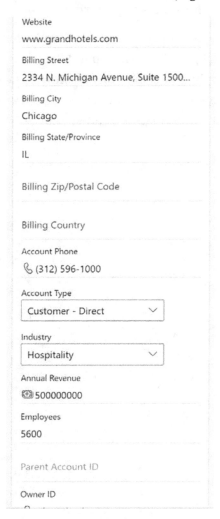

Figure 12-34. *Editing account information in Salesforce from Copilot for sales*

3. Once changes are made, you can select Update
    (Update) to reflect the changes.

These changes will reflect in real time to Sales Cloud, making it easier for you to maintain the latest changes at Salesforce without leaving Outlook.

Opportunity View and Updates

Important opportunity or sales deals can also be updated using Copilot for sales. This is further ensuring that maintenance of accurate information is no more a laborious task for you.

1. Click any opportunity in the Opportunities action card to view the opportunity information. Here, you would notice a generative AI–based summary generated by Copilot for sales along with opportunity details (Figure 12-35).

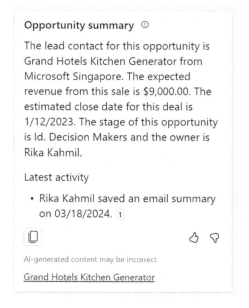

Figure 12-35.   *Opportunity summary for a Salesforce object in Copilot for sales*

2. Like the Account and Contact, you can edit the
opportunity information by clicking More actions
(⋯) and selecting Edit object (Figure 12-36).

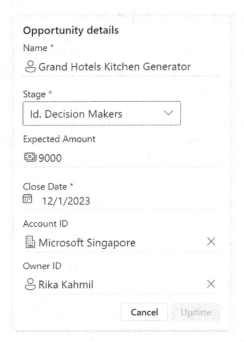

Figure 12-36. *Opportunity details form to update a Salesforce object
from Copilot for sales*

3. Once changes are made, select Update (Update) as
shown in Figure 12-36 to reflect the changes.

Note   that you can work with your admin to add more fields to this
view; please refer to CRM-based settings in the previous chapter.

Save Outlook Activities to Salesforce

Using Copilot for sales, you can easily save Outlook activities to Salesforce.
We will begin by learning to save an email, followed by learning to save
a meeting. This feature allows you to reduce operational overhead of
manually adding an activity in Sales Cloud.

1. Log in to Outlook Office, either through app or
    browser experience.

2. Select an email of a customer that you wish to
    review and use for this experiment.

3. At the email view, click the Apps (⊞) icon to open the
    app add-in available and select the Copilot for sales
    (▨) icon.

4. This will launch Copilot for sales with relevant
    customer information and key email info.

5. You can save the customer email from the Copilot
    Sales pane to Salesforce. Select the Save (Save)
    button at the pane (Figure 12-37).

Save email to Salesforce ⊙

Save

Figure 12-37. *Save email to Salesforce from Copilot for sales*

6. Copilot for sales will list the objects where you may
    want to connect the email. It will list the accounts
    and opportunities, where you can also save without
    connecting to the object (Figure 12-38).

Figure 12-38. *Save email with the connected object in Salesforce*

7. Select the relevant object; I have selected the account object and choose to click Save to reflect changes.

8. You will notice a confirmation email being saved with the Saved tag (Figure 12-39).

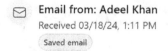

Figure 12-39. *Saved email tag after saving email in Salesforce*

You can also save and connect the email by clicking any of the relevant records in the action card. To use this option, follow these steps:

1. In the Copilot for Sales pane, choose the record (account or opportunity) and click the More actions (⋯) icon (Figure 12-40).

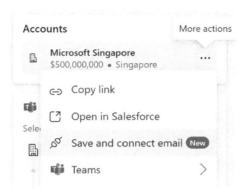

Figure 12-40. *Save and connect from Copilot for sales action cards*

2. This will reduce the number of clicks we performed and further improve user experience.

The other Outlook activity critical in customer engagements is meetings. To save meeting activities in sales cloud, change your view to calendars (⊞) at Outlook and choose an available time slot for the meeting. Once selected, follow these steps to learn the feature:

1. Open a new event in the Outlook calendar.

2. Fill in the required information, such as meeting title, date, and time, physical or virtual with the team's link and description of the meeting (Figure 12-41).

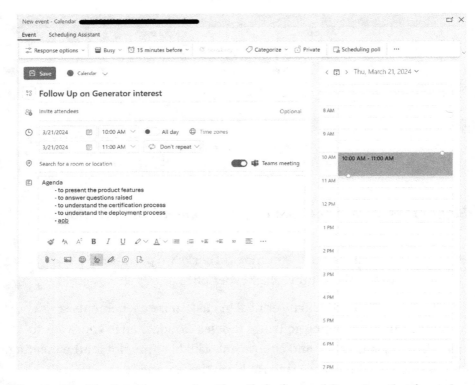

Figure 12-41. *Setting meeting details before adding Copilot for sales*

3. Invite the attendees; please be careful when adding an attendees as you need to send the meeting invite before being able to save. It is recommended to take precautions and add attendees wisely.

4. Click More actions (⋯) and choose Copilot for sales (⬤) from the add-ins drop-down.

5. This will enable the familiar Copilot for sales pane in the meeting invite. Notice that you cannot save the meeting yet in Sales cloud until you have sent the meeting to the customer (Figure 12-42).

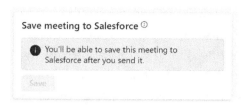

Figure 12-42. *Disabled saving to Sales cloud at the meeting with Copilot for sales*

6. Send the meeting to the customer, open the meeting invite, and click More actions (⋯) to choose Copilot for sales (🖌) from the add-ins drop-down. This time, you can see the Save meeting to Salesforce enabled (Figure 12-43).

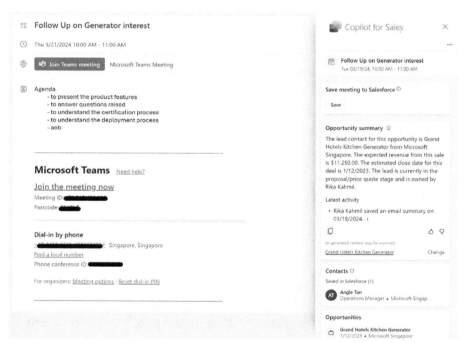

Figure 12-43. *Enabled save meeting to Salesforce with Copilot for sales*

7. Notice that you have an opportunity summary detailed automatically. The match is made or suggested based on keywords; however, by linking the meeting to the right opportunity, Copilot for sales can be coached to display the relevant summary in the future.

8. Click Save to view the Connect to an object action card. You can choose the relevant object where tracking of this meeting would be most relevant.

9. Click Save to reflect the changes as shown in Figure 12-44.

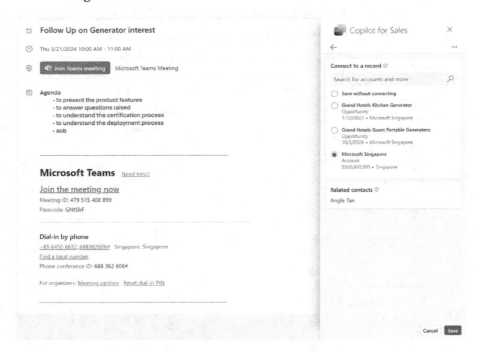

Figure 12-44. *Connecting the meeting to a Salesforce object using Copilot for sales*

10. Once the meeting is saved, you will see a saved
meeting sign under the meeting title at Copilot for
sales (Figure 12-45).

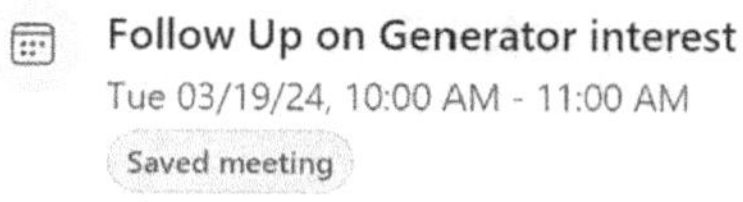

Follow Up on Generator interest
Tue 03/19/24, 10:00 AM - 11:00 AM
Saved meeting

Figure 12-45. *Saved meeting tag after saving the meeting in Salesforce*

12.1.5 AI Suggestion for CRM Actions

This feature is an excellent application of AI where Copilot for sales can
understand the email's context and identify important updates needed
especially for sales opportunity. In the example, I have used a scenario
where the customer has emailed about changes in the customer budget,
which affects the amount in Sales Cloud and the date planned to close
the deal. Copilot for sales powered by AI can detect such request and
offer a list under Suggested actions – an action card for you to review and
apply. For this example, you need an email with such content. Let's see the
example email I have used:

1. Choose the email with content where either the
budget or the intent to close has been discussed.
Figure 12-46 shows a sample email I prepared
for demo where the customer has mentioned the
changes in budget and closure date.

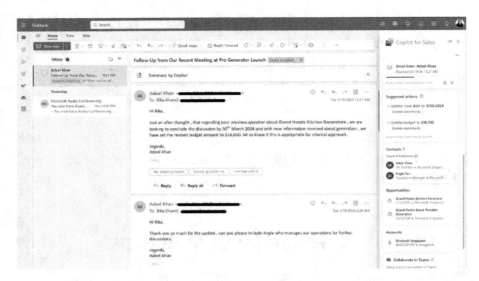

Figure 12-46. *Email with the amount and close date info for Salesforce updates*

2. Notice the new "Suggested Action card" in the Copilot for sales pane listing the auto identified actions (Figure 12-47).

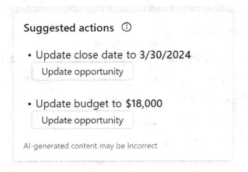

Figure 12-47. *Suggested actions action card for Salesforce updates in Copilot for sales*

3. If you click these suggestions, Copilot for sales will ask for a related opportunity with suggested opportunities as shown in Figure 12-48. Select the relevant opportunity to perform the update.

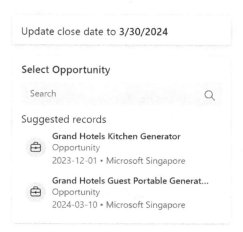

Figure 12-48. *Select opportunity for suggested updates in Salesforce from Copilot for sales*

4. The other way can be to choose the relevant opportunity listed under the action card from the main Copilot for sales pane (Figure 12-49). This way, you can reduce the selection step mentioned earlier.

Figure 12-49. *Opportunity list under the Opportunity action card for Salesforce*

5. By clicking the opportunity, Copilot for sales
    will display the Opportunity view with Copilot
    suggestions to update the relevant fields (Amount
    for Budget Amount and Close Date for opportunity
    close date). You can edit the opportunity in the
    Copilot for sales pane and perform the update
    (Figure 12-50).

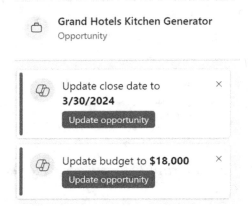

Figure 12-50. *Copilot suggested update to Salesforce for user review*

6. You can also perform updates by clicking Update
    opportunity (Update opportunity) to open the opportunity
    record in the Salesforce environment and perform
    updates.

12.1.6 Teams with Copilot for Sales

The integration between Copilot for sales and Microsoft Teams allows sellers
to leverage teams' collaborative excellence to be infused in sales processes
and help accelerate deals with easy collaboration. In this section, you will
explore and learn how you can use Copilot for sales with MS Teams.

We will begin with in-pane experience that is called Collaboration Space and later explore the features available during teams' meetings.

Collaboration Space

Microsoft Copilot for sales Collaboration Space provides an out-of-the-box environment for sales collaboration that's built on Microsoft Teams. The feature provides two out-of-the-box templates and reduces the setup overhead for versatile personas coming together to achieve impressive results.

- **Account Team**: The template is created for smooth teamwork within account teams and with customers. When used by a team and connected to a Salesforce account, the template offers a perfect space to work together with account team members and customers.

- **Deal Room**: The template is designed for concentrated cooperation on deal-related tasks. Connected to a Salesforce opportunity and used at the channel level, this template offers a specific area for effective teamwork.

There are several ways you can apply these templates; you can experience them by following these steps:

1. Log in to Outlook Office, either through app or browser experience.

2. Select an email of a customer that you wish to review and use for this experiment.

3. At the email view, click the Apps (▦) icon to open the app add-in available and select the Copilot for sales (●) icon.

4. This will launch Copilot for sales with relevant customer information and key email info.

5. Browse below to find the Collaboration Space action card. The card contains already connected teams' channel as well as templates for you to set up. If you are setting up for the first time, you will only notice the templates (Figure 12-51).

Figure 12-51. *Collaboration Space action card with Salesforce objects in Copilot for sales*

6. Hover your mouse over the account name (in this case, Microsoft Singapore) to activate the account template (Figure 12-52).

Figure 12-52. *Set up an account team with the Salesforce account using Copilot for sales*

7. Click "Set up account team" to start finalizing the
    template settings (Figure 12-53).

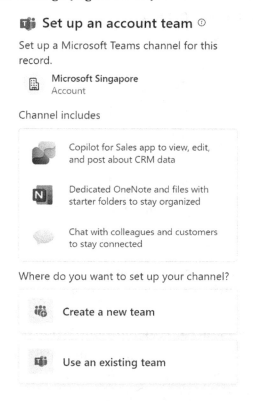

Figure 12-53. *Set up an account team configuration using the*
Salesforce account in Copilot for sales

8. The template will include the Copilot for sales app
    view to view the object details, OneNote for notes,
    and storage for file/folder management.

9. You can choose to either create a new team or use
    an existing team's channel.

10. Choosing a new team will require additional
     information about the team's channel such as
     joining policy (Figure 12-54).

Figure 12-54. *New team joining policy for the Salesforce account
team's channel*

11. The creator will be added by default as a team
     member; the remaining can be added later. Please
     note that you will require the Salesforce admin
     to enable the account/opportunity team's setup
     (Figure 12-55). You can find guidance at `https://`
     `trailhead.Salesforce.com/content/learn/`
     `projects/protect-your-data-in-Salesforce/`
     `set-up-account-teams`.

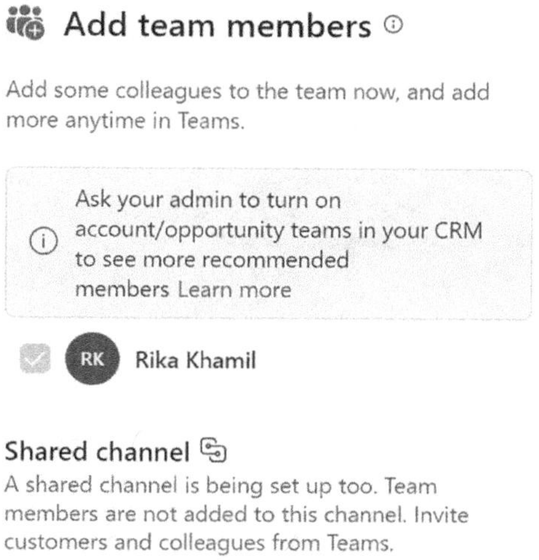

👥 Add team members ⓘ

Add some colleagues to the team now, and add more anytime in Teams.

> ⓘ Ask your admin to turn on account/opportunity teams in your CRM to see more recommended members Learn more

☑ **RK** Rika Khamil

Shared channel 🔗
A shared channel is being set up too. Team members are not added to this channel. Invite customers and colleagues from Teams.

Figure 12-55. *Adding team members for the account template*

12. Once all users are added, click Create team (Create team)
    to begin the creation of the new team's channel.
    Upon completion, the Copilot for sales pane will
    provide a link to open the team's channel directly by
    clicking the Open in Teams (Open in Teams) button.

13. A new team channel is created. As an owner of the
    channel, you can further maintain the engagement
    and activities. Also, the Salesforce tab has been
    added by default; however, you would require the
    teams' integration enabled by the Salesforce admin
    as shown in Figure 12-56.

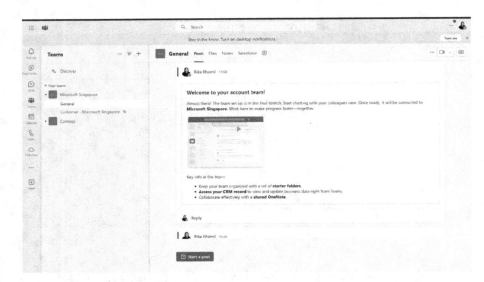

Figure 12-56. *Account template deployed at MS Teams with the Salesforce tab*

14. In the channel, you can also create a post using Copilot for sales and share Salesforce object details as shown in Figure 12-57.

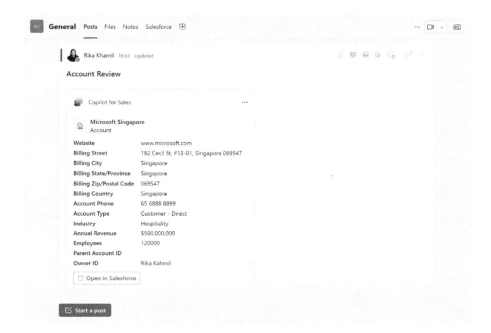

Figure 12-57. *Posting Salesforce object information in the account channel*

To create a deal room, you can follow these steps:

1. In the Copilot for sales pane, hover the mouse over the opportunity title under the Collaboration with Teams action card (Figure 12-58).

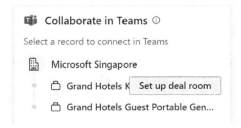

Figure 12-58. *Set up deal room for Salesforce opportunity*

2. Click Set up deal room to start configuring the deal
    room channel (Figure 12-59).

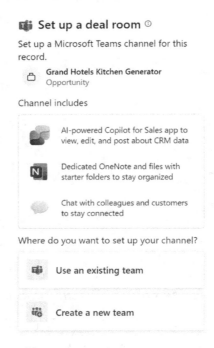

Figure 12-59. *Configuring the deal room for Salesforce opportunity*

3. The process from here onward is like the account
    team's settings in the case of creating a new
    team's channel. Let's select the "Use an existing
    team" option.

4. This will present a list of team's channels already
    existing. You can choose the channel where you
    want to set up the deal room. Typically, for the
    opportunity deal room, it should be under the
    account's team channel (Figure 12-60).

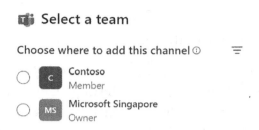

Tﬁ Select a team

Choose where to add this channel ⓘ   ☰

○ [C] **Contoso**
           Member

○ [MS] **Microsoft Singapore**
            Owner

Figure 12-60. *Choosing a channel for the Salesforce opportunity deal room*

5. Proceed by clicking Next (Next) to channel privacy details. If you choose Standard, you will get AI features enabled in the channel (Figure 12-61).

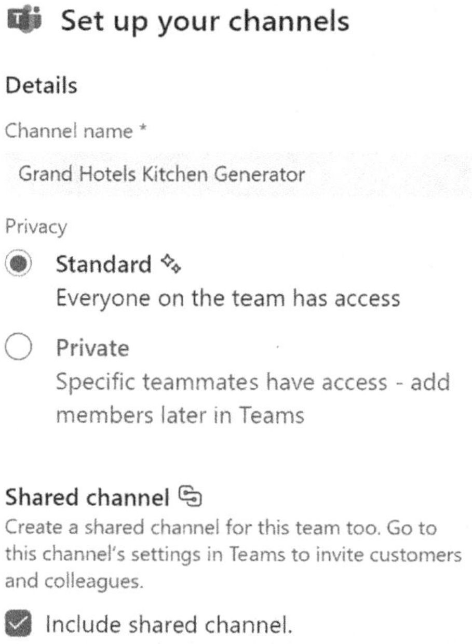

Tﬁ Set up your channels

Details

Channel name *

Grand Hotels Kitchen Generator

Privacy

◉ **Standard** ⚡
    Everyone on the team has access

○ **Private**
    Specific teammates have access - add
    members later in Teams

Shared channel ⌷
Create a shared channel for this team too. Go to
this channel's settings in Teams to invite customers
and colleagues.

☑ Include shared channel.

Figure 12-61. *Channel privacy settings for Salesforce opportunity*

6. Please carefully choose the privacy settings according to sensitivity of deals.

7. Click Set up team (Set up team) to begin channel creation. Upon completion, the Copilot for sales pane will provide a link to open the team's channel directly by clicking the Open in Teams (Open in Teams) button.

8. A new channel is now available under accounts. You can now collaborate with confidence and reduce communication barriers between teams (Figure 12-62).

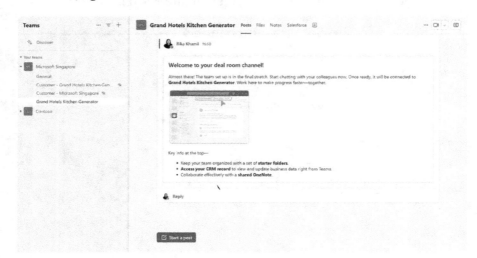

Figure 12-62. *New deal room channel created with Salesforce opportunity*

To use Copilot for sales in a post, you need to perform the following actions:

1. Click the Start a post (Start a post) button to open the post editor.

2. In the post editor, prepare the remaining details
    such as the subject and message and look for the
    Copilot for sales icon as shown in Figure 12-63.

Figure 12-63. *Edit a post in the teams' channel with the
Salesforce object*

3. By clicking the Copilot for sales icon, a pop-up
    will be displayed where you can choose the object
    required that you wish to share with the team.
    Choose the recently updated object or select
    Advanced search to find the object of interest
    (Figure 12-64).

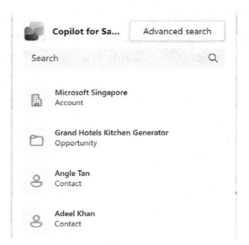

Figure 12-64. *Copilot for sales with Salesforce objects*

4. Once you have decided or found the relevant record, you can post in the channel, and all channel users will be able to view the information (Figure 12-65).

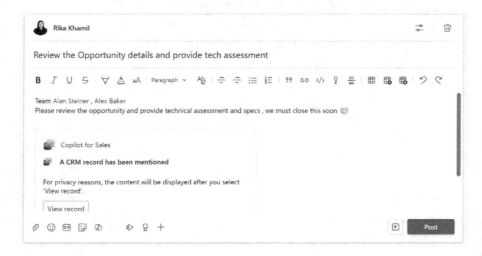

Figure 12-65. *Posting with Salesforce opportunity details*

5. Notice the View record (View record) button; this
    ensures that only users having access to the
    opportunity object in Salesforce can view the
    information in the channel.

6. Users with access to the channel and Salesforce
    object will be able to see the information in the post
    (Figure 12-66).

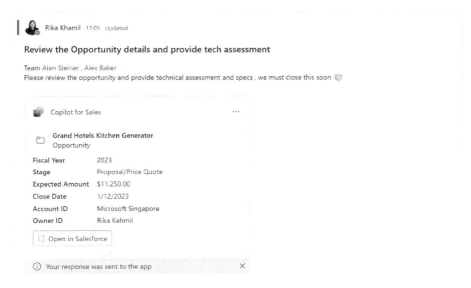

Figure 12-66. *Post with Salesforce opportunity details*

Through these templates, you can collaborate and work with peers
effectively in managing customer engagements. With the Copilot for sales
ability to share object information as part of a post, you do not have to
launch Salesforce for each time.

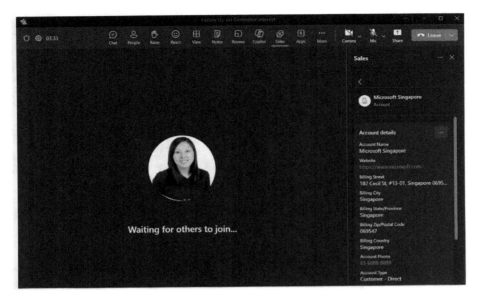

Figure 12-68. *Copilot for sales with the connected Salesforce object in Teams meeting*

7. As you learned in the Copilot for sales pane in Outlook, you can update the object details right from the teams meeting or choose to copy the link to the object or open the object in Salesforce (Figure 12-69).

Figure 12-69. *Actions available for Salesforce with Copilot for sales*

Once the meeting is completed, Copilot will prepare a summary as shown in Figure 12-70 and send you a teams chat message about the ready summary for your review. We will cover the remaining steps in the next section.

Figure 12-70. *Summary notification from Copilot for sales*

Post Teams Meeting

Once your team's meeting summary is ready, you can start using Copilot for sales in a post-meeting scenario. This setting allows you to recap, review mentions of keywords, and analyze the transcript for further actions. We can begin our review experience through the main meeting event or by opening the summary. Let's review these features:

1. Open the meeting you concluded with attendees and had Copilot for sales enabled.

2. Choose the Recap (Recap) tab from the top menu.

3. This will open the Recap view with access to objecting, content, and other features (Figure 12-71).

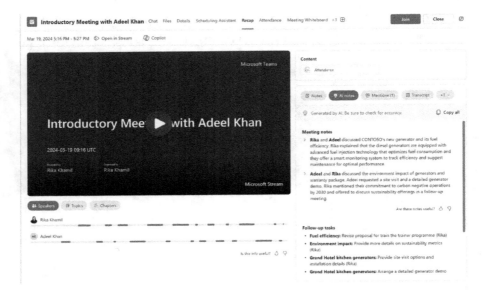

Figure 12-71. *Recap meeting view*

4. Review the AI notes; notice how Copilot has applied
    generative AI and created a summary note that can
    be expanded (Figure 12-72).

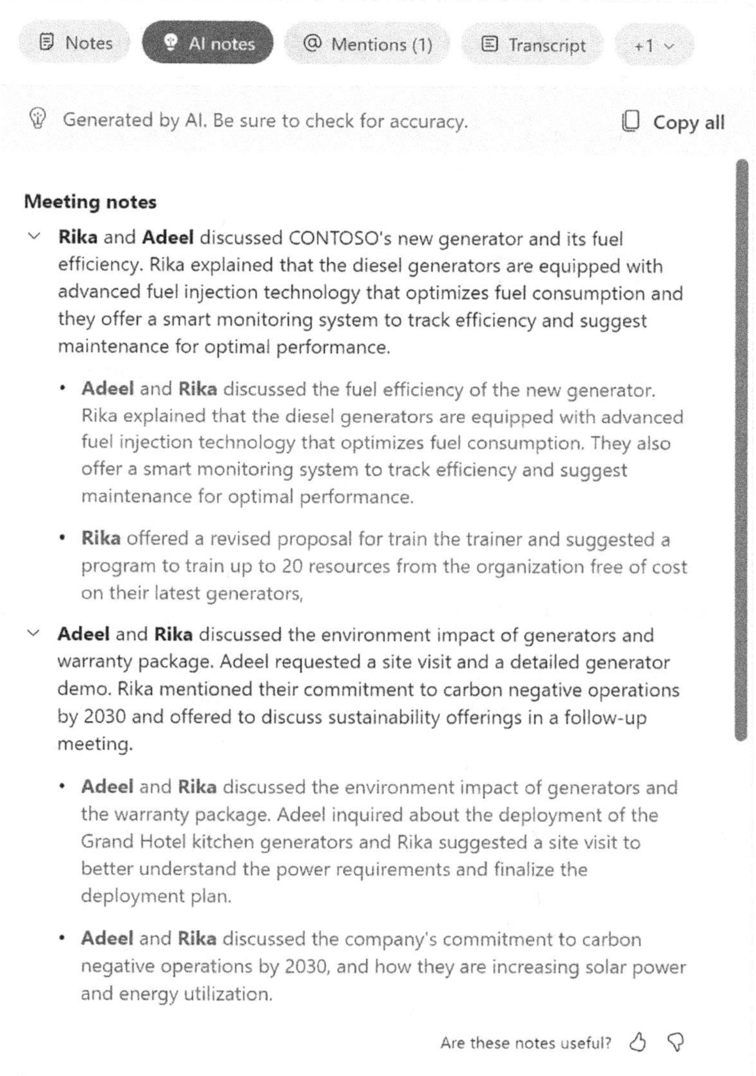

Notes   💡 AI notes   @ Mentions (1)   🗒 Transcript   +1 ⌄

💡 Generated by AI. Be sure to check for accuracy.   📋 Copy all

Meeting notes

⌄ **Rika** and **Adeel** discussed CONTOSO's new generator and its fuel efficiency. Rika explained that the diesel generators are equipped with advanced fuel injection technology that optimizes fuel consumption and they offer a smart monitoring system to track efficiency and suggest maintenance for optimal performance.

- **Adeel** and **Rika** discussed the fuel efficiency of the new generator. Rika explained that the diesel generators are equipped with advanced fuel injection technology that optimizes fuel consumption. They also offer a smart monitoring system to track efficiency and suggest maintenance for optimal performance.

- **Rika** offered a revised proposal for train the trainer and suggested a program to train up to 20 resources from the organization free of cost on their latest generators,

⌄ **Adeel** and **Rika** discussed the environment impact of generators and warranty package. Adeel requested a site visit and a detailed generator demo. Rika mentioned their commitment to carbon negative operations by 2030 and offered to discuss sustainability offerings in a follow-up meeting.

- **Adeel** and **Rika** discussed the environment impact of generators and the warranty package. Adeel inquired about the deployment of the Grand Hotel kitchen generators and Rika suggested a site visit to better understand the power requirements and finalize the deployment plan.

- **Adeel** and **Rika** discussed the company's commitment to carbon negative operations by 2030, and how they are increasing solar power and energy utilization.

Are these notes useful? 👍 👎

Figure 12-72. *Meeting notes created by AI*

5. Review the follow-up actions captured by AI
    (Figure 12-73).

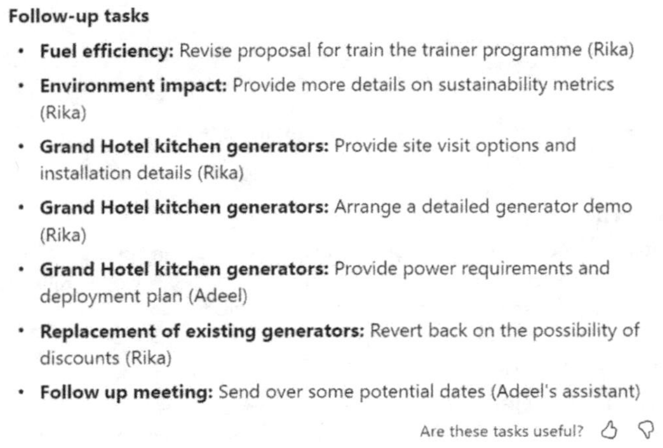

Follow-up tasks

- **Fuel efficiency:** Revise proposal for train the trainer programme (Rika)
- **Environment impact:** Provide more details on sustainability metrics (Rika)
- **Grand Hotel kitchen generators:** Provide site visit options and installation details (Rika)
- **Grand Hotel kitchen generators:** Arrange a detailed generator demo (Rika)
- **Grand Hotel kitchen generators:** Provide power requirements and deployment plan (Adeel)
- **Replacement of existing generators:** Revert back on the possibility of discounts (Rika)
- **Follow up meeting:** Send over some potential dates (Adeel's assistant)

Are these tasks useful? 👍 👎

Figure 12-73. *Follow-up tasks created by AI*

6. Click + and select Copilot for sales to open the Copilot for sales view (Figure 12-74).

Figure 12-74. *Copilot for sales in a post-meeting scenario*

7. You will be presented with highlights, and if any action required task creation, AI would suggest them (Figure 12-75).

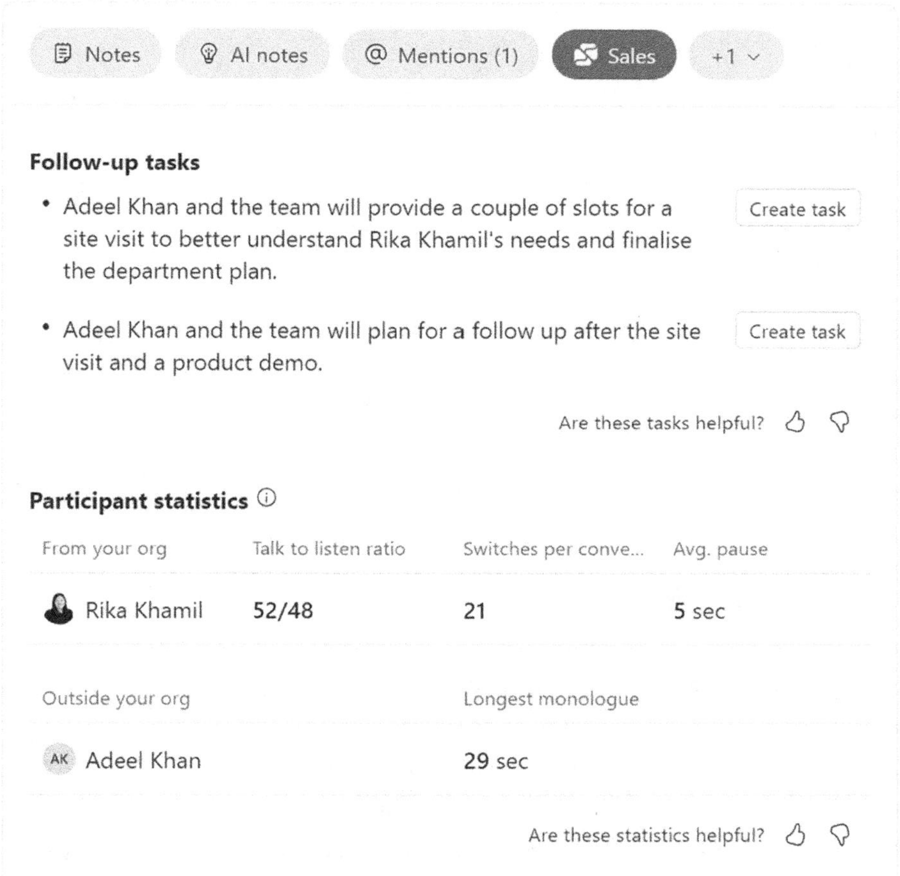

Figure 12-75. *Follow-up task creation from Copilot for sales*

8. In addition, Copilot for sales also provides statistics that can help you improve conversations during meetings.

9. Click Create task (Create task) to create actions in Salesforce directly; you can set necessary details of tasks and optimize task creation and assignment through a single interface (Figure 12-76).

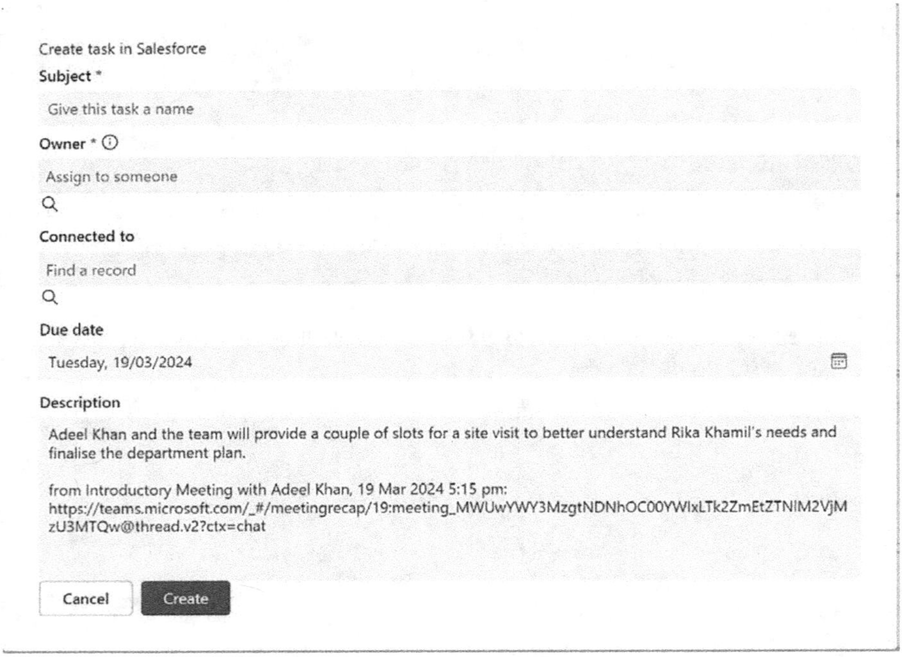

Create task in Salesforce

Subject *

Give this task a name

Owner * ⓘ

Assign to someone

Q

Connected to

Find a record

Q

Due date

Tuesday, 19/03/2024   🗓

Description

Adeel Khan and the team will provide a couple of slots for a site visit to better understand Rika Khamil's needs and finalise the department plan.

from Introductory Meeting with Adeel Khan, 19 Mar 2024 5:15 pm:
https://teams.microsoft.com/_#/meetingrecap/19:meeting_MWUwYWY3MzgtNDNhOC00YWIxLTk2ZmEtZTNIM2VjM zU3MTQw@thread.v2?ctx=chat

Cancel   Create

Figure 12-76. *Task creation in Salesforce using Copilot for sales*

Once the meeting notes are available, you can use them in Copilot for sales Outlook experience to send a summary of meeting to the customer. To view the experience, open the Outlook and Copilot for sales app with an email, select the Draft a reply option, and notice the new default prompt that can help you send the meeting summary to the attendees. By clicking the drop-down option, you can choose the meeting summary relevant for the conversation (Figure 12-77).

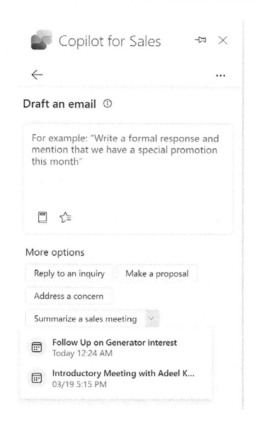

Figure 12-77. *Sending a meeting summary as an email reply*

Also, you can use the meeting summary to generate a pitch in a Word document as shown in Figure 12-78. To experience this feature, open an unfamiliar Word document and click the Copilot icon (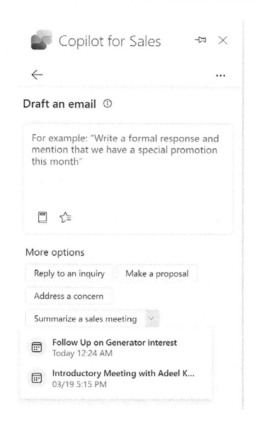) and type your prompt. To refer to the meeting, type "/" and select "Sales Meeting" from the pop-up menu.

Figure 12-78. *Accessing Sales meetings in Word*

Upon selecting Sales meetings, Word will list all available meetings that you can use (Figure 12-79).

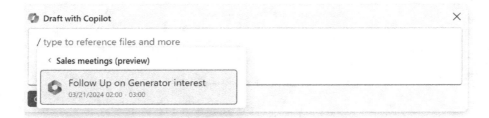

Figure 12-79. *Using a meeting transcript to generate content in Word*

This is truly a cross-platform integration of enterprise applications with the intelligent use of generative AI. Copilot for sales deeply holds promise to change the way you or your sales team work and shall empower them to accelerate success in their role.

12.2 Summary

This chapter delved into the integration of Microsoft Copilot for sales with Salesforce, a leading customer relationship management (CRM) platform. The chapter began with an overview of Salesforce, emphasizing its role in unifying various organizational departments to effectively engage with customers. It highlighted the Sales Cloud module, designed to support the sales process from lead acquisition to sale closure, offering features like account and contact management, opportunity management, lead management, and sales data.

The chapter then discussed the setup process and explored the Copilot for sales experience, highlighting how it enhances the Salesforce user experience through features accessible from Outlook and Teams, powered by generative AI.

We also learned about various experiences all the way from first login to email summarization to drafting email responses with CRM data. The chapter later explored CRM actions that can be performed without opening the Salesforce interface. The chapter provided step-by-step instructions for these features, illustrating how Copilot for sales seamlessly integrates with M365 to offer a unique and efficient user experience.

The last part of the chapter discussed AI-suggested CRM actions, highlighting how generative AI can understand email context and suggest important updates for sales opportunities. It also touched upon the integration of Copilot for sales with Teams, facilitating collaboration and accelerating deal closures through features like Collaboration Space and post-meeting summaries.

In this chapter, I have attempted to provide a comprehensive guide to leveraging Microsoft Copilot for sales with Salesforce, enhancing the sales process through AI-powered features and integrations with M365 applications.

The next chapter will discuss Microsoft Copilot for sales with Dynamics 365 and in-app Copilot experience available for Dynamics 365 users.

CHAPTER 13

Microsoft Copilot for Sales with Dynamics

Microsoft Dynamics 365 is a world-leading suite of business applications that empowers your organization's different departments, from marketing to sales to customer service, with the tools they need to effectively engage with customers. It's an integrated platform that provides a unified, holistic view of your customers.

One of the key modules in Microsoft Dynamics 365 is the Sales module, designed to support the sales process from the acquisition of a new lead through the close of a sale. The Sales module offers a wide range of features for users, including account and contact management, opportunity management, lead management, sales analytics, and more. These features enable your sales team to build strong relationships with customers, take actions based on intelligent insights, and close deals positively faster.

As practiced in the previous chapters, this chapter will highlight and discuss the features of Copilot for sales and Sales Copilot built into the Dynamics 365 sales module, assuming you have a fair understanding of Outlook, Teams, and Dynamics 365 Sales. It is recommended to spend some time learning the basic concepts of sales and sales module of Dynamics 365 before deep diving into the chapter further.

© Adeel Khan 2024
A. Khan, *Introducing Microsoft Copilot for Managers*, Inside Copilot,
https://doi.org/10.1007/979-8-8688-0419-9_13

If you are starting the book from this chapter and new to the concept of Copilot, I would encourage you to spend some time at reading Chapter 1. Also, since Copilot for sales works closely with M365 Copilot, I suggest reading Part II of this book to better appreciate and understand the features.

It is also assumed that you have completed the setup as discussed in the previous chapter. It is recommended to read this chapter after Chapter 11 for better understanding and continuation.

13.1 Copilot for Sales Experience

The section will discuss Dynamics 365 Sales user experience with Modern Work apps. In this section, you will also learn the various features and experiences available from Outlook and Teams interfaces, simplifying user access to sales- and relationship-related information, powered by generative AI.

Both Dynamics 365 Sales and Microsoft Modern Work are leaders in their domains, and they work better together. In this section, you will learn how using Copilot for sales brings best of both Microsoft clouds together for you to seamlessly experience rich features and capabilities without compromising on customer personalization. We will begin our experience from first time login and expand on various features available during the time of this book's writing.

13.1.1 First Login

In the first exercise, you are going to log in to Copilot for sales from Outlook experience. As discussed earlier, Outlook experience is critical and foundational to the overall Sale Copilot experience as your gateway to choose and sign in to your CRM of choice can only be done through the Outlook app.

For the experiment, I have signed up a developer access to Dynamics 365 Sales. You can either sign up for a developer account or use your own organization's Dynamics 365 Sales account. The following are the step-by-step guide to try your first Copilot for sales experience:

1. Log in to Outlook Office, either through app or browser experience.

2. Confirm the settings mentioned in Chapter 11 Section 11.1.3 for Dynamics 365 Sales.

3. Select an email of a customer that you wish to review and use for this experiment.

4. At the email view, click the Apps (⊞) icon to open the app add-in available (Figure 13-1).

Figure 13-1. *List of apps available at Outlook*

5. Please note that the list can be different based on your setup; however, you can see Copilot for sales (⬛) that is required for the next steps.

6. Click the Copilot for sales () icon to launch the Copilot side pane as shown in Figure 13-2.

Figure 13-2. *Copilot for sales side pane in Outlook*

7. Click the "Sign in to your CRM" and select Dynamics 365 Sales for this experience (Figure 13-3).

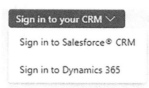

Figure 13-3. *Selecting the CRM of choice, Sales Copilot*

8. In the next step, you will be asked to choose the
    correct environment of Dynamics 365 sales. Choose
    a production, according to your organization
    policies (Figure 13-4).

Figure 13-4. *Selecting Dynamics 365 Sales environment for
Sales Copilot*

9. Using single sign-on, Copilot will sign in with your
    Dynamics 365 sales profile and start loading action
    cards in the Copilot for sales pane (Figure 13-5).

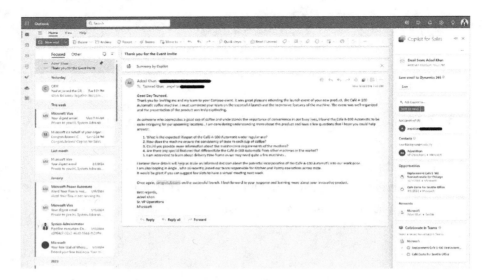

Figure 13-5. *Copilot for sales with action cards in Outlook*

Your Copilot for sales is ready for consumption; we will continue using Copilot for sales and learn the features now with ease.

13.1.2 Email Summary with CRM Context

The second experience you are going to learn is to use the summary feature. The Copilot summary you learned in Part II was generated using content available only in the email (or in an email chain); however, now with CRM data to refer, the summary is going to be more relevant to the current customer situation. Follow the steps to experience the context-based summarization:

1. Log in to Outlook Office, either through app or browser experience.

2. Select an email of a customer that you wish to review and use for this experiment.

3. Notice the Summary by Copilot (🖺) option at the top of the selected email; click to begin the summarization.

4. It may take a few seconds to complete; once ready, as shown in Figure 13-6, you will be provided with an initial summary of the email along with an indication that this summary is generated "With sales insights added."

Figure 13-6. *Summary generated with Sales insights added in Outlook Sales Copilot*

5. Do verify the summary and validate as it is AI generated and can be incorrect.

6. You can now expand further on the summary and assess key points with links to Dynamics 365 Sales records. Click Go to Sales (🖺 Go to Sales) to open the side pane.

7. The Copilot for sales pane will be launched with identified information as shown in Figure 13-7. In the example I have used, some of the email contacts and accounts already exist in Dynamics 365 Sales. Copilot for sales was able to identify and provide key info with Dynamics 365 Sales record reference.

Figure 13-7. *Copilot for sales with key email information in Outlook*

8. If you are comfortable with the key email info, you can choose either to save directly in Dynamics 365 Sales, copy the summary, or perhaps change the language of the summary. Click More actions (⋯) to expand the options (Figure 13-8).

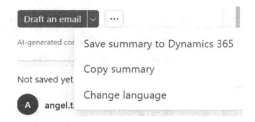

Figure 13-8. *Options with summary in Copilot for sales in Outlook*

9. Select "Save Summary to Dynamics 365 Sales" first.
    Copilot for sales will showcase the record where you
    want to save the information at Dynamics 365 Sales.
    Choose the record suitable (Figure 13-9).

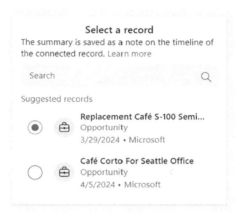

Figure 13-9. *Select a record for the summary to be saved in Copilot for sales at Outlook*

10. Notice that we did not find our account listed in
    the record list. To find any available record, use the
    search bar to find with title. For example, I wanted
    to reflect the summary at the account level, hence
    searching for Microsoft and choosing the account
    record from the results (Figure 13-10).

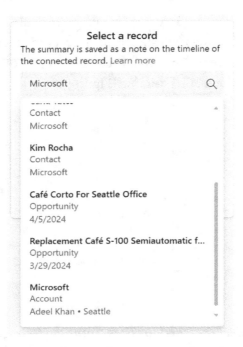

Figure 13-10. *Searching for a relevant record to connect the summary from Copilot for sales*

11. Click Save (Save) to reflect the connection with selected record, and you will find the summary in interaction timelines (Figure 13-11).

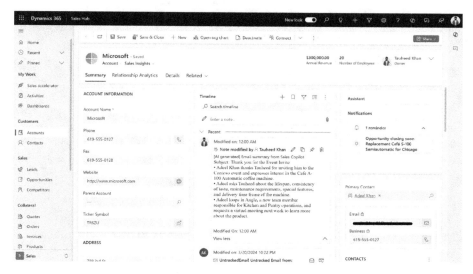

Figure 13-11. *Copilot generated email summary reflected to interaction timelines of Dynamics 365 sales*

12. Next, click the three dots (⋯) and experience the change language feature. Notice that the save summary is grayed out as you have already copied the summary at the related record (Figure 13-12).

Figure 13-12. *Grayed out save summary, Copilot for sales Outlook experience*

13. Click "Change language"; this will prompt the user to select the language they need "key info summary" to be prepared. Experiment with a few languages you know and analyze the results (Figure 13-13).

Figure 13-13. Changing the language for the key info summary, Copilot for sales in Outlook

13.1.3 Draft an Email Response with CRM Context

In this section, you will experience generating a draft email response with CRM data. We discussed and experienced Copilot's ability to generate draft responses to emails in Part II; you will now expand the experience with CRM data. This will make your draft more aligned with customer information and interaction history, personalized with useful information available in CRM. Follow the steps to experience the CRM-based draft response:

1. Log in to Outlook Office, either through app or browser experience.

2. Select an email of a customer that you wish to review and use for this experiment.

3. Click the Reply button to draft the response (Figure 13-14).

Figure 13-14. *Draft options with Sales Copilot*

4. At the draft bar, you can choose any of the given
    default prompts or provide a custom prompt. Let's
    choose a custom prompt to experiment.

5. This will open a Copilot prompt box where you can
    provide a custom instruction to Copilot regarding
    the reply (Figure 13-15).

Figure 13-15. *Custom prompt using Copilot for sales in Outlook*

6. You can provide a prompt relevant to address the
    customer response. In my case, I provided the
    response shown in Figure 13-16.

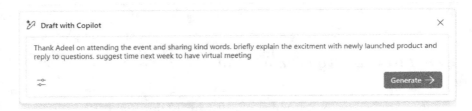

Figure 13-16. *Providing a custom prompt to draft a reply with Copilot for sales*

7. Click Generate to view the draft; you can also set other features such as tone and length like Outlook Copilot experience.

8. Review the draft, and if you find it relevant, select Keep it or Regenerate (Figure 13-17).

Figure 13-17. *Draft generated by Copilot for sales in Outlook*

This is one way of generating a draft reply; let's experience the other way of drafting a reply using the Copilot for sales pane.

1. Log in to Outlook Office, either through app or browser experience.

2. Select an email of a customer that you wish to review and use for this experiment.

3. At the email view, click the Apps (⊞) icon to open the app add-in available and select the Copilot for sales (●) icon.

4. This will launch Copilot for sales with relevant customer information and key email info as experienced in the previous section.

5. Click Draft an email (Draft an email ⌄). Like Outlook-based experience, you will be presented with an option to provide a custom prompt or choose a default prompt. There are a few more options available to save the prompt (☆≡) or review suggestions (▯) (Figure 13-18).

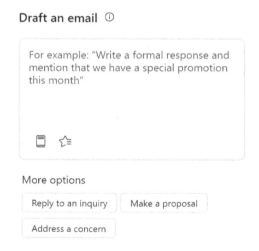

Draft an email ⓘ

> For example: "Write a formal response and mention that we have a special promotion this month"
>
> ▯   ☆≡

More options

Reply to an inquiry   Make a proposal

Address a concern

Figure 13-18. *Draft options using the Copilot for sales pane*

6. Click the suggestion (🗔) icon to view the AI-powered
    prompt suggestions that you can use as a draft
    prompt (Figure 13-19).

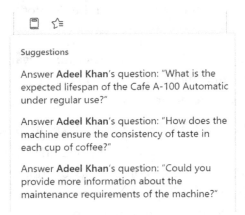

Figure 13-19. *AI-powered suggestions for a custom prompt in Copilot for sales Outlook experience*

7. These suggestions are great help to start
    understanding how you can interact with Copilot
    and generate drafts of your interest.

8. Let's choose "Reply to an inquiry" and analyze the
    results. Copilot will leverage the data in Dynamics
    365 Sales and draft a response (Figure 13-20).

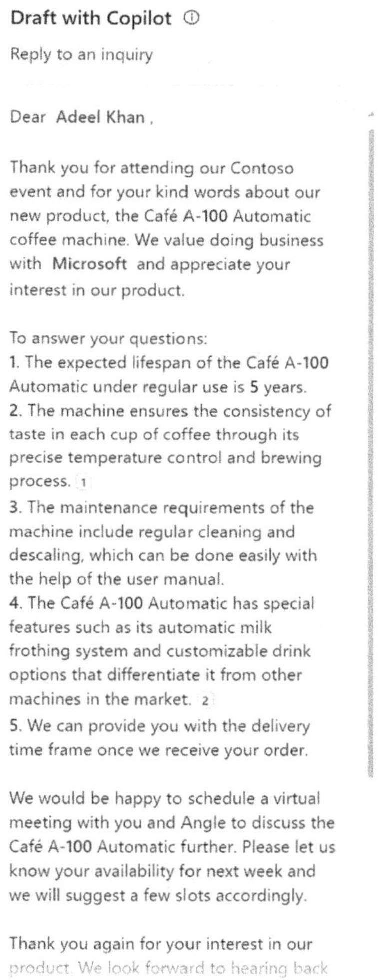

Draft with Copilot ⓘ

Reply to an inquiry

Dear Adeel Khan ,

Thank you for attending our Contoso
event and for your kind words about our
new product, the Café A-100 Automatic
coffee machine. We value doing business
with Microsoft and appreciate your
interest in our product.

To answer your questions:
1. The expected lifespan of the Café A-100
Automatic under regular use is 5 years.
2. The machine ensures the consistency of
taste in each cup of coffee through its
precise temperature control and brewing
process. 1
3. The maintenance requirements of the
machine include regular cleaning and
descaling, which can be done easily with
the help of the user manual.
4. The Café A-100 Automatic has special
features such as its automatic milk
frothing system and customizable drink
options that differentiate it from other
machines in the market. 2
5. We can provide you with the delivery
time frame once we receive your order.

We would be happy to schedule a virtual
meeting with you and Angle to discuss the
Café A-100 Automatic further. Please let us
know your availability for next week and
we will suggest a few slots accordingly.

Thank you again for your interest in our
product. We look forward to hearing back

Figure 13-20. *Draft generated using the Copilot for sales pane*

9. Analyzing the response, Copilot for sales has
leveraged Dynamics 365 Sales data and prepared a
lot better draft response. The response has citation
as well, so you can validate reasons during the
review of the draft.

10. You can further improve the draft response; you can choose Adjust Draft (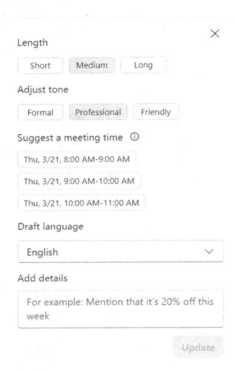) to set the additional attributes (Figure 13-21).

Length   ×

[Short] [Medium] [Long]

Adjust tone

[Formal] [Professional] [Friendly]

Suggest a meeting time ⓘ

[Thu, 3/21, 8:00 AM-9:00 AM]

[Thu, 3/21, 9:00 AM-10:00 AM]

[Thu, 3/21, 10:00 AM-11:00 AM]

Draft language

[English   ∨]

Add details

[For example: Mention that it's 20% off this
week]

[Update]

Figure 13-21. *Adjust draft attributes using Copilot for sales*

11. Play with the options, such as the Add a meeting option, and analyze the changes in the draft.

12. Once you are satisfied with the draft, click the Copy (▢) icon to copy the draft that can be used to reply to the customer email at Outlook.

In this exercise, you generated a draft reply using two options. The exercise also covered various attributes and settings offered for preparing a reply to customers. To combine best of M365 and Copilot for sales, you can apply coaching by Copilot (Figure 13-22) to further improve the draft reply.

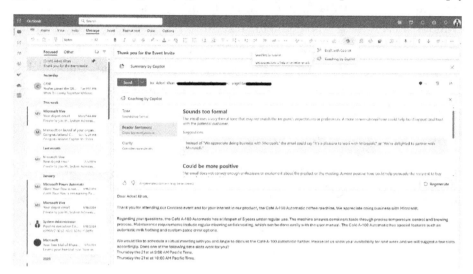

Figure 13-22. *Applying coaching at the final draft created using Sales Copilot*

Refer to Part II where I have discussed the Coaching feature.

13.1.4 CRM Actions from Copilot for Sales Pane

In this exercise, you will learn about how to perform CRM-related actions from the Copilot for sales pane. You will learn how to save the interaction in Dynamics 365 Sales, how to update record information, and how to get a summary of active associated opportunities in Dynamics 365 Sales.

Create a New Record

Copilot for sales allows users to create a new table record. This feature has been recently added to the Copilot for sales pane. There are two ways to create a record available at the time of writing this book. The list of available tables depends on the form settings discussed in Chapter 11.1.3. An admin can allow creation of records through the Copilot for sales pane or allow creation through a link to Dynamics 365 sales. Using the settings discussed in the previous chapter, I have set the configurations for records as listed in Table 13-1.

Table 13-1. *Form setting summary*

Record	Create Inside Pane	Create by Opening Dynamics	Edit Inside Pane
Contact	Yes	No	Yes
Account	No	Yes	Yes
Opportunity	Yes	Yes	Yes

Keep Table 13-1 in mind while exploring the creation feature as the options available will vary based on the settings.

1. Log in to Outlook Office, either through app or browser experience.

2. Select an email of a customer that you wish to review and use for this experiment.

3. At the email view, click the Apps (▦) icon to open the app add-in available and select the Copilot for sales (◆) icon.

4. This will launch Copilot for sales with relevant customer information and key email info.

5. The first way is to create from the top menu. At the top menu, you will find an Add (+) icon. Click the icon (Figure 13-23).

Figure 13-23. *Create a new record icon at the menu in Copilot for sales*

6. This will open the record selector as shown in Figure 13-24. You will find the records allowed for the creation listed. For options where only one mode of creation is allowed, you will see a Create record action, whereas for the option with both inside and link selected, you will see create options to choose.

Figure 13-24. *Choosing the record type for creation in Copilot for sales*

7.   You can select the create record (+ Create record)
     action to launch the create contact form
     (Figure 13-25). I have discussed the form setup in
     Chapter 11.

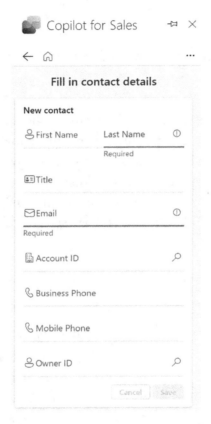

Figure 13-25. *New record form in Copilot for sales*

8.   When you select the Create in CRM (⬀ Create in CRM)
     action, you will be taken to the New Account
     creation form at Dynamics 365 CRM.

9. The second option is to select the add (+) at the top of the action card of a record. Similar behavior will be experienced (Figure 13-26).

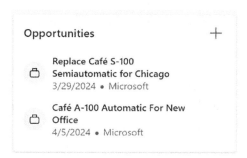

Figure 13-26. *Add a new opportunity from the action card in Copilot for Sales*

Add New Contact Details

At times, a new stakeholder, decision-maker, or influencer is introduced via email that needs to be captured at CRM, but manual efforts and context switching make it harder for sellers to perform such timely updates. Using Copilot for sales, sellers will not only be advised that there is a new contact that does not exist in Dynamics 365 Sales but also presented with an opportunity to add new contacts seamlessly, without worrying about losing focus or switching interface.

1. Select a contact from the Contacts action card. This is where you would notice contacts that are already in CRM as well as new contacts introduced through email. You can choose to add new contacts directly to Dynamics 365 Sales by choosing "Add to Dynamics 365 Sales" as shown in Figure 13-27.

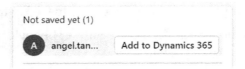

Figure 13-27. *Adding a new contact in Dynamics 365 Sales from Copilot for sales*

2. Copilot will display a new contact form where you can enter the details of the new contact and save the record to Dynamics 365 Sales (Figure 13-28).

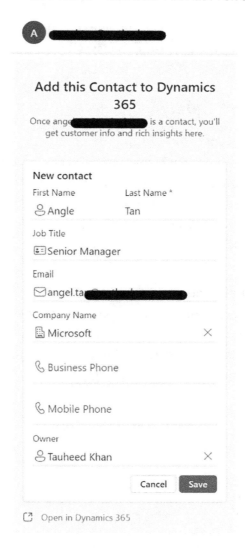

Figure 13-28. *New contact to Dynamics 365 Sales using Copilot for sales*

3.   Click Save to reflect the changes to Dynamics 365 Sales.

This feature allows you to capture new stakeholders' information with ease, without losing context or focus; sellers can now add new stakeholders in Dynamics 365 Sales with ease.

Update Account Details

When it comes to email communication, important account information often requires updates within Dynamics 365 Sales; however, manual work can be hard and time-consuming for sellers. Sellers can now easily keep their customer account details up to date and accurate, right from Outlook using Copilot for sales. This smooth integration not only improves data quality but also makes it easy for sellers to perform such updates frequently.

1. Select the Account action card in Copilot for sales and click record. This will expand the account view in Copilot for sales. You can view the account information with default fields and opportunities with the account (Figure 13-29).

Figure 13-29. *Account view in Copilot for sales with Dynamics 365 Sales information*

2. Click More actions (⋯) and select Edit record

(✎ Edit record) to edit the information of the account

(Figure 13-30).

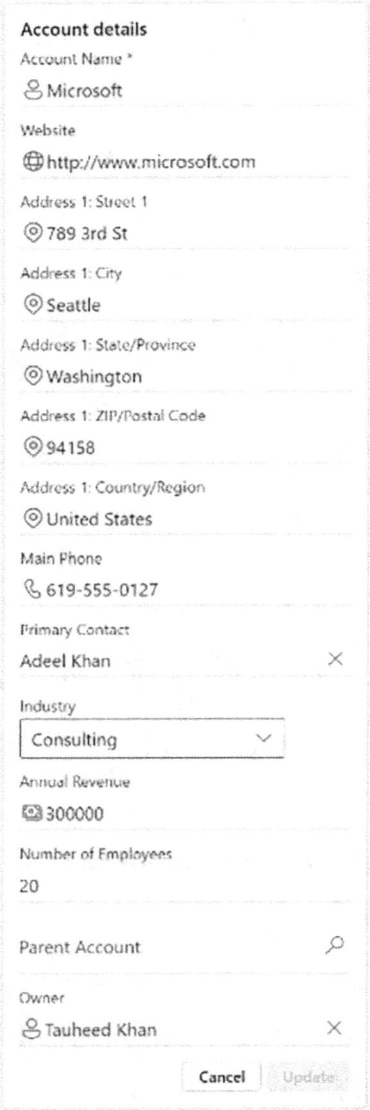

Account details

Account Name *

  👤 Microsoft

Website

  🌐 http://www.microsoft.com

Address 1: Street 1

  📍 789 3rd St

Address 1: City

  📍 Seattle

Address 1: State/Province

  📍 Washington

Address 1: ZIP/Postal Code

  📍 94158

Address 1: Country/Region

  📍 United States

Main Phone

  📞 619-555-0127

Primary Contact

  Adeel Khan   ✕

Industry

  Consulting   ⌄

Annual Revenue

  💰 300000

Number of Employees

  20

Parent Account   🔍

Owner

  👤 Tauheed Khan   ✕

    Cancel Update

Figure 13-30. *Editing the account information in Dynamics 365 Sales from Copilot for sales*

3. Once changes are made, you can select Update
   (Update) to reflect the changes.

These changes will reflect in real time to Dynamics 365 Sales, making it easier for you and your sales team to maintain latest changes at Dynamics 365 Sales without leaving Outlook.

Update Contact Details

Contacts need to have accurate and current information in Dynamics 365 Sales, just like accounts. Copilot for sales lets sellers update their contact details right from Outlook, without any hassle, following the similar process as we experienced in the update account exercise:

1. Click Contact that is saved in Dynamics 365 Sales to open the Contact view.

2. You can add private notes to contacts that are saved only at Copilot for sales (Figure 13-31).

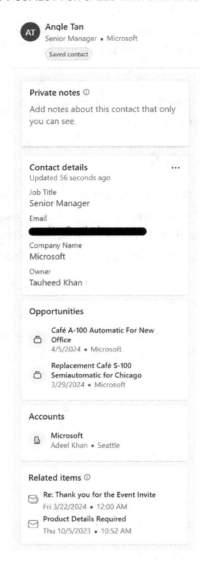

Figure 13-31. *Contact information with private notes with Dynamics 365 Sales information*

3. Note that you do not have to save the private notes, they will be automatically saved.

4. Review the contact's related account and related
    items to familiarize yourself with contact
    information. Click More actions (⋯) and select
    "Edit Record" to perform editing actions and Update
    (Update) to reflect changes (Figure 13-32).

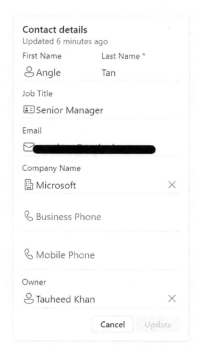

Figure 13-32. *Edit contact details in Dynamics 365 Sales using
Copilot for sales*

Opportunity View and Updates

Important opportunity or sales deals can also be updated using Copilot for
sales. This is further ensuring that maintenance of accurate information is
no more a laborious task for you:

1. Click any opportunity in the Opportunities
    action card to view the opportunity information.
    Here, you would notice a generative AI–based
    summary generated by Copilot for sales along with
    opportunity details (Figure 13-33).

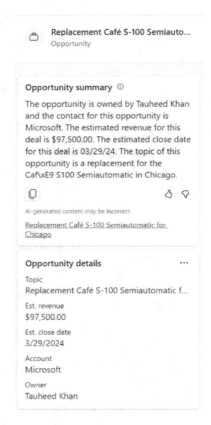

Figure 13-33. *Opportunity summary for Dynamics 365 Sales records in Copilot for sales*

2. Like the Account and Contact, you can edit the
    opportunity information by clicking More actions
    (...) and selecting Edit Record (Figure 13-34).

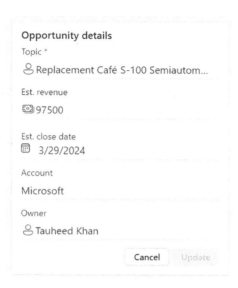

Figure 13-34. *Opportunity detail form to update Dynamics 365 Sales records from Copilot for sales*

> 3.   Once changes are made, select Update (Update) to
>   reflect the changes as shown in Figure 13-34.

Note that you can work with your admin to add more fields to this
view; please refer to CRM-based settings in the previous chapter.

Save Outlook Activities to CRM

Using Copilot for sales, you can easily save Outlook activities to Dynamics
365 Sales. We will begin by learning to save an email, followed by learning
to save a meeting. This feature allows you to reduce operational overhead
of manually adding activity in Dynamics 365 Sales.

> 1.   Log in to Outlook Office, either through app or
>   browser experience.

2. Select an email of a customer that you wish to review and use for this experiment.

3. At the email view, click the Apps (⊞) icon to open the app add-in available and select the Copilot for sales (🔵) icon.

4. This will launch the Copilot for sales with relevant customer information and key email info.

5. You can save the customer email from the Copilot Sales pane to Dynamics 365 Sales. Select the Save (Save) button at the pane (Figure 13-35).

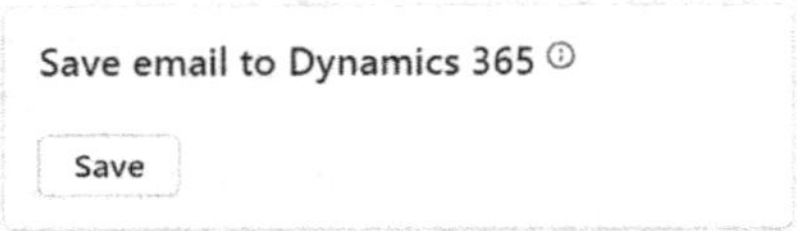

Save email to Dynamics 365 ⓘ

Save

Figure 13-35. *Save email to Dynamics 365 Sales from Copilot for sales*

6. Copilot for sales will list the records where you may want to connect the email. It will list accounts and opportunities where you can also save without connecting to the record (Figure 13-36).

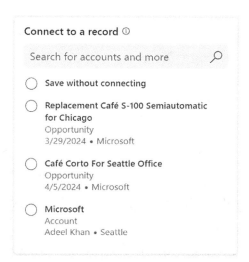

Figure 13-36. *Save email with the connected record in Dynamics 365 Sales*

7. Select the relevant record. I have selected the account record and choose to click Save to reflect changes.

8. You will notice a confirmation email being saved with the Saved tag (Figure 13-37).

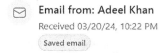

Figure 13-37. *Saved email tag after saving email in Dynamics 365 Sales*

You can also save and connect the email by clicking any of the relevant records in the action card. To use this option, follow these steps:

1. In the Copilot for Sales pane, choose the record (account or opportunity) and click the More actions (⋯) icon (Figure 13-38).

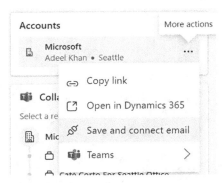

Figure 13-38. *Save and connect from Copilot for sales action cards*

2. This will reduce the number of clicks we performed and further improve user experience.

The other Outlook activity critical in customer engagements is meetings. To save meeting activities in Dynamics 365 Sales, change your view to calendars (▦) at Outlook and choose an available time slot for the meeting. Once selected, follow these steps to learn the feature:

1. Open a new event in the Outlook calendar.

2. Fill in the required information, such as meeting title, date, and time, physical or virtual with the team's link and description of the meeting.

3. Invite the attendees; please be careful when adding an attendees as you need to send the meeting invite before being able to save. It is recommended to take precautions and add attendees wisely.

4. Click More actions (⋯) and choose Copilot for sales (🔴) from the add-ins drop-down.

5. This will enable the familiar Copilot for sales pane in the meeting invite.

6. The Copilot for sales pane will provide an option to save the meeting to a record in Dynamics 365 sales or select an opportunity to connect the meeting with an opportunity (Figure 13-39).

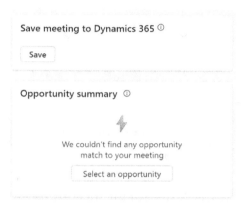

Figure 13-39. *Save meeting or connect opportunity in Copilot for sales*

7. You can click Save (Save) or select an opportunity (Select an opportunity) to begin the record selection process similar to what we discussed in the email scenario.

8. You can also connect and save in one click by selecting the record from the action card. Since in my example this email is related to new sales opportunity, hence I will track it under the Opportunity view. To save and connect, I will click More actions (⋯) at the opportunity record and select Save and connect (Figure 13-40).

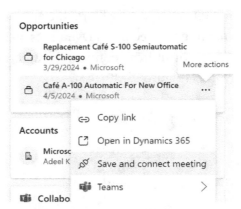

Figure 13-40. *Save and connect meeting event to record in Dynamics Sales 365 using Copilot for sales*

9. Next time when you open the meeting invite and Copilot for sales, you will find a summary of opportunity presented. We will discuss opportunity later in the section (Figure 13-41).

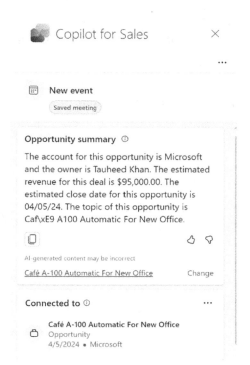

Figure 13-41. *Meeting invite with the opportunity summary in Copilot for sales*

13.1.5 AI Suggestion for CRM Actions

This feature is an excellent application of AI where Copilot for sales can understand the email's context and identify important updates needed especially for sales opportunity. In the example, I have used a scenario where the customer has emailed about changes in the customer budget, which affects the estimated revenue in Dynamics 365 Sales, and date planned to close the opportunity. Copilot for sales, powered by AI, can detect such request and offer a list under Suggested actions action card for you to review and apply. For this example, you need an email with such content. Let's see the example email I have used:

1. Choose the email with content where either the
    budget or the intent to close has been discussed.
    Figure 13-42 shows a sample email I prepared
    for demo where the customer has mentioned the
    changes in budget and closure date.

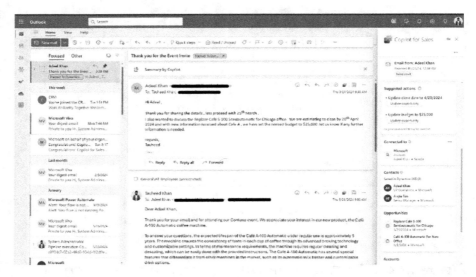

Figure 13-42. *Email with revenue and close date info for Dynamics
365 Sales updates*

2. Notice the new Suggested actions action card in
    Copilot for sales pane, listing the auto identified
    actions (Figure 13-43).

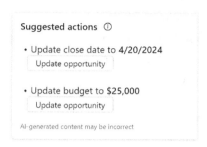

Figure 13-43. *Suggested actions action cards for Dynamics 365 Sales updates in Copilot for sales*

3. If you click these suggestions, Copilot for sales will ask for a related opportunity with suggested records. Select the relevant opportunity to perform the update (Figure 13-44).

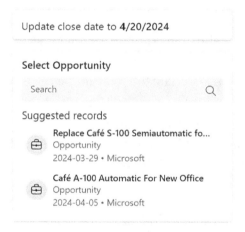

Figure 13-44. *Select opportunity for suggested updates in Dynamics 365 Sales from Copilot for sales*

4. The other way can be to choose the relevant
    opportunity listed under the action card from
    the main Copilot for sales pane. This way, you
    can reduce the selection step mentioned earlier
    (Figure 13-45).

Figure 13-45. *Opportunity list under the opportunity action card for
Dynamics 365 Sales*

5. By clicking the opportunity, Copilot for sales
    will display the Opportunity view with Copilot
    suggestions to update the relevant fields (Est.
    Revenue for Budget and Est. Close Date for
    opportunity close date). You can edit the
    opportunity in the Copilot for sales pane and
    perform the update (Figure 13-46).

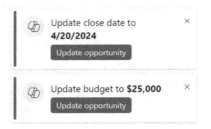

Figure 13-46. *Copilot suggested update to Dynamics 365 Sales for
user review*

6. You can also perform updates by clicking Update
   opportunity (Update opportunity) to open the opportunity
   record in the Dynamics 365 Sales environment and
   perform updates.

13.1.6 Teams with Copilot for Sales

The integration between Copilot for sales and Microsoft Teams allows
sellers to leverage teams' collaborative excellence to be infused in sales
processes and help accelerate deals with easy collaboration. In this
section, you will explore and learn how you can use Copilot for sales
with MS Teams. We will begin with in-pane experience that is called
Collaboration Space and later explore the features available during teams'
meetings.

Collaboration Space

Microsoft Copilot for sales Collaboration Space provides an out-of-the-box
environment for sales collaboration that's built on the Microsoft Teams.
The feature provides two out-of-the-box templates and reduces the setup
overhead for versatile personas coming together to achieve great results:

- **Account Team**: The template is created for smooth
  teamwork within account teams and with customers.
  When used by a team and connected to a Dynamics
  365 Sales account, the template offers a perfect space
  to work together with account team members and
  customers.

- **Deal Room**: The template is designed for concentrated
  cooperation on deal-related tasks. Connected to a
  Dynamics 365 Sales opportunity and used at the
  channel level, this template offers a specific area for
  effective teamwork.

There are various ways you can apply these templates; you can experience them by following these steps:

1. Log in to Outlook Office, either through app or browser experience.

2. Select an email of a customer that you wish to review and use for this experiment.

3. At the email view, click the Apps (⊞) icon to open the app add-in available and select the Copilot for sales (🍂) icon.

4. This will launch the Copilot for sales with relevant customer information and key email info.

5. Browse below to find the Collaboration Space action card. The card contains already connected teams' channel as well as templates for you to set up. If you are setting up for the first time, you will only notice the templates (Figure 13-47).

Figure 13-47. *Collaboration Space action card with Dynamics 365 Sales records in Copilot for sales*

6. Hover your mouse over the account name (in this case, Microsoft) to activate the account template (Figure 13-48).

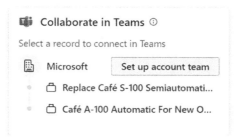

Figure 13-48. *Set up an account team with the Dynamics 365 Sales account using Copilot for sales*

7. Click "Set up account team" to start finalizing the template settings (Figure 13-49).

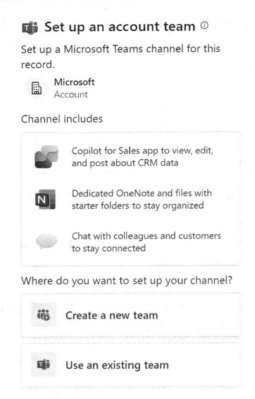

Figure 13-49. *Set up an account team configuration using the Dynamics 365 Sales account in Copilot for sales*

8. The template will include the Copilot for sales app view to view the Record details, OneNote for notes, and storage for file/folder management.

9. You can choose to either create a new team or use an existing team's channel.

10. Choosing a new team will require additional information about the team's channel such as joining policy (Figure 13-50).

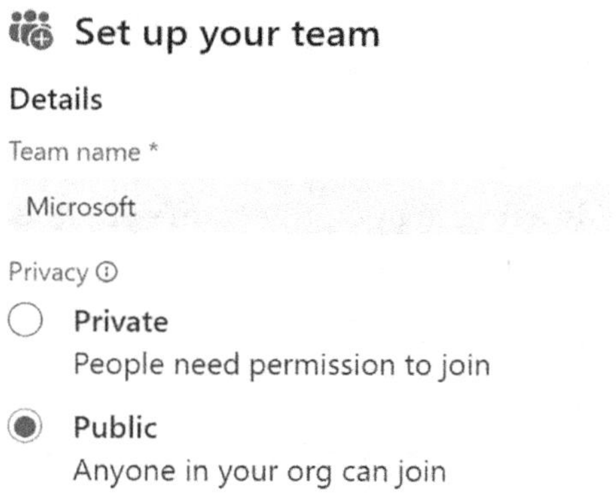

👥 Set up your team

Details

Team name *

Microsoft

Privacy ⓘ

○ **Private**
People need permission to join

◉ **Public**
Anyone in your org can join

Figure 13-50. *New team joining policy for the Dynamics 365 Sales account team's channel*

11. The creator will be added by default as a team member; the remaining can be added later (Figure 13-51).

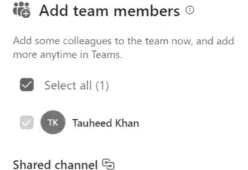

👥 Add team members ⓘ

Add some colleagues to the team now, and add more anytime in Teams.

☑ Select all (1)

☑ 🟣 **TK** Tauheed Khan

Shared channel 🔗
A shared channel is being set up too. Team members are not added to this channel. Invite customers and colleagues from Teams.

Figure 13-51. *Adding team members for the account template*

12. Click Create team (Create team) to begin the creation of the new team's channel. Upon completion, the Copilot for sales pane will provide a link to open the team's channel directly by clicking the Open in Teams (Open in Teams) button.

13. As shown in Figure 13-52, a new team channel is created. As an owner of the channel, you can further maintain the engagement and activities. Also, the Dynamics tab has been added by default.

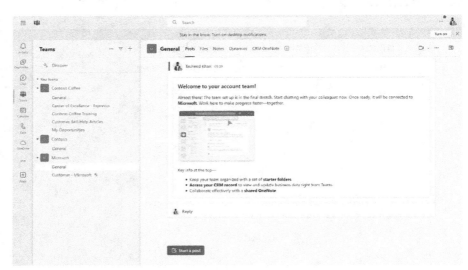

Figure 13-52. *Account template deployed at MS Teams with the Dynamics tab*

14. In the channel, you can also create a post using Copilot for sales and share sales Record details (Figure 13-53).

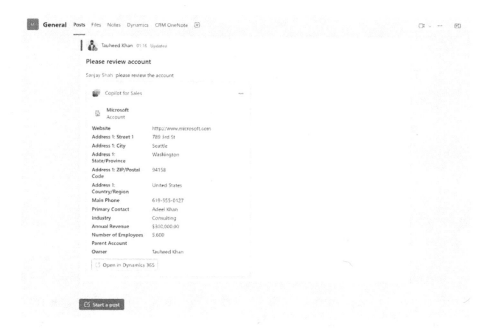

Figure 13-53. *Posting Dynamics 365 Sales record information in the account channel*

15. Next time you view the Copilot for sales pane for the same accounts or contacts, you will notice that the account channel will be listed under Collaboration Space as shown in Figure 13-54.

Figure 13-54. *Listing of connected Teams channel in the collaboration action card*

You can also apply an account template by clicking More actions (⋯) at the account record and selecting Teams (Figure 13-55). As I have already created a team's channel, Copilot is also listing the existing channel details.

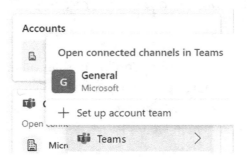

Figure 13-55. *Set up an account team from the Accounts action card*

To create a deal room, you can follow these steps:

1. In the Copilot for sales pane, hover the mouse over the opportunity title under the Collaboration with Teams action card (Figure 13-56).

Figure 13-56. *Set up deal room for Dynamics 365 Sales opportunity*

2. Click Set up deal room to start configuring the deal
    room channel (Figure 13-57).

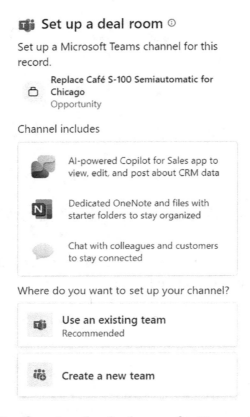

Figure 13-57. *Configuring the deal room for Dynamics 365 Sales opportunity*

3. The process from here onward is like the account team's settings in the case of creating a new team channel. Let's select the "Use an existing team" option.

4. This will present a list of teams' channels already existing. You can choose the channel where you want to set up the deal room. Typically, for the opportunity deal room, it should be under the account's team channel as shown in Figure 13-58.

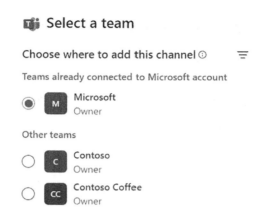

Figure 13-58. *Choosing a channel for the Dynamics 365 Sales opportunity deal room*

5. Proceed by clicking Next (Next) to channel privacy details. If you choose Standard, you will get AI features enabled in the channel (Figure 13-59).

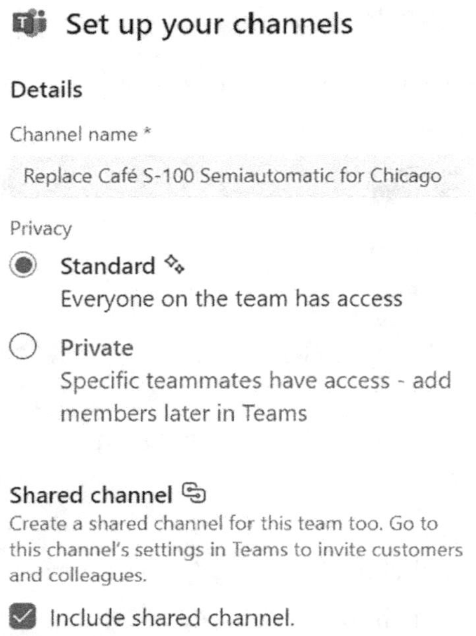

🗔 Set up your channels

Details

Channel name *

Replace Café S-100 Semiautomatic for Chicago

Privacy

◉ **Standard** ✢
Everyone on the team has access

◯ **Private**
Specific teammates have access - add
members later in Teams

Shared channel 🔗
Create a shared channel for this team too. Go to
this channel's settings in Teams to invite customers
and colleagues.

☑ Include shared channel.

Figure 13-59. *Channel's privacy settings for Dynamics 365 Sales opportunity*

6. Please carefully choose the privacy settings according to sensitivity of deals.

7. Click Set up team (Set up team) to begin channel creation. Upon completion, the Copilot for sales pane will provide a link to open the team's channel directly by clicking the Open in Teams (Open in Teams) button.

8. A new channel is now available under accounts. You can now collaborate with confidence and reduce communication barriers between teams (Figure 13-60).

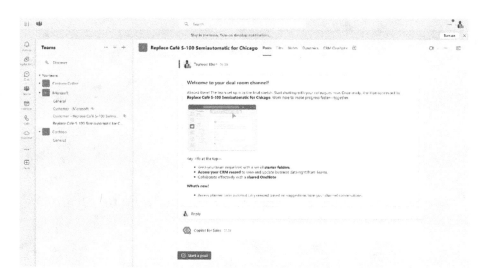

Figure 13-60. *New deal room channel created with Dynamics 365 Sales opportunity*

You can also create a deal room by selecting the opportunity from the opportunity action card; click More actions (⋯), select teams, and choose to set up a deal room.

To use Copilot for sales in a post, you need to perform the following actions:

1. Click the Start a post (🖉 Start a post) button to open the post editor.

2. In the post editor, prepare the remaining details such as the subject and message and look for the Copilot for sales icon as shown in Figure 13-61.

Figure 13-61. *Edit a post in the teams' channel with the Dynamics 365 Sales record*

3. By clicking the Copilot for sales icon, a pop-up
    will be displayed where you can choose the record
    required that you wish to share with the team.
    Choose the recently updated record or select
    Advanced search to find the record of interest
    (Figure 13-62).

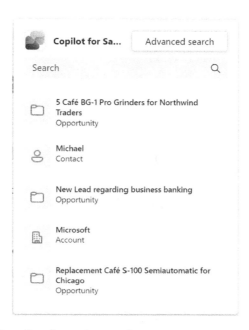

Figure 13-62. *Copilot for sales with Dynamics 365 Sales records*

4. Once you have decided or found the relevant record,
    you can post in the channel, and all channel users
    will be able to view the information as shown in
    Figure 13-63.

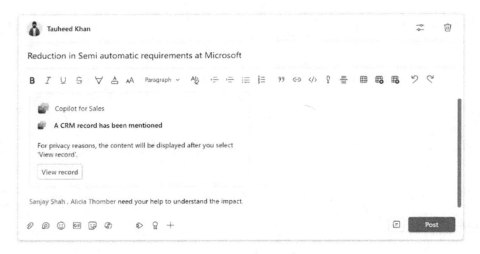

Figure 13-63. *Posting with Dynamics 365 Sales opportunity details*

5. Notice the View record (View record) button; this ensures that only users having access to the opportunity record in Dynamics 365 Sales can view the information in the channel.

6. Users with access to the channel and Dynamics 365 Sales record will be able to see the information in the post (Figure 13-64).

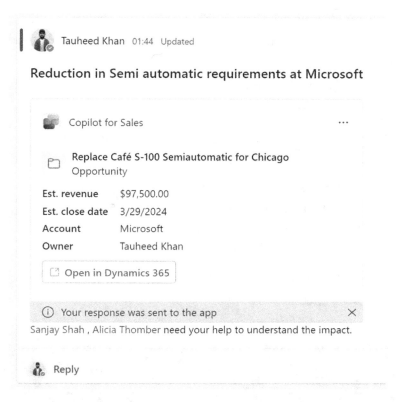

Figure 13-64. *Post with Dynamics 365 Sales opportunity details*

Through these templates, you can collaborate and work with peers effectively in managing customer engagements. With the Copilot for sales ability to share record information as part of a post, you do not have to launch Dynamics 365 Sales for each time.

During Teams Meeting

You can use sales Copilot during the virtual meetings with customers or peers in Microsoft Teams. This feature allows you to interact with customers and refer or reflect the latest information. To be able to use

Copilot for sales, you need to have the transcription on as required by
Copilot for Teams as well. Let's follow these steps to learn about the
feature:

1. Open Microsoft Teams as app or browser
   experience.

2. Open the previously organized meeting where you
   have added Copilot for sales.

3. Recall the steps defined in Section 13.1.4 under
   "Save Outlook Activities to Dynamics 365 Sales."
   Meetings like that can be ready for Copilot for sales
   usage during the meeting.

4. When the meeting is in flight, click the Copilot for
   sales (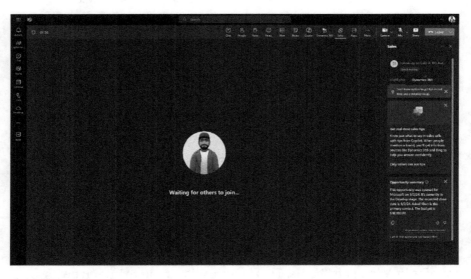) icon to open the Copilot for sales pane
   (Figure 13-65).

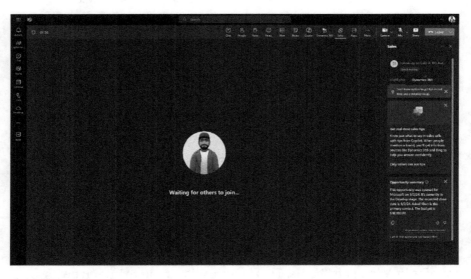

Figure 13-65. *Copilot for sales with real-time highlight and*
Dynamics 365 Sales tab

5. The Highlight tab displays real-time tips helpful for sellers as well as a summary of opportunity records connected (Figure 13-66).

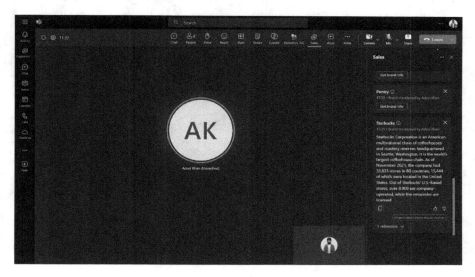

Figure 13-66. *Brand identification from conversations by Copilot for Sales*

6. At the Dynamics 365 tab, you will find the record you connected during the meeting setup at Outlook. In my case, I can see opportunity record details as shown in Figure 13-67.

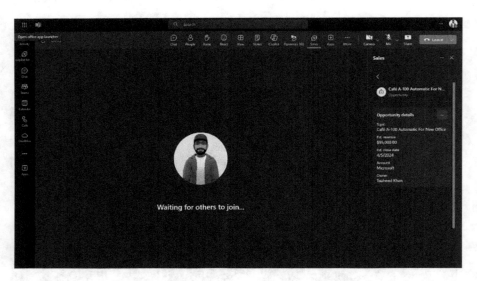

Figure 13-67. *Copilot for sales with the connected Dynamics 365 record in Teams meeting*

    7.   As you learned with the Copilot for sales pane in Outlook, you can update the record details right from the teams meeting or choose to copy the link to record or open the record in Dynamics 365 Sales (Figure 13-68).

Figure 13-68. *Actions available for Dynamics 365 Sales with Copilot for sales*

    8.   For Dynamics 365 users, the record editing can also be performed using the Dynamics (   ) add-in. Although it is not a Copilot feature, it helps you perform access to a similar capability (Figure 13-69).

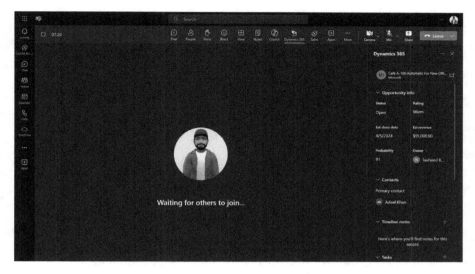

Figure 13-69. *Editing a record using the Dynamics 365 app in MS Teams*

Once the meeting is completed, Copilot will prepare a summary and send you a teams chat message about the ready summary for your review (Figure 13-70). We will cover the remaining steps in the next section.

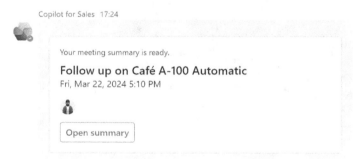

Figure 13-70. *Summary notification from Copilot for sales*

Post Teams Meeting

Once your team's meeting summary is ready, you can start using Copilot for sales in a post-meeting scenario. This setting allows you to recap, review mentions of keywords, and analyze the transcript for further actions. We can begin our review experience through the main meeting event or by opening the summary. Let's review these features:

1. Open the meeting you concluded with attendees and had Copilot for sales enabled.

2. Choose the Recap (Recap) tab from the top menu.

3. This will open the Recap view with access to recording, content, and other features as shown in (Figure 13-71).

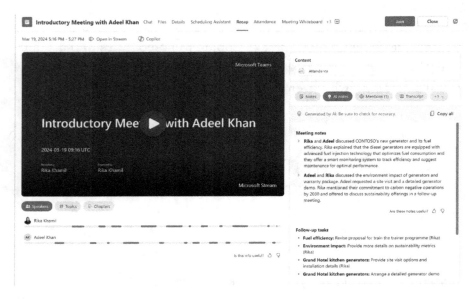

Figure 13-71.   Recap meeting view

4. Review the AI notes; notice how Copilot has applied
   generative AI and created a summary note that can
   be expanded (Figure 13-72).

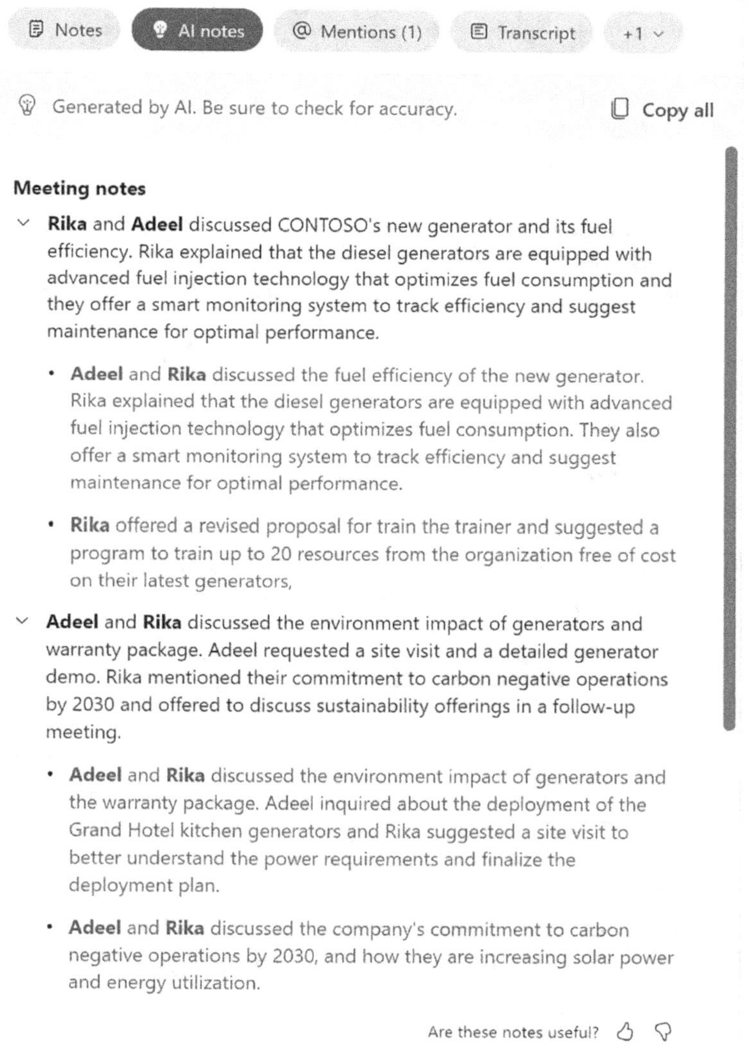

Figure 13-72. Meeting notes created by AI

5. Review the follow-up actions captured by AI (Figure 13-73).

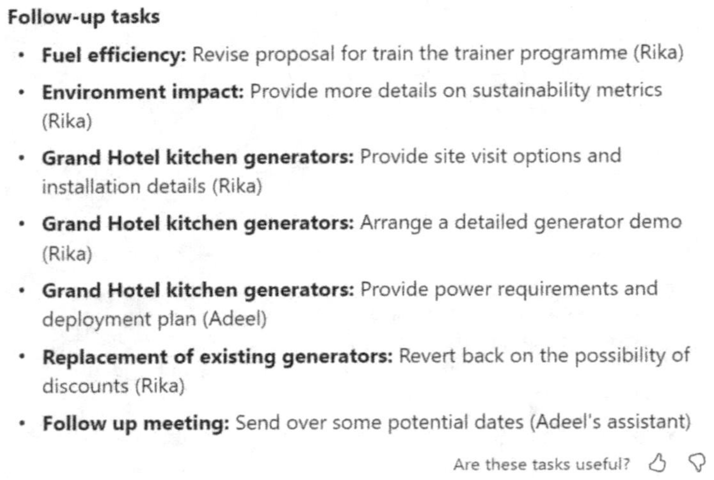

Follow-up tasks
Fuel efficiency: Revise proposal for train the trainer programme (Rika)
Environment impact: Provide more details on sustainability metrics (Rika)
Grand Hotel kitchen generators: Provide site visit options and installation details (Rika)
Grand Hotel kitchen generators: Arrange a detailed generator demo (Rika)
Grand Hotel kitchen generators: Provide power requirements and deployment plan (Adeel)
Replacement of existing generators: Revert back on the possibility of discounts (Rika)
Follow up meeting: Send over some potential dates (Adeel's assistant)
Are these tasks useful?

Figure 13-73. *Follow-up tasks created by AI*

6. Click + and select Copilot for sales to open the Copilot for sales view (Figure 13-74).

Notes
AI notes
Mentions (1)
Transcript
+1
Sales
Generated by AI. Be sure to check for accuracy.

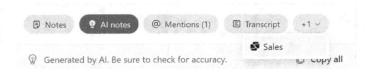

Figure 13-74. *Copilot for sales in a post-meeting scenario*

7. You will be presented with highlights, and if any action required task creation, AI would suggest them (Figure 13-75).

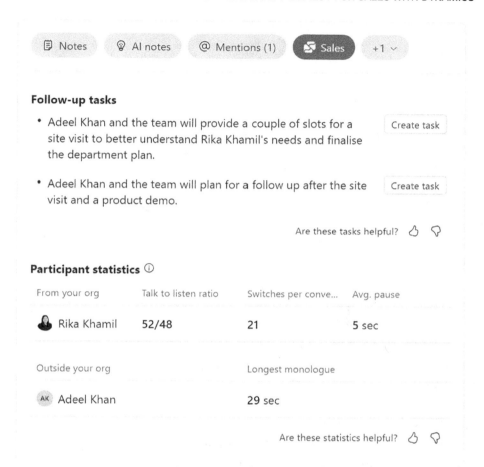

Figure 13-75. *Follow-up task creation from Copilot for sales*

8. In addition, Copilot for sales also provides statistics that can help you improve conversations during meetings.

9. Click Create task (Create task) to create actions in Dynamics 365 Sales directly; you can set necessary details of tasks and optimize task creation and assignment through a single interface (Figure 13-76).

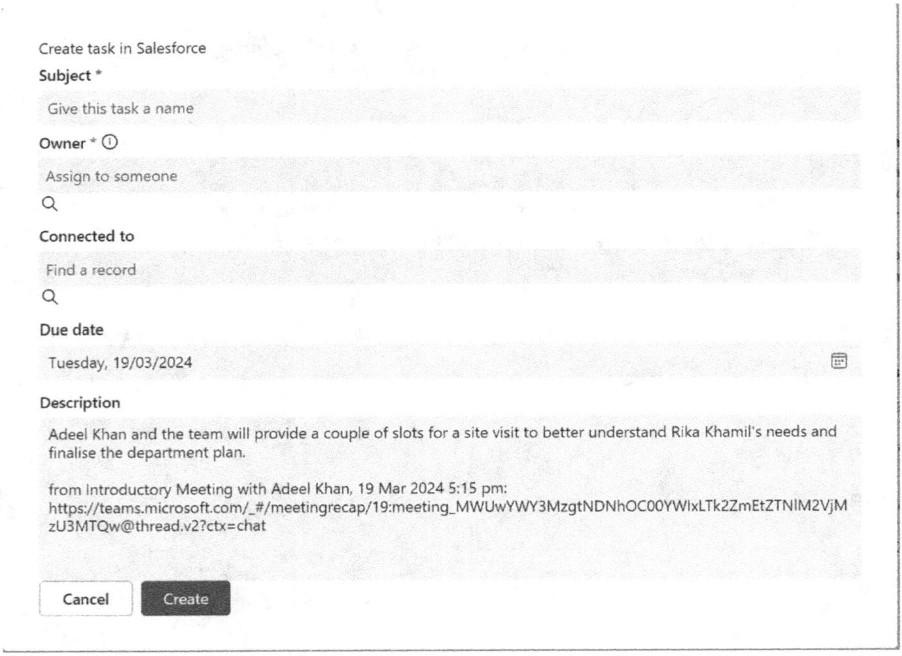

Create task in Salesforce

Subject *

Give this task a name

Owner * ⓘ

Assign to someone

🔍

Connected to

Find a record

🔍

Due date

Tuesday, 19/03/2024   📅

Description

Adeel Khan and the team will provide a couple of slots for a site visit to better understand Rika Khamil's needs and finalise the department plan.

from Introductory Meeting with Adeel Khan, 19 Mar 2024 5:15 pm:
https://teams.microsoft.com/_#/meetingrecap/19:meeting_MWUwYWY3MzgtNDNhOC00YWIxLTk2ZmEtZTNlM2VjM
zU3MTQw@thread.v2?ctx=chat

Cancel   Create

Figure 13-76. *Task creation in Dynamics 365 Sales using Copilot for sales*

Once the meeting notes are available, you can use them in Copilot for sales Outlook experience to send a summary of meeting to the customer. To view the experience, open the Outlook and Copilot for sales app with an email, select the Draft a reply option, and notice the new default prompt that can help you send the meeting summary to the attendees. By clicking the drop-down option, you can choose the meeting summary relevant for the conversation (Figure 13-77).

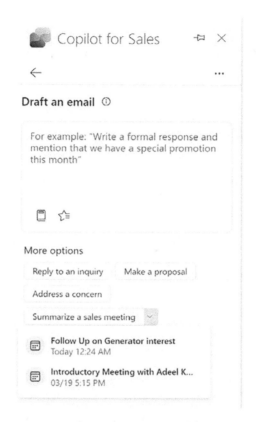

Figure 13-77. *Sending a meeting summary as an email reply*

Also, you can use the meeting summary to generate a pitch in a Word document. To experience this feature, open a new Word document and click the Copilot icon (🔵) and type your prompt. To refer to the meeting, type "/" and select "Sales Meeting" from the pop-up menu (Figure 13-78).

Figure 13-78. *Accessing Sales meetings in Word*

Upon selecting Sales meetings, Word will list all available meetings that you can use as shown in Figure 13-79.

Figure 13-79. *Using a meeting transcript to generate content in Word*

This is truly a cross-platform integration of enterprise applications with the intelligent use of generative AI. Copilot for sales truly holds promise to change the way you or your sales team work and shall empower them to accelerate success in their role.

13.2 Sales Copilot for Dynamics 365 Sales Apps

This section will discuss Dynamics 365 Sales user experience and showcase how users of Dynamics 365 Sales can benefit from Copilot within Sales apps. In this section, you will also learn the various features available

434

as part of interface enhancements within the Dynamics 365 sales app. We will cover Copilot actions available at the time of this book's writing.

The experience of Copilot in Dynamics 365 Sales app has been grouped into three experience categories: Get Info, Ask Questions, and Stay ahead. We will experience the default prompts available in these categories. In addition to these categories, Dynamics 365 Sales also offers the ability to draft emails and assist in creating personalized responses using customer data from Dynamics 365 Sales.

With the familiar Copilot chat pane, you can experiment with your own prompts and learn different ways of interacting with Sales data in Dynamics 365 CRM.

13.2.1 Get Info

Get Info is a category of prompts that helps you access relevant information about your sales data quickly and easily (Figure 13-80). You can use natural language queries to ask Copilot about your accounts, leads, and opportunities. You can use default prompts in this category to get news about the top accounts or a list of opportunities. Let's experience some of them in the next section.

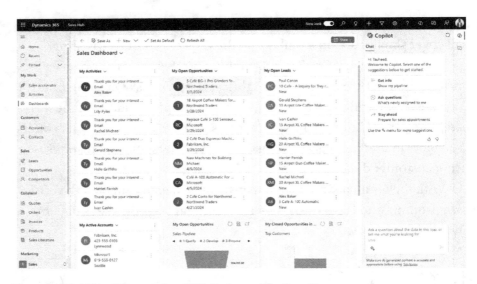

Figure 13-80. *Dynamics 365 Sales with Copilot*

These default prompts are going to be improved regularly as the Copilot feature will mature; hence, I do not intend to cover them one by one, but rather share the concept and working, so you can use them in your CRM interactions.

Getting Account-Related News

For businesses where the customer's information is available in the public domain, or customers are publicly listed corporates, it is critical to stay informed and aware of the news circulating about them. Traditionally, sellers who wish to keep an eye on the latest news updates relevant to their customers had to perform this action outside CRM and manually. With Copilot for sales and its native integration with Bing search, sellers can now get the top news right inside the CRM interface. The most recent news that includes or refers to your accounts, selected by Bing, can help you either to start a conversation or have a sight on the latest developments with your account. Follow these steps to experience this feature:

1. Log in to the Dynamics 365 Sales app.

2. At the landing screen, look for the Copilot (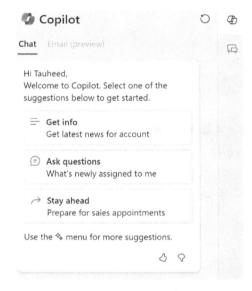) icon at the top menu or at the right-side pane ( ), if the Copilot pane is not automatically opened.

3. This will bring you to the familiar Copilot pane, but this time in the Dynamics 365 Sales environment as displayed in Figure 13-80.

4. By default, you will be presented with three prompts, one from each category. Notice if the Get Info prompt is related to news or not. If so, you can click the prompt to get the updates (Figure 13-81).

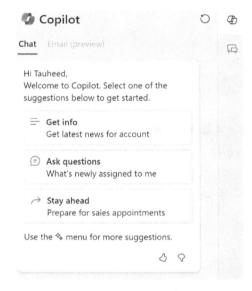

Figure 13-81. *Auto-suggestions at login for Copilot in Dynamics 365 Sales*

5. If that's not the case, which is possible, you can click the prompt guide (✧✦) icon, choose Get info, and subsequently select "Get latest news for account" (Figure 13-82).

Figure 13-82. *Selecting the Get latest news for account prompt from the prompt guide*

6. Click the send (▷) icon to begin the news collection process, and in a few seconds, Copilot will list the top news/articles found relevant to your accounts (Figure 13-83).

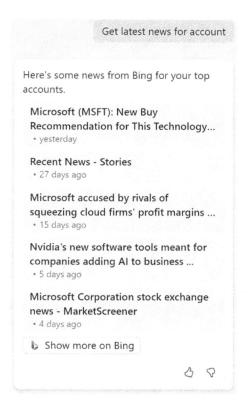

Figure 13-83. *Latest news for accounts*

7. Similarly, if you want to get news about a specific
    account, you can also apply the same prompt but
    ends with "/" to select the specific account as shown
    in Figure 13-84.

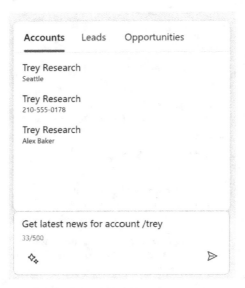

Figure 13-84. *Selecting a specific account for news*

8. Lastly, if you open an account view and select the same prompt (Figure 13-85), Copilot will automatically select the account in view and provide the outcome.

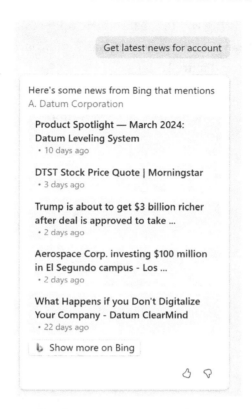

Figure 13-85. *News for the account in view*

Show Pipeline

This prompt will help get the list of opportunities sorted by estimated closed date. This can help get the latest list of assigned opportunities without moving to Opportunity views.

1. Log in to the Dynamics 365 Sales app.

2. At the landing screen, look for the Copilot ( ) icon at the top menu or at the right-side pane ( ), if the Copilot pane is not automatically opened.

3. This will bring you to the familiar Copilot pane, but this time in the Dynamics 365 Sales environment as displayed in Figure 13-80.

4. Click the prompt guide (⬥) icon, choose Get info, and subsequently select "Show my pipeline" (Figure 13-86).

Figure 13-86. *Show pipeline prompt in Dynamics 365 sales Copilot*

5. This will draft the prompt in the prompt chat box; select the send (▷) icon to begin the listing process (Figure 13-87).

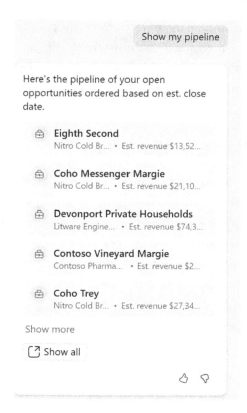

Figure 13-87. *Top five open opportunities based on close date*

6. Select Show more (Show more) to expand the list to
    the top ten opportunities by est. closed date or select
    Show all (⌃ Show all) to browse to "My Open
    Opportunity View" as shown in Figure 13-87.

7. Note that the default view is the list of opportunities
    based on estimated date in ascending order, that is,
    the oldest est.

8. Hover the mouse over any of the opportunity listed, and you will notice the summarize (✧ Summarize) suggestion. You can click the suggestion to generate the summary of opportunity. We will cover the summary as the next topic.

Opportunity-Related Information

Using the prompt, you can gather opportunity-related information with ease. We will begin with the summary feature. Summarization is a key feature of Copilot, and we have been learning about various summarizations throughout this chapter as well as this book. The purpose is to bring concise, impactful information to sellers, so they can gain more information in lesser time. The summary feature is available with leads and opportunities. We will begin with the opportunities first as in the previous exercise, we talked about accessing a summary through the "Show my pipeline" prompt output.

1. As discussed in the previous topic, one way to accessing the summary is to hover the mouse over the listed opportunities under the Show my pipeline prompt. This will trigger the summarization preparation by Copilot (Figure 13-88).

Figure 13-88. *Summarize the opportunity from the Show my pipeline list*

2. The next option of getting a summary is to click the prompt guide (✧) icon, choose Get info, and subsequently select Summarize opportunity (Figure 13-89).

Figure 13-89. *Summarize opportunity prompt from the prompt guide*

3. In the Copilot chat, complete the prompt by typing "/" and selecting the relevant opportunity (Figure 13-90).

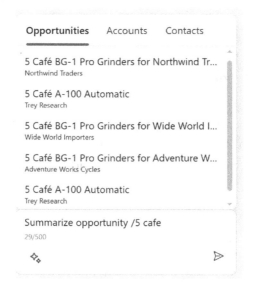

Figure 13-90. *Selecting an opportunity for summarization*

4. Select the send (▷) icon to begin the
    summarization. If Copilot finds a resembling topic,
    it will require additional confirmation of the exact
    opportunity (Figure 13-91).

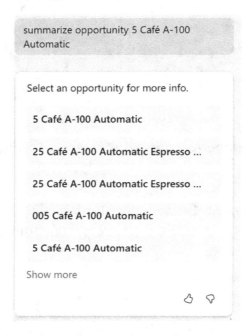

Figure 13-91. *Opportunity with a similar topic*

5. You can also type the prompt directly without using
    the prompt guide route; use either "/" to select
    the opportunity or provide the topic in inverted
    commas "" (Figure 13-92).

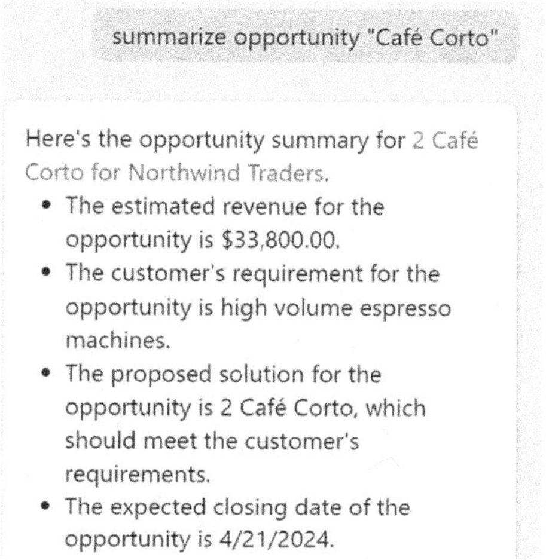

summarize opportunity "Café Corto"

Here's the opportunity summary for 2 Café
Corto for Northwind Traders.
- The estimated revenue for the
  opportunity is $33,800.00.
- The customer's requirement for the
  opportunity is high volume espresso
  machines.
- The proposed solution for the
  opportunity is 2 Café Corto, which
  should meet the customer's
  requirements.
- The expected closing date of the
  opportunity is 4/21/2024.

Figure 13-92. Summarize by typing a prompt with inverted commas

6.   Finally, if you open an opportunity view or
     opportunity record, Copilot will display the first
     opportunity summary (in view) or displayed
     opportunity summary.

While you have learned to generate a summary of opportunities in
many ways, let's spend some time and learn the insights typically available.
The summary generated will focus on attributes selected during the
setup. This includes information from the opportunity, account, contact,
competitor, and opportunity product–related records out of the box. If
you have configured additional fields in the opportunity data model and
you want to use the information in the summary, you can easily get the
attributes included through the CRM admin. Please refer to Chapter 11
where I have covered the Dynamics CRM configuration discussing the
subject.

Figure 13-93 shows the two sample summaries of opportunities for
different accounts and different stages.

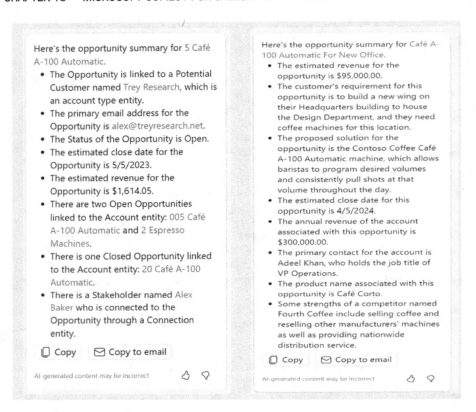

Figure 13-93. *Samples of opportunity summary*

Notice the information changes along with references, and detailing varies based on the way information is captured in Dynamics 365 Sales. It is worth noting that summaries will get better and better as seller will start using Dynamics 365 more and update information with ease as discussed in the previous section of this chapter.

Also, there is a related prompt that has been recently added, and at the time of writing this book, it was still under preview. This prompt can help you get the relevant product information, if your organization maintains product-related documentations at Dynamics 365 sales (Figure 13-94).

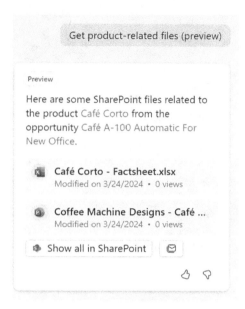

Figure 13-94. *Product-related files for the opportunity*

I found this feature very useful as it can reduce time lost searching for relevant documentations.

Lead-Related Information

The summary feature with leads works like the opportunity except the focus record is "lead". You can use the default prompt under the prompt guide. If you type or select "Summarize lead," Copilot will provide you a list of leads assigned to you (Figure 13-95).

Figure 13-95. *List of leads assigned for the summary*

You will also notice the familiar Summarize (✧ Summarize) when you hover the mouse over the lead record. You can also generate a summary by typing a prompt at the Copilot chat window with "/" to select the lead record or mention the lead topic under inverted commas "". Once you open the lead view, Copilot will create a summary and display it by default (Figure 13-96).

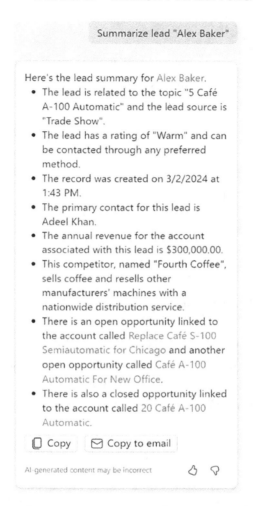

Figure 13-96. Lead summary generated using Copilot prompts

13.2.2 Ask Questions

Asking a question allows users to engage with Copilot to extract information and answers to questions about accounts, contacts, or leads. You can ask questions to track the changes happening to records or if there is any new developments.

What's Changed

You can also use question prompts to get information about the records. Prompts such as "What's changed with lead" will get a shorter time-based summary as shown in Figure 13-97.

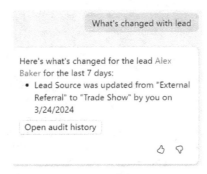

Figure 13-97. *Duration-based summary of a lead*

Your user profile must have access to the audit summary to get such summary. You can also get a summary based on the last login by using a suggested prompt "What's changed since I last logged 1 day ago." This prompt works for both lead and opportunity and helps you generate shorter time-based summary.

What's New

The next set of prompts in the prompt guide allows you to find new actions and activities associated with your profile. This includes getting a summary view of all related sales records as well as tracking new assignments.

1. Open the Copilot pane in Dynamics Sales 365.

2. Click the prompt guide (✧) icon, choose ask questions, and subsequently select "What's new with my sales records" (Figure 13-98).

Figure 13-98. *Tracking sales records using Copilot*

3. This will draft the prompt in the prompt chat box; select the send (▷) icon to begin the detailing process (Figure 13-99).

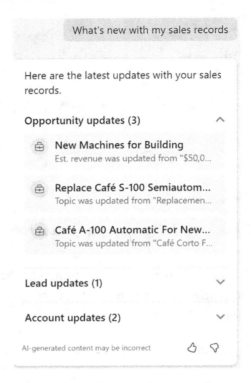

Figure 13-99. *Latest updates from sales records*

4. Review the content, and if you need to get more details, hover the mouse over the related record and select Get updates (✧ Get updates) (Figure 13-100).

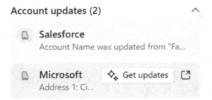

Figure 13-100. *Get updates from newly updated sales records*

5. This will bring the details of the account that have changed in the last seven days (Figure 13-101).

Figure 13-101. *Account changes in the last seven days*

6. The next prompt you can use is to find a new assignment. You can use the default prompt of "What's newly assigned to me" or type the same to get a summary of new assignments (Figure 13-102).

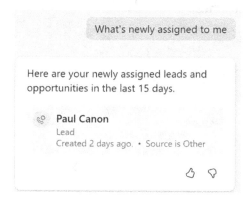

Figure 13-102. *Finding new assignments*

13.2.3 Stay Ahead

The last category I want to cover is the Staying ahead. This is using AI-assisted capabilities to help our sellers better prepare for upcoming meetings and ensure no customer inquiry remains unreplied.

Prepare for Sales Meeting

This feature helps you to review the relevant information about your leads and customers before your scheduled sales meetings. While using CRM you can see their recent activities, interactions, notes, and tasks, as well as insights from LinkedIn and Dynamics 365 Sales Insights, Copilot will help you review the key points based on recent interactions and activities.

1. Open the Copilot pane in Dynamics Sales 365.

2. Click the prompt guide (✧) icon, choose to stay ahead, and subsequently select *"Prepare for sales appointments"* as shown in Figure 13-103. The native integration with Outlook will allow meeting synchronization and the ability to use Copilot to prepare for these meetings.

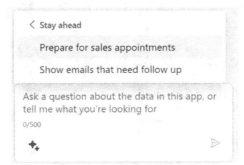

Figure 13-103. *Stay ahead with preparation for sales appointments*

3. This will bring the sales appointment list where you can select the specific appointment you need Copilot help (Figure 13-104).

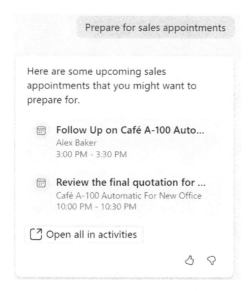

Figure 13-104. Sales appointment listing in Copilot

4. Hover the mouse over the appointment and select Prepare (✧ Prepare) to start the Copilot supported preparation process.

5. You can also type "Prepare for "<Meeting Subject>" if you would like to type (Figure 13-105).

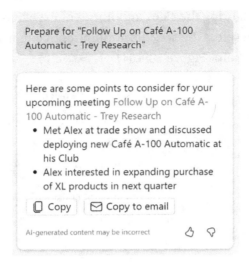

Figure 13-105. *Points to consider for preparation*

6. Copilot will require the meeting to be synchronized or saved under the sales record as well as some notes available in the interaction history to generate these points.

Unreplied Emails

Copilot shows you emails that you haven't replied to yet and that are related to the record you're viewing. If you're in the grid view such as the dashboard or view, Copilot shows you all your unreplied emails. The emails must meet these conditions to be on the list: They've been in your inbox for three to seven days without a reply. After seven days, they disappear from the list Copilot prepares. They express a buying intent, a question, a query, or an action item. They have a lead or an opportunity as the regarding field.

1. Open the Copilot pane in Dynamics Sales 365.

2. Click the prompt guide (✦◆) icon, choose to stay ahead, and subsequently select "Show emails that need follow-up."

3. You can also type "unreplied emails" to share your intent with Copilot.

4. Copilot will bring the list of such emails limiting to the last seven days as shown in Figure 13-106.

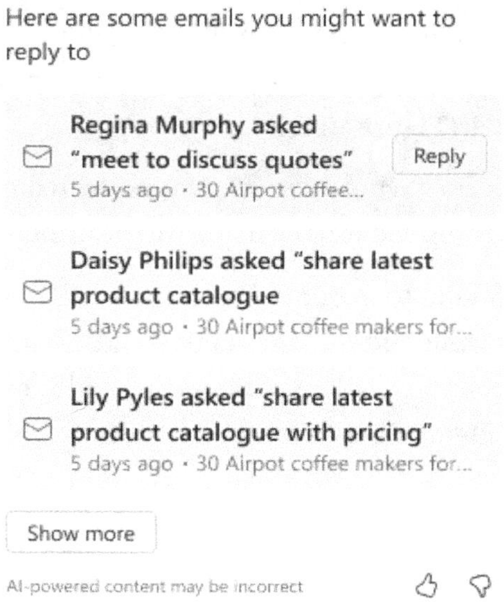

> Here are some emails you might want to reply to
>
> ✉ **Regina Murphy asked "meet to discuss quotes"**   `Reply`
> 5 days ago · 30 Airpot coffee...
>
> ✉ **Daisy Philips asked "share latest product catalogue**
> 5 days ago · 30 Airpot coffee makers for...
>
> ✉ **Lily Pyles asked "share latest product catalogue with pricing"**
> 5 days ago · 30 Airpot coffee makers for...
>
> `Show more`
>
> AI-powered content may be incorrect   👍 👎

Figure 13-106. *Unreplied emails for the last seven days*

5. As experienced in the previous sections, hovering the mouse over an email and selecting Reply (`Reply`) will allow you to respond to the email using the Dynamics 365 sales editor.

13.2.4 Replying to Email

As part of the core Copilot feature, replying to an email is an essential feature. Using Dynamics 365 Sales Copilot, you can also reply to emails from the Dynamics 365 sales interface.

1. Log in to the Dynamics 365 Sales app.

2. At the landing screen, look for the Copilot ( ) icon at the top menu or at the right-side pane ( ), if the Copilot pane is not automatically opened.

3. This will bring you to the familiar Copilot pane, but this time in the Dynamics 365 Sales environment as displayed in Figure 13-80.

4. Select a record where you want to reply to emails or find out unreplied emails using the prompt.

5. Once you land to the email reply, you will notice that the Copilot email tab is active and, similar to our previous Outlook experience, provides familiar options (Figure 13-107).

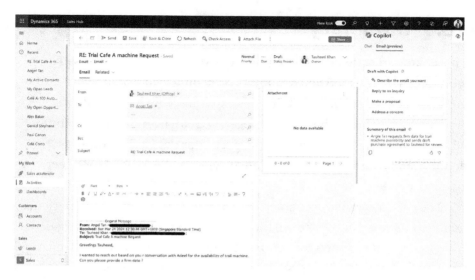

Figure 13-107. *Reply to emails with Copilot assistance*

6. As we have covered this extensively in the previous sections, I will not cover the feature details; however, I recommend you play around and familiarize yourself with the features.

7. Note that emails created would be sent to the audience in To, CC, or BCC. Please be careful not to use customer interactions for playing with this feature.

13.3 Summary

This chapter discussed the integration of Microsoft Copilot for sales with the Dynamics 365 Sales module, providing a comprehensive guide for users to enhance their sales experience through AI-driven insights and actions. The chapter began with an overview of Dynamics 365, emphasizing its role in unifying customer data across different departments, thereby offering a holistic view that is crucial for effective customer engagement.

The core focus of the chapter was on the Copilot for sales experience, detailing the user journey from the initial login to utilizing AI-suggested CRM actions. It outlined the seamless interaction between Dynamics 365 Sales and Microsoft Modern Work apps, particularly Outlook and Teams, and how Copilot for sales leverages generative AI to simplify access to sales and relationship-related information.

The chapter then covered key features such as email summary and response creation, performing CRM actions from Outlook with the help of AI suggestions, and lastly discussed the Teams integration with Copilot for sales and how it helps sellers to remain in customer context.

The chapter concluded with a walk-through of the Sales Copilot for Dynamics 365 Sales apps, highlighting the "Get Info," "Ask Questions," and "Stay Ahead" features that enable users to interact with sales data efficiently.

The chapter served as a practical guide for users to effectively integrate Copilot for sales into their Dynamics 365 Sales workflow, harnessing the power of AI to optimize their sales operations and customer relationships.

CHAPTER 14

Microsoft Copilot for Service

The service function is the backbone of any organization. It is the bridge that connects the company to its customers, ensuring that their needs and concerns are addressed promptly and effectively. A robust service function not only enhances customer satisfaction but also contributes to the overall growth and success of the organization. If I say that it is the service function that ensures you maintain customers profitably for longer period, I would not be wrong.

The service function can be divided into a back office and a front office. While the front office enables customers to reach out from their preferred mode of communication with ease and focus on maximizing solving problems at first interaction, the back-office service teams often grapple with the challenge of managing a high volume of complex and difficult instances. Emails are a critical part of business correspondence, and Microsoft Outlook plays a pivotal role in managing these communications.

Similarly, the back office in the majority of organizations leverages established platforms such as Dynamics 365, Salesforce, ServiceNow, Zendesk, and others to organize, orchestrate, and manage service-related engagements. However, many critical roles at times sit outside these platform users' persona, and collaborating with them remains a challenge. That is where Microsoft Teams is enabling various profiles and bringing them to a unified instance-focused, client-driven collaboration.

© Adeel Khan 2024
A. Khan, *Introducing Microsoft Copilot for Managers*, Inside Copilot,
https://doi.org/10.1007/979-8-8688-0419-9_14

Microsoft Copilot for Service is a Microsoft AI–powered assistant that helps different roles in the service landscape to use Microsoft 365 and CRM platforms to provide high-quality service. It gets data from the organization's CRM platforms (Microsoft Dynamics Service or Salesforce), large language models (LLMs), Microsoft Graph, Microsoft 365 apps, and the Internet. This combination of AI features into the service process aims to change how service operations will communicate with customers.

This chapter is a foundational chapter for the next two chapters as you would have experienced in Copilot for Service; it will begin with Copilot for Service prerequisites and setup-related details. The subsequent chapters will highlight and discuss the features of Copilot for Service with Dynamics Customer Service 365 and other industry-leading CRMs (Salesforce, ServiceNow, Zendesk).

It is assumed the readers have fair understanding of Outlook, Teams, and CRM platforms of choice. It is also recommended to spend some time learning the basics of the Customer Service module in CRM solutions deployed at your organization before deep diving into later chapters.

If you are starting the book from this chapter and new to the concept of Copilot, I would encourage you to spend time at reading Chapter 1. Also, since Copilot for Service works closely with M365 Copilot, I suggest reading Part II of this book to better appreciate and understand the features.

14.1 Setting Up Copilot for Service

In this section, we begin with guidance on how to set up Copilot for service. We will explore the licensing options available for organizations to begin Copilot for Service procurement and the deployment options available and deep dive into the enablement of Copilot for service personas.

14.1.1 Licensing Options

Organizations setting up Copilot for Service will have a variety of options to procure and deploy the AI-powered assistant. As with any other Microsoft product, I foresee changes in licensing introduced as the product becomes generally available; however, I will discuss them based on the CRM solutions your organization has and assume that essential M365 licenses are already available:

- **Dynamics 365 Customer Service Install Base**: If your organization has a Dynamics 365 Customer Service **Enterprise** license, you can enable Copilot in Dynamics Customer Service with an existing license; however, for the Copilot for Service add-in of Outlook and teams, you will have to sign up for an additional Copilot for Service license.

  The Dynamics 365 Customer Service Enterprise license includes summarizing cases, ask a question, draft emails, and Copilot analytics features. However, to utilize the full capabilities of Microsoft Copilot for Service, a separate license is required.

- **Non-Dynamics 365 Customer Service Install Base**: If your organization has any one of the CRM (Salesforce, Zendesk, ServiceNow), there could be further two scenarios. First, if your organization does not have a Microsoft 365 license, you would need to purchase a Microsoft 365 for **Enterprise** license as well as Copilot for Service license. The second scenario could be where your organization uses non Microsoft CRM and also have Microsoft 365 licenses, you can purchase

Microsoft Service Copilot. However, you must have a Microsoft 365 for Enterprise license and an **Entra** (previously known as Azure Active Directory) account, which gives you access to Microsoft 365 apps like Outlook and Teams.

These are the licensing options available at the time of writing this book; it is always best to check the latest licensing options as they can change based on market needs.

14.1.2 M365 Deployment Options

Once your licensing is sorted, we can proceed to explore the deployment options. As discussed in Microsoft Copilot for Service, Copilot for Service can be deployed through two primary methods, admin deployed and user deployed. The choice between admin-deployed and user-deployed methods depends on the organization's needs and preferences. If the organization prefers centralized control and uniformity, the admin-deployed method would be more appropriate. If the organization values flexibility and individual customization, the user-deployed method would be a better choice.

Admin Deployed

The admin-deployed method allows administrators to install Copilot for Service as an integrated app on multiple platforms or as an individual add-in on a single platform. The setup can be initiated from either the Microsoft 365 admin center or Microsoft AppSource to install it in Outlook and assign users. In the admin-deployed method, administrators have the authority to install Copilot for Service as an integrated application across multiple platforms or as an individual add-in on a single platform.

Here are the summarized steps required for deploying using the admin-deployed method. Please note that for the admin-deployed option, you need to be a Microsoft 365 administrator to perform these actions:

1. Log in to https://admin.microsoft.com/.

2. From the site navigation, click the Settings (⚙ Settings) menu.

3. Under the submenu, click the Integrated apps (Integrated apps) option.

4. This option allows the admin to purchase and deploy Microsoft 365 apps developed by Microsoft or Microsoft Partner.

5. At the Integrated apps page, select the Get apps (⊞ Get apps) icon to open the app source.

6. Search for "Copilot for Service" to list Copilot for Service apps as shown in Figure 14-1.

Figure 14-1. *AppSource Copilot for Service app listing*

7. Click the Get it now (Get it now) icon under "Copilot for Service in Microsoft Outlook" to begin the deployment.

8. You will need to repeat the following actions with "Copilot for Service" later. "Copilot for Service in Microsoft Outlook" is a prerequisite of the "Copilot for service" teams app.

9. The Get it now will require a confirmation about the terms of use and privacy; review if required, or you can proceed with the acceptance based on your organization's policies.

10. This will take you to the admin center to complete the remaining steps.

11. This step begins with validating the user group for deployment. This is where the admin-deployed option is helpful as the admin has full control over the selection options. In my case, I have chosen a couple of users in an organization to benefit from Copilot for Service; however, it can vary based on the number of licenses or number of personas in your organization (Figure 14-2).

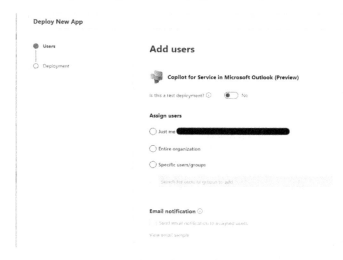

Figure 14-2. *Admin-deployed option, selecting users for Copilot for Service*

12. The final step is regarding app permissions. Copilot for Service will leverage the Internet and send data over the Internet to Microsoft-hosted Azure OpenAI services. It is critical to review this step based on the organization's policies and procedures. If Copilot

for Service is already approved by your enterprise
security team, please select accept permissions for
both apps and proceed as shown in Figure 14-3.

Figure 14-3. *Admin-deployed option, reviewing and accepting
permissions for Copilot for Service*

13. Before completing deployment, review all the
options selected and click the Finish deployment
(Finish deployment) button to proceed with deployment
(Figure 14-4).

Figure 14-4. *Admin-deployed option, reviewing and finishing deployment for Copilot for Service*

14. Once deployment is completed, the system will provide a confirmation.

15. Please note that it could typically take up to six hours for any app to appear in Outlook. However, for my deployment, the app was available immediately (Figure 14-5).

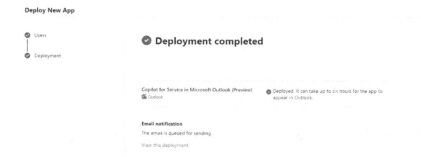

Figure 14-5. *Admin-deployed option, deployment completion for Copilot for Service*

The next set of actions is required to be executed from the MS Teams admin center. At the time of writing this book, "Copilot for Service" teams add-in deployment was not supported through the admin center, and I had to perform these actions at the MS Teams admin center.

1. Log in to https://admin.teams.microsoft.com/.

2. Browse to Teams apps (⊞ Teams apps) and then select the Manage apps (▮ Manage apps) menu option.

3. Under "All Apps," search for "Copilot for Service." This will list the app as shown in Figure 14-6.

Figure 14-6. *Adding Copilot for Service team's add-on*

4. Click the app and select Assignment from the tab to assign the app to users (Figure 14-7).

Figure 14-7. *Assigning Copilot for Service to users in teams*

5.   Click Assign App (Assign app) to set the policy.

6.   The next prompt will allow the admin to enable
     users to install the app (Figure 14-8).

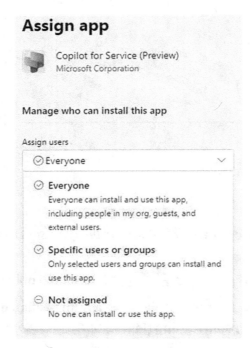

Figure 14-8. *Copilot for Service MS Teams policy*

This setup completes the admin-deployed Copilot for Service enablement for service personas. However, still the administrator needs to perform additional actions that can vary based on CRM of your organization.

User Deployed

The user-deployed method empowers individual users to install the Copilot for Service for Microsoft Outlook application from Microsoft AppSource.

The option is suitable for organizations where flexibility is provided to choose based on individual needs. Please note that the Outlook add-in is a user-deployed installation, not an admin-deployed one, and it has limited features. User-deployed add-ins don't have the Copilot for Service banner notifications that show up at the top of new or reply to emails (you will experience this later in the chapter).

Also, the meeting invites don't automatically include the Copilot for Service app. But you can add Copilot for Service to the meeting yourself to get meeting summaries.

The user needs to perform the following actions to enable the Microsoft Copilot for Service Outlook add-in, provided your tenant administrator has allowed downloading add-ins:

- Open the Outlook app or browser experience.

- Select the Apps (⊞) icon from the side menu.

- Select the Add apps (Add apps ⊞) button to search for the "Copilot for Service in Microsoft Outlook" app.

- At AppSource, search for the "Copilot for Service in Microsoft Outlook" app.

- Choose the Add (Add) option to add and enable Copilot for Service.

In summary, the choice between admin-deployed and user-deployed methods depends on the organization's needs and preferences. If the organization prefers centralized control and uniformity, the admin-deployed method would be more appropriate. If the organization values flexibility and individual customization, the user-deployed method would be a better choice.

Microsoft Teams Settings

After completing the Outlook setup, the tenant admin needs to perform two actions so that you can leverage the Copilot for Service in Microsoft Teams environment. Here are the two actions required. The first action is only required if you have not set up Microsoft Copilot for Sales.

1. Log in to `https://admin.teams.microsoft.com/`.

2. Select the Meetings (🗓 Meetings) menu from the options and then select the Meeting policies (| Meeting policies) option.

3. Choose the appropriate policy, or in case the admin wants to enable this for all organizations, choose "Global (Org-wide default)."

4. In the policy, ensure the "Transcription" option is on under "Recording & transcription" (Figure 14-9).

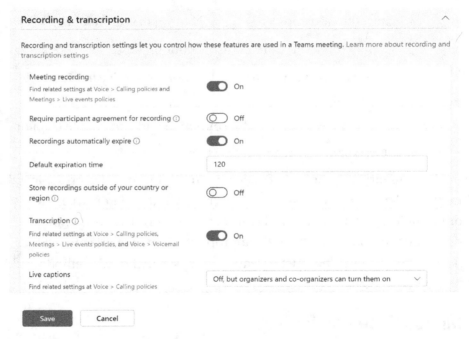

Figure 14-9. Setting the Teams meeting policy for Copilot for Service

5. Ensure to click Save after making the change in case the transcription was not on.

6. Next, at the main menu, select the Teams apps (⊞ Teams apps) option and select Setup policies (❙ Setup policies).

7. Choose the appropriate policy, or in case the admin wants to apply this for all organizations, choose "Global (Org-wide default)."

8. Under "Pinned App," select the Add apps (+ Add apps) icon.

9. This will open the search box where the admin can search for "Copilot for Service." Add the app-to-app bar list (Figure 14-10).

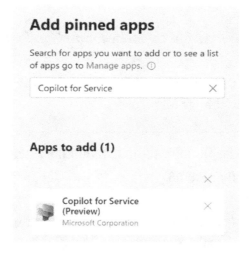

Figure 14-10. *Pinning Copilot for Service in Teams*

10. Choose the appropriate location of the Copilot for Service app and click Save to reflect the change (Figure 14-11).

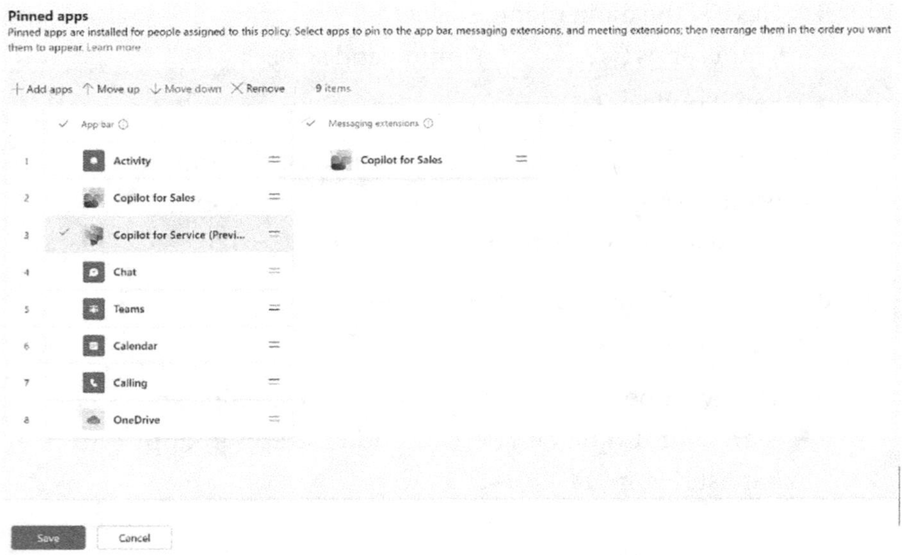

Pinned apps

Pinned apps are installed for people assigned to this policy. Select apps to pin to the app bar, messaging extensions, and meeting extensions; then rearrange them in the order you want them to appear. Learn more

+ Add apps	↑ Move up	↓ Move down	✕ Remove 9 items

	✓ App bar ⓘ		✓ Messaging extensions ⓘ	
1	🔲 Activity	=	🔳 Copilot for Sales	=
2	Copilot for Sales	=		
3	✓ Copilot for Service (Previ...	=		
4	💬 Chat	=		
5	📑 Teams	=		
6	📅 Calendar	=		
7	📞 Calling	=		
8	OneDrive	=		

Save   Cancel

Figure 14-11. *Pinned apps in policy for all Copilot for Service users*

11. Confirm the changes and wait for some time to reflect the change for all users.

Please note that the Outlook setup is mandatory before setting up Copilot for Service in teams.

This marks the completion of the deployment setup. In the next section, we will finalize the setup-related activities based on the CRM deployed at your organization.

14.1.3 CRM-Based Settings

This section will discuss the remaining steps required for setting up working Copilot for Service. We will begin with discussing activities required for the Dynamics 365 Customer Service install base and complete with a discussion of activities required for the Salesforce install base.

Settings for Dynamics 365

The organization where Dynamics 365 Customer Service is used as primary CRM, following activities are required by users having a system administrator role. Tenants in North America have Copilot enabled by default; however, the tenants in other parts of the world require the following actions to enable the experience in Dynamics 365 Customer Service as well as Copilot for Service. Here are the steps needed to be performed in the Dynamics 365 Customer Service app:

1. Log in to `https://admin.powerplatform.microsoft.com/`.

2. Select the Dynamics 365 Customer Service environment.

3. Select Settings from the top menu and click User+ Permissions to select the users you wish to allow using Copilot for Service.

4. Assign the "Copilot for Service User" or "Copilot for Service Administrator" role based on the user profile (Figure 14-12).

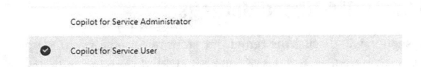

Copilot for Service Administrator

✓   Copilot for Service User

Figure 14-12. *Copilot for Service roles required to be assigned*

Save the changes and switch to the "Customer Service Admin Center" app for the next actions:

1. From the menu, select Productivity under Agent Experience.

2. Notice the Copilot "Copilot help pane" and "Summaries" settings (Figure 14-13).

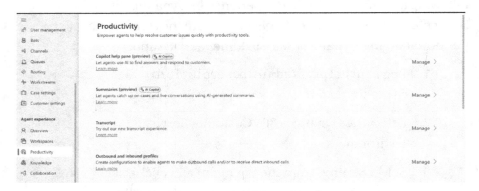

Figure 14-13. *Copilot help pane and Summaries settings in Dynamics 365 Customer service*

3. Check the agreement of terms based on your organization's policy. Again, it is best to ensure that the data movement that is required for Copilot is something your organization has reviewed and accepted (Figure 14-14).

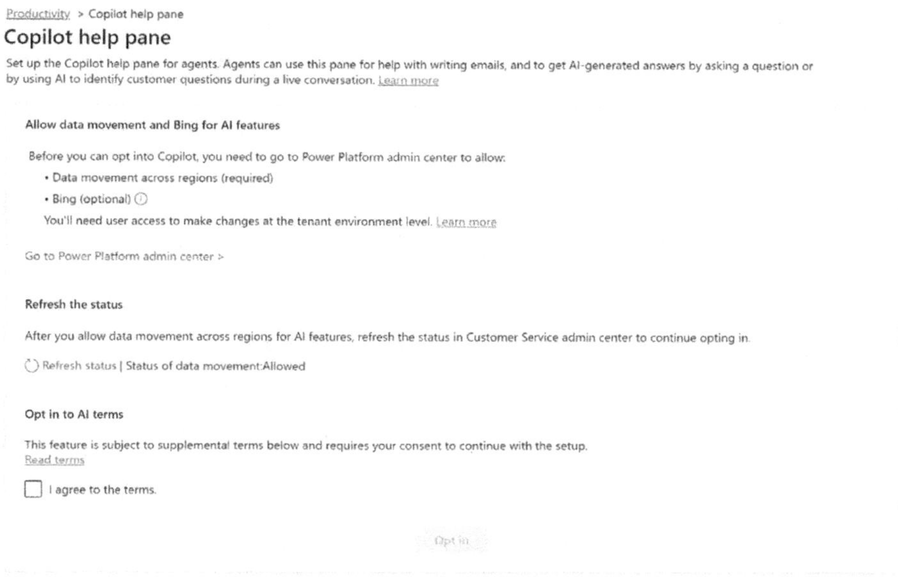

Productivity > Copilot help pane

Copilot help pane

Set up the Copilot help pane for agents. Agents can use this pane for help with writing emails, and to get AI-generated answers by asking a question or by using AI to identify customer questions during a live conversation. Learn more

Allow data movement and Bing for AI features

Before you can opt into Copilot, you need to go to Power Platform admin center to allow:

- Data movement across regions (required)
- Bing (optional) ⓘ

You'll need user access to make changes at the tenant environment level. Learn more

Go to Power Platform admin center >

Refresh the status

After you allow data movement across regions for AI features, refresh the status in Customer Service admin center to continue opting in.

⟳ Refresh status | Status of data movement:Allowed

Opt in to AI terms

This feature is subject to supplemental terms below and requires your consent to continue with the setup.
Read terms

☐ I agree to the terms.

Opt in

Figure 14-14. *Copilot help pane configuration*

4.   Click Opt in (Opt in) to reflect the changes and
settings made as shown in Figure 14-14. It may take
some time before you will start experiencing the
Copilot help pane in Dynamics 365 Customer
Service experience.

5.   Perform similar actions under the Summarize
option as well.

Next is to enable the rich text AI feature for Customer Service apps.
Admins can follow these steps to enable this feature:

1.   Log in to http://make.powerapps.com.

2.   Select the right environment where Dynamics 365
Customer Service apps are deployed.

3. First, you can edit the Customer Service Hub app
    by clicking the edit icon in the app list as shown in
    Figure 14-15.

Figure 14-15. *Editing Customer Service Hub app*

4. In the App edit screen, click Settings (⚙ Settings) and
    select the feature section.

5. At the feature menu, search for rich text and ensure
    that you enable the "Turn on generative AI in
    emails" option (Figure 14-16).

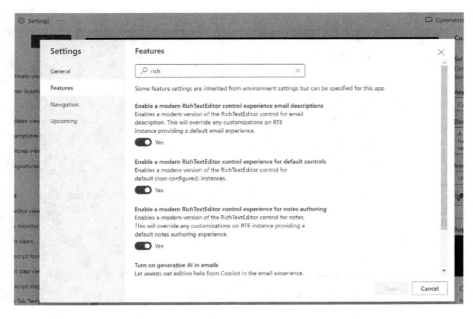

Figure 14-16. *Generative AI in emails feature*

6. Save and publish the app.

7. Repeat the same steps with Customer Service workspace.

The final steps of settings are required at the Copilot for Service app under MS Teams. To set up further, your admin can follow these steps:

1. Log in to MS Teams' client or web portal.

2. Select the App (⊞) icon from the side menu and search for "Copilot for Service."

3. The other option is the click on More actions (•••), and from the pop-up menu, choose the Copilot for Service (🔶) icon (Figure 14-17).

Figure 14-17. *App selection menu in Teams for Copilot for Service*

4. This will open the Copilot for Service app where you can access the Settings tab (Figure 14-18).

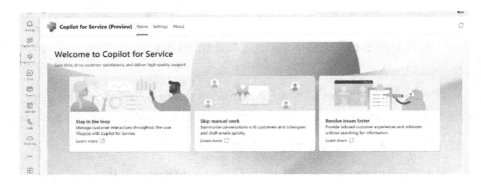

Figure 14-18. *Copilot for Service app form settings*

5. Choose the Settings (Settings) tab from the top to open
   the settings page.

6. Choose Copilot AI (✦ Copilot AI) under Tenant and
   ensure Copilot AI is on as shown in Figure 14-19.

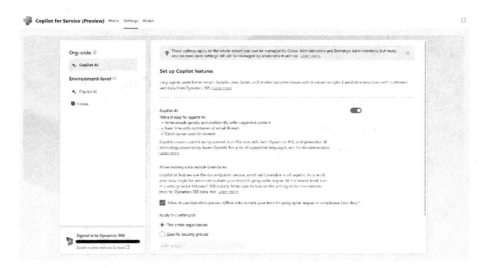

Figure 14-19. *Enabling Copilot at Org-wide using the Copilot for
Service app with Dynamics*

2. Select the App (⊞) icon from the side menu and search for "Copilot for Service."

3. The other option is the click on More actions (•••), and from the pop-up menu, choose the Copilot for Service (🞇) icon (Figure 14-25).

Figure 14-25. *App selection menu in Teams for Copilot for Service*

4. This will open the Copilot for sales app where you can access the Settings tab (Figure 14-26).

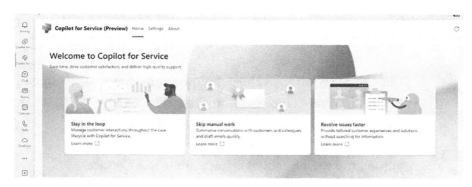

Figure 14-26. *Copilot for Service app*

5. Choose the Settings (Settings) tab from the top to open the settings page.

6. Choose Copilot AI (✦ Copilot AI) under Environment
   and ensure Copilot AI is on as shown in
   Figure 14-27.

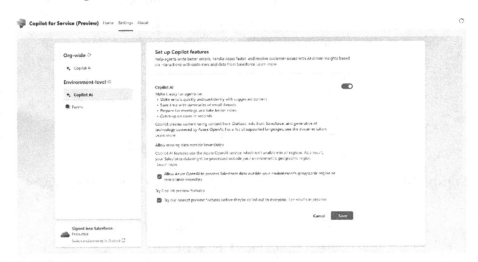

Figure 14-27. *Enabling Copilot at the environment level using*
Copilot for Service

7. You will be required to check "Allow Azure Open
   AI" as shown in Figure 14-27 to allow the Copilot
   process data from Salesforce outside geo. If your
   tenant is outside the United States, you will require
   this feature to be enabled if you want to use Copilot
   for Service.

8. If you want to try new preview features, check the
   box. This is an optional setting.

9. Once settings are completed, choose Save (⊘ Save)
   to reflect the changes.

10. The admin can set up form-level details for Salesforce objects such as contact, account, or case as shown in Figure 14-28. This setup is similar to Copilot for sales; however, to keep both discussions independent, I am repeating the concepts here.

Figure 14-28. *Adding objects to Copilot for Service*

11. The admin can choose fields that will be used for display under Copilot for Service as well as option to edit these objects (Figure 14-29). The admin can also add additional objects if required.

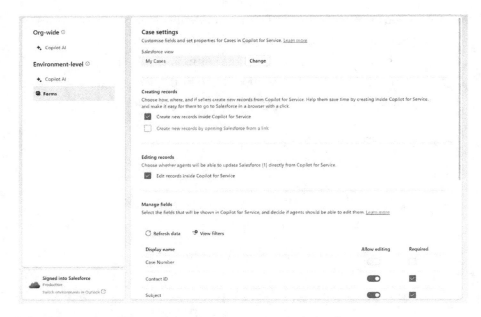

Figure 14-29. *Object form setting using Copilot for Service*

12. Note that by default the Create new feature is not enabled. You need to check the option if you want to enable the creation of new objects from the Outlook Copilot for service pane.

13. Ensure to Publish (⊘ Publish) the form settings once complete.

With these steps, your Copilot for Service is ready to work with the Salesforce solution. The users having access to Copilot will now be able to use Copilot for Service in Outlook or Teams.

14.2 Agent-Facing Deployment

Copilot for service also offers a unique opportunity to deploy the generative AI–powered assistant into supported CRM. This is called the agent-facing deployment. This deployment allows organizations to set up Copilot with one or multiple customer support solutions and deploy them into an agent-facing platform, so the agent can take advantage of the Copilot assistant in a familiar interface of customer support CRM. In the following steps, we will cover the integration with Salesforce and ServiceNow; similar steps would be applied for Zendesk or any future supported CRM platform.

Please note these steps may be suitable for CRM developers and admin working groups as they may require permissions as well as working knowledge of how Power Platform/CRM works.

The prerequisite for these steps is to have an environment ready for agent-facing Copilot configurations. An environment is a logical space where you can keep, organize, and share your organization's business data. The Copilots that you build are kept in an environment. Environments can also have different roles, security needs, and audiences, and each environment is made in a different location. Copilot created through this exercise will also be stored in an environment. Please refer to Microsoft Learn to understand more about environments and the type of environment required for agent-facing Copilot creation: `https://learn.microsoft.com/en-us/microsoft-copilot-service/admin-working-with-environments`.

The essentials to remember are as follows: your environment should be in the United States, and Dataverse (a SaaS service to store and manage data) is enabled in the environment.

14.2.1 Configuring Agent-Facing Copilot for Service

In this section, we will cover how to configure agent-facing Copilot; we will first configure Copilot with content sources, finalize the configuration and behavior, and lastly publish agent Copilot:

1. Log in to `https://servicecopilot.microsoft.com/`.

2. A landing page will appear with guidance to create agent-facing Copilot for service as shown in Figure 14-30.

Figure 14-30. *Agent-facing Copilot deployment landing page*

3. Click the Create a Copilot for agents (Create a copilot for agents) button to proceed as shown in Figure 14-30.

4. This will begin the wizard Copilot setup. The first
    step requires you to provide the name of your
    Copilot for agent. Then select an environment and
    language. Currently, only English is supported,
    but other languages will be added in the future
    (Figure 14-31).

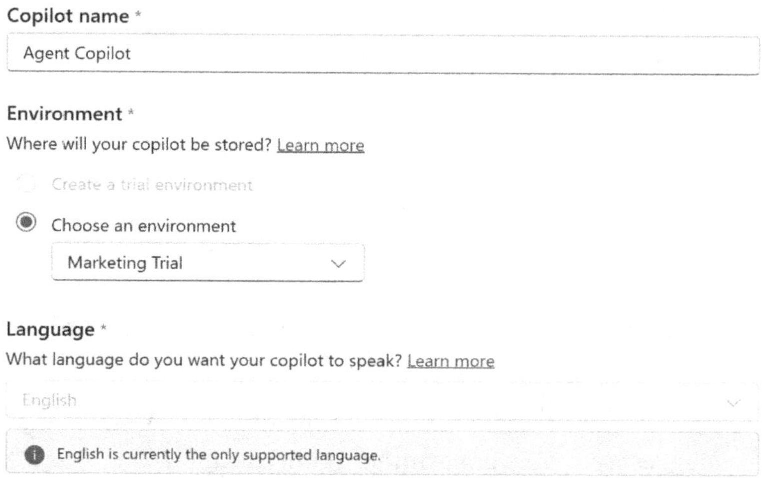

Copilot name *

Agent Copilot

Environment *

Where will your copilot be stored? Learn more

◯ Create a trial environment

◉ Choose an environment

Marketing Trial ⌄

Language *

What language do you want your copilot to speak? Learn more

English ⌄

ⓘ English is currently the only supported language.

Figure 14-31. *First step of essential configurations for agent-*
facing Copilot

5. Based on your sign-up and license, you may have
    a trial environment available. In my case, I had
    to choose the right environment. I created an
    environment specifically for Copilot for Service that
    is hosted in the United States and has Dataverse
    enabled (Figure 14-32).

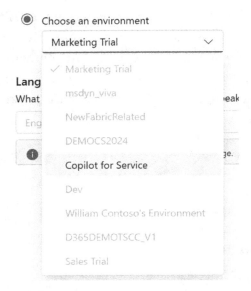

Figure 14-32. *Environment selection for agent-facing Copilot*

6.   When I click the environment selection, the system
     suggests suitable environments and disables
     nonsuitable ones as shown in Figure 14-32.

7.   Click Next (　Next　) to proceed to the second step
     of configuration.

8.   This step is referred to as connect to content, where
     you will select the content sources for Copilot
     references and consumption. The content in these
     sources will be grounded for Copilot, so agent
     Copilot can respond to queries and questions asked
     in real time (Figure 14-33).

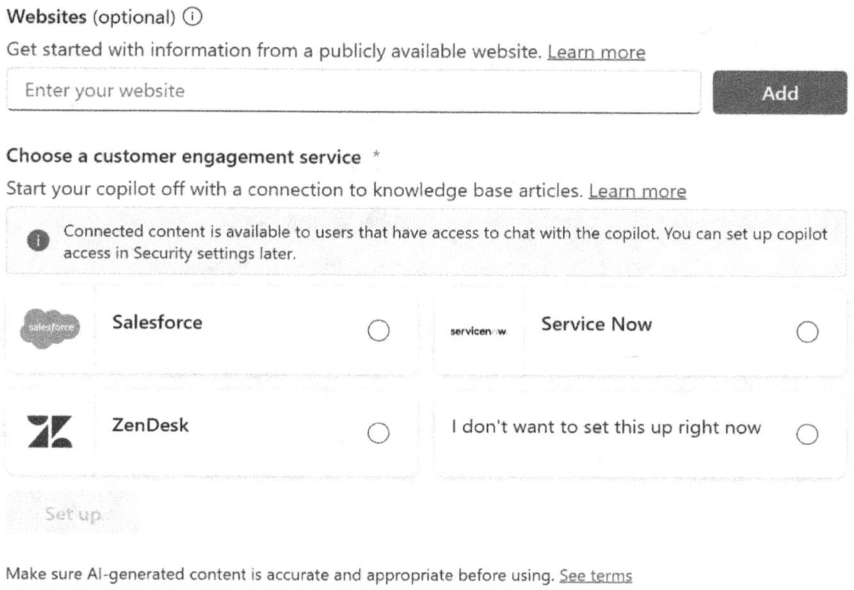

Websites (optional) ⓘ

Get started with information from a publicly available website. Learn more

| Enter your website | **Add** |

Choose a customer engagement service *

Start your copilot off with a connection to knowledge base articles. Learn more

> ⓘ Connected content is available to users that have access to chat with the copilot. You can set up copilot
> access in Security settings later.

| salesforce Salesforce | ○ | servicenow Service Now | ○ |
| ZenDesk | ○ | I don't want to set this up right now | ○ |

Set up

Make sure AI-generated content is accurate and appropriate before using. See terms

Figure 14-33. *Content source selection for agent-facing Copilot*

9. Note that you can also add more sources and configure the details later.

10. If you want to set up the details now, you can provide a public website address under the Websites section and click Add to reflect. This could be your organization's website where your products/services and general FAQs are already available.

11. For the connection to the CRM source, select the CRM of choice. Once selected, you will be provided with the Set up button to provide additional connection details (Figure 14-34).

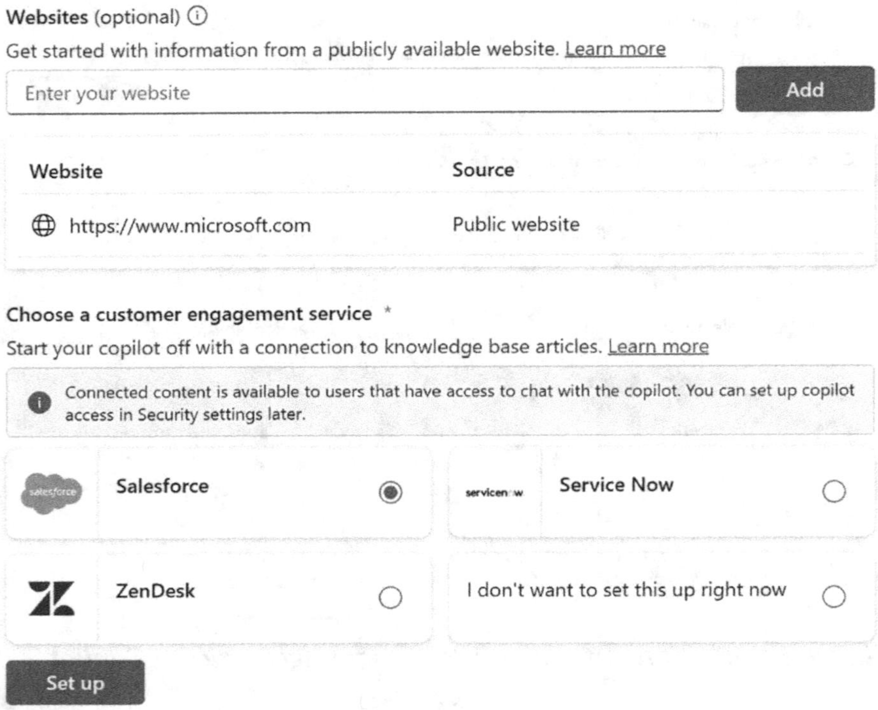

Websites (optional) ⓘ

Get started with information from a publicly available website. Learn more

Enter your website	Add

Website	Source
🌐 https://www.microsoft.com	Public website

Choose a customer engagement service *

Start your copilot off with a connection to knowledge base articles. Learn more

> ⓘ Connected content is available to users that have access to chat with the copilot. You can set up copilot access in Security settings later.

Salesforce	⦿	Service Now	◯
ZenDesk	◯	I don't want to set this up right now	◯

Set up

Figure 14-34. *Setup with supported CRMs*

12. The setup will require the user to sign in to create a connection with CRM (Figure 14-35).

Connection setup   ✕

Salesforce   Sign in

Figure 14-35. *Connection setup to CRM*

13. Similar connection settings are required in the case of other CRM solutions as well (Figure 14-36).

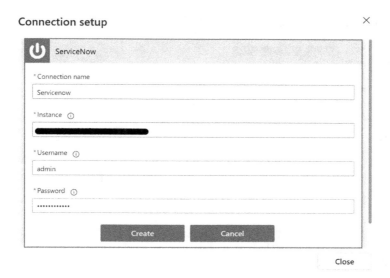

Figure 14-36. *Connection setup with ServiceNow*

14. Once the content setting is completed, you will notice
     a connection confirmation (✅ Connected successfully)
     after the setup option.

15. Select Create to (⬛ Create ⬛) begin Copilot creation.
     Please note that you can create only one Copilot per
     environment. Once your Copilot is ready, you will
     be redirected to the Copilot for Service console
     (Figure 14-37).

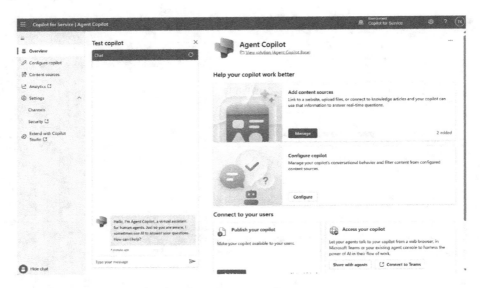

Figure 14-37. *Copilot for Service console*

16. At the Copilot for service console, you can further configure the agent conversation style, such as how to greet, how to respond when an answer is not found, or what to filter from content (Figure 14-38).

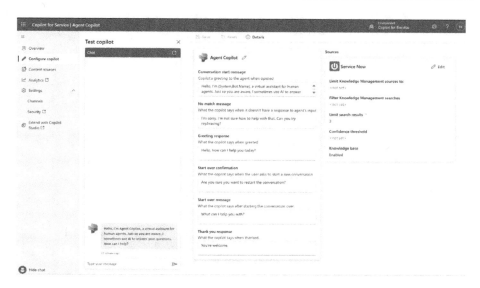

Figure 14-38. *Configuring agent Copilot behavior*

17. Select Content sources (📑 Content sources) from the side
navigation to update or add additional data sources
(Figure 14-39).

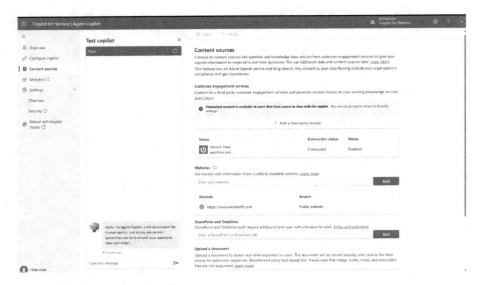

Figure 14-39. *Adding additional data sources to agent Copilot*

18. You can add an internal SharePoint site link
    to enrich the responses further or upload the
    document directly for Copilot to respond.

Once your agent Copilot is ready with configurations, you can Publish
(Publish) from the home page.

14.2.2 Embedding Agent Copilot for Service

There are multiple options you can choose to deploy or host agent Copilot.
You can choose Microsoft Teams, your custom website, or a third-party
agent console.

1. Log in to `https://servicecopilot.`
   `microsoft.com/`.

2. Choose agent Copilot's environment if it is not
   automatically selected.

3. From the side navigation, choose Settings
   (⚙ Settings) and submenu channels (Channels)
   (Figure 14-40).

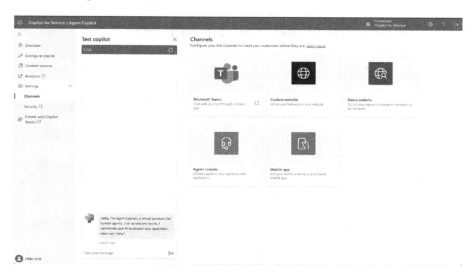

Figure 14-40. *Channels available for agent Copilot deployment*

4. Experiment with channel options; however, I will
   discuss how to add to Salesforce.

5. To add to Salesforce, you need to choose the agent
   console as an option.

6. This will provide a token endpoint and embed code
   that can be copied for the next steps (Figure 14-41).

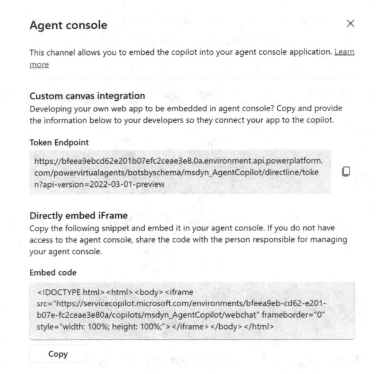

Figure 14-41. *Agent console setup*

7. Copy the "iFrame" embed code as shown in Figure 14-41.

8. Log in to the Salesforce environment and select setup.

9. Under setup, find the "Visualforce" object as shown in (Figure 14-42).

Figure 14-42. *Salesforce setup and Visualforce Pages*

10. Click New and set the details as per need. The most
     important here is to paste the iFrame details copied
     from Copilot for Service embed code (Figure 14-43).

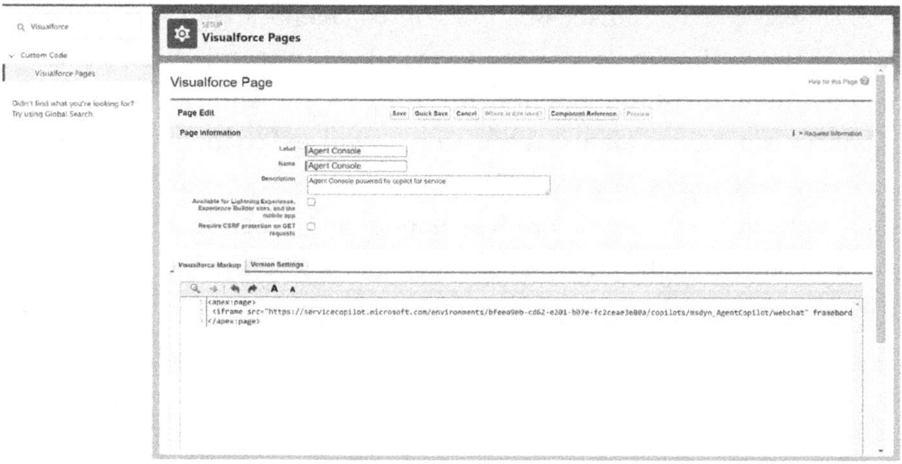

Figure 14-43. *Setting up Visualforce*

This marks the completion of setup. You will be able to use agent-facing Copilot now in Salesforce agent experience. In the next chapter, we will discuss the usage.

14.3 Summary

In this chapter, we expanded our Copilot journey with Microsoft Copilot for Service. The chapter introduced Microsoft Copilot for Service, an AI assistant for personas that connects to service solutions and provides insights across productivity platforms like Outlook and Teams.

The chapter discussed the licensing and deployment options and listed the process of setting up the environment. We learned how organizations can procure Copilot for Service licenses based on their current CRM system. We also explored how Copilot for Service can be deployed as an integrated app or an individual add-in on multiple platforms, such as Outlook and Teams.

The chapter also covered how the CRM-based settings differ between Dynamics 365 Customer Service and Salesforce Service cloud.

Lastly, the chapter discussed the setup of agent-facing deployment. This allows Copilot for service to be expanded to agents consoles and provides them real-time support while they engage with customers.

As we move on to feature discussion in the next chapters, you can choose to read either Microsoft Copilot for Service with Salesforce or Microsoft Copilot for Service with Dynamics 365 depending on the platform your organization has chosen.

CHAPTER 15

Microsoft Copilot for Service with Salesforce

Salesforce is a global customer relationship management (CRM) platform that connects companies and customers. As discussed earlier in Copilot for Service, it's a unified CRM platform that allows all your organization's various departments, such as marketing, service, commerce, and service, to interact with customers efficiently and with a consistent, shared view of customer priorities.

One of the key modules in Salesforce is the Service Cloud, a module designed to support the service ecosystem of an organization, with a wide variety of features and capabilities, addressing the organization's ability to address service-related engagements such as case ticket management, resource management, and customer interaction management.

This chapter will explain and show the features of Copilot for service, as you have done in the previous chapters. You should have a good knowledge of Outlook, Teams, and Salesforce service cloud before starting this chapter. It is a good idea to learn the basic concepts of Service and the Service cloud features of Salesforce before you continue with this chapter.

© Adeel Khan 2024
A. Khan, *Introducing Microsoft Copilot for Managers*, Inside Copilot,
https://doi.org/10.1007/979-8-8688-0419-9_15

Before you continue with this chapter, if you have not read about the Copilot concept before, I recommend that you go back and read Chapter 1. Also, since Copilot for service is integrated with M365 Copilot, I advise reading Part II of this book to have a better understanding and appreciation of the features.

It is also assumed that you have completed the setup as discussed in the previous chapter.

15.1 Copilot for Service Experience

This section will explain how Salesforce users can improve their experience and outcomes with Copilot for Service. In this section, you will also discover the different features and options that are available from Outlook and Teams interfaces, which make it easier for users to access information about service and relationships, powered by generative AI.

Salesforce is a leading CRM platform, but Microsoft Modern Work dominates the productivity side of the world with Fortune 500 and most of the large enterprise markets using Outlook and Teams as their core productivity platforms.

Remember that the aim of this book is to discuss the Copilot for Service features with Salesforce and not to discuss or cover the Salesforce Service cloud features. It is assumed that the readers of this chapter either have working knowledge or are gaining the knowledge of Service cloud in parallel.

You will discover how Copilot for service enables you to combine the strengths of both platforms in a way that you have never seen before. We will start our journey from the first login experience and explore the various features that are available at the time of writing the book.

15.1.1 First Login

In the first section, you are going to log in to Copilot for service from Outlook experience. For the chapter, I have signed up a developer access to Salesforce Service cloud. You can either sign up for a developer account or use your own organization's Salesforce account.

The following are the step-by-step guide to experience your first Copilot for service experience:

1. Log in to Outlook Office, either through app or browser experience.

2. Confirm the settings mentioned in the previous chapter, Section 14.1.3, for Salesforce.

3. Select an email of a customer or a sample email that you wish to review and use for this experience.

4. At the email view, click the Apps (▦) icon to open the app add-in available (Figure 15-1).

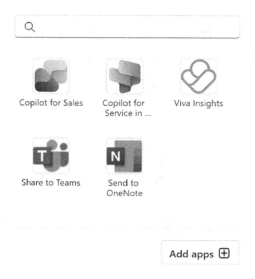

Figure 15-1. *List of apps available at Outlook*

5. Please note that the list can be different based on your setup; however, you will need Copilot for service ( ) for the next steps.

6. Click the Copilot for service ( ) icon to launch the Copilot side pane (Figure 15-2).

Figure 15-2. Copilot for service side pane in Outlook

7. Click "Sign in to your CRM" and select Salesforce for this experience (Figure 15-3).

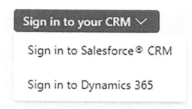

Figure 15-3. *Selecting the CRM of choice, Copilot for Service*

8. In the next step, you will be asked to choose the
    correct environment of Service cloud as shown in
    Figure 15-4. Choose the production, according to
    your organization policies.

Figure 15-4. *Selecting a Salesforce environment*

9. For the login process, Copilot for service will be
    required to launch the Salesforce login screen.
    You will be required to allow the launch of a new
    window (Figure 15-5).

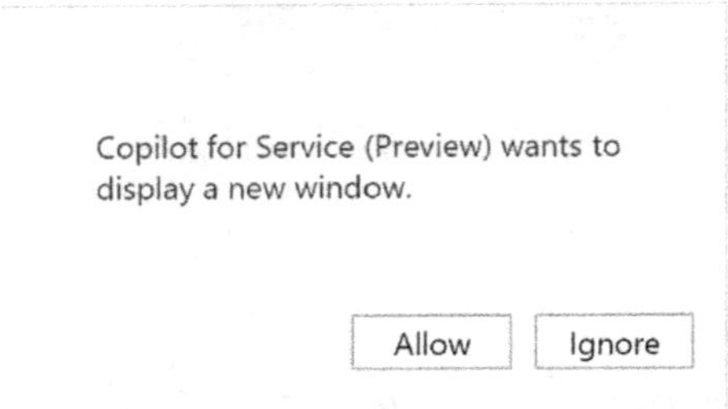

Copilot for Service (Preview) wants to
display a new window.

Allow   Ignore

Figure 15-5. *Allow the login screen launch, Copilot for service*

10. This will take you to the Salesforce login screen;
     provide credentials accordingly (Figure 15-6).

Figure 15-6. *Salesforce login screen*

11. Microsoft will be leveraging the Power Platform
     Salesforce connector to fetch information from
     Service cloud. For that, Power Platform requires
     confirmation for the first time only. Click Allow to
     proceed forward as shown in Figure 15-7. You will
     also require a permission in case you log out or
     change environments of Salesforce.

Figure 15-7. *Power Platform access for Copilot*

12. Lastly, Salesforce requires validation of the access
     provided to the Power Platform connector. Select
     Allow access to proceed (Figure 15-8).

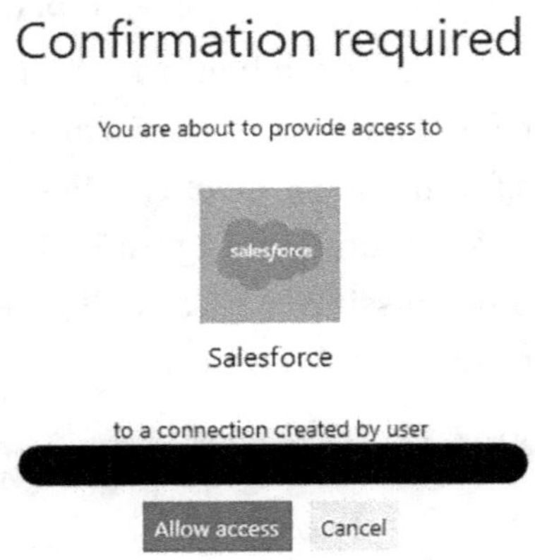

Confirmation required

You are about to provide access to

Salesforce

to a connection created by user

Allow access   Cancel

Figure 15-8. *Connector validation for Copilot*

13. Once completed, you will be able to see the Copilot
    for service information pane filled with related
    information (Figure 15-9).

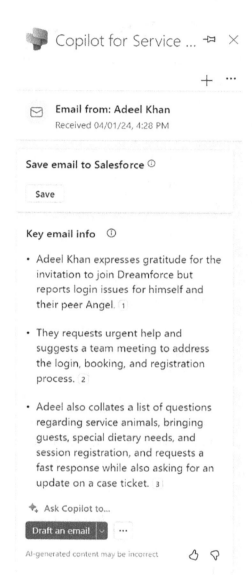

Figure 15-9. *Copilot for service with action card in Outlook*

Your Copilot for service is ready for consumption; we will continue using Copilot for service and learn the features now with ease.

15.1.2 Email Summary with CRM Context

The second experience you are going to learn is to use the key email info feature. The Copilot summary you learned in Part II was generated using content available only in the email (or in an email thread), but with no CRM-related data.

With Copilot for Service, you can now get key email information summarized using AI. It is important to remember that an email with less than 180 words will not be summarized. To experience this feature, you can perform the following actions:

1. Log in to Outlook Office, either through app or browser experience.

2. Select an email of a customer that you wish to review and use for this experiment.

3. Click the Copilot for service (🍃) icon or select the App (▦) icon to open the app list and select the Copilot for Service app.

4. The Copilot for service pane will be launched with identified information. In the example I have used, one of the email contacts is already available at Service Cloud. Copilot for service will identify and provide the key email info (Figure 15-10).

Figure 15-10. *Copilot for service with key email information in Outlook*

5. If you are comfortable with the key email info, you can choose either to save directly in Salesforce, copy the summary, or change the language of summary. Click More actions (⋯) to expand the options (Figure 15-11).

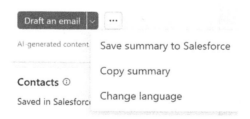

Figure 15-11. *Options with a summary in Copilot for service in Outlook*

6. Select "Save summary to Salesforce" first as shown in Figure 15-11. Copilot for service will display a search form where you can find the relevant object record (Figure 15-12).

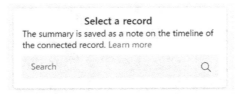

Figure 15-12. *Select an object for the summary to be saved in Salesforce*

7. You can search using account titles, contact names, case subjects, or case numbers (Figure 15-13).

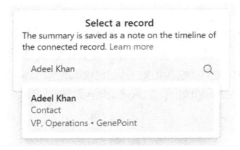

Figure 15-13. *Search results for Salesforce object selection*

8. Click Save (Save) to reflect the changes at Salesforce.

9. Next, click the three dots (⋯) and experience the change language feature. Notice that the Save summary is grayed out as you have already copied the summary at the related object (Figure 15-14).

Figure 15-14. *Grayed out Save summary, Copilot for service Outlook experience*

10. Click "Change language"; this will prompt the user to select the language they need "key info summary" to be prepared. Experiment with a few languages you know and analyze the results (Figure 15-15).

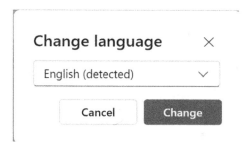

Figure 15-15. *Changing language for the key info summary, Copilot for service in Outlook*

15.1.3 Draft an Email Response with CRM Context

In this section, you will experience generating a draft email response with CRM data. We discussed and experienced Copilot's ability to generate draft responses to emails in Part II; you will now expand the experience with CRM data. This will make your draft more aligned with customer information and activities, personalized with useful information available in CRM such as account information, case information, or knowledge articles. Follow the steps to experience the CRM-based draft response:

1. Log in to Outlook Office, either through app or browser experience.

2. Select an email of a customer that you wish to review and use for this experiment.

3. At the email view, click the Apps (⊞) icon to open the app add-in available and select the Copilot for service (⬤) icon.

4. This will launch Copilot for service with relevant customer information and key email info as experienced in the previous section (Figure 15-16).

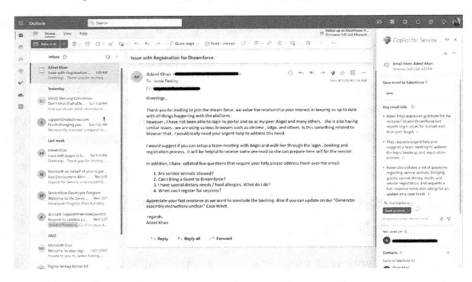

Figure 15-16. *Copilot for service pane with related information*

5. Click Draft an email (Draft an email ▾). You can either provide a custom prompt or choose from any of the default options (Figure 15-17).

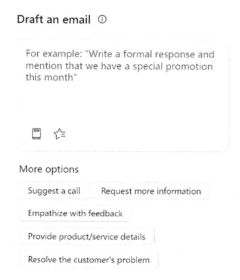

Figure 15-17. *Draft options using the Copilot for service pane*

6. There are several prompts' options available out of the box. They can be very useful to quickly prepare a draft response with specific service-related focus. You can also click the familiar suggestion (⊡) icon to see AI-powered suggestions (Figure 15-18).

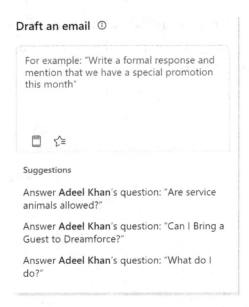

Draft an email ⊙

For example: "Write a formal response and mention that we have a special promotion this month"

Suggestions

Answer **Adeel Khan**'s question: "Are service animals allowed?"

Answer **Adeel Khan**'s question: "Can I Bring a Guest to Dreamforce?"

Answer **Adeel Khan**'s question: "What do I do?"

Figure 15-18. *AI-powered suggestions generated by Copilot for Service*

7. You can choose the "Resolve the customer's problem" option as in the original email the customer has asked several questions and analyzed the results. Copilot will leverage knowledge articles available at Salesforce and draft response (Figure 15-19).

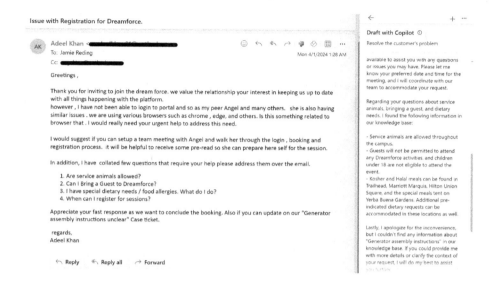

Figure 15-19. *Draft generated using the Copilot for service pane*

8. Analyzing the response, Copilot for service has leveraged Salesforce knowledge articles to find relevant information and prepared a draft response (Figure 15-19).

9. You can further improve the draft response; you can choose Adjust Draft (⚏) to set the additional attributes as shown in Figure 15-20.

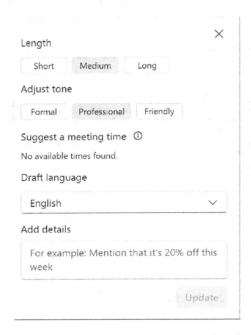

Figure 15-20. Adjust draft attribute using Copilot for Service

10. Play with the options and analyze the changes
    in draft.

11. Once you are satisfied with the draft, click the Copy
    (⧉) icon to copy the draft that can be used to reply
    to the customer email at Outlook.

You can also initiate the Copilot for service powered draft when you
click the Reply or Reply all button:

1. Click the Reply or Reply all button.

2. Notice the Outlook suggestions to use Copilot
   for service for draft response preparation
   (Figure 15-21).

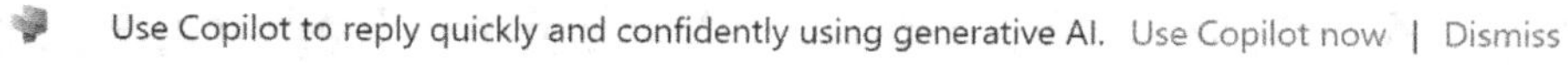

Use Copilot to reply quickly and confidently using generative AI. Use Copilot now | Dismiss

Figure 15-21. *Outlook suggestion to draft response using Copilot for service*

3. This will open the Copilot for service pane where you can use the previously discussed options.

4. With the draft action card, this time you will find the Add to email (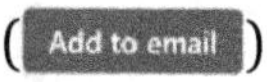 Add to email) option that will directly copy the drafted content to email.

In this exercise, you generated a draft reply using two options. The exercise also discussed various attributes and settings offered for preparing a reply to customers.

To combine best of M365 and Copilot for service, you can apply Coaching by Copilot to further improve the draft reply. Refer to Part II where I have discussed the Coaching feature in detail (Figure 15-22).

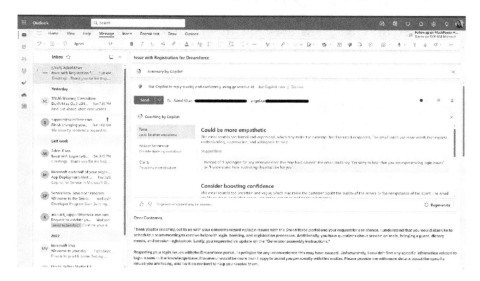

Figure 15-22. *Applying coaching at the final draft created using Copilot for Service*

15.1.4 CRM Actions from Copilot for Service Pane

In this exercise, you will learn about how to perform CRM-related actions from the Copilot for service pane. You will learn how to save the interaction in Salesforce, how to update object information, and how to get a summary of active associated cases in Service Cloud.

Create New Objects

Copilot for service allows users to create a new record. This feature has been recently added to the Copilot for service pane. The objects available for the create feature depend on the settings discussed in Chapter 14, Section 14.1.3. There are two ways to create a record:

1. Log in to Outlook Office, either through app or browser experience.

2. Select an email of a customer that you wish to review and use for this experiment.

3. At the email view, click the Apps (⊞) icon to open the app add-in available and select the Copilot for service (🔵) icon.

4. This will launch the Copilot for service with relevant customer information and key email info.

5. The first way is to create from the top menu. At the top menu, you will find an Add (+) icon. Click the icon (Figure 15-23).

Figure 15-23. *Create new object icon at the menu in Copilot for Service*

6. This will open an object selector. This screen offers an addition of objects that are allowed to be created from the Copilot for service pane through form settings as discussed in Chapter 14, Section 14.1.3. I have set up initially to only allow a contact and case to be added; however, I can also add an account or any custom objects (Figure 15-24).

Choose which type of object to create

Contact   + Create record

Case   Create ∨

Figure 15-24. Choosing the object type for creation in Copilot for Service

7. The Create record will allow the user to create a record from the Copilot pane. If the admin has chosen the record creation to happen at CRM only, the Create in CRM opens up with an object. If the admin has configured both options of creation, the Copilot pane will provide a drop-down with options to choose.

8. This list of objects can be modified through form settings discussed in Chapter 14, Section 14.1.3.

9. Select the create option to launch the create contact
   form. We will cover the creation of contact later in
   the chapter (Figure 15-25).

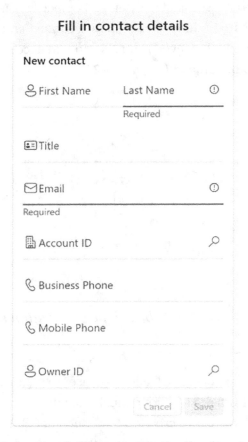

Figure 15-25. New contact form in Copilot for Service

10. The second option is to select the add (+) at the top
    of the action card. Each object enabled with the
    creation feature will have the add option available
    with the associated action card (Figure 15-26).

Figure 15-26. *Add a new contact from the Contacts action card in Copilot for Service*

Add New Contact Details from Suggestions

Sometimes, a new person who has a stake, a say, or an impact on the engagement is brought in through email, and they need to be added to CRM. But it is hard for the user to do such updates in time when they must switch contexts and do it manually. With Copilot for service, you will not only get a suggestion that there is a new contact that is not in Salesforce but also a chance to add them easily, without losing attention or changing the interface.

1. Select a contact from the Contacts action card. This is where you would notice contacts that are already in CRM as well as new contacts introduced through email as shown in Figure 15-27. You can choose to add new contacts directly to Service cloud by choosing "Add to Salesforce."

Figure 15-27. *Adding a new contact in Salesforce from Copilot for Service*

2. Copilot will display a new contact form where you can enter the details of the new contact and save the object to Salesforce (Figure 15-28).

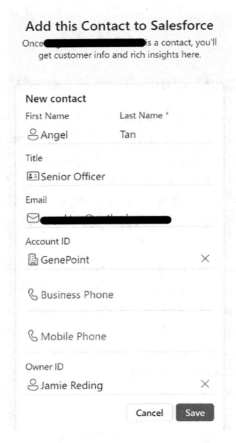

Figure 15-28. *New contact to Salesforce using Copilot for Service*

3. Click Save to reflect the changes to Salesforce.

This feature allows you to capture the new stakeholders' information with ease, without losing context or focus; users can now add new stakeholders in Service Cloud with ease.

Update Contact Details

Contacts need to have accurate and current information in Salesforce. Copilot for service lets users update their contact details right from Outlook, without any hassle, following an easy process. You can experience the same using the following steps:

1. Click Contact that is saved in Salesforce to open the Contact view.

2. You can add private notes to contacts that are saved only at Copilot for Service (Figure 15-29).

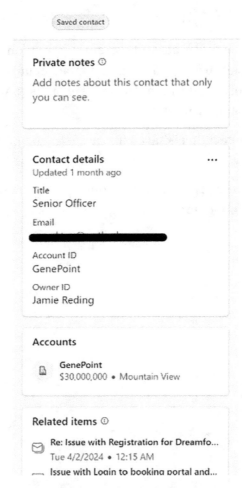

Figure 15-29. *Contact information with private notes with Salesforce information*

3. Note that you do not have to save the private notes; they will be automatically saved.

4. Review the contact's related account and related items to familiarize yourself with the contact information. Click More actions (⋯) and select "Edit Object" to perform editing actions and Update (Update) to reflect changes.

Add New Case

Using the Copilot for service pane, you can now add a case directly to Service cloud and initiate the workflow associated with new case creation. To experience this feature, you can follow these steps:

1. Log in to Outlook Office, either through app or browser experience.

2. Select an email of a customer that you wish to review and use for this experiment.

3. At the email view, click the Apps (▦) icon to open the app add-in available and select the Copilot for service (🐟) icon.

4. This will launch Copilot for service with relevant customer information and key email info.

5. The first way is to create from the top menu. At the top menu, you will find an Add (+) icon. Click the icon (Figure 15-30).

Figure 15-30. *Create a new object from Copilot for Service*

6.   This will open an object selector. This screen
currently offers an addition of objects that are
allowed to be created from the Copilot for service
pane (Figure 15-31).

Figure 15-31. *Choosing the object type for creation in Copilot
for Service*

7.   Notice that Case create has multiple options as
during the setup, we selected an option to either add
a case from the pane or get a link to create a case in
CRM (Figure 15-32).

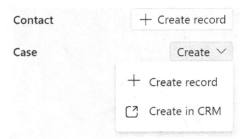

Figure 15-32. *Case creation options at Copilot for service*

8. This allows the user to have multiple options
    suitable in the business settings.

9. The Create record option will open the case form,
    allowing the user to provide relevant information
    (Figure 15-33).

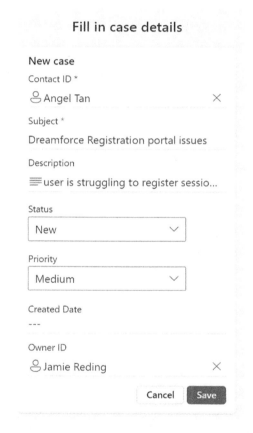

Figure 15-33. Case creation from Copilot for service

10. Click Save (Save) to create a case at service cloud.

11. At the creation of case, the Copilot for service pane will display the case summary view with the new case ticket ID and other information (Figure 15-34).

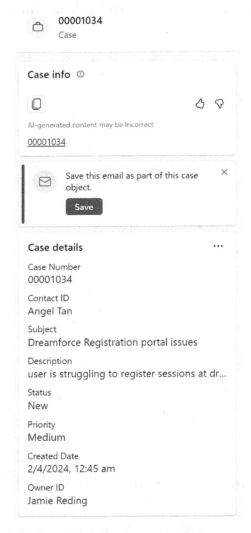

Figure 15-34. *Case created at Service cloud*

12. Notice the suggestion to save the email associated
with this case. We will discuss this feature later in
the section.

Manage Account Details

Users can manage accounts such as edit the information of existing ones
or add new using Copilot for Service. This smooth integration not only
improves data quality but also makes it easy for users to perform such
actions frequently.

1. To add a new account, click the Add icon at the main
view of Copilot for service.

2. The remaining experience is similar to what has
been discussed in the "Create New Objects" section.

3. Once the new account is added, you can update the
details as well.

4. Select the Account action card in Copilot for service
and click Object. This will expand the account view
in Copilot for Service. You can view the account
information with default fields (Figure 15-35).

Figure 15-35. *Account view in Copilot for service with Service Cloud information*

5. Click More actions (⋯) and select Edit object
   (∕ Edit object) to edit the information of the account.
   Notice that only fields set editable during form
   settings are allowed to change (Figure 15-36).

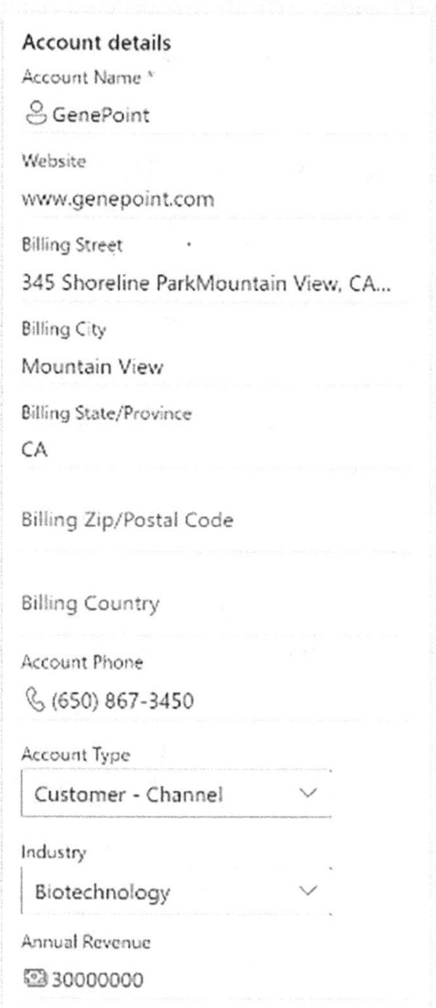

Account details

Account Name *

  ⊖ GenePoint

Website

www.genepoint.com

Billing Street   ·

345 Shoreline ParkMountain View, CA...

Billing City

Mountain View

Billing State/Province

CA

Billing Zip/Postal Code

Billing Country

Account Phone

  📞 (650) 867-3450

Account Type

Customer - Channel   ∨

Industry

Biotechnology   ∨

Annual Revenue

  📷 30000000

Figure 15-36. *Editing the account information in Salesforce from Copilot for Service*

6. Once changes are made, you can select Update 
   (Update) to reflect the changes.

These changes will reflect in real time to Service Cloud, making it easier for you to maintain the latest changes at Salesforce without leaving Outlook.

Save Outlook Activities to Salesforce

Using Copilot for service, you can easily save Outlook activities to service cloud. We will begin by learning to save an email, followed by learning to save a meeting. This feature allows you to reduce operational overhead of manually adding an activity in Service Cloud.

1. Log in to Outlook Office, either through app or browser experience.

2. Select an email of a customer that you wish to review and use for this experiment.

3. At the email view, click the Apps (⊞) icon to open the app add-in available and select the Copilot for service (🔵) icon.

4. This will launch Copilot for service with relevant customer information and key email info.

5. You can save the customer email from the Copilot for Service pane to Salesforce. Select the Save (Save) button at the pane (Figure 15-37).

Figure 15-37. *Save email to Salesforce from Copilot for Service*

6. Copilot for service will list the objects where you may want to connect the email. It will list the accounts, where you can also save without connecting to an object (Figure 15-38).

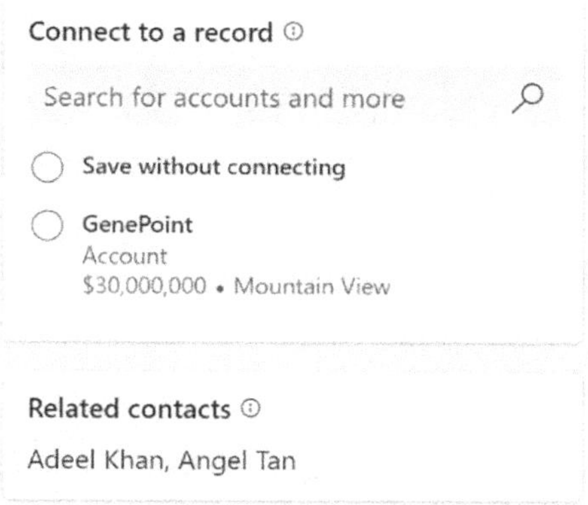

Connect to a record ⊙

Search for accounts and more   🔎

○ Save without connecting

○ GenePoint
  Account
  $30,000,000 • Mountain View

Related contacts ⊙

Adeel Khan, Angel Tan

Figure 15-38. *Save an email with a connected object in Salesforce*

7. If you don't find a relevant object listed, you can search for the account or case using the search bar (Figure 15-39).

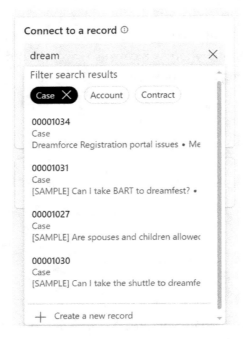

Figure 15-39. *Searching in objects added to Copilot for service*

8. Notice in the list, each object included in the form
    settings will be available to search and connect
    an email.

9. Select the relevant object; I have selected the Case
    Object and choose to click Save to reflect changes
    (Figure 15-40).

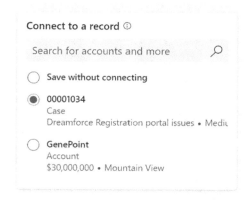

Figure 15-40. *Connecting an email with a case*

10. You will notice a confirmation email being saved
    with the Saved tag (Figure 15-41).

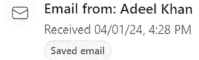

Figure 15-41. *Saved email tag after saving email in Salesforce*

11. Also, the main Copilot view will display the case
    summary action card (Figure 15-42).

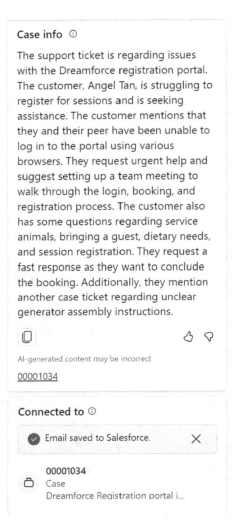

Case info ⓘ

The support ticket is regarding issues
with the Dreamforce registration portal.
The customer, Angel Tan, is struggling to
register for sessions and is seeking
assistance. The customer mentions that
they and their peer have been unable to
log in to the portal using various
browsers. They request urgent help and
suggest setting up a team meeting to
walk through the login, booking, and
registration process. The customer also
has some questions regarding service
animals, bringing a guest, dietary needs,
and session registration. They request a
fast response as they want to conclude
the booking. Additionally, they mention
another case ticket regarding unclear
generator assembly instructions.

AI-generated content may be incorrect

00001034

Connected to ⓘ

Email saved to Salesforce.   ✕

00001034
Case
Dreamforce Registration portal i...

Figure 15-42. *Case summary of the connected case with email*

You can also save and connect the email by clicking any of the relevant
records in the action card. To use this option, follow these steps:

1. In the Copilot of Service pane, choose Account and click the More actions (···) icon as shown in Figure 15-43.

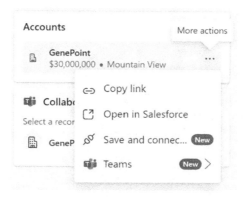

Figure 15-43. *Save and connect from Copilot for service action cards*

2. This will reduce the number of clicks we performed and further improve user experience.

The other Outlook activity critical in customer engagements is meetings. To save meeting activities in Service cloud, change your view to calendars (▦) at Outlook and choose an available time slot for the meeting. Once selected, follow these steps to learn the feature:

1. Open a new event in the Outlook calendar.

2. Fill in the required information, such as meeting title, date, and time, physical or virtual with the team's link and description of the meeting (Figure 15-44).

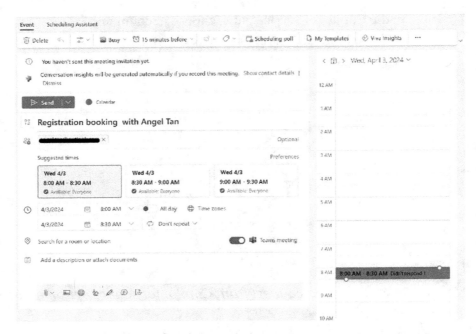

Figure 15-44. *Setting meeting details before adding Copilot for Service*

3. Invite the attendees; please be careful when adding an attendees as you need to send the meeting invite before being able to save. It is recommended to take precautions and add attendees wisely.

4. Click More actions (⋯) and choose Copilot for service (🖼) from the add-ins drop-down.

5. The rest of the experience of saving the meeting is like saving the email.

6. Carefully review the content, especially the contact details to whom you are sending the meeting request.

546

7. Once sent, you will find similar information as experienced in the email scenario (Figure 15-45).

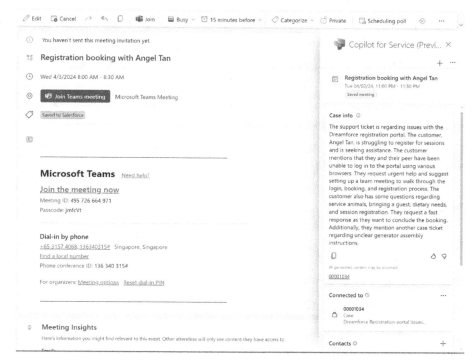

Figure 15-45. *Meeting activity saved in Service cloud*

15.1.5 Teams with Copilot for Service

The integration between Copilot for service and Microsoft Teams allows you to leverage teams' collaborative excellence to be infused in service processes and help accelerate deals with easy collaboration. In this section, you will explore and learn how you can use Copilot for service with MS Teams. We will begin with in-pane experience that is called Collaboration Space and later explore the features available during teams' meetings.

Collaboration Space

Microsoft Copilot for service Collaboration Space provides an out-of-the-box environment for service collaboration that's built on Microsoft Teams. The feature provides an out-of-the-box template to set up an account team and reduce the overhead for versatile personas coming together to achieve impressive results.

The account team template is designed for effective collaboration among account teams and with customers. When a team uses it and connects it to a Salesforce account, the template provides an ideal space to cooperate with account team members and customers.

There are several ways you can apply this template; you can experience them by following these steps:

1. Log in to Outlook Office, either through app or browser experience.

2. Select an email of a customer that you wish to review and use for this experiment.

3. At the email view, click the Apps (▦) icon to open the app add-in available and select the Copilot for service (⬤) icon.

4. This will launch Copilot for service with relevant customer information and key email info.

5. Browse below to find the Collaboration Space action card. The card contains already connected teams' channel as well as templates for you to set up. If you are setting up for the first time, you will only notice the templates as shown in Figure 15-46.

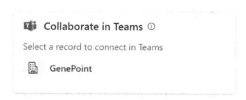

Figure 15-46. *Collaboration Space action card with an account name*

6. Hover your mouse over the account name (in this case, GenePoint) to activate the account template (Figure 15-47).

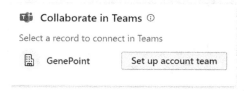

Figure 15-47. *Set up an account team with the Salesforce account using Copilot for Service*

7. Click "Set up account team" to start finalizing the template settings.

8. Follow the guided steps to create the account team. If you need a step-by-step guide, please refer to Chapter 12, Section 12.1.6.

During Teams Meeting

You can use Microsoft Copilot for service during the virtual meetings with customers or peers in MS Teams. This feature allows you to interact with customers and refer or reflect the latest CRM information. To be able to use Copilot for service, you need to have the transcription on as required by Copilot for Teams as well. Let's follow these steps to learn about the feature:

1. Open Microsoft Teams as an app or browser experience.

2. Open the previously organized meeting where you have added Copilot for Service.

3. Recall the steps defined in Section 15.1.4 under "Save Outlook Activities to Salesforce." Meetings like that can be ready for Copilot for service usage during the meeting.

4. When the meeting is in flight, click the Copilot for service (⬛) icon to open the Copilot for service pane as shown in Figure 15-48.

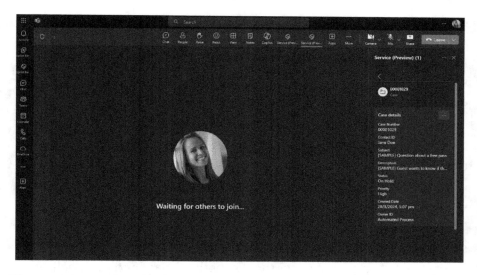

Figure 15-48. *Copilot for service with real-time highlight and Salesforce tab*

5. This will showcase the related object information during the meeting that you can view and update as required.

6. All changes made will reflect immediately to the service cloud.

7. You can also leverage Copilot to transcript and generate meeting minutes using M365 Copilot features.

At the time of writing this book, Copilot for service is in preview mode and expected to have a lot more features coming in the near future.

15.2 Summary

In this chapter, we explored the integration of Microsoft Copilot with Salesforce's Service Cloud, offering a comprehensive guide for enhancing service experiences through the power of generative AI.

The chapter also covered Copilot for Service experience, detailing the seamless login process and the innovative features accessible from Outlook and Teams interfaces. The chapter deep dived into the user experience, highlighting the ease of accessing Copilot's functionalities within the familiar Microsoft ecosystem.

The chapter extensively covered how Copilot for Service can summarize key email information with CRM context, enhancing the user's ability to draft email responses that are both relevant and personalized. The chapter also discussed actions that user can perform through Copilot for service pane.

Furthermore, the chapter covered the Teams integration, which facilitates collaboration and accelerates service processes through Microsoft Teams. The Collaboration Space feature was introduced, providing a template for setting up account teams and enhancing cooperation with customers.

The next chapter will discuss Copilot for service experience with Dynamics 365 Customer Service that offers in-app CRM experience along with Copilot for service experience in Outlook and Teams.

CHAPTER 16

Microsoft Copilot for Service with Dynamics 365 Customer Service

Dynamics 365 Customer Service is a leading customer relationship management (CRM) platform that bridges the gap between businesses and customers. As we mentioned before in Copilot for Service, it's an integrated CRM platform that enables all your organization's different departments, such as marketing, sales, commerce, and service, to operate, connect, and communicate with customers effectively and with a common, shared understanding of customer needs and aspirations.

Dynamics 365 is one of the main modules in Dynamics 365 first-party modules. It is a module that helps the service ecosystem of an organization to manage and organize service-related processes with many features and capabilities that are helping the organization to deal with customer interactions. The prime objective of the module is to simplify the customer support and service journey and optimize operational efficiency in solving customer problems.

© Adeel Khan 2024
A. Khan, *Introducing Microsoft Copilot for Managers*, Inside Copilot,
https://doi.org/10.1007/979-8-8688-0419-9_16

This chapter will demonstrate and discuss how to use Copilot for service with the Dynamics 365 module. As the chapter's focus is on Copilot features, it is assumed that you are familiar with Outlook, Teams, and the essential Dynamics 365 Customer Service module. It is helpful to understand the fundamental principles of service engagements and the Dynamics 365 features before you proceed with this chapter. Leverage great documentation and learning paths available at the Microsoft Learn site to familiarize yourself with the Dynamics 365 module if you are new to the subject (`https://learn.microsoft.com/en-us/training/dynamics365/customer-service`).

Also, if you are new to the Copilot concept, I recommend that you read Chapter 1 and Part II of this book to have a better understanding and appreciation of the features.

Lastly, the features discussed in this chapter are not enabled out of the box and require administrative actions and approvals. Please review and complete the setup requirements discussed in Chapter 14.

16.1 Copilot for Service Experience

This section will discuss how Copilot for Service can help Dynamics 365 Customer Service users enhance their interactions and customer engagements. In this section, you will learn about the various features and options that are available from the familiar interface of Outlook and Teams, enabling you to access information about customers and relationships with ease.

We will start our journey from the first login experience and explore the various features that are available at the time of authoring this book.

16.1.1 First Login

In the first exercise, you are going to log in to Copilot for service from an Outlook experience. For this chapter, I have signed up a developer access to Dynamics 365 Customer Service. You can either sign up for a developer account or use your own organization's Dynamics 365 Customer Service account.

The following are the step-by-step guide to try your first Copilot for service experience:

1. Log in to Outlook Office, either through app or browser experience.

2. Confirm the settings mentioned in the previous chapter, Section 14.1.3, for Dynamics 365.

3. Select an email of a customer or a sample email that you wish to review and use for this experience.

4. At the email view, click the Apps (▦) icon to open the app add-in available (Figure 16-1).

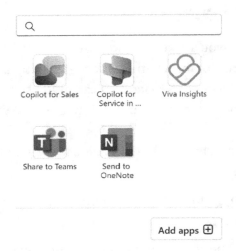

Figure 16-1. *List of apps available at Outlook*

5. Please note that the list can be different based on
    your setup; however, you will need Copilot for
    service (🟦) for the next steps.

6. Click the Copilot for service (🟦) icon to launch the
    Copilot side pane (Figure 16-2).

Figure 16-2. *Copilot for service side pane in Outlook*

7. Click the "Sign in to your CRM" and select Dynamics
365 for this experience as shown in Figure 16-3.

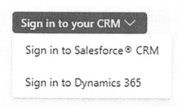

Figure 16-3. *Selecting the CRM of choice, Copilot for Service*

8. In the next step, you will be asked to choose the
    correct environment of Dynamics 365. You will see
    the list of all environments available to your profile.
    Select the environment where you have customer
    service–related security roles assigned (Figure 16-4).

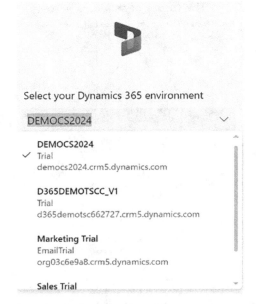

Figure 16-4. *Selecting a Dynamics 365 environment*

9. Once selected, click Get started (Get started) to begin
    the login process. D365 leverages a single sign-on
    method, meaning your tenant ID credentials will be
    used, and based on the organization setup, you will
    be logged in to the D365 environment.

10. You will see a Copilot for service pane loaded
    with various action cards and actions as shown
    in Figure 16-5. One of the action cards should

automatically display "key email info" that is key
highlights summarized from the email or email
thread. If you don't see the key info action cards,
there can be two reasons discussed as follows.

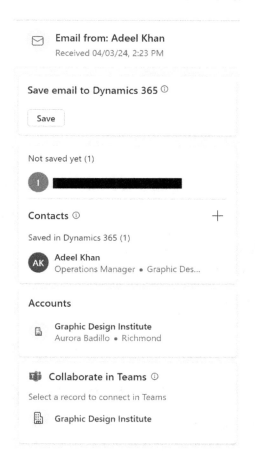

Figure 16-5. *Copilot for Service pane without key email info*

11. First, ensure that your admin has enabled
the Copilot feature at the environment level
as discussed in Chapter 14, Section 14.1.3
(Figure 16-6).

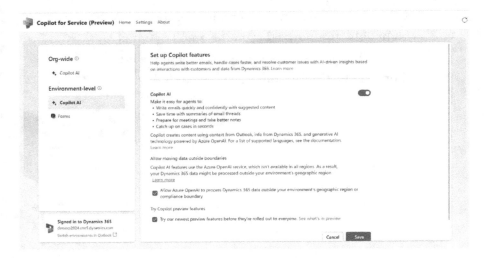

Figure 16-6. *Environment-level Copilot feature enablement*

12. Second, the email content and thread word count
    are less than 180 words. Copilot will not use the key
    email info for emails shorter than 180 words.

Once verified, your Copilot for service is ready for consumption;
we will continue using Copilot for service and learn the features now
with ease.

16.1.2 Email Summary with CRM Context

The second experience you are going to learn is to use the key email info
feature. The Copilot summary you learned in Part II was generated using
content available only in an email (or in an email thread), but with no
CRM-related data. With Copilot for Service, you can now get key email
information summarized using AI. It is important to remember that an

email with less than 180 words will not be summarized. To experience this
feature, you can perform the following actions:

1.   Log in to Outlook Office, either through app or
     browser experience.

2.   Select an email of a customer that you wish to
     review and use for this experiment.

3.   Click the Copilot for service ( ) icon or select the
     App ( ) icon to open the app list and select the
     Copilot for Service app.

4.   The Copilot for service pane will be launched with
     identified information. In the example I have used,
     one of the email contacts is already available at
     Dynamics 365. Copilot for service will identify and
     provide key email info (Figure 16-7).

Figure 16-7. *Copilot for service with key email information*
in Outlook

5. If you are comfortable with key email info, you can
    choose either to save directly in Dynamics 365
    Customer Service, copy the summary, or change the
    language of summary. Click More actions (⋯) to
    expand the options (Figure 16-8).

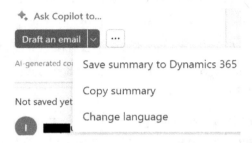

Figure 16-8. *Options with summary in Copilot for service in Outlook*

6. Select "Save Summary to Dynamics 365" first.
    Copilot for service will display a search form
    where you can find the relevant record as shown in
    Figure 16-9.

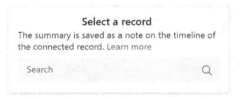

Figure 16-9. *Select record for summary to be saved in Dynamics 365*

7. You can search using account titles, contact names,
    case subject, or case number (Figure 16-10).

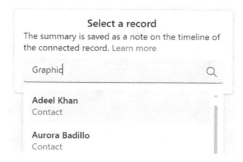

Figure 16-10. *Search results for Dynamics 365 record selection*

8. Click Save (Save) to reflect the changes at
    Dynamics 365 Customer Service.

9. Next, click the three dots (⋯) and experience the
    change language feature. Notice that the save
    summary is grayed out as you have already copied
    the summary at the related record (Figure 16-11).

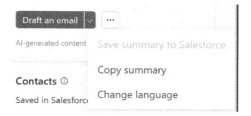

Figure 16-11. *Grayed out save summary, Copilot for service Outlook*
experience

10. Click "Change language"; this will prompt the
    user to select the language they need the "key
    info summary" to be prepared. Experiment with
    a few languages you know and analyze the results
    (Figure 16-12).

Figure 16-12. Changing language for the key info summary, Copilot for service in Outlook

16.1.3 Draft an Email Response with CRM Context

In this section, you will experience generating a draft email response with CRM data. We discussed and experienced Copilot's ability to generate draft responses to emails in Part II; you will now expand the experience with CRM data. This will make your draft more aligned with customer information and activities, personalized with useful information available in CRM, such as account information, case information, and knowledge articles. Follow the steps to experience the CRM-based draft response:

1. Log in to Outlook Office, either through app or browser experience.

2. Select an email of a customer that you wish to review and use for this experiment.

3. At the email view, click the Apps (▦) icon to open the app add-in available and select the Copilot for service (🌑) icon.

4. This will launch the Copilot for service with relevant customer information and key email info as experienced in the previous section (Figure 16-13).

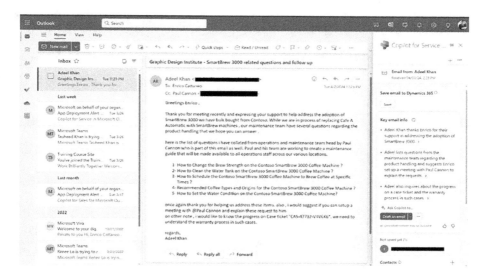

Figure 16-13. *Copilot for service pane with related information*

5. Click Draft an email (Draft an email ⌄). You can either
    provide a custom prompt or choose from any of the
    default options (Figure 16-14).

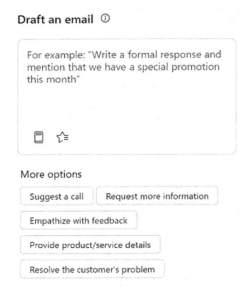

Figure 16-14. *Draft option using the Copilot for service pane*

6. There are several prompts' options available out of
    the box. They can be extremely useful to quickly
    prepare a draft response with specific service-
    related focus. You can also click the familiar
    suggestion (⬚) icon to see AI-powered suggestions
    as shown in Figure 16-15.

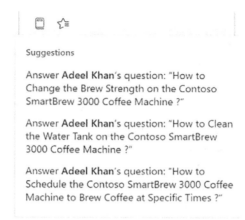

Figure 16-15. *AI-powered suggestions generated by Copilot for Service*

7. You can choose the "Resolve the customer's
    problem" option as in the original email the
    customer has asked several questions first
    and analyzed the results. Copilot will leverage
    knowledge articles available at Dynamics 365 and
    draft response (Figure 16-16).

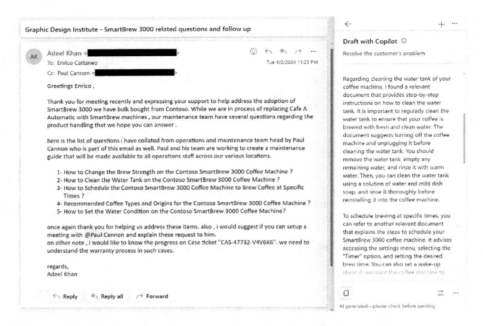

Figure 16-16. *Draft generated using the Copilot for service pane*

8.   Analyzing the response, in my scenario, Copilot for
     service leveraged Dynamics 365 knowledge articles
     to find relevant information and prepared a draft
     response. The responses were well drafted but still
     needed review and updates.

9.   You can further improve the draft response; you can
     choose Adjust Draft (☲) to set the additional
     attributes (Figure 16-17).

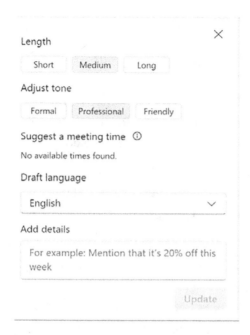

Figure 16-17. *Adjust draft attribute using Copilot for Service*

10. Play with the options and analyze the changes in draft.

11. Once you are satisfied with the draft, click the Copy (⬚) icon to copy the draft that can be used to reply to the customer email at Outlook.

You can also initiate the Copilot for service powered email draft when you click the Reply or Reply all button:

1. Click the Reply or reply all button.

2. Notice the Outlook suggestions to use Copilot for service for draft response preparation (Figure 16-18).

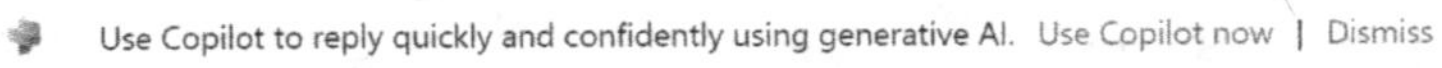

Use Copilot to reply quickly and confidently using generative AI. Use Copilot now | Dismiss

Figure 16-18. *Outlook suggestion to draft response using Copilot for service*

3. This will open the Copilot for service pane where you can use the previously discussed options.

4. With the draft action card, this time you will find the Add to email (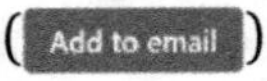 Add to email) option that will directly copy the drafted content to email.

In this exercise, you generated a draft reply using two options. The exercise also discussed various attributes and settings offered for preparing a reply to customers.

To combine best of M365 and Copilot for service, you can apply Coaching by Copilot to further improve the draft reply. Refer to Part II where I have discussed the Coaching feature (Figure 16-19).

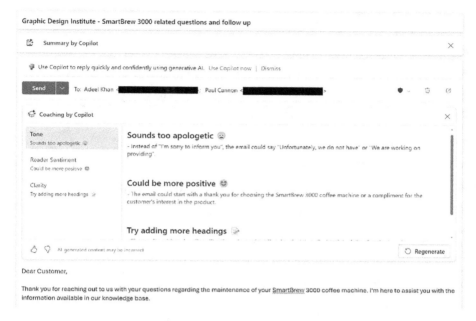

Figure 16-19. *Applying coaching at the final draft created using Copilot for Service*

16.1.4 CRM Actions from the Copilot for Service Pane

In this exercise, you will learn about how to perform CRM-related actions from the Copilot for service pane. You will learn how to save the interaction in Dynamics 365, how to update record information, and how to get a summary of active associated cases.

Create New Records

Copilot for service allows users to create a new record. This feature has been recently added to the Copilot for service pane. The tables available for the create feature depend on the settings discussed in Chapter 14, Section 14.1.3. There are two ways to create a record:

1. Log in to Outlook Office, either through app or browser experience.

2. Select an email of a customer that you wish to review and use for this experiment.

3. At the email view, click the Apps (⊞) icon to open the app add-in available and select the Copilot for service (🔧) icon.

4. This will launch the Copilot for service with relevant customer information and key email info.

5. The first way is to create from the top menu. At the top menu, you will find an Add (＋) icon. Click the icon (Figure 16-20).

Figure 16-20. *Create a new record icon at the menu in Copilot for Service*

6. This will open a record selector. This screen currently lists tables where creation from the Copilot for service pane is allowed. Each of the table records offers different types of creation option (Figure 16-21).

572

Choose which type of record to create

Figure 16-21. *Choosing the record type for creation in Copilot for Service*

7. The Create record will allow the user to create a record from the Copilot pane; the Create in CRM opens a CRM form in the browser to add the record. If the user has configured both options of creation, the Copilot pane will provide a drop-down with options to choose from (Figure 16-22).

Figure 16-22. *Option to choose creation experience in Copilot for service*

8. This list of record types can be modified
    through form settings discussed in Chapter 14,
    Section 14.1.3.

9. Select the create option to launch the create contact
    form. We will cover the creation of contact later in
    the chapter (Figure 16-23).

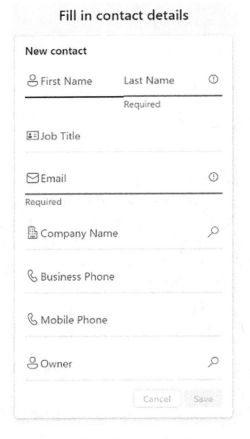

Figure 16-23. *New contact form in Copilot for Service*

10. The second option is to select the add (+) at the top of the action card. Each table enabled with the creation feature will have the add option available with the associated action card (Figure 16-24).

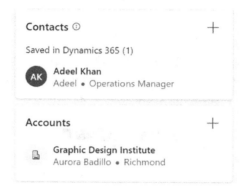

Figure 16-24. *Add a new record from action cards in Copilot for Service*

Add New Contact Details from Suggestions

Occasionally, a new contact who is involved or introduced in the engagement joins the email thread, and for better coverage they need to be captured at CRM. But it is difficult for the user to make such changes promptly when they must switch contexts. With Copilot for service, you will get not only a recommendation that there is a new contact that is missing from Dynamics 365 but also an opportunity to add them quickly, without breaking the focus or changing interface.

1. Select a contact from the Contacts action card. This is where you would notice contacts that are already in CRM as well as new contacts introduced through email. You can choose to add new contacts directly to Dynamics 365 by choosing "Add to Dynamics 365" (Figure 16-25).

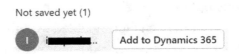

Figure 16-25. *Adding a new contact in Dynamics 365 from Copilot for Service*

2. Copilot will display a new contact form where you can enter the details and save the record to Dynamics 365 (Figure 16-26).

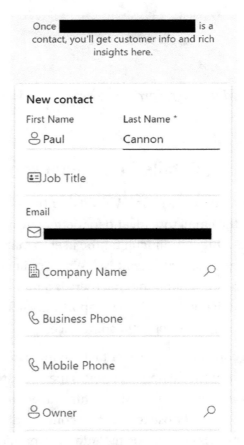

Figure 16-26. *New contact to Dynamics 365 using Copilot for Service*

   3.   Click Save to reflect the changes to Dynamics 365.

With this feature, you can easily enter the information of new stakeholders without getting distracted. You can now create new stakeholders in Dynamics 365 with no trouble.

Update Contact Details

Having up-to-date and correct information for contacts in Dynamics 365 Customer Service is important. Copilot for service enables the user to change their contact details directly from Outlook with a simple process. You can try it out using these steps:

   1.   Click Contact that is saved in Dynamics 365 to open the Contact view.

   2.   You can add private notes to contacts that are saved only at Copilot for Service (Figure 16-27).

Figure 16-27. *Contact information with private notes with Dynamics 365 information*

3. Note that you do not have to save the private notes, they will be automatically saved.

4. Review the contact's related account and related
    items to familiarize yourself with contact
    information. Click More actions (⋯) and select "Edit
    Record" to perform editing actions and Update
    (Update) to reflect changes (Figure 16-28).

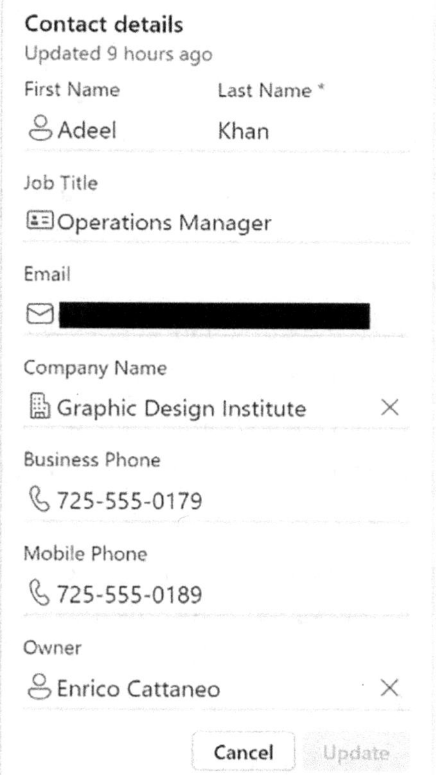

Contact details
Updated 9 hours ago

First Name   Last Name *

👤 Adeel   Khan

Job Title

📇 Operations Manager

Email

✉ ████████████████████

Company Name

🏢 Graphic Design Institute   ✕

Business Phone

📞 725-555-0179

Mobile Phone

📞 725-555-0189

Owner

👤 Enrico Cattaneo   ✕

Cancel   Update

Figure 16-28. *Edit contact details in Dynamics 365 using Copilot*
for Service

Add New Case

Using the Copilot for service pane, you can now add a case directly to Dynamics 365 and initiate the workflow associated with new case creation. To experience this feature, you can follow these steps:

1. Log in to Outlook Office, either through app or browser experience.

2. Select an email of a customer that you wish to review and use for this experiment.

3. At the email view, click the Apps (⊞) icon to open the app add-in available and select the Copilot for service (⬤) icon.

4. This will launch the Copilot for service with relevant customer information and key email info.

5. The first way is to create from the top menu. At the top menu, you will find an Add (+) icon. Click the icon.

6. This will open a record selector. This screen currently offers addition of records that are allowed to be created from the Copilot for service pane (Figure 16-29).

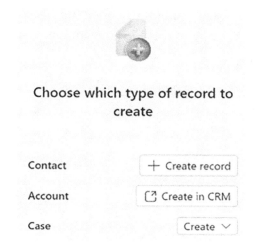

Figure 16-29. *Choosing the record type for creation in Copilot for Service*

7.   Notice that Case create has multiple options as
      during the setup, we selected an option to either add
      a case from the pane or get a link to create a case in
      CRM (Figure 16-30).

Figure 16-30. *Case creation options at Copilot for service*

8.   This allows the user to have multiple options
      suitable in the business settings.

9. The create record option will open the case form, allowing the user to provide relevant information (Figure 16-31).

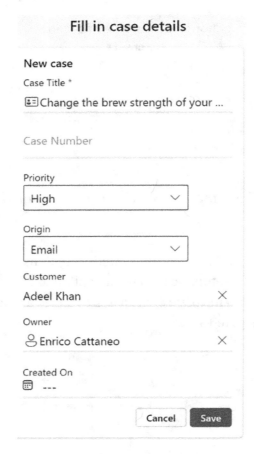

Figure 16-31. *Case creation from Copilot for service*

10. Click Save (Save) to create a case at Dynamics 365 as shown in Figure 16-31.

11. At the creation of case, the Copilot for service pane
     will display the case summary view with the new
     case ticket ID and other information (Figure 16-32).

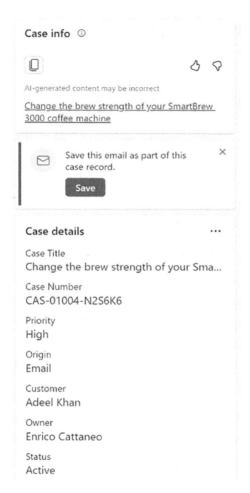

Figure 16-32. *Case created at Dynamics 365*

12. Notice the suggestion to save the email associated
     with this case. We will discuss this feature later in
     the section.

13. Also, the case info action card does not have a summary as we don't have much information about the ticket available at this point.

Manage Account Details

Users can manage accounts such as edit the information of existing ones or add new using Copilot for Service. This smooth integration not only improves data quality but also makes it easy for users to perform such actions frequently.

1. To add a new account, click the Add icon at the main view of Copilot for service.

2. The remaining experience is similar to what has been discussed in the "Create New Records" section.

3. Once the new account is added, you can update the details as well.

4. Select the Account action card in Copilot for service and click Record. This will expand the account view in Copilot for Service. You can view account information with default fields (Figure 16-33).

Figure 16-33. *Account view in Copilot for service with Dynamics 365 information*

5.   Click More actions (⋯) and select Edit record

(✎ Edit record) to edit the information of the account.

Notice that only fields set editable during form

settings are allowed for change.

6. Once changes are made, you can select Update
    (Update) to reflect the changes.

These changes will reflect real time on Dynamics 365, making it easier
for you to maintain latest changes at Dynamics 365 Customer Service
without leaving Outlook.

Save Outlook Activities to Dynamics 365 Customer Service

Using Copilot for service, you can easily save Outlook activities to
Dynamics 365. We will begin by learning to save an email, followed by
learning to save a meeting. This feature allows you to reduce operational
overhead of manually adding an activity in Dynamics 365.

1. Log in to Outlook Office, either through app or
    browser experience.

2. Select an email of a customer that you wish to
    review and use for this experiment.

3. At the email view, click the Apps (⊞) icon to open
    the app add-in available and select the Copilot for
    service (●) icon.

4. This will launch Copilot for service with relevant
    customer information and key email info.

5. You can save the customer email from the Copilot
    for Service pane to Dynamics 365 Customer Service.
    Select the Save (Save) button at the pane
    (Figure 16-34).

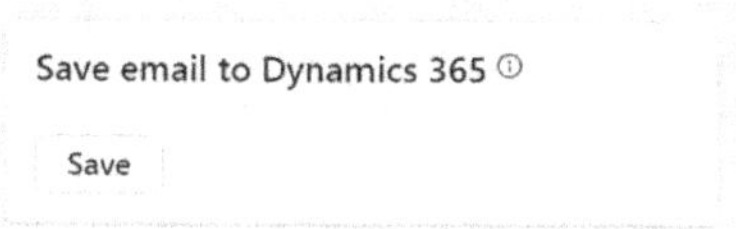

Save email to Dynamics 365 ⓘ

Save

Figure 16-34. *Save email to Dynamics 365 Customer Service from Copilot for Service*

6. Copilot for service will list the records where you may want to connect the email. It will list the accounts, where you can also save without connecting to a record (Figure 16-35).

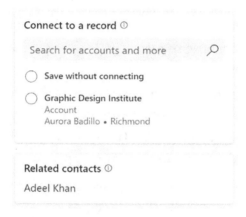

Figure 16-35. *Save email with a connected record in Dynamics 365 Customer Service*

7. If you don't find a relevant record listed, you can search for the account or case using the search bar (Figure 16-36).

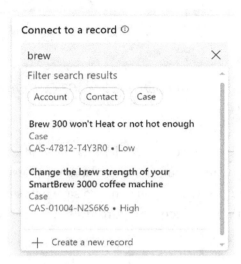

Figure 16-36. *Searching in records added to Copilot for service*

8. You can also initiate to create a new record by selecting the Create new (+ Create a new record) option as shown in Figure 16-36. This will take you through the experience we discussed in the previous section.

9. Notice in the preceding list, each record included in the form settings will be available to search and connect an email.

10. Select the relevant record, I have selected the Case Record, and click save to reflect changes (Figure 16-37).

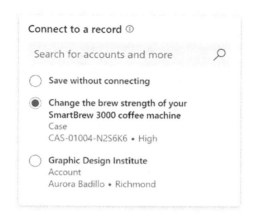

Figure 16-37. *Connecting email with a case*

11.   You will notice a confirmation email being saved
with the Saved tag (Figure 16-38).

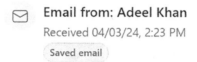

Figure 16-38. *Saved email tag after saving email in Dynamics 365
Customer Service*

12.   Also, the main Copilot view will display the case
summary action card as well as the connected to
action card (Figure 16-39).

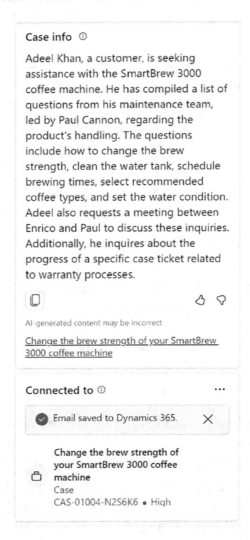

Case info ⓘ

Adeel Khan, a customer, is seeking assistance with the SmartBrew 3000 coffee machine. He has compiled a list of questions from his maintenance team, led by Paul Cannon, regarding the product's handling. The questions include how to change the brew strength, clean the water tank, schedule brewing times, select recommended coffee types, and set the water condition. Adeel also requests a meeting between Enrico and Paul to discuss these inquiries. Additionally, he inquires about the progress of a specific case ticket related to warranty processes.

AI-generated content may be incorrect

Change the brew strength of your SmartBrew 3000 coffee machine

Connected to ⓘ   ...

✓ Email saved to Dynamics 365.   ✕

Change the brew strength of your SmartBrew 3000 coffee machine
Case
CAS-01004-N2S6K6 • High

Figure 16-39. *Case summary of the connected case with an email*

You can also save and connect the email by clicking any of the relevant record in the action card. To use this option, follow these steps:

1. In the Copilot of Service pane, choose an account and click the More actions (⋯) icon (Figure 16-40).

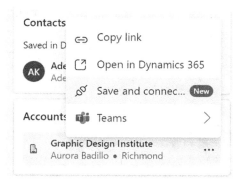

Figure 16-40. *Save and connect from Copilot for service action cards*

2. This will reduce the number of clicks we performed and further improve user experience.

The other Outlook activity critical in customer engagements is meetings. To save meeting activities in Dynamics 365, change your view to calendars (▦) at Outlook and choose an available time slot for a meeting. Once selected, follow these steps to learn the feature:

1. Open a new event in the Outlook calendar.

2. Fill in the required information, such as meeting title, date, and time, physical or virtual with the team's link and description of the meeting.

3. Invite the attendees; please be careful when adding an attendees as you need to send the meeting invite before being able to save. It is recommended to take precautions and add attendees wisely.

4. Click More actions (⋯) and choose Copilot for service (🌸) from the add-ins drop-down.

5. The rest of the experience of saving the meeting is like saving the email where you will be provided with an option to save the meeting in Dynamics 365 (Figure 16-41).

Save meeting to Dynamics 365 ⊙

Save

Figure 16-41. *Save meeting to Dynamics 365*

6. Carefully review the content, especially the contact details to whom you are sending the meeting request.

7. Once sent, you will find similar information as experienced in the email scenario (Figure 16-42).

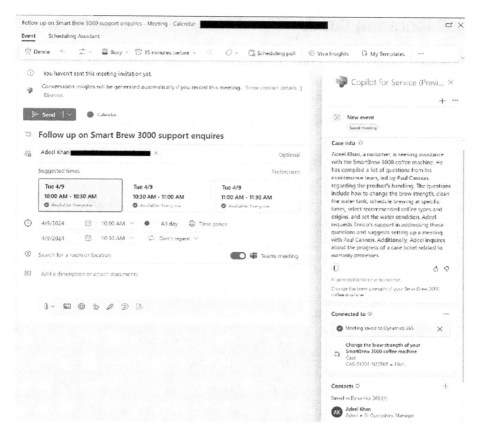

Figure 16-42. *Meeting activity saved in Dynamics 365*

16.1.5 Teams with Copilot for Service

The integration between Copilot for service and Microsoft Teams
allows you to leverage teams' collaborative excellence to be infused in
service processes and help accelerate deals with easy collaboration.
In this section, you will explore and learn how you can use Copilot for
service with MS Teams. We will begin with pane experience that is called
Collaboration Space and later explore the features available during teams'
meetings.

Collaboration Space

Microsoft Copilot for service Collaboration Space provides an out-of-the-box environment for service collaboration that's built on Microsoft Teams. The feature provides an out-of-the-box template to set up an account team and reduce the overhead for versatile personas coming together to achieve impressive results.

The account team template is designed for effective collaboration among account teams and with customers. When a team uses it and connects it to a Dynamics 365 account, the template provides an ideal space to cooperate with account team members and customers.

There are several ways you can apply this template; you can experience them by following these steps:

1. Log in to Outlook Office, either through app or browser experience.

2. Select an email of a customer that you wish to review and use for this experiment.

3. At the email view, click the Apps (▦) icon to open the app add-in available and select the Copilot for service (🌑) icon.

4. This will launch the Copilot for service with relevant customer information and key email info.

5. Browse below to find the Collaboration Space action card. The card contains already connected teams' channel as well as templates for you to set up. If you are setting up for the first time, you will only notice the templates as shown in Figure 16-43.

Figure 16-43. *Collaboration Space action card with an account name*

6. Hover your mouse over the account name (in this case, Graphic Design Institute) to activate the account template (Figure 16-44).

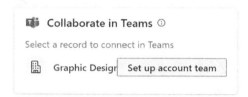

Figure 16-44. *Set up an account team with the Dynamics 365 account using Copilot for Service*

7. Click "Set up account team" to start finalizing the template settings.

8. Follow the guided steps to create the account team. If you need a step-by-step guide, please refer to Chapter 13, Section 13.1.6

During Teams Meeting

You can use Microsoft Copilot for service during virtual meetings with customers or peers in MS Teams. This feature allows you to interact with customers and refer or reflect latest CRM information. To be able to use

Copilot for service, you need to have the transcription on as required by Copilot for Teams as well. Let's follow these steps to learn about the feature:

1. Open Microsoft Teams through app or browser experience.

2. Open the previously organized meeting where you have added Copilot for Service.

3. Recall the steps defined in Section 16.1.4 under "Save Outlook Activities to Dynamics 365." Meetings like that can be ready for Copilot for service usage during the meeting.

4. When meeting is in flight, click the Copilot for service (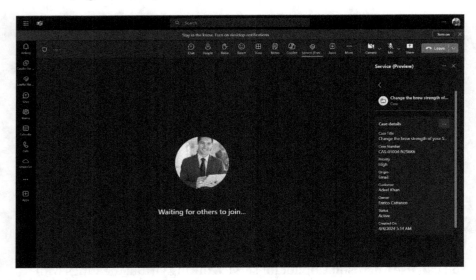) icon to open the Copilot for service pane (Figure 16-45).

Figure 16-45. *Copilot for service with real-time highlight and Dynamics 365 Customer Service tab*

5. This will showcase the related record information during the meeting that you can view and update as required.

6. All changes made will reflect immediately to the Dynamics 365.

7. You can also leverage Copilot to transcript and generate meeting minutes using M365 Copilot features.

At the time of the book's writing, Copilot for service is in preview mode and expected to have a lot more features coming in the near future.

16.2 Service Copilot for Dynamics 365 Customer Service Apps

This section will discuss the Dynamics 365 Customer Service Hub and Customer Service workspace app user experience and highlight how users of these apps can benefit from Copilot embedded in Dynamics. I will cover the Copilot actions available at the time of this book's writing.

The experience of Copilot in Dynamics 365 allows users to ask questions, summarize content, draft email, and support customer inquiries while engaged in conversation. I will share the experience based on sample data that can be easily loaded in the test environment.

16.2.1 Ask a Question

Asking a question allows the customer service app users to engage with Copilot to extract information and answers to questions based on knowledge articles available in Dynamics CRM. Users can ask a variety of questions such as

- **Direct Question**: From the knowledge sources your organization has provided, Copilot displays the best answer.

- **Follow-Up Turn-by-Turn Questions**: You can have natural, back-and-forth conversations with Copilot and give it more directions if its first answer isn't helpful enough.

- **A Better Response**: You can ask Copilot to also rewrite responses based on more instructions, such as "Can you condense your response?" or "Can you try a response explaining each of the steps you mentioned?"

This allows users to experience an interaction similar to what they would have with an experienced colleague or a manager to solve specific problems. To experience this feature, we can perform the following steps:

1. Log in to the Dynamics 365 Customer Service Hub or Customer Service workspace.

2. At the landing screen, look for the Copilot (▨) icon at the top menu or at the right-side pane (⌖), if the Copilot pane is not automatically opened.

3. This will bring you to a familiar Copilot pane, but this time in the Dynamics 365 app (Figure 16-46).

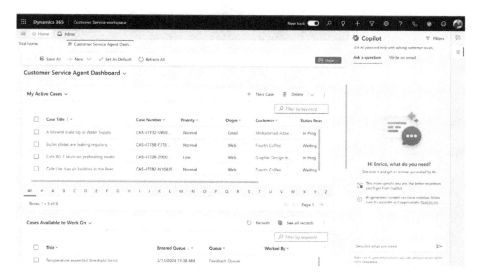

Figure 16-46. *Copilot pane in the Customer Service app*

4. In the Copilot pane, you can ask a question related to customer problems. The answers will be based on the knowledge articles available in CRM.

5. You can type the following question if the sample data is loaded:

   "what is return and exchange policy"

6. Copilot will find the related information and address the question in natural language as shown in Figure 16-47.

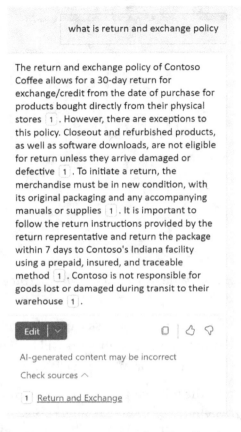

Figure 16-47. *Response to a question by Copilot in service*

7.   Notice the Check sources and the citation in
     Figure 16-47. In the customer support business, it is
     critical to ensure that you validate the citation and
     ensure there are no assumptions made by Copilot.

8.   You can follow up with more details or specific
     questions on the matter. For example, I validated
     the customer situation with the following prompt to
     understand better:

"so if already 10 days have passed, return is no more accepted?"

9. The Copilot returned with the response and guided me to consult additional resources or team as this could be a sensitive matter and may require escalation (Figure 16-48).

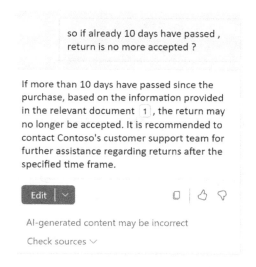

Figure 16-48. *Follow-up question with Copilot in Customer Service*

10. Finally, I ended with another prompt, but this time I requested Copilot to create a checklist out of information that is available so as a user I can be better prepared to manage return and exchange.

    "Can you create step by step check list for accepting return or exchange from customer"

11. This created a nice step-by-step checklist with instructions that I can use in such events (Figure 16-49).

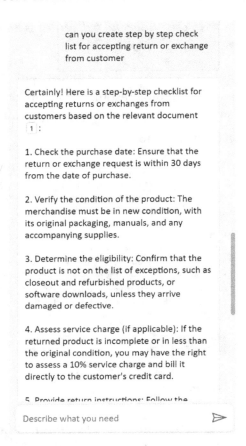

Figure 16-49. *Step-by-step instruction created with Copilot*

This feature can really help onboard and bring customer-facing agents up to speed with policies, procedures, and what-if scenarios, leveraging an existing knowledge base. Later, we will learn the "ask question" experience once an agent is in a live conversation/chat with a customer.

16.2.2 Summarize Content

The summarization feature has been introduced at various interfaces in customer services. The feature enables users to quickly understand the gist of targeted information without spending a long time to browse through details. We will experience and learn about the summarization for case and contact records. I will cover the conversation summary in agent experience later in the chapter.

1. Log in to the Dynamics 365 Customer Service Hub or Customer Service workspace.

2. At the landing screen, look for the Copilot (🔲) icon at the top menu or at the right-side pane (⓪), if the Copilot pane is not automatically opened.

3. This will bring you to a familiar Copilot pane, but this time in the Dynamics 365 app.

4. Browse to Contact and select any contact with some interactions already recorded as shown in Figure 16-50.

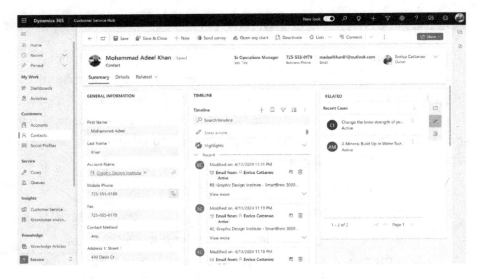

Figure 16-50. *Contact record with interactions in timelines*

5. Notice the new Highlights ( Highlights) icon in
    timelines. Click the icon to initiate the
    summarization of timeline activities and
    interactions (Figure 16-51).

Figure 16-51. *Summary of timeline interactions*

6. This bulleted summary can now be reviewed or
    copied for sharing purposes. The summary is also
    time stamped for chronological references.

Let's switch to the case view and select a case with interactions and
activities:

1. Open a case form with a case having interactions
    and activities (Figure 16-52).

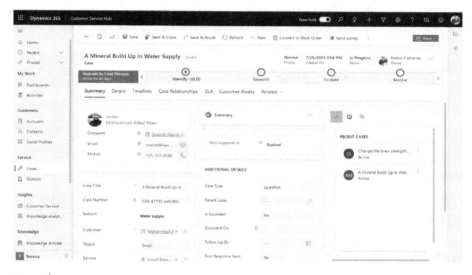

Figure 16-52. *Case record with summary*

2. Click the Summary (Summary) icon to generate the
    summary of the case.

3. Copilot will generate a summary detailed enough
    to capture the important highlights and takeaways
    (Figure 16-53).

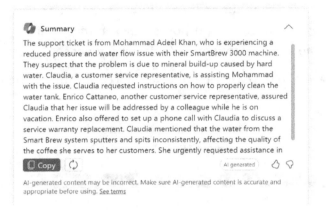

Figure 16-53. *Case summary generated using Copilot*

4. The timeline at the case is also enabled to generate the highlight or summary of interactions (Figure 16-54).

Figure 16-54. *Case timeline summary generated using Copilot*

This is another useful feature that can reduce manual summary preparation time and help create initial draft for sharing or to understand the current state much faster.

16.2.3 Draft an Email

One of the main features of Copilot is to help you draft an email. You can use the integrated Copilot to compose and respond to emails from the Dynamics 365 interface.

There are two ways you can experience this feature. The first experience is based on the Copilot pane as shown in Figure 16-55, which by now you must have experienced many times (even in this book as we covered the pane-based email drafting experience in many chapters including this one). The Copilot customer service pane draft introduces few more out-of-the-box prompts to address from customer service lens.

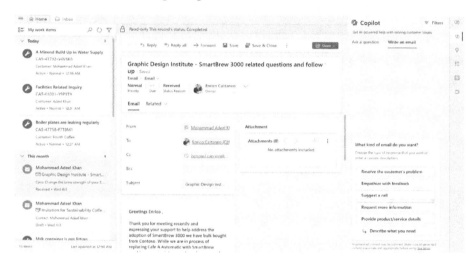

Figure 16-55. *Draft a response through the Copilot pane*

As we have experienced this feature many times, I recommend you evaluate this feature on your own. Please ensure you are not using a customer email or contact while evaluating this feature.

The other feature is new in Dynamics 365, that is, to draft an email using an email editor. This feature requires the admin of Dynamics 365 to enable "Turn on generative AI in emails" for the app. A step-by-step guide is discussed in Chapter 14, Section 14.1.3.

Perform the following steps to experience this feature:

1. Log in to the Dynamics 365 Customer Service Hub or Customer Service workspace.

2. At the landing screen, look for the Copilot ( ) icon at the top menu or at the right-side pane ( ), if the Copilot pane is not automatically opened.

3. This will bring you to a familiar Copilot pane, but this time in the Dynamics 365 app.

4. First, you can open a new email activity from either the activity view, account, contact, or case timelines.

5. You will notice the Copilot feature enabled in the rich text editor (Figure 16-56).

Figure 16-56. *Copilot feature in rich text editor*

6. This will allow you to create an email draft by using a prompt or adjust your drafted email.

7. Click the draft with Copilot to open the ready prompt or provide a custom prompt (Figure 16-57).

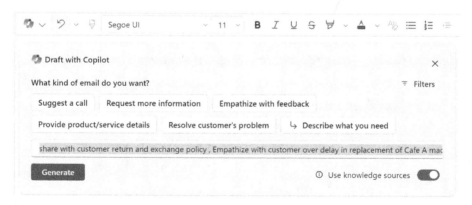

Figure 16-57. *Draft an email with Copilot in the rich text editor*

8. I used the following prompt to engage knowledge
    article content as well by choosing the "Describe
    what you need" option (Figure 16-58):

    *"share with customer return and exchange policy,
    Empathize with customer over delay in replacement
    of Cafe A machine. also suggest 10% discount on next
    purchase of preferred coffee blend."*

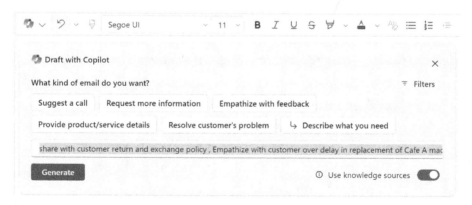

Figure 16-58. *Custom prompt with knowledge article support*

9.   Click Generate to begin the drafting process.

10. This resulted in a draft prepared with knowledge
     article content. Copilot successfully added the
     content in the conversation and addressed my
     request effectively (Figure 16-59).

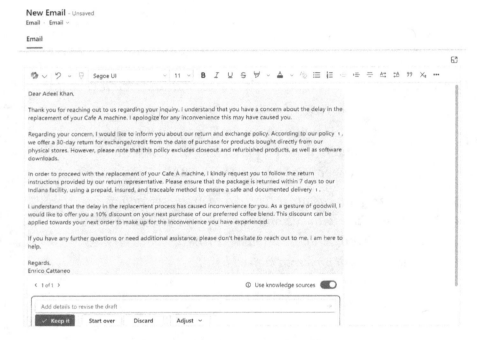

Figure 16-59. *Draft generated using knowledge article content*

11. As experienced previously, you can review and
     decide to keep the draft, start over again with some
     additional information, discard completely, or
     adjust the tone or length of response. Also, you will
     be provided with a list of citations to ensure that the
     right content is used (Figure 16-60).

Figure 16-60. *Working with a generated draft*

This will reduce the time to respond to customer queries over email and promises to improve the email content quality that can lead to better customer engagement and satisfaction.

16.2.4 Copilot Experience During Chat

For the Omni-channel agents in contact centers, Copilot adds some additional features that I will discuss in this section. To experience these features, you must have an Omni-channel setup with chat enablement. If you don't have a setup ready, sign up for a trial instance, and you can experience a chat interaction and interface through the Customer Service workspace app. We will begin our experience assuming the chat conversation has already started with an agent as shown in Figure 16-61.

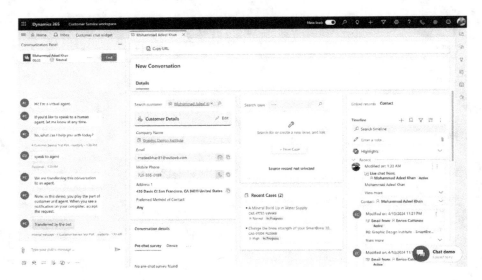

Figure 16-61. *Agent console during live chat*

We will begin our learning from chat options:

1. At the chat option, notice the addition of the Copilot
   (⬡) icon. This will allow the agent to leverage
   Copilot features during the chat session.

2. The click on the icon will summarize the
   conversation. This will provide a quick detail of the
   conversation and key highlights (Figure 16-62).

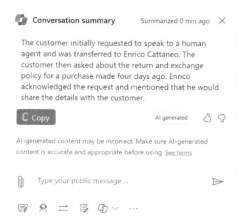

Figure 16-62. *Conversation summary using Copilot*

3. The customer has inquired about the return and exchange policy; to find the answer, we can click the Copilot (⑳) icon at the side pane and open the Copilot pane with the Ask a question interface. We can either copy and paste the customer question or use our own words to describe the customer ask (Figure 16-63).

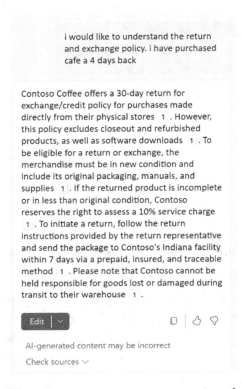

Figure 16-63. *Addressing a customer query using the Copilot pane*

4. If the agent likes to make some adjustments to this
   draft, they can click Edit (Edit); however, if the response
   is acceptable and ready to be sent, the agent can click
   the drop-down ( ) icon and select Send to customer
   (Figure 16-64).

Figure 16-64. *Sending response to a customer at chat*

5. This will transfer the response to a chat session and
    send to the customer, reducing the number of clicks
    for the agent.

6. The other features of Copilot such as the case
    summary and timeline highlights are similar to
    customer service hub experience.

7. Once the chat session ends with the customer, CRM
    will generate a refreshed summary and suggest an
    option to create a case if required (Figure 16-65).

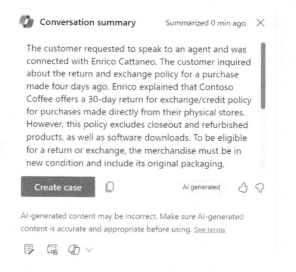

Figure 16-65. *Conversation summary at the end of the chat session*

8. This feature can be extremely helpful to fill "call
    wrap-ups" forms that is commonly used in contact
    centers.

9. The summary will be automatically added to the
    description of the new case.

These are the features available at the time of writing this book; however, it is expected to have many new features added in the next cycle of the product release.

16.3 Summary

In this chapter, we explored the integration of Microsoft Copilot with Dynamics 365 Customer Service, offering a comprehensive guide for enhancing service experiences through the power of generative AI.

The chapter also covered Copilot for Service experience, detailing the seamless login process and the innovative features accessible from Outlook and Teams interfaces. The chapter deep dived into the user experience, highlighting the ease of accessing Copilot's functionalities within the familiar Microsoft ecosystem.

The chapter extensively covered how Copilot for Service can summarize key email information with CRM context, enhancing the user's ability to draft email responses that are both relevant and personalized. The chapter also discussed actions user can perform using Copilot for service pane.

The chapter covered the Teams integration, which facilitates collaboration and accelerates service processes through Microsoft Teams. The Collaboration Space feature was introduced, providing a template for setting up account teams and enhancing cooperation with customers.

The last part of the chapter discussed the Copilot experience with Dynamics 365 Customer Service. The in-app experience, offering a wide range of features such as ask a question, summarize information, or intelligently draft an email with knowledge article content from within Dynamics 365 workspace.

This marks the completion of business application Copilot that is currently available for multiple CRMs. There are Copilot features for Dynamics 365 Marketing and Field Services users that are worth exploring. However, now that you have gained the Copilot knowledge, those features will become easy to learn and use.

PART V

Extending Copilot Experience

The last part of this book will introduce you to the concept of extending Copilot experience. So far, I have discussed how to leverage out-of-the-box, ready-to-use Copilots; however, there will always be organization-specific needs that are beyond out-of-the-box Copilots. Using extensions and Copilot Studio, you will learn how to expand the impact of Copilot in your own unique business processes.

Chapter 17: This chapter delves into Microsoft Copilot Studio, a platform that allows users to extend the Microsoft 365 Copilot experience or build custom Copilot bots for internal or external audiences. It discusses the transition from Power Virtual Agent to Copilot Studio and its integration with Power Platform services like Dataverse and Power Automate. The chapter outlines various use cases such as travel and project automations and LOB (line of business) automations, highlighting the flexibility of Copilot Studio in addressing business problems through natural language interactions. The chapter concludes with a detailed guide on creating custom plugins using Copilot Studio, enabling users to build conversational plugins, task plugins, and custom connector–based plugins for a more personalized Copilot experience.

Chapter 18: The final chapter of the book reflects on the transformative impact of generative AI and Microsoft Copilot on the future of work. It emphasizes how these technologies are reshaping the way we approach tasks, from drafting emails to responding to complex requests for proposals. The chapter concludes with a forward-looking perspective on the collaboration between humans and AI, urging business managers to adapt to these changes to remain competitive in a rapidly evolving workplace.

CHAPTER 17

Microsoft Copilot Studio

So far in the book, we have discussed many out-of-the-box or ready-to-use Copilots. These Copilots are AI powered and understand our instructions or ask in natural languages. In addition to offering out-of-the-box and ready-to-use Copilots, Microsoft has also introduced a platform where you and your team can build or extend the Copilot experience. Microsoft Copilot Studio is a SaaS (software as a service) platform where business users or pro developers can extend the Microsoft 365 Copilot experience or build a custom Copilot bot that can serve internal or external audience.

Previously known as Power Virtual Agent, Copilot Studio is part of the Microsoft Power Platform family, having native integration to Power Platform services like Dataverse and Power Automate. However, as in the case of Power BI, Copilot Studio is also a stand-alone service and requires separate licensing.

Copilot Studio can help you and your team solve business problems in a new way, where end users may not require going through a traditional application interface, but rather use natural language to either get the information they need or perform the action they want.

Let's discuss some of the common use cases customers of Microsoft Copilot Studio have already deployed in production and using these custom experiences in daily business operations:

© Adeel Khan 2024
A. Khan, *Introducing Microsoft Copilot for Managers*, Inside Copilot,
https://doi.org/10.1007/979-8-8688-0419-9_17

1. **Travel Automation**: Copilot Studio can help organizations to facilitate travel and ticket booking. This solution can integrate with travel APIs or platforms for fetching and booking travel options, manage user itineraries within M365, automate expense reporting, and support group travel coordination. The solution can be secure and compliant with privacy regulations.

2. **Project Automation**: Copilot Studio can help organizations build a project inquiry and collaboration experience from M365 Chat. Users can inquire about the project status, retrieve pending tasks or invoices, and understand various KPIs.

3. **LOB Automations**: Copilot Studio can help expand interaction with information stored in LOB (line of business) solutions, such as Dynamics 365, Salesforce, ServiceNow, or SAP, and surface your business data. Users can inquire information in these systems and get answers to their data-centric questions from the familiar M365 Chat.

4. **External User Facing**: Copilot Studio can help organizations build external-facing bots that can be hosted at websites or chat channels. These bots can help end users fetch information from existing knowledge base and perform actions. The audience or end users of these bots can be citizens, retail consumers, or partners.

If you notice, these experiences are typically categorized in two, expanding the experience of M365 Chat or building a new experience altogether. Copilot Studio allows you to address use cases in these two disciplines and offers flexible licensing to help you choose the right solution track.

In the next section, we will cover these two categories or offerings in detail and experience some examples to learn about them.

17.1 Licensing and Accessing Studio

Licensing has become a fluid conversation especially when the products and services are evolving to new needs. At the time of writing this book, for the purpose of extending M365 Chat experience, there is no additional license required, and users can log in to Copilot Studio and build a plugin (we will discuss this later in the section). However, for the custom experience, such as HR bots or customer-facing bots, organizations can procure a Copilot Studio license, which allows building generative AI–powered bots and hosting these bots at various channels.

You can access Copilot Studio in two ways: either as a web app on its own or as an app within Teams. The two versions have mostly the same features. But you might prefer one version over the other depending on how you want to use Copilot Studio.

You can visit the `http://copilotstudio.microsoft.com` web app to access the Copilot Studio, or you can add a Copilot Studio app in Microsoft Teams to access the studio features as shown in Figure 17-1. At the time of writing this book, the team's app is still titled "Power Virtual Agent," so try both Copilot Studio and Power Virtual Agent to find and add the app.

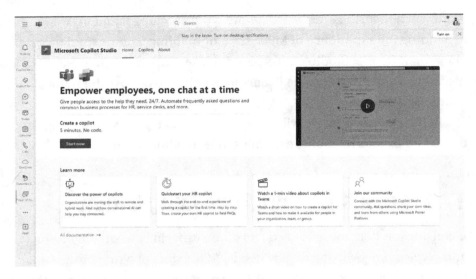

Figure 17-1. *Microsoft Copilot Studio in Teams*

17.2 Extending M365 Copilot

This section will discuss how you can extend M365 Chat Copilot to surface business data from line-of-business applications. This feature requires users to have access to M365 Copilot license and of course the LOB application, such as Dynamics 365, Salesforce, ServiceNow, or SAP.

To understand the concept of extension, it is important to understand what plugins are. A plugin is a tool that allows chat experience to be enhanced by enabling integration with business data in various line-of-business applications. They are add-ons that can be added or custom created to surface the information as well as perform actions.

M365 Chat can be further extended by either enabling out of the box plugins or build a custom plugin using Microsoft Copilot Studio.

Note   Another way of surfacing business data is through teams'
extension; it is primarily a pro developer journey, hence not discussed
in this chapter.

17.2.1 Out-of-the-Box Plugins

There are various out-of-the-box plugins available, and the list will
continue to expand in the future as increased solution providers see
value in bringing AI-powered, natural language experience to users in the
familiar interface of M365 Copilot Chat. We will discuss the Microsoft-
powered plugins in this section to learn with ease and experiment with
setup you may already have.

Before diving deep into the world of plugins, let's quickly learn how to
access them:

1. Access M365 Chat through teams as shown in
   Figure 17-2.

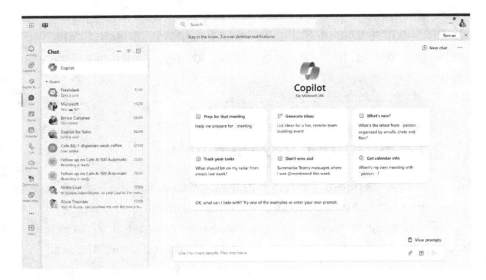

Figure 17-2. *Accessing M365 Chat through teams*

2. Click the plugin (⊞) icon near chat. This will open
    the list of plugins already available/published by
    your IT admin (Figure 17-3).

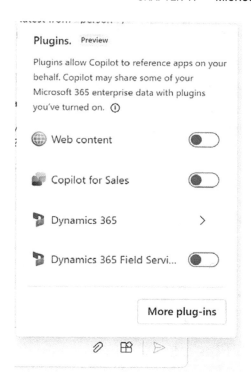

Figure 17-3.   *Chat with plugins*

3.   Users can toggle on/off to enable the plugin activation during the chat session. These plugins can be activated by your admin through integrated apps.

The process of enabling the plugins is similar to what has been discussed in detail under Copilot for sales and service administration. The only difference is that the admin can sort or search the plugins by filtering through "Copilot-ready" attributes as shown in Figure 17-4. Please refer to Chapter 11 or 14 to understand the process.

Figure 17-4. *Available plugins for M365 Chat*

Dynamics 365 Plugins

Plugins for Microsoft Dynamics applications such as Dynamics 365 Sales, Customer Service, Field Service, and Supply Chain are available out of the box. At the time of writing this book, plugin feature is available in preview mode; the feature offers M365 chat user to surface data from Dynamics 365 Dataverse tables for the preceding app without any additional integration.

A user is required to have access to these apps, and the interaction with data is only available with information user profile have access to. We will explore this feature further in the following exercise. Your admin must have deployed and made the Dynamics plugin available to your user. Please ensure this access is already granted before starting the following steps:

1. Access M365 Chat through teams.

2. Click the plugin (⊞) icon near chat. This will open
    the list of plugins already available/published by
    your IT admin.

3. First, ensure that the Dynamics sales plugin is
    switched off. If you have more than one sales
    environment, your view will see the expand (>) icon;
    else, you would only see a single toggle
    (Figure 17-5).

Figure 17-5. *Reviewing the plugin activation*

4. Click the expand (>) icon and ensure the
    switch is off.

5. Type the following prompt in the chat box and
    observe the results:

    "List all leads assigned to me"

6. You will notice that M365 Copilot chat was not able
    to recognize the content store or source and hence
    did not provide helpful information (Figure 17-6).

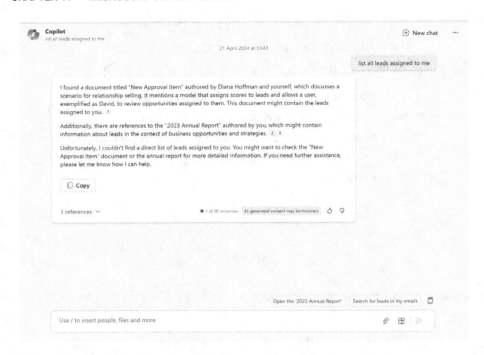

Figure 17-6. *Inquiring lead information without a plugin*

7. Now, click the plugin (⊞) icon near chat and toggle on the Dynamics 365 sales plugin. Since I have two environments, my view allows me to enable the plugin at a selected environment. This can be useful if you wish to first experiment with the UAT (User Acceptance Testing) environment before enabling for production (Figure 17-7).

Figure 17-7. *Enabling the Dynamics 365 Sales plugin*

8. Ask the same question again and observe the results:

   "List all leads assigned to me"

9. This time, you will notice that M365 chat was able to answer the question and surfaced the lead information from Dynamics 365 sales (Figure 17-8).

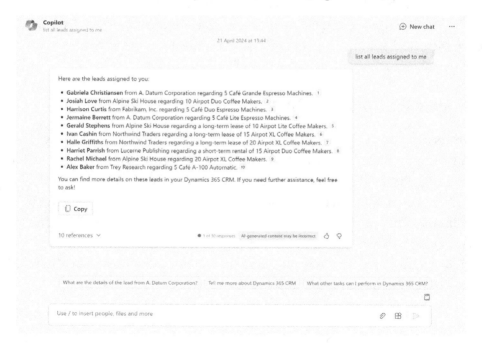

Figure 17-8. *Surfacing lead information through M365 Chat*

10. You can now ask a follow-up question or experiment with additional prompts to explore and interact with data that is available in the Dynamics 365 sales data model.

11. Here are a few examples that you can use to explore further:

    "Find all Dynamics 365 Sales contacts named [First Name/Last Name]"

    "What is the business phone for [Full Name of Contact or Lead]?"

    "What is the email for account [Account Name]?"

Use these prompts with your lead, contact, or account names and appreciate the ease of access to information this plugin brings.

Similar to sales, you can deploy and activate Customer Service, Field Service, and Supply Chain plugins and inquire about information in your natural language.

Power Platform Plugins

Users can also use plugins to surface information from various line-of-business applications such as Salesforce, ServiceNow, or SAP. This is made possible with native integration to the Power Platform ecosystem and certified connectors. The familiar connector architecture is leveraged by plugins to either bring information from these data sources or help create a specific behavior or experience in your M365 Copilot chat. There are built-in plugins using Power Platform connectors, and users can also build custom plugins that we will discuss in the next section.

Built-in plugins are available for some of the most popular SaaS solutions as well as for Power Automate. Let's explore first the SaaS solution Jira plugin; the experience would be similar for other first-party plugins with a difference in prompts to engage the plugin or surface information.

If you are new to Jira, you can sign up for a trial account using your work email ID. You can browse to the board and create a sample scrum board as shown in Figure 17-9 that will provide you with sample data to test the scenario.

Figure 17-9. *Create a board with the sample data in Jira*

Once the Jira sample board is set up or if you have an existing board, you can resume to the following exercise:

1. Access M365 Chat through teams.

2. Click the plugin (⊞) icon near chat. This will open the list of plugins already available/published by your IT admin.

3. Choose the More plugins (More plugins) button to open the list of plugins available with Microsoft Copilot (Figure 17-10).

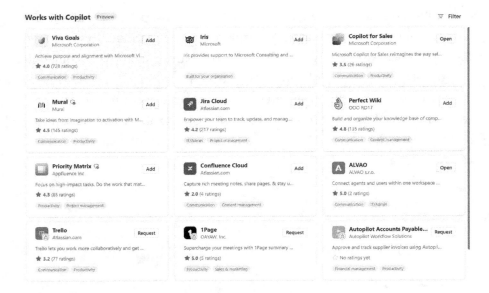

Figure 17-10. *First-party plugins that can work with M365 Copilot*

4. Since we want to experiment with Jira Cloud, choose the Add (Add) option with Jira Cloud.

5. This will open the Jira Cloud app and ask where to open the app (Figure 17-11).

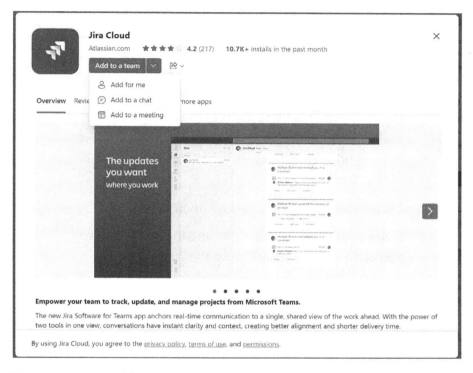

Figure 17-11. *Adding Jira Cloud to teams*

6. Select Add for me (⊖ Add for me).

7. This will open the Jira Cloud in chat and ask for sign-in with your Jira user ID (Figure 17-12).

Figure 17-12. *Sign in to Jira from teams*

8. Once signed in to Jira, you will receive the confirmation message (Figure 17-13).

Figure 17-13. Confirmation of signing in to Jira Cloud

9. You are now ready to use the Jira Cloud plugin with M365 Chat.

10. Let's go back to M365 Chat and open plugins.

11. Ensure the Jira plugin is active and toggled on before you can ask a question (Figure 17-14).

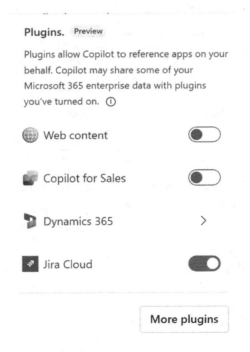

Figure 17-14. Jira Cloud plugin enabled for chat

12. Try the following prompt and observe the results:

    "What ticket is assigned to me in Jira"

13. This prompt will trigger the Jira plugin, and with
    the help of generative AI, you will receive the
    information in a natural language tone as shown in
    Figure 17-15.

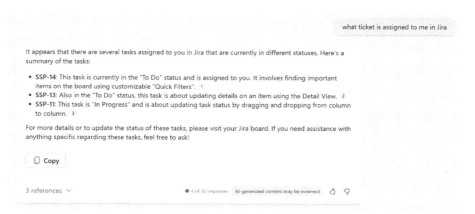

Figure 17-15. *Prompt response from Jira Cloud using the first-
party plugin*

14. Some of the first-party plugins offer more than
    inquiry capabilities. Here, in the case of Jira, if
    you ask a summarization question as shown in
    Figure 17-15, you get the opportunity to take actions
    on the ticket as well. Use the following prompt and
    replace the ticket number "SSP-14" with tickets
    assigned to you:

    "Summarize the ticket SSP-14 in Jira"

15. Notice that in the output, you will not only get the summary but also the distinct options to perform the required next actions (Figure 17-16).

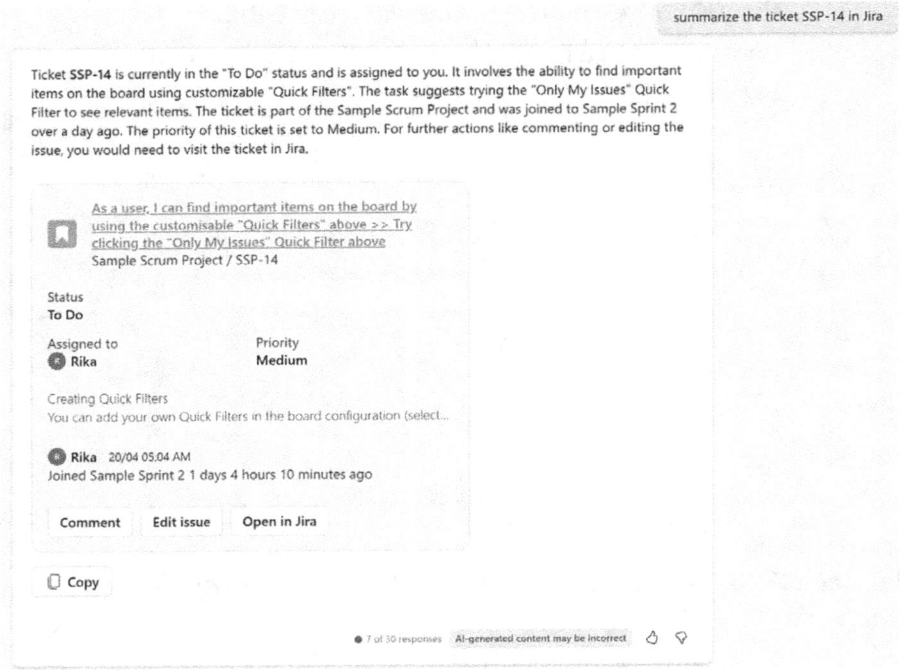

Figure 17-16. *Action card with a ticket summary from Jira Cloud*

16. Play with more prompts and familiarize how you can use M365 chat to access information with ease.

First-party plugins offer a great gateway to surface as well as perform actions (in some cases). It is bound to change the way we work and interact with the data in business applications. While we are not covering the other SaaS applications, the experience remains more or less the same. In the next section, Copilot actions will be discussed that open up extensibility to a whole new world and enable us to use Power Platform connectors to fetch information from various sources and use generative AI to deliver results in natural language.

17.2.2 Copilot Actions

As an organization, you can further expand Microsoft 365 Copilot extensibility by creating Copilot actions. Copilot Studio provides an authoring interface that can allow citizen developers to surface data using Power Platform connectors or pro developers to build OpenAI plugins to address various use cases. Using Power Platform connectors, citizen developers can build conversational actions, AI plugins, task plugins, and custom connector–based plugins. I will discuss each of these in detail in this section; however, to keep the context for business users, I will cover the conversational action in detail and provide a short guide on others.

Conversational

Conversational actions allow users to build topics that can surface information from various data sources and use generative AI to generate answers to the user's questions. The action is designed and managed under the Copilot Studio environment and leverages Power Platform connectors to access information from source systems.

Let's build a simple use case to surface information from Microsoft Dataverse. I have selected this example due to simplicity and ease of experimentation. We will learn how to access information in one of Dataverse core tables "Account" and apply generative AI to answer user query about the data in the table. While Dataverse has been added as a knowledge source and it would be rare to build such scenario, use this example to familiarize yourself with the process of constructing the conversational action and replicate with your organization's own third-party business solution.

We will perform the following steps to learn about this feature:

1. Log in to the Copilot Studio environment by accessing the web address: `https://copilotstudio.microsoft.com`.

2. Once landed in the studio, select the appropriate environment at the top-left corner. Revise the Chapter 7 Power Apps or Chapter 8 Power Automate chapter to recall the concept of environments.

3. From the right-side menu, select (⊕) Create. This will take you to the Create landing page as shown in Figure 17-17.

Figure 17-17. *Copilot Studio extended landing page*

4. Notice that there are several templates available out of the box that can easily spin a new custom Copilot experience for you; we will discuss and experience them later in the chapter. For now, you can click at the New Microsoft Copilot action.

5. By clicking the new Copilot action as shown
    Figure 17-18, the system will prompt you to choose
    the Copilot experience you wish to extend. At
    Microsoft Build in May 2024, Microsoft announced
    the public preview of the out-of-the-box Copilot
    extension, meaning that you can now extend
    the Copilot for sales with additional connectors
    as well. (Figure 17-19). This option will be only
    available for environments where you have both
    Copilots deployed. For the time being, let's choose
    the Copilot for Microsoft 365 for our current
    experiment.

Figure 17-18. *New Microsoft Copilot action option*

Which Copilot would you like to extend? (preview)   ✕

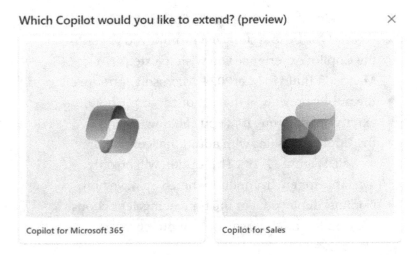

Copilot for Microsoft 365   Copilot for Sales

Figure 17-19. *Selecting the Copilot experience for extension*

6. You will be provided with options to choose the type
    of Copilot action intended (Figure 17-20). Choose
    the conversation for this experiment.

Figure 17-20. *Action type intended for extension*

7. You can also land to a similar screen with less clicks. At the home screen of Copilot or under the Copilot (☉) menu, you can find M365 Copilot (●) along with other Copilots. Select Copilot for Microsoft 365 and choose Add actions (+ Add action) from the landing page as shown in Figure 17-21.

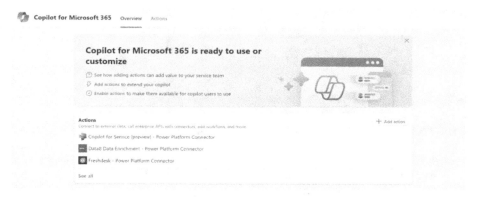

Figure 17-21. *Add action from the Copilot for M365 landing page*

8. The unique attribute of the conversational action is their ability to be triggered for custom topics and extend the topic coverage under unified Copilot for M365 experience, making M365 Copilot reach beyond the Microsoft ecosystem into business applications and providing role-specific information with ease.

9. Since this is being done for the first time, Copilot Studio would ask to create a conversational action solution; the purpose of the solution is to allow the ability to publish the ready topics and manage them easily (Figure 17-22).

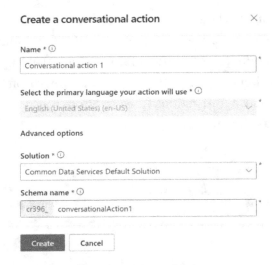

Figure 17-22. *Conversational action solution*

10. Provide a name that can be easily referred to and recalled – I am using "CP1" – and click Create.

11. Once created, you will be automatically transferred to the conversation plugin solution environment where you can start configuring the topics (Figure 17-23).

Figure 17-23. *Conversation plugin solution environment*

12. Click the Topics (Topics) menu option to open the topic management interface. This is where you will define and manage several topics that the conversational action would handle. For the first time, it will intelligently take you to the topic configuration studio as shown in Figure 17-24.

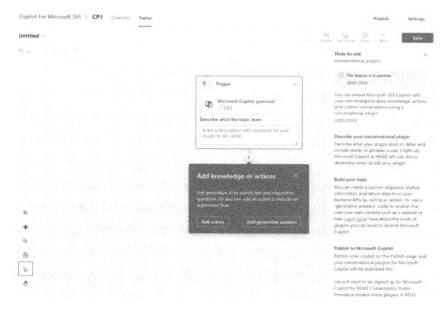

Figure 17-24. *Topic configuration studio*

13. Click the Details (ⓘ) icon to first provide details about the topic as shown in Figure 17-25.

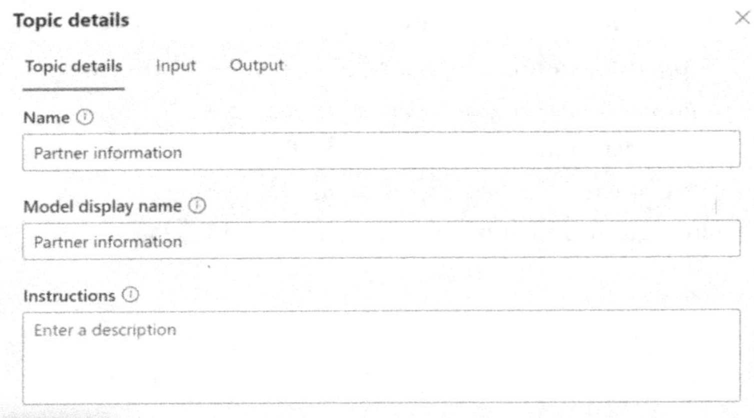

Topic details   ✕

Topic details   Input   Output

Name ⓘ

Partner information

Model display name ⓘ

Partner information

Instructions ⓘ

Enter a description

Figure 17-25. *Topic details*

14. As explained in the beginning of the section, we will configure a simple topic to retrieve information from the accounts table in Microsoft Dataverse and apply generative AI to respond to a user query. We need to ensure that details are provided accordingly, and they will be displayed to users in Copilot chat and also used by the Copilot engine to determine the start of action.

15. It is important to remember that you cannot use any user actions such as button, question, or response in the conversation action.

16. Set up the details of Trigger. Add a description and click Edit to include conversation starters as shown in Figure 17-26.

Figure 17-26. *Description of the topic*

17. Click the Add (⊕) icon to add the next action to include Call an action and invoke the Power Platform connector for Dataverse (Figure 17-27).

Figure 17-27. *Adding action to the conversation*

18. Click Connector and search for "list rows from selected environment" (Figure 17-28).

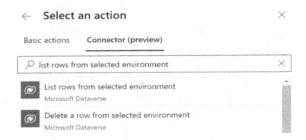

Figure 17-28. *Dataverse action to list rows for the conversation plugin*

19. Choose the list rows action and provide information about the environment, table, and other attributes. Learn about these actions at attributes from the Microsoft Power Platform documentation as they are the same (Figure 17-29).

Figure 17-29. *Connector action configuration for the conversation action*

20.   Click each attribute, and the studio will provide easy access to environments and tables. Select the appropriate environment where you have Dataverse with an accounts table.

21.   Click the Add (⊕) icon again to add the next action from the Advanced submenu. Select Generative answers (Figure 17-30).

Figure 17-30. *Generative answers in the conversation plugin*

22.   In the configuration of action, select "Activity.Text" in the input field. The user question is going to be stored in this system variable, and by passing this to the generative answer, you are asking AI to take the question as an input (Figure 17-31).

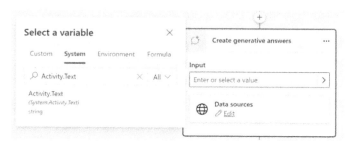

Figure 17-31. *Passing the user query to the generative AI*

23. Click Edit under data sources to open the data source configuration. Select Custom data and choose the output of the Dataverse action as the input. This is where we are providing the data source, so answers can be prepared based on the data (Figure 17-32).

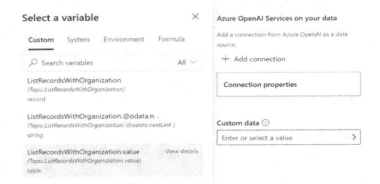

Figure 17-32. *Selecting data source for the conversation plugin*

24. We can choose other data source options as well; I will discuss these in the "custom Copilot section".

25. Name the action that can easily guide the user to understand the topic covered. I have named this topic "Partner information."

26. You can publish the top from the authoring interface by clicking the Publish button at the top bar as shown in Figure 17-33.

Figure 17-33. Publishing the solution with topics

27. Or you can save the topic and move back to the overview; clicking Publish makes all actions available in M365 Copilot as shown in Figure 17-34.

Figure 17-34. Publishing all the topics in the solution

Once published and available, you can now use the plugin at Microsoft 365 Copilot chat just like first-party plugins.

To experience the prompt, log in to Microsoft Teams and access M365 Copilot Chat:

1. Click the plugin (⊞) icon near chat. This will open the list of plugins already available/published by your IT admin. This list should also include the new partner information plugin created (Figure 17-35).

Figure 17-35. *Conversation plugin made available with M365 Copilot chat*

2. Use the following prompt but replace the name of the account with the account name in your Dataverse table, that is, replace "British Gypsum" with a relevant account name:

    "*Partner city for account name British Gypsum*"

3. Observe that now Copilot would bring information and create a response in a natural language; it also provides you a link to Dataverse records for verification (Figure 17-36).

Figure 17-36. *Action response in M365 Copilot Chat*

Experiment with a few more questions and improve the conversation starters for better outcomes.

Prompt, Flow, and Connector Plugins

In the conversation action, while we use the same connectors as Power Platform, the design and orchestration experience were available at Copilot Studio. The other three types of Copilot actions leverage the Power Platform skill set and interface to configure extensibility experience. I will briefly discuss them here as any citizen developer with intermediate or advanced Power Platform knowledge can quickly understand the working design.

1. Log in to the Copilot Studio environment by accessing the web address: `https://copilotstudio.microsoft.com`.

2. Once landed in the studio, select the appropriate environment at the top-left corner. Revise the Chapter 7: Power Apps or Chapter 8: Power Automate to recall the concept of environments.

3. From the right-side menu, select (⊕) Create. This will take you to the Create landing page.

4. Click the New Microsoft Copilot action to launch a Copilot selector. Select Copilot for M365 and then Prompt (≡≉) as shown in Figure 17-37.

Figure 17-37. *Working with prompt action*

5. This type of action uses AI prompts to analyze the content or provide insights on the dataset. For example, a common use case I noticed in the industry is to score the candidate resume based on specific criteria provided in the prompt.

6. Once you click the prompt, it will open a Prompt editor which is powered by AI Builder. as shown in Figure 17-38.

Figure 17-38. *AI prompt builder*

7. Once ready, you can assess the prompt with sample data before publishing and making it available at teams (Figure 17-39).

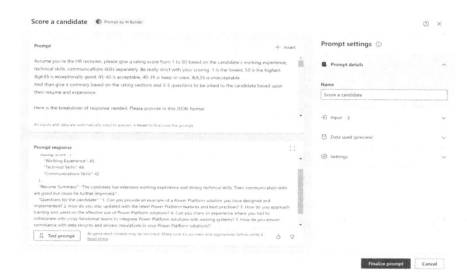

Figure 17-39. *Scoring candidate using the AI prompt*

8. Finalize the prompt by creating an AI plugin (Figure 17-40).

Figure 17-40. *Creating an AI plugin*

9. The final action will be available under the action tab (Figure 17-41).

Figure 17-41. *Action tab with the list of actions available with Copilot for M365*

10. Once available, you will be able to activate the plugin from M365 Copilot chat.

The other type of Copilot action is known as the flow action. The flow action ( ) will leverage Power Automate flow capabilities and allow users to perform various actions. By selecting the flow, you will be transferred to the Power Automate studio as shown in Figure 17-42 with the flow having a new Copilot-specific trigger and Copilot-specific output.

Figure 17-42. *Task plugins using Power Automate flow*

This opens a huge transformation opportunity where you can configure a custom plugin to not only surface information from multiple sources but also provide the capability to execute actions using Power Platform connectors.

Lastly, the connector action allows you to deploy connectors with third-party solutions to retrieve or perform an action. This allows Copilot to use generative AI and trigger connector-based actions from Copilot for M365; the feature is currently under preview and may go through a few revisions before being finalized. Figure 17-43 highlights the connector configuration process that will enable the feature under Copilot for M365.

Figure 17-43. *Configuring a connector with Copilot for M365*

The extensibility feature is in preview at the time of this book's writing; the features are evolving and adding more capabilities for citizen developers to use M365 Copilot chat as a unified assist for personal productivity across solutions. The features discussed in this section can change in the future; however, the concepts you have learned will remain the same. May 2024 Microsoft build had a major upgrade to various products, and Copilot Studio received several upgrades. While this section is documented to introduce you to the features, I would urge you to understand the core concept as it will continue to remain the same. Keep an eye on the latest updates from Microsoft to ensure you learn the new features as they are released.

17.3 Custom Copilot Bot

The section will discuss how to configure custom Copilots that can be hosted for internal or external audience. So far in the chapter, we have Microsoft Copilot Chat extensibility that allows us to surface business data using various out-of-the-box or custom plugins; however, Microsoft Copilot Chat for M365 is a prebuilt AI assistant designed to help users navigate and utilize Microsoft 365 services more effectively.

On the other hand, custom Copilots built using Copilot Studio offer a more personalized and flexible solution. Copilot Studio allows citizen developers and pro developers to build their own AI assistants tailored to their specific needs. These custom Copilots can be designed to understand and respond to specific domains, tasks, or industries, providing a highly customized user experience. They can be integrated into various data sources, platforms, and workflows, making them a versatile tool for many different use cases.

For Microsoft Copilot Chat for M365, extensibility means the ability to continuously update and improve the assistant's capabilities based on user feedback and evolving needs. This ensures that the assistant remains relevant and useful as the M365 services continue to grow and change. For custom Copilots, extensibility refers to the ability to expand and adapt the assistant's capabilities over time. As the needs of the users or the requirements of the application change, developers can easily update the custom Copilot to meet these new demands. This flexibility and adaptability are key advantages of custom Copilots, allowing them to provide long-term value in a wide range of scenarios.

Custom Copilots can be targeted to various audiences; we can typically categorize them into internal users, such as compliance officers, HR managers, or finance managers, or external users, such as website-visiting customers, public service user citizens, or suppliers/partners using chat channels for fast inquiries and actions.

17.3.1 Custom Copilot and Environment

Before we dive deep into the custom Copilot creation process, let's quickly refresh the concept of environments. With Microsoft Copilot Studio, you can create Copilots in different environments and easily switch between them. An environment is a space to store, manage, and share your organization's business data. The Copilots you create are stored in an environment. Environments may also have dissimilar roles, security requirements, and target audiences, and each environment is created in a separate location.

There are many strategies for using multiple environments. For example, your admin can create separate environments that correspond to specific teams or departments in your organization, each containing the relevant data and Copilots for each audience. You can also configure all your Copilots in a single environment if you don't need or want to use different ones.

Microsoft recommends using a non-default production environment for Copilots that you want to deploy to production. While it's not strictly necessary to use Dataverse for a Copilot bot, it can certainly enhance the bot's capabilities and make it more useful and versatile. However, the specific requirements might vary based on your organization's needs and the specific use case of the bot.

17.3.2 Templates and Copilot for Copilot Creation

At Microsoft Build 2024, Microsoft has introduced many changes in Copilot Studio, two specifics to new Copilot creation. The first one is the Copilot for Copilot, which may seem humorous, but that's the reality. The second is the prebuilt templates. The templates for building custom Copilots, though they are not discussed in the book, but I would highly recommend you play with them. These templates are easy to use and can be super helpful in learning the custom Copilot bot creation process.

The Copilot for Copilot works exactly like what you have learned in Power Apps, Power Automate, or Power Pages. You provide a prompt and maker Copilot help you set up the foundations. The interface as shown in Figure 17-44 is similar to other power experiences. This is a great update to the product as it streamlines the overall experience.

Figure 17-44. *Maker Copilot and templates for Copilot Studio*

You can provide a prompt or use sample prompts provided to kick-start the experience. However, we will learn to build the Copilot first in a traditional way, so we can understand the concept; later, you can easily leverage the maker Copilot to fast-track the bot creation process.

17.3.3 Custom Copilot for Internal Users

Copilot Studio can be used to configure custom Copilot bots for various internal functions and audiences. When we say internal users, the audience is your organization's employees having Microsoft Entra–based authentication setup as well as access to organization artifacts that can be used by a custom Copilot bot. There are several use cases that we have already started witnessing at the customer's organization, leveraging Copilot Studio to configure intelligent generative AI–powered bots to facilitate internal user groups. Some of the common use cases are, but not limited to, the following:

- **Employee Onboarding**: The bot can provide new employees with information about the company, answer FAQs, and guide them through the onboarding process.

- **IT Support**: The bot can assist in troubleshooting common IT issues, reducing the workload on the IT department.

- **Knowledge Base**: The bot can serve as a searchable knowledge base, providing employees with quick answers to their questions about company policies, procedures, or specific job functions.

- **Project Management**: The bot can integrate with project management tools to provide updates on project status, deadlines, and tasks.

- **HR Assistance**: The bot can answer common HR-related questions, guide employees through processes like leave application, and gather feedback.

Setting Up New Internal Copilot Bot

In this section, we will learn how to build a Copilot bot and host the newly created bot in teams, making access to the custom bot easy for our peers and colleagues.

In this example, we will consider an employee onboarding scenario; you can build any other use case depending on the availability of content and information.

To begin this exercise, follow these steps:

1. Start with logging to `https://copilotstudio. microsoft.com/`.

2. Choose the right environment from top left to configure your Copilot bot.

3. Select Create (⊕) and then New Copilot (New copilot) to configure the new experience.

4. This will start a wizard, where first you need to provide the name of the bot and the default language of the Copilot; choose "Employee Buddy" as the name and English as the default language. There are many languages supported, and this list will continue to grow in the future (Figure 17-45).

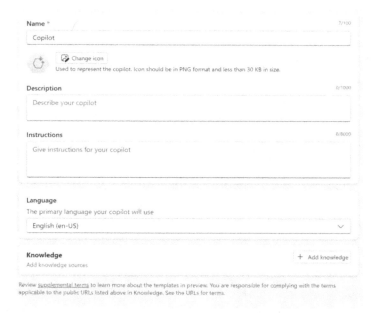

Figure 17-45. *Create a Copilot wizard*

5. The instruction section is also critical as it sets the tone of Copilot. For example, in the case of

employee onboarding, I would set the following instructions:

"You are new employee buddy and tasked to make them feel great about joining the organization. You are kind and helpful, you empathise with them and help them find best resources. your tone is friendly and chatty."

6. After setting up, the configuration looks as shown in Figure 17-46. You can always improve the descriptions as needed.

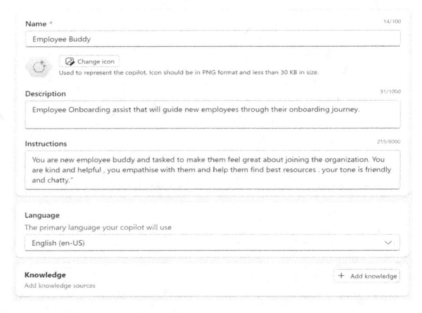

Figure 17-46. *Employee buddy configuration*

7. The knowledge section is the area where you can add various data sources to power Copilot.

8. Click Add knowledge (+ Add knowledge) to set the knowledge sources that could be anything from a

document at OneDrive or third-party solutions
(Figure 17-47).

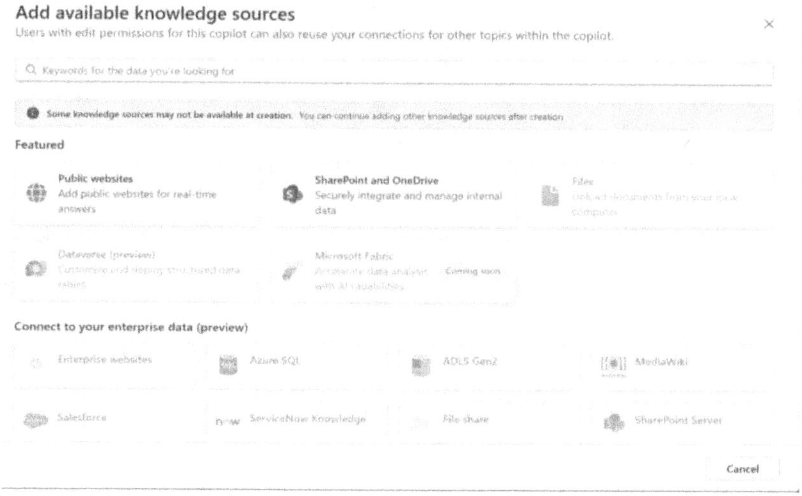

Figure 17-47. *Knowledge sources for Copilot*

9. Notice that at the time of creation, you can only set up public websites or SharePoint and OneDrive. The rest of the knowledge sources will be enabled once Copilot is created.

10. Cancel this option and proceed with the creation of Copilot by clicking the Create ( Create) button.

11. Once Copilot is ready, you will land at the Copilot build experience that has been recently upgraded with new look and feel as shown in Figure 17-48.

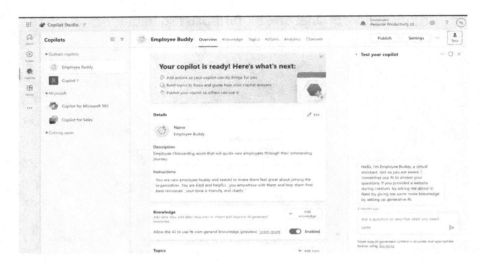

Figure 17-48. *Copilot build interface*

12. At the top of the screen as shown in Figure 17-48, notice access to features like Knowledge, Topic, Actions, Analytics, and others. You can also access them if you scroll down. The other important feature is Test ( ) that allows you to test Copilot. You can further review and expand by clicking ⋯ where you will find options to import, export, or demo a website to test Copilot.

13. Let's quickly understand the purpose of each tab or feature explained in Table 17-1.

Table 17-1. *Copilot feature explanation*

Feature	Description
Knowledge	This feature provides a comprehensive database of information, enabling Microsoft Copilot to answer a wide range of queries.
Topics	This refers to the various subject areas that Copilot can discuss. These topics can be custom or system defined.
Actions	This feature allows Copilot to perform specific tasks by integrating with Power Platform connectors or by invoking Power Automate flow.
Analytics	This feature provides the ability to analyze the performance of Copilot. There is a built-in report powered by Power BI to help understand performance against key areas like customer satisfaction, sessions, billing, and boost conversation.
Channel	This feature allows the deployment of Copilot at various supported channels.

14. Going back to our use case, we can now start improving our "employee buddy" to help the new hires. For that, our custom Copilot will require knowledge of policies and procedures. These policies and procedures can be preexisting in your organization as SharePoint portal or documents. I will share how to add these resources to our custom Copilot.

15. At the main screen as shown in Figure 17-48, either click the Knowledge tab or scroll down to the Knowledge section and click Add knowledge (+ Add knowledge) as shown in Figure 17-49.

Figure 17-49. *Adding a data source for knowledge*

16. To use generative AI, ensure the switch of AI is enabled as shown in Figure 17-49.

17. By clicking Add knowledge, you will be presented with data sources as experienced at the time of Copilot creation. Notice in Figure 17-50 that now all data sources are enabled. The recent changes at the platform have enabled many out-of-the-box sources and opened up exciting opportunities of automation.

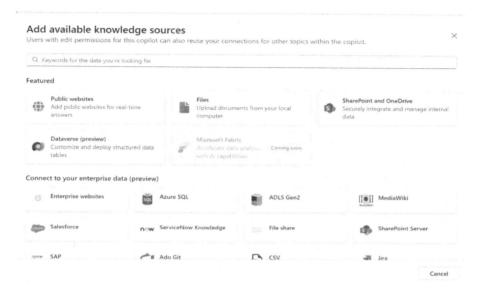

Figure 17-50. *Available data sources for knowledge*

18. I am assuming that our organization has employee onboarding–related content available at the internal SharePoint site and has a few documents. We will set up these sources to empower our Copilot. For the experiment, you can set up a sample employee onboarding SharePoint site and use Copilot in MS Word to generate a few sample policy documents.

19. First, set up the SharePoint source. Click the SharePoint and OneDrive (⬛) option as shown in Figure 17-50.

20. You will be presented with the Add option; provide the link of the internal SharePoint site, and click the Add (⬛ Add) button (Figure 17-51).

Figure 17-51. *Add SharePoint and OneDrive*

21. Once added, you will be able to provide additional context about the site and what information it serves (Figure 17-52).

Figure 17-52. *Adding additional context to the source*

22. This feature can be especially useful as it would help the author of Copilot maintain links with user-friendly details.

23. Once all the SharePoint and OneDrive sources are added, click the Add (Add) button at the bottom.

24. At the completion, you will find the new source listed under the Knowledge section (Figure 17-53).

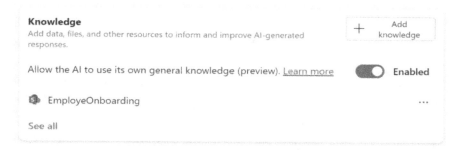

Figure 17-53. *New source added to knowledge*

25. Repeat the action described earlier, and instead of SharePoint, use file (📄) upload.

26. I have added three documents and provided names and descriptions (Figure 17-54).

Figure 17-54. *Uploading files as a source*

27. Uploaded files will be grounded, and the output as well as files is stored in local Dataverse in your environment.

28. All sources with their current status will be listed under Knowledge (Figure 17-55).

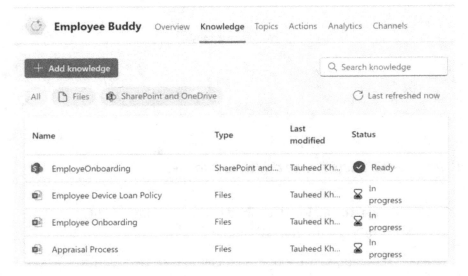

Figure 17-55. *Knowledge sources provided to Copilot*

29. It is recommended not to publish Copilot until all sources are ready. This will ensure that Copilot has access to all information.

We can now test our Copilot using the test window. Based on the data sources, I can ask some questions and analyze the results. The first question I asked is about the appraisal process, not challenging Copilot much. Copilot successfully answered with citation (Figure 17-56).

Figure 17-56. *Testing Copilot with questions and queries*

30.   I also asked a question to summarize a content posted at the sample onboarding site. The results were again very impressive (Figure 17-57).

Figure 17-57. *Summary of SharePoint content*

31. Based on the content and site you have provided, ask questions and learn how to engage with the content and custom Copilot.

32. If you need to set up additional settings, you can click Settings (Settings) at the top to either reset some of the settings like the Copilot information we provided or set generative AI–related settings (Figure 17-58).

Figure 17-58. *Settings of Copilot*

33. One of the key features/settings in generative AI is the Copilot content moderation settings. This sets what we call the temperature and how creative generative AI can be while responding to the query (Figure 17-59)

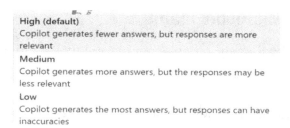

High (default)
Copilot generates fewer answers, but responses are more relevant

Medium
Copilot generates more answers, but the responses may be less relevant

Low
Copilot generates the most answers, but responses can have inaccuracies

Figure 17-59. *Content moderation settings*

34. There are several other features available in settings that as a business user or citizen developer you may not have to interact with. The security feature is important to know as for internal Copilots it has to be set with Entra ID as shown in Figure 17-60. I will cover this later in the external Copilot experience.

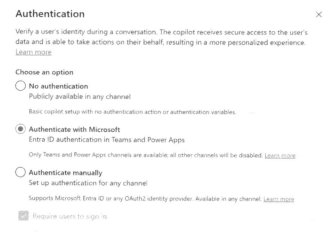

Authentication   ✕

Verify a user's identity during a conversation. The copilot receives secure access to the user's data and is able to take actions on their behalf, resulting in a more personalized experience. Learn more

Choose an option

○ No authentication
Publicly available in any channel

Basic copilot setup with no authentication action or authentication variables.

◉ Authenticate with Microsoft
Entra ID authentication in Teams and Power Apps

Only Teams and Power Apps channels are available; all other channels will be disabled. Learn more

○ Authenticate manually
Set up authentication for any channel

Supports Microsoft Entra ID or any OAuth2 identity provider. Available in any channel. Learn more

☐ Require users to sign in

Figure 17-60. *Authentication settings*

Our custom Copilot is ready for deployment. The internal bots can be made available through Microsoft Teams which allow end users to access Copilot with ease. In the next section, I will discuss how to host Copilot at teams.

Hosting at Microsoft Teams

Now that Copilot is ready, it's time to host Copilot. For internal users, the best platform to host would be Microsoft Teams as users can find it easy to access the new bot and have a familiar environment of Teams to interact with the Copilot bot. Follow these steps to deploy the bot in teams:

1. Log in to Copilot Studio and open the employee buddy bot.

2. Click the Settings (⚙ Settings) menu option and select Security (Security).

3. This is where you can define the type of authentication required to access this Copilot along with other security features. This is the key configuration that differentiates between internal and external bots (Figure 17-61).

Figure 17-61. *Security options available with custom Copilot*

4. For the internal user–facing bot, click the authentication tile. This will open Authentication settings (Figure 17-62).

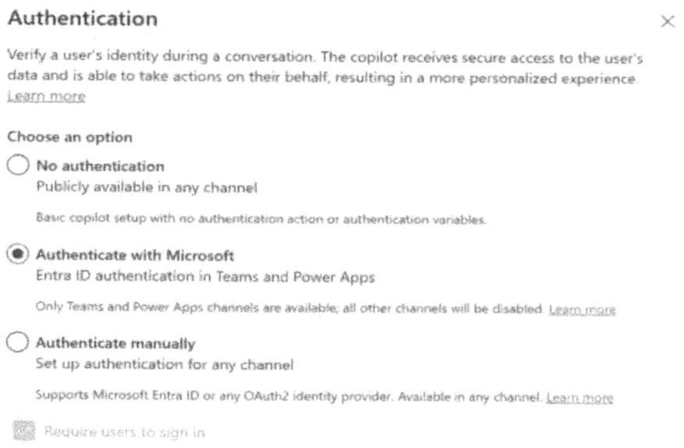

Figure 17-62. *Authentication settings*

5. For hosting at Teams, you will choose the Authenticate with Microsoft. This will use the Entra ID and authenticate the user at the initiation of bot conversation. Also, it restricts hosting of this bot at public channels.

6. Save the settings and select Channels (Channels) from the top menu.

7. This is where you will be deploying our Copilot bot to Teams. Choose the Teams tile from the Channels option to open settings (Figure 17-63).

Figure 17-63. *Channels available with Entra ID authentication*

8. Select Turn on Teams (Turn on Teams) to begin teams' integration with Copilot.

9. Once completed, you will be notified about the completion of hosting (Figure 17-64).

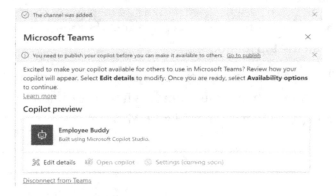

Figure 17-64. *Custom Copilot hosted in Teams*

10. The last action before this bot becomes available is to publish Copilot. Note that publishing can happen before or after the security and channel hosting; however, it is best to do it later.

11. Click Publish (Publish) in the menu followed by
     Publish (⬆ Publish) at the prompt to complete
     the action.

12. Once publishing is complete, go back to Channels
     ➤ Teams and select Open Copilot (🗊 Open copilot) to
     experience newly created Copilot in teams.

13. At Teams, you will be provided with add screen
     where you can finalize the deployment action and
     add an employee onboarding bot to teams for
     interaction (Figure 17-65).

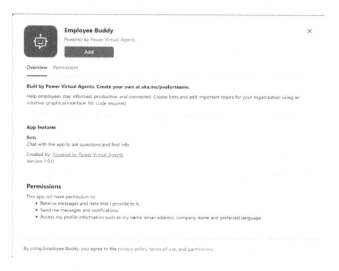

Figure 17-65. *Adding Copilot bot in Teams*

14. Ask questions about employee onboarding and
     observe the results (Figure 17-66).

Figure 17-66. *Active Copilot bot in teams*

You can share Copilot with your peers or submit Copilot for organization-wide access by selecting Settings ➤ Security ➤ Availability.

17.3.4 Custom Copilot for External Users

One of the most common uses of Copilot Studio or its predecessor Power Virtual Agent is to empower external-facing platforms with intelligent bots, which can answer the user's questions as well as perform actions. Many organizations today use Copilot Studio–powered bots to address their "always present/always available" needs and reduce or offload repetitive conversations from human agents or interfaces.

With Copilot Studio, you can configure external-facing bots, just like we configured internal-facing bots. The difference comes from how we host these bots, how we authenticate, and of course the use case. Some of the common use cases I have seen in the industry are as follows:

- **Customer Support**: The bot that can answer common customer queries, provide information about products or services, and guide users through processes like placing an order or tracking a shipment

- **Sales Assistance**: The bot that can provide product recommendations based on user preferences, answer questions about products, and assist with the purchasing process

- **User Engagement**: The bot that can engage users through interactive content, games, quizzes, or personalized recommendations

- **Feedback Collection**: The bot that can collect user feedback on products, services, or user experience, offering valuable insights for business improvement

- **Appointment Scheduling**: The bot that can aid users in scheduling appointments, making reservations, or booking services

In this section, we will not discuss the common generative AI features as they are similar to what is available for internal-facing bots; our focus of discussion will be at plugin actions and channels.

Setting Up New Copilot Bot

With generative AI infusion in Copilot bots, setting up custom Copilot bots has become easier and has reduced time to production. In this section, we will learn how to set up an external-facing Copilot and learn how to use generative AI to quickly gauge information from websites and answer user questions. We will begin our experience with setting up a new custom Copilot.

1. Start with logging in to `https://copilotstudio.microsoft.com/`.

2. Choose the right environment from top left to configure your Copilot bot.

3. Select Create (⊕) and then New Copilot (New copilot) to configure the new experience.

4. This will start a wizard where first you need to set up initial details such as the name of the Copilot bot, default language, and instruction. Choose "Xbox" as the name and English as the default language and perform the following instructions:

    "You are Xbox support provider. You are funny and use gaming terms while responding to user. you are helpful and give suggestions on new games and devices."

5. Once the initial setup is configured, your settings should look similar to Figure 17-67.

Figure 17-67. *Setting Xbox Copilot*

6. Under the Knowledge, let's add the link of the Xbox public website: `www.xbox.com/en-SG/`.

⊕   Add public websites   ×

How to choose websites:
  • If your site is external, make sure it's indexed or found by Bing.
  • Don't use sites with forums or comments from end users; this can reduce the relevancy of answers.
  • Don't include query strings, more than two levels of depth, or the character " in your URL.

Webpage link

| Enter a link | Add |

Link	Name	Description
⊕ https://www.xbox.com/en-SG/	xbox singapore	This knowledge source searches information

This generative AI feature uses Bing Search. Your data will flow outside your organization's compliance and geo boundaries. Customer's use of Bing search is governed by the Microsoft Services Agreement and the Microsoft Privacy Statement.

| Back | | Add | Cancel |

Figure 17-68. *Adding the public website of Xbox*

7. You can add multiple websites here; ideally, these websites are under a similar category, for example, I can add the EA sports website to further help my users get information about EA sports games.

8. Click the Add (Add) button to include the website to Knowledge as shown in Figure 17-69.

Knowledge (1)   ＋ Add knowledge
Add knowledge sources

⊕ xbox singapore   ⋮

Figure 17-69. *Public website added to Xbox Copilot*

9. Click Create (Create) at the top to begin the Xbox bot creation.

10. Once provisioned, you will land to the Copilot configuration studio where you can define and orchestrate the custom bot experience for end users.

11. At the Copilot configuration studio, you can test the created Copilot and its ability to "Bing search" content from the Xbox website. Ideally, the Test panel should be visible; if not, browse the main page and find Test Copilot (🎤) to launch the Test panel (Figure 17-70).

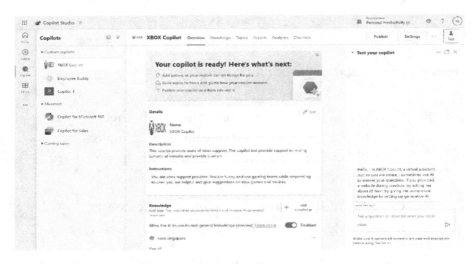

Figure 17-70. *Testing the Copilot bot using the Test panel*

12. Let's ask a question about the latest game consoles available. I am trying to be vague to evaluate the bot's ability to understand by question. You can ask "*What is the latest device available.*"

13. Observe the result as shown in Figure 17-71; more often than not, you will find Copilot answers the question appropriately as in my case.

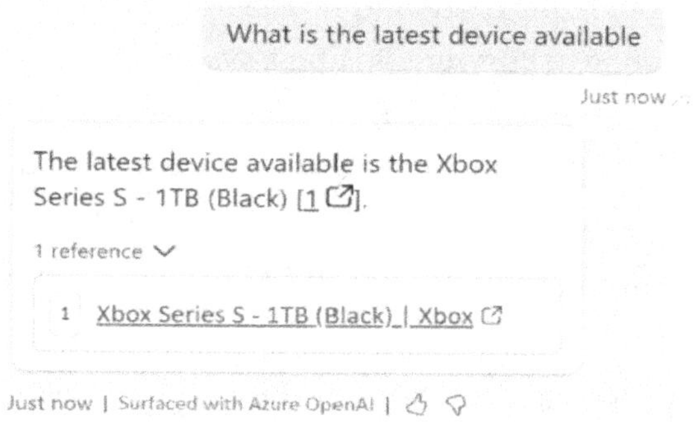

What is the latest device available
Just now
The latest device available is the Xbox Series S - 1TB (Black) [1].
1 reference
1 Xbox Series S - 1TB (Black) | Xbox
Just now | Surfaced with Azure OpenAI |

***Figure 17-71.** Bot answering a question using generative AI*

14. As I set up the instruction of Copilot to be helpful and a gaming expert, I followed up with the prompt "*is this any good?*" Copilot responded with recommendations as shown in Figure 17-72.

XBOX Copilot
Settings
Conversational boosting
Test your copilot
Trigger
On Unknown Intent
Create generative answers
Input
Data sources
Condition
All other conditions
New condition

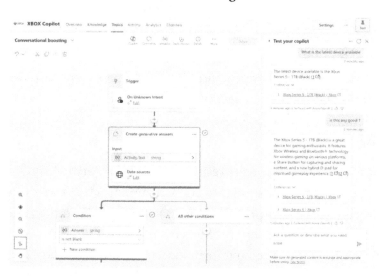

***Figure 17-72.** Following up with additional questions*

15. Observe Figure 17-72 and notice that these questions are answered using a system topic called "conversational boosting," where every time a user provides a prompt where Copilot does not find any defined topic, it will trigger the conversational boosting topic and try finding answers using data sources.

16. As experienced in out-of-the-box Copilots, citation is a regular feature of Copilot and in this case as well provided us with the citation on the source of information.

17. This example demonstrates the amazing ability of generative AI to consume external information and address end-user queries with available information. No new knowledge base, documentation, or training is required to enable this experience.

The remaining features of generative AI are consistent with what I have already covered in an earlier section.

Actions

The other generative AI usage available that can be very handy is actions. Actions are conceptually similar to conversational actions we discussed in the previous section; however, they are managed differently, and in fact you cannot use conversational actions in custom Copilot.

Actions allow you to fetch information from various sources and surface to users while you do not have to explicitly call out a topic or inputs required. At the time of writing this book, the feature is in public preview. Actions can be based on prebuilt connector actions, custom connection actions, Power Automate cloud flows, AI Builder prompt, or

Bot Framework. To use actions, you will require generative mode selected that can be set under Settings ➤ Generative AI. This allows your action to be called automatically in response to a relevant user query.

Let's perform the following steps to configure a simple action using the MSN Weather connector. While this may not be practical reference to our use case of "Xbox helper", it is one of the least dependent use case to build. Hence, I have chosen the MSN connector use case to share with you the concept. Once the concept is clear, you can use any connector or other features as and when needed.

1. Start with logging in to `https://copilotstudio.microsoft.com/`.

2. Choose the right environment from top left to configure your Copilot bot.

3. Select Xbox Copilot we created, or you can start afresh and create a new Copilot bot.

4. From the top tab, select Actions (Actions) to create a new action.

5. At the Action area, select Add an action (+ Add an action).

6. This will begin a wizard to set up a new plugin action (Figure 17-73).

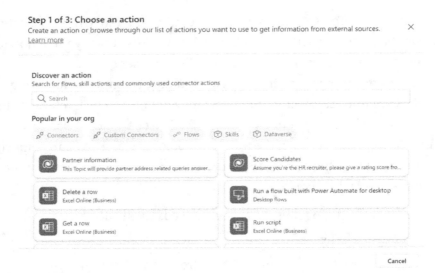

Figure 17-73. *Action wizard for custom Copilot*

7. The first configuration required is to select the
    action with the connector. In this case, we will
    choose the MSN Weather connector and the action
    Get current weather (Figure 17-74).

Figure 17-74. *Get current weather action*

8. The next step is to validate the connection. The platform will validate the connection and enable usage for this Copilot. Click Next (Next) to proceed.

9. The last step is important. Here, you need to configure the inputs and outputs of this connector that generative AI will use. The inputs will be dynamically extracted from the user sentence, and the outputs will be used to create the generative answer (Figure 17-75).

Figure 17-75. *Action inputs and outputs*

10. For this exercise, we will leave it as is at the review and finish page, and select Finish (Finish) to create the action.

11. Once the action is created, you will be able to find it listed at the Action page (Figure 17-76).

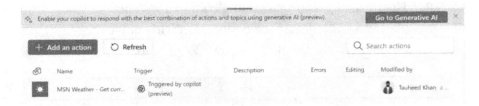

Figure 17-76. *Action added to custom Copilot*

12. As you can notice in Figure 17-76 and in the
     experience as well, the system is recommending
     choosing the generative mode; go to Settings ➤
     Generative AI and select generative mode as shown
     in Figure 17-77.

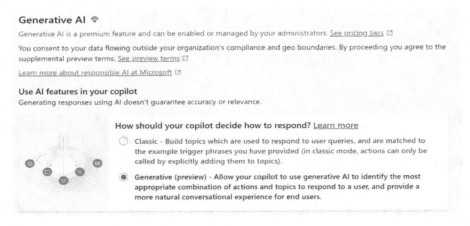

Figure 17-77. *Setting mode of Copilot as generative*

13. Save the changes to reflect the change.

14. To assess our plugin action, go to the Test panel
     and ask a question about temperature. I used the
     following question to inquire about my hometown:
     "what is temperature in Karachi right now."

As expected, the Plugin action identified the intent and responded to my question (Figure 17-78). I loved the answer as it still made reference to gaming (as I used Xbox Copilot).

Figure 17-78. *Action activated through a prompt*

15. Let's change the prompt and include the unit; I used the following prompt: *"what is temperature in Karachi right now? give answer in Celsius."* This prompt will force the generative AI to change the unit to Celsius in an answer as shown in Figure 17-79.

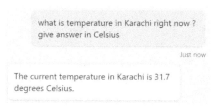

Figure 17-79. *Changing units using the prompt*

16. As part of the output, there are numerous weather-related attributes available, for example, I asked a question about wind speed in Singapore as shown in Figure 17-80, and the action executed with success.

Figure 17-80. *Asking additional questions about the weather*

This is another useful generative AI feature that can reduce manual orchestration and integration with external data sources and help us automatically chain the inputs from the user prompt as well. There are several examples available already today going beyond out-of-the-box connectors as well; however, they would be more suitable for a pro-developer discussion. As a business user or citizen developer, it is good to know that the pace of transformation today can match the pace of business needs.

Channels

We briefly discussed about various channels available to host our Copilot bot in the previous section. Let's discuss them in detail. You can host the Copilot bot for external users at several channels. These channels range from websites to advanced integration with a direct line speech.

Each of the channel requires different setup to be configured. These configurations are generally available to pro developers or advanced citizen developers who understand the host channel details as well.

As a business user, it is worth noting the available options, so you can devise a user engagement plan and also expand the reach to users at different channels. You can also host the same bot at various channels simultaneously, making it truly omni-channel (Figure 17-81).

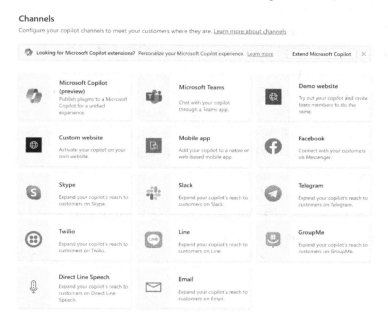

Figure 17-81. *Channels available for external hosting*

By default, authentication is set to use Teams and Power Apps, hence binding bots to be used by internal users; however, you can change it to either have no authentication or different types of authentication service. Figure 17-81 displays the list of available channels at the time of publishing. The list is expected to grow in the future.

17.4 Summary

In this chapter, we delved into the capabilities of Microsoft Copilot Studio, a platform that allows users to extend the Microsoft 365 Copilot experience or build custom Copilot bots for both internal and external audiences.

The chapter began with an overview of licensing and accessing the studio, followed by a detailed examination of the out-of-the-box plugins available and the process for creating custom plugins.

The chapter further explored the concept of a custom Copilot, discussing its application for internal users and the considerations for extending it to external users. The chapter discussed the process of configuring bots powered with generative AI and how we can use existing data as a source of information for Copilot bots.

This chapter also marked the end of this part where we learned about Copilot Studio and how the future of work can truly transform using intelligent conversational bots in various scenarios.

CHAPTER 18

Copilot, Generative AI, and Future of Work

We mark the end of this book with the shortest chapter that is written partly using Microsoft Copilot and further edited by myself. What we have experienced so far through this book is the beginning of a new era where the way we used to work is destined to change. From preparing an email response to responding to complex RFP (Request for Proposals) or preparing an enterprise project, every single function at our organization and every single role in our corporates will have new SOPs, new KPIs, and new challenges to address. The integration of generative AI into tools such as M365 Copilot, Copilot in Power Platform, Copilot for Sales, Copilot for Service, and the newly unveiled Copilot for Finance is transforming mundane tasks into opportunities for creativity and efficiency.

In this book, we learned how the introduction of Microsoft Copilot for M365 will revolutionize the way we used productivity tools. M365 Copilot serves as an intelligent assistant within the Microsoft 365 ecosystem, leveraging the power of AI to draft emails, create documents, and analyze data with unprecedented speed and accuracy. It's not just about automating tasks; it's about augmenting human capabilities and allowing professionals to focus on the strategic aspects of their work.

© Adeel Khan 2024
A. Khan, *Introducing Microsoft Copilot for Managers*, Inside Copilot,
https://doi.org/10.1007/979-8-8688-0419-9_18

We experienced Copilot in Power Platform services. Copilot in Power Platform empowers users to build apps, automate workflows, and analyze data through a conversational interface. It's a step toward democratizing development, enabling users with little to no coding experience to bring their ideas to life.

We learned about sales and service Copilots. Copilots act as real-time advisors, providing insights and recommendations that help close deals faster and deliver exceptional customer service. These AI-driven tools are not just support systems; they are going to be the partners that will enhance the human touch in every interaction.

Microsoft has also announced that Copilot for Finance, though not covered in this book but it is a significant milestone in financial management. By analyzing trends and generating forecasts, this AI assistant aids finance professionals in making informed decisions, ensuring the financial health of their organizations. Importantly, it is also agnostic to the core platform organizations use.

Like Microsoft's, other organizations also share the same transformation vision such as Salesforce, which is also embracing generative AI to infuse the Copilot experience into its offerings. By integrating AI into their platforms, these companies are setting a new standard for customer relationship management and enterprise resource planning.

The future of work is undeniably intertwined with AI. As these technologies become more sophisticated, the role of the business manager will shift from overseeing operations to strategizing and innovating. Embracing this change is not just important; it's imperative for staying competitive in a world where the only constant is change itself.

In conclusion, the rise of Microsoft Copilots and generative AI heralds a new dawn for the workplace. The future of work will be characterized by a collaboration between humans and AI, where each complements the other's strength. For business managers, the time to adapt is now, for the workplaces of tomorrow will be built on the decisions made today.

APPENDIX A

Prompt Exercise

Bing Chat is an AI-powered chat assistant that is changing the way we access public information. It is designed to be available to everyone. However, access might depend on a few factors such as Internet connectivity, device compatibility, adherence to conversation guidelines, and regional restrictions. As long as these conditions are met, anyone can interact with Bing Chat. Let's begin a short exercise by opening `https://bing.com` at Microsoft Edge. Once the page is open, select Chat from the available tabs to land to the Bing Chat landing page as shown in Figure A-1.

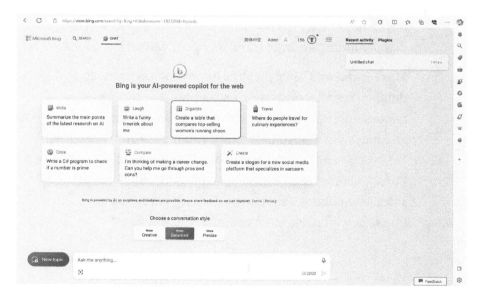

Figure A-1. *Bing Chat landing page*

© Adeel Khan 2024
A. Khan, *Introducing Microsoft Copilot for Managers*, Inside Copilot,
https://doi.org/10.1007/979-8-8688-0419-9

This landing page provides some of the default prompts that are quite useful in terms of understanding how to engage Bing Chat Copilot, but we will do our own exercise here. We will choose the conversation styles and provide a set of prompts to understand how to engage Copilot. Bing Chat Copilot offers three conversation styles to cater to different user needs:

- **More Creative**: This style encourages imaginative and innovative responses, ideal for brainstorming sessions or when you're seeking out-of-the-box ideas. For instance, if you're looking for a unique marketing strategy, you may prompt: "Let's create a virtual reality experience that takes customers on a journey through the production process of your product."

- **More Balanced**: This style provides a mix of creativity and precision, making it suitable for everyday business conversations. For example, if you're discussing how to improve team productivity, you may prompt: "Consider implementing a mix of flexible work hours, regular team-building activities, and an open feedback system."

- **More Precise**: This style aims to provide accurate and detailed responses, perfect for technical or business-related queries. For instance, if you're asking for an analysis of a business report, you may prompt: "Microsoft annual report shows a 15% increase in sales but a 7% increase in expense, suggesting which product sales is impacting increase and what operations is impacting increase in expenses."

These styles allow you to customize your interaction with Copilot based on your specific needs and preferences. Let's begin performing our preparatory hands-on for the book. In this exercise, we will experience various prompts and use the three modes of Bing Chat to generate drafts for our work.

A.1 Creative Mode

Let's choose the creative mode and ask the following prompts. In this exercise, we have suggested interconnected prompts to show another exciting ability of Copilot; it can remember the conversation and provide near human interaction experience. This means that we can create prompts that may refer to the output of the previous prompt. Let's experiment with this idea:

- "Write a 300-word story about a company named 'Eco Innovations' that aims to reduce the digital waste across Asia Pacific."

- "Based on a story, can you come up with possible slogans for the company?"

- "Create five potential products or services this company can offer."

These prompts will create a conversational journey where Copilot will first create a story, then based on the story generate a set of slogans and finally create potential products or services this company can offer. All of mentioned artifacts using public data generated on the fly, in context and improving as we continue to provide or ask more questions as shown in Figure A-2. Also, notice that Copilot will also provide references of the information or suggestions; this is also an important aspect of suggestions as it provides authenticity and reasoning.

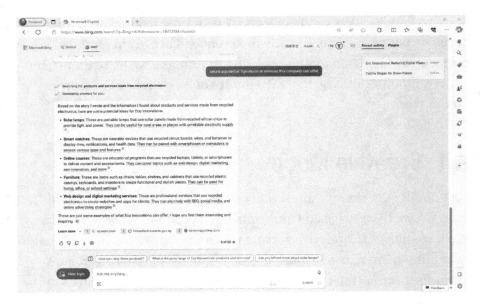

Figure A-2. *Prompt response and references*

A.2 Balanced Mode

For the next topic, you can choose the balanced mode. This style combines creativity and accuracy, making it ideal for regular business discussions. You can use the following prompts to generate a balanced outcome; it is advised to select New Topic each time you use a prompt.

- "Provide a brief overview of the concept of Supply Chain Management."

- "Explain the impact of digital transformation on business operations."

- "Generate a short essay on the role of artificial intelligence in business decision-making."

Analyze the results generated and notice how comprehensive they are. Most importantly, you have the ability to suggest if you disagree with the results, hence enabling Bing Chat Copilot to learn from its mistakes.

A.3 Precise Mode

The last mode we want you to experiment is the precise mode. This mode is for when we want Bing to be more factual and concise. Choosing this conversational style will provide shorter, more direct, and more accurate answers, using facts, data, or logic. Copilot will also avoid any unnecessary or irrelevant information. This mode is ideal for finding information, getting answers, or solving problems. Let's try a few prompts under the precise mode:

- "What is Fibonacci series?"

- "Explain the application of Fibonacci series in business."

- "Write a Python program that asks the user for a number, n, and prints the Fibonacci series up to the nth term."

In this exercise, you will notice that not only the information was precise but also to the point where Copilot returned information based on facts rather than imagination as shown in Figure A-3. Also, we learned the Copilot ability to generate Python code that can be copied and further modified or validated.

APPENDIX A   PROMPT EXERCISE

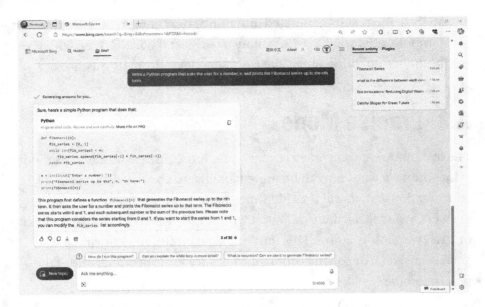

Figure A-3. *Python code generation using a prompt*

APPENDIX B

Flow Configuration

This appendix covers the flow configuration of custom flow created in Chapter 8. Please note that some of these configurations would be environment specific, such as the email address of the approver.

1. Configuration of the Dataverse trigger

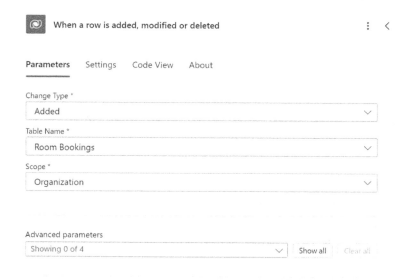

2. Configuration of the approval action; please select your current user in "Assigned To."

© Adeel Khan 2024
A. Khan, *Introducing Microsoft Copilot for Managers*, Inside Copilot,
https://doi.org/10.1007/979-8-8688-0419-9

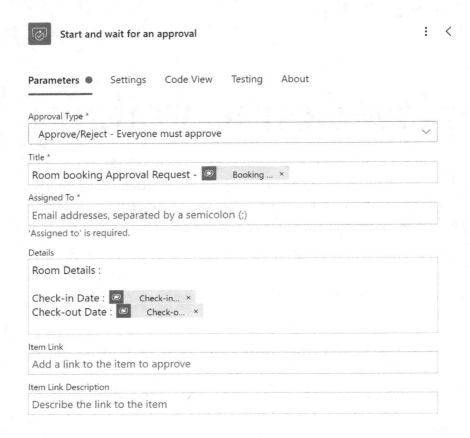

3. Condition control

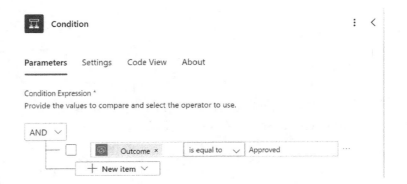

4.   Email action in case of approval

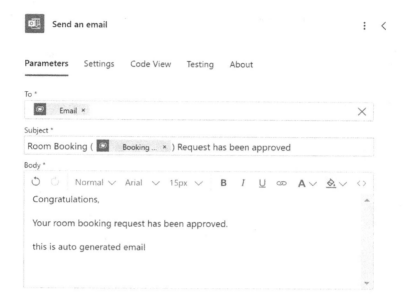

5.   Email action in case of rejection

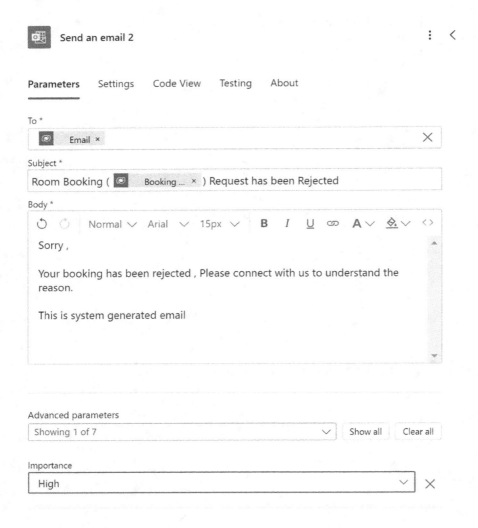

As most of this information is self-explanatory, we will not document them in the book. However, it is recommended to review these connectors and actions at Microsoft Learn.

Index

A, B

C

© Adeel Khan 2024
A. Khan, *Introducing Microsoft Copilot for Managers*, Inside Copilot,
https://doi.org/10.1007/979-8-8688-0419-9

T, U, V

W, X, Y, Z

GPSR Compliance
The European Union's (EU) General Product Safety Regulation (GPSR) is a set
of rules that requires consumer products to be safe and our obligations to
ensure this.

If you have any concerns about our products, you can contact us on

ProductSafety@springernature.com

In case Publisher is established outside the EU, the EU authorized
representative is:

Springer Nature Customer Service Center GmbH
Europaplatz 3
69115 Heidelberg, Germany